The SOUTHERN BAPTIST CONVENTION

The SOUTHERN BAPTIST CONVENTION

A Sesquicentennial History

JESSE C. FLETCHER

Nashville, Tennessee

4211-67
0-8054-1167-4

Dewey Decimal Classification: 286.132
Subject Heading: SOUTHERN BAPTIST CONVENTION / BAPTISTS—HISTORY
Library of Congress Card Catalog Number: 94-8576

Scripture quotations are from the King James Version of the Bible.

Library of Congress Cataloging-in-Publication Data
Fletcher, Jesse C.
        The Southern Baptist Convention : a sesquicentennial history / by Jesse
C. Fletcher.
            p.   cm.
        Includes bibliographical references and index.
        ISBN 0-8054-1167-4
        1. Southern Baptist Convention—History.   2. Baptists—United
States—Church history.   I. Title.
        BX6462.3.F54   1994
        286'.132'09—dc20
                                                                                94-8576
                                                                                CIP

To my mentors
Jesse N. Fletcher, father
John D. Barbee, pastor
Robert A. Baker, teacher
Baker J. Cauthen, leader

Contents

Publisher's Note

This book is being published in conjunction with the 150th anniversary in 1995 of the Southern Baptist Convention's founding. This denominational history is the result of long and extensive planning.

In 1985 the Inter-Agency Council (IAC), at the request of the Executive Committee of the Southern Baptist Convention, appointed a Workgroup to coordinate agency sesquicentennial events. The Workgroup recommended the publication of this history. The following persons have composed this Workgroup:

Minette Drumwright, ch., 1985–94 (Foreign Mission Board)

James L. Powell, 1985– , ch. 1994– (Stewardship Commission)

Robert E. Bingham, 1985–90 (Home Mission Board)

John Bloskas, 1985–89 (Annuity Board)

Ellis M. Bush, 1985–93 (coordinator, Bold Mission Thrust)

Wallace W. Buckner, 1990–94 (Home Mission Board)

Lamar Cooper, 1985–95 (Christian Life Commission)

Michael S. Day, 1991– (Brotherhood Commission)

Charles Deweese, 1990– (Historical Commission)

Carl Duck, 1985–93 (Nashville Baptist Association)

Jim Freedman, 1993– (Nashville Baptist Association)

Leonard E. Hill, 1985–94 (Executive Committee)

Lloyd Householder, 1985–92 (Sunday School Board)

Hollis E. Johnson III, 1985– (Southern Baptist Foundation)

Don Kammerdiener, 1994– (Foreign Mission Board)

Martin King , 1993– (Home Mission Board)

Richard McCartney, 1985– (Radio & Television Commission)

Tom Miller, 1993– (Annuity Board)

Frank G. Schwall, Jr., 1989–93 (Annuity Board)

Jerry Self, 1985– (Education Commission)

James H. Smith, 1985– (Brotherhood Commission)

Don H. Stewart, 1985–91 (Seminaries)

A. Ronald Tonks, 1985–90 (Historical Commission)

Marshall Walker, 1992– (Sunday School Board)

June Whitlow, 1985– (Woman's Missionary Union)

Reginald M. McDonough, ex officio, 1985–87 (Executive Committee)

Ernest E. Mosley, ex officio, 1987– (Executive Committee)

Dr. Jesse Fletcher graciously agreed to undertake this monumental project and has done an exceptional work. Additionally, a reading committee, consisting of the following members, read the final manuscript and made suggestions as appropriate: James L. Powell, ch., Charles Deweese, H. Leon McBeth, Richard McCartney, Don Stewart, and June Whitlow.

In 1988 the Executive Committee appointed a Sesquicentennial Celebration Committee to coordinate all aspects of this celebration. The following persons have served on this committee:

John Sullivan, ch., 1988–

Minette Drumwright, vice-ch., 1988–94

James L. Powell, vice-ch., 1994–

Catherine Allen, events coordinator, 1993–94

Joel C. Gregory, 1988–94

James N. Griffith, 1988–

Warren C. Hultgren, 1988–

Earl Kelly, 1988–

Lynn E. May, Jr., 1988–

H. Leon McBeth, 1988–

Dorothy E. Sample, 1988–

James L. Sells, 1988–93

Charles W. Sullivan, ex officio, 1988–89

Sam W. Pace, ex officio, 1989–91

David Hankins, ex officio, 1991–93

Fred H. Wolfe, ex officio, 1993–

This demonstrates the truly cooperative nature of this work covering the history of our denomination. As the publisher of record, I wish to thank all those, particularly those mentioned above, who have participated in making this volume possible.

Charles A. Wilson
Publisher
Broadman & Holman

Acknowledgments

The author of any project of this scope is soon deeply grateful for all who have previously plowed the ground, whether by field or by furrow. While required to go back to many of the same sources and sometimes coming to different conclusions, this author wants to confess his indebtedness to this company.

More specifically, I want to thank my special assistants, Glendy (Mrs. Don R.) Whitehead, Charlene (Mrs. Kenneth) Archer, and my graduate assistant, the Reverend Donny Harbers. Without their dedication and good humor, this would have been a much tougher task. In addition, I want to express my sincere appreciation to H. Leon McBeth, professor of church history at Southwestern Baptist Theological Seminary, for advising so generously on historical matters and to Genevieve Greer, retired book editor for the Foreign Mission Board, for editing advice. None of these to whom I am so indebted, however, should have to bear responsibility for the final result. That is mine alone.

Librarians at Southern Baptist Theological Seminary, Southwestern Baptist Theological Seminary, the Historical Commission, Southern Baptist Convention, and Hardin-Simmons University's Richardson library have given invaluable help. I want to express special appreciation to Southern's Ron Deering; Southwestern's Carl Wrotenberry, Bob Phillips and Alan Lefever; the Historical Commission's Lynn May, Charles Deweese, Carol Woodfin (now at Palm Beach Atlantic College), and Bill Sumners; and Hardin-Simmons' Alice W. Specht.

Special gratitude is reserved for Minette Drumwright of the Foreign Mission Board who has chaired the interagency group working under the SBC Sesquicentennial Committee to bring this project to completion. Her faith and encouragement have been unfailing.

And finally, to my wife, family, and friends who have endured my preoccupation with this effort over the past four years and yet offered continued support, I love you.

Jesse C. Fletcher
Logsdon School of Theology,
Hardin-Simmons University

Introduction

The end of one era and the beginning of a new one infuses life with narrative meaning. Writer Lance Morrow says, "Delineated time is history's narrative framework—the way to make sense out of beginnings, middles, and ends."[1] This truth makes the Southern Baptist Convention's sesquicentennial, 150 years, almost eight generations, a uniquely propitious time to try to review its own history, to tell its story.

A people numbering more than 15 million gathered in more than 38,000 churches organized into a national organization that includes work in every state of the Union and over 120 countries deserves to have that story told. Not only is the Southern Baptist Convention's century and a half of struggle and achievement relatively unknown to those **outside their fell**owship, it is surprisingly unappreciated within its own widespread and diverse ranks.

With roots lodged in churches first established by English exiles in the Netherlands in 1609 and in America in 1639, Baptists appeared in the southern states around 1696. They gradually merged the diverse traditions of their early American experience by uniting Calvinistic convictions with a more modified theology, and traditional, ordered ecclesiologies with experiential, frontier-evangelistic expressions of faith. With many of their numbers passionately involved in the American Revolution, they carved out a place on the American scene and began to prosper.

Baptists located in the southern states developed a strong sensitivity for their region with its predominantly agrarian economy and, unfortunately, the institution of slavery. Though a product of New England commercialism, this cruel tradition found fertile ground in the South's agricultural base and soon became the undergirding reality of southern culture. As Baptists grew in the South they became increasingly identified with their culture.

Baptists, those in the North and South, were at first highly suspicious of organizations other than the local church. The first Baptist Association in the United States was not founded until 1707 in Philadelphia and the first such connection in the South did not appear until 1751 in Charleston. A denominational body on a national scale finally emerged in 1814 under the mandate of foreign missions. When it did, however, southern churches were among the most enthusiastic participants.

This initial agreement fell victim three decades later to antislavery convictions that surfaced first among Baptists in England and then found their way in an even more zealous form to New England. Organized as abolitionists, people holding these convictions mounted an unrelenting campaign against the South's "peculiar institution." After several unsuccessful tries, their leaders in 1845 persuaded the mission boards of the national Baptist body to refuse to appoint a slaveholder as a missionary. This set the stage for the southern churches, defensive and feeling discredited in organizations they had helped create and nurture, to demand their own denominational structure. The Southern Baptist Convention was the result.

Growing slowly at first with major setbacks coming from the war between the states and the pain of reconstruction, they began to define themselves as a denomination in the late nineteenth century and finally to grow in the mid-twentieth century.

The Challenges of Growth

And grow they did. Beyond all expectations they rode the crest of westward expansion and created an infrastructure of institutions to become the largest denomination outside Roman Catholicism in the United States. Led by a corporate-wise Sunday School Board and an aggressive and unifying foreign and home mission enterprise and undergirded by a remarkable ministerial training and educational matrix, they finally overcame the segregated aftermath of their beginnings and became a national force to be reckoned with both in their economic clout and in their political influence.

Known both admiringly and derisively as Southern Baptists, they have, since World War II, been identified by that name more in a doctrinal and ecclesiastical way than in a regional sense. From their organization in 1845, however, they have been beset with internal battles and an uneasy diversity. Statesmanship, compromise, and overriding common interests enabled them to overcome each challenge.

By far the biggest threat to their amazing union and remarkable progress came in the last two decades of their century and a half of existence. Starting over an old 1920s battleground surrounding biblical interpretations of Genesis and inroads of liberalism perceived in SBC educational institutions, the issue was this time politicized by a group of politically-wise "Conservatives" who in 1979 successfully elected a president committed to shifting power from a traditional leadership bloc composed of both moderates and conservatives to a highly organized group of conservative pastors with strong ties to an aggressive national political movement. Led by the president of a Bible college and a state court judge and traveling under the banner of Biblical inerrancy, the conservatives won every SBC presidential election from 1979 through 1990. This was critical because presidents controlled the appointment of the committees that determined nominations for trustees of Southern Baptist institutions.

Concurrent to this battle was another battle over categories. Many Baptist state papers, in an effort to respond to the sensitivities of both groups, would refer to one as fundamental/conservative and the other as conservative/moderate. Obviously, it was awkward and confusing. The first group used "liberal" as a pejorative for the second group, while the second group used "fundamentalist" as a pejorative for the first group. This study, in an effort to avoid pejoratives, uses the word "conservative" for the forces that successfully challenged in 1979 and the word "moderate" for those who resisted.

By 1990 the challengers had secured majorities on all their Boards, restructured the Christian Life Commission, and placed their own people in the presidencies of Southeastern Seminary and the Home Mission Board. In 1990 they pressed for changes of agenda and leadership in all Convention sponsored institutions and agencies. It was obvious that the "conservative resurgence," as its leaders defined their movement, had achieved its objectives.

Their ten-year march to dominance had not been easy. Displaced moderates mounted determined counterattacks at each convention during this time period, but failed repeatedly by an average 45 percent to 55 percent vote. Since a significant percentage of funds flowing through SBC coffers came from the more moderate churches, the question of how long they would stay in harness was critical. A rash of alternative programs and institutions came in the years leading up to the sesquicentennial.

Conservatives were divided between those who wanted these dissident groups to exit the convention and those who argued for continued inclusion. Conversely, moderate leaders tried to keep a coalition between those within their ranks who were pressing for a new denomination and those who wanted to nurture the alternate programs and yet stay within the Southern Baptist Convention.

As they approached their sesquicentennial, Southern Baptists began to harvest the negative perceptions held by others who had watched their fierce infighting. In a 1992 commencement address to graduates of Southern Baptist Theological Seminary, former President Jimmy Carter, the nation's most visible Southern Baptist, said, "When I tell people I am a Southern Baptist, it is treated with something of a joke. The term Southern Baptist is related to schism and incompatibility."[2] Carter, whose sympathy lay with the moderates, was referring to the continuing division and turmoil resulting from conservative reforms and moderate alternatives. Television journalist Bill Moyers, himself a graduate of Southwestern Baptist Theological Seminary, said, "Onlookers shake their heads at how a people so disputatious could be defined by a common name; those of us who wear it shrug our shoulders at the anomalies and schisms and go on punching (usually each other)."[3] While speaking of Baptists in general, a 1987 Moyers-produced public broadcasting television special probed Southern Baptist problems in particular.

The Need for Historical Perspective

Throughout the most recent controversy there has been evidence of a dearth of historical understanding. The desire to "get back to the vision and values of our founding fathers" has been sounded by both sides of the issue, despite startling contradictions in terms of just what might be meant. In 1992, conservative theologian Timothy George said, "The conflict of visions in the SBC encompasses not only different views of the Bible but also diverse claims about relative degrees of fidelity to the Baptist tradition."[4]

While the pressure of an anniversary as significant as a sesquicentennial undoubtedly birthed the commissioning of this volume, the controversy itself identified the need for a review of how Southern Baptists really came into being, how they have evolved, and just what principles have been persistently at the heart of their being. After all, Southern Baptist state conventions operate half a hundred colleges and universities and dozens of hospitals, children's homes, and geriatric centers, and the Convention itself presides through its agencies over hundreds of publications, not to mention a communications network and a national and worldwide mission program. The whole enterprise cries out to be understood—at least by its own.

But the task is more complicated than simply telling the story of origins and developments. The highly decentralized nature of Baptists as a people, inherent in both their beginnings and their beliefs, makes a focal point difficult to find. A multitude of stories within the story involving institutions, agencies, individuals, controversies, and movements has to be woven into any cogent narrative of the Southern Baptist Convention.

In addition, some Baptists have long been infected with a desire to trace their lineage back through all of Christian history to the life and times of Christ. Baptists have on numerous occasions, as shall be evident, rejected the doctrinal need as well as the historical viability for successionism, but many of their number have never escaped the emotional need. That has highlighted the task of identifying the characteristics in a fellowship of Christians that reveals it as Baptist or at least a legitimate forerunner of Baptists.

For a dozen years now, however, looking back has been subordinate to looking inward. Baptists have had different agendas for identifying a mainline Southern Baptist church. For most, positions such as a regenerate church membership, baptism by immersion, soul competency, the priesthood of the believer, the Bible as the sole basis for faith and practice, freedom of religion, and separation of church and state are necessary to pass history's muster. Some have added to this list women's rights and a more inclusive policy toward persons and positions in defining a mainline Southern Baptist church.

For others, biblical inerrancy, an evangelistically modified Calvinism, a pastor-centered authority, and a less stringent view of church and state, along with prayer in schools, moral legislation, right-to-life advocacy, and male authority figures are the appropriate additions to the historic positions.

Not surprisingly, these two groups have more often than not found little room or motivation for compromise despite so much still held in common. Yet Southern Baptists' current struggles make a review of their common history more important than ever before despite the difficulty. Baptist history winds in and out of all of the forces and events that occupy the same time periods. Political currents, economic factors, geographical realities, technological breakthroughs, and demographic ebbs and flows have all left their marks.

Even the fact that such a need has been recognized over and over and resulted in histories and historical essays in great numbers offers difficulty (though no one would want this task without their existence) because many of them were written with a particular spin or bias, especially evident in the very earliest efforts and the most recent. Commenting on the recent trend, Susan Harding observes, "It seems they have nothing in common, that they do not occupy the same narrative planet."[5]

Thoughtful historians admit that unrecognized biases can permeate the most careful and rigorously objective efforts. They also realize that histories are colored by the issues in place at their writing. This truth has made this writer uniquely sensitive to the subtle and not-so-subtle pressures of the controversy still being played out. The sobering reality that the way the story is told is capable of shaping Baptist identity has given this author a determination to tell it as fairly and accurately as possible.

Writing this story in this period in Southern Baptist life also confronts the human tendency to look for code words or key positions in granting a valid reading to any work. This tendency, unfortunately, can be found on all sides of Southern Baptists' current controversy. Accepting both the burden of rigorous objectivity and the risk of rejection by a severely polarized constituency has been a personal pilgrimage.

Despite these complications, the task is needed, not just because of the time frame of an anniversary or even the reverberations of conflict, but because a continued effort to understand oneself and environment is critical to growth and inherent in the Christian experience. This conviction evidently constrained those who asked the author for a narrative that can be read with profit by the average Baptist. The desire to offer those who will make up the rank and file, both the dominant and the dissenting, of Southern Baptist's future the necessary historical perspective for their unfolding experience is both a goal and a prayer.

On the surface the readability constraint may limit the contribution this publication can make to the ongoing task of "doing" Southern Baptist history. This author hopes that several new findings and sources plus the opportunity to weave latter-day events into an ongoing narrative can offer an overview perspective that will help offset this limitation. Because of the political climate and the author's determined effort to avoid undue bias, only materials published or collected in libraries have been used. No personal interviews with any principals have been sought. On the other hand, published materials based on such interviews have admittedly been invaluable. But in this author's mind, the fact they had been published and are subject to review and challenge is the critical difference.

While the beginnings of Baptist life continue to be debated and theories refined, the historical beginning of the Southern Baptist Convention is easy to establish. It convened in Augusta, Georgia, on May 8, 1845, and adopted a constitution on May 10, establishing an organization that has lasted 150 years.

But it was a long and winding road to Augusta. And it has been a wild and challenging ride since.

1

Roots and Reasons

1609–1845

It has been said that there are only three ways to tell a story. One can start at a perceived beginning and write to the end. One can start at the end and write backward to the beginning. Or one can start at the crucial event in the story and write backward to the beginning and forward to the end. The latter method has the advantage when there is some ambiguity about beginnings, when the crucial event dictates the focus, and when the end is an arbitrary point in an ongoing story. A history of the Southern Baptist Convention meets all three conditions and this narrative starts with the crucial event. It took place during five days in May in 1845 in historic Augusta, Georgia.

Located ninety miles up the Savannah River from the port of Savannah, Augusta had once been the capital of Georgia, but was still at the heart of its commercial activity and the growing Baptist presence in that area. Eli Whitney had built his first cotton gin just outside Augusta in 1793. With its dogwood and azaleas, Augusta was one of the loveliest points in the Southern states but, in a contrast of symbols, it became the arsenal of the South in the approaching conflict. A century and a half later it was just down river from a nuclear weapons plant.

The Convention at Augusta

The 293 individual "delegates"[1] who gathered in Georgia during those late spring days were motivated by deeply held religious convictions, but they also were subject to a sectional and social bias that soon engulfed the region they represented in the bloodiest of all civil wars.

The implications of their political persuasion was little more than a small cloud on their horizon when these Baptists from nine states met at the Baptist church in Augusta. Their meeting was in response to a call issued by Virginia Baptists less than a month before to consider breaking with their national Baptist body in favor of a southern organization because of discriminating procedures imposed by northern abolitionists.

Brevity of time between the call for "consultation" and the event itself probably prevented more Baptists from attending. All but fifty-two of the delegates were from Georgia and South Carolina, with 139 and 102 respectively. Virginia was a distant third.

An accurate understanding of the character of this gathered body requires some attention to those who were not there. No women registered for these proceedings. Neither were any black members of the churches at the meeting. This is significant because on the rolls of their various congregations both groups probably outnumbered the white males who were there.

Women played a serious role in Baptist life and had for many years. But history paid scant attention to the role of Catherine Scott in Roger Williams' Baptist decision, Martha Stearns Marshall's role as a frontier preacher in the Sandy Creek movement, Mary Webb's role in establishing America's first Baptist missionary society in Boston, or even Lydia Turner's role in the conversion of W. B. Johnson, who later presided over this organization. It was obvious that though Baptists in the South represented a union of the regular and separate traditions of its American heritage, the Separates' openness to women's ministries had been largely overcome by the Regulars' practice of denying the same.[2] Yet Judson College in Alabama and what became Mary Hardin-Baylor College in Texas were even then being founded by Baptists to encourage literacy and leadership among women.

Nor were any black Baptists present. This should provoke little surprise since in all but a few significant instances their status was that of slave. While the First African Baptist Church of Richmond, Virginia, which J. B. Jeter had helped bring into existence, was being replicated in other places, for the most part blacks were members of southern Baptist churches.[3]

Who was there as well as who was not there reflected the cultural identification peculiar to southern Baptist life. That cultural union would mark the Baptist Convention for decades to come. It was to be all but inseparable from a white male-dominated culture dependent upon agriculture, especially cotton. It was a culture marked at that time by slavery and for years following by its demeaning aftermath.

Personalities, Histories, and Drives

This story's crucial event is more than a time and place. It is also personalities, histories, and drives. It involves roots and reasons. Understanding those involves writing the story back toward its beginnings as far as the records will allow.

Delegates who gathered at Augusta were for the most part an impressive group of educated, experienced, mature, and cultured believers. Their leader, as was quickly recognized, was William Bullein Johnson of South Carolina. Pastor of the Baptist church in Edgefield, Johnson had already helped fashion some dramatic beginnings. He had once been pastor of a church in Savannah and knew the Augusta area well.

Johnson was joined there by a host of impressive persons including Richard Fuller of Beaufort, South Carolina, who had achieved some fame for defending the institution of slavery from a scriptural point of view in a debate with a northern Baptist, Francis Wayland. Their debate was published in a book called *Domestic Slavery Considered as a Scriptural Institution.*[4]

Two years later, Fuller became pastor of the Seventh Baptist Church of Baltimore, where he helped those on both sides of the issue try to understand each other. Since Maryland would remain in the Union, Fuller's views must have modified enough to allow him a significant hearing. The fact that they did so reflects the ambivalence that ran up and down the borders toward the issue that was beginning to divide the fledgling United States of America.

Neither Johnson nor Fuller overshadowed Basil Manly, Sr., president of the University of Alabama. He would help found Southern Baptist Theological Seminary within the next decade, as well as Furman University. His son, Basil, became one of the original faculty members of the seminary and another son, Charles, became president of Furman University. Education was well represented at the consultative gathering, with nearby Mercer University's financial agent, C. D. Mallory, and several Mercer students.

There was only one delegate from Kentucky, but he brought a measure of fame with him. Isaac McCoy had distinguished himself as a missionary among the Indians in Kentucky. He went to the consultation to protect a vested interest (he led the Indian Missionary Association which drew much of its support from the churches represented in the consultative convention), but he also brought an evangelistic frontier flavor that would increasingly mark the young organization and, in tension with the educated traditions of the majority of the founders, constitute an abiding fault-line.

Perhaps the most influential group came from Virginia. They were led by the indomitable pastor of the First Baptist Church of Richmond, Dr. Jeremiah Bell Jeter. In his autobiography, Jeter described the perilous trip to Augusta. The delegation left Richmond by train to journey down through the lowlands and tidewater to Wilmington, North Carolina, where they embarked on a steamship down the Cape Fear River to the Atlantic and then started the perilous coastal ocean voyage to Charleston, South Carolina. A fierce storm tossed their little ship until the Virginians feared for their lives. Jeter, characteristically impressed by his delegation, said that had the ship been lost it would have dealt a terrible blow to Virginia Baptist life. But they did land at Charleston and then took an arduous overland trip to Augusta.[5]

It is doubtful that in 1845 the trip was easy for anyone except those in the immediate area. The complex reasons that motivated these Baptist leaders to make their way to Augusta, however, is more significant than any of the attendant circumstances.

At the risk of oversimplification, these reasons may be understood in terms of three intertwining historical roots. Even a cursory understanding of the roots can shed light on the strong dynamics at work in the hearts and minds of those who convened in Augusta, as well as the antecedents that would shape their subsequent history.

First, the nearest thing to a taproot was a growing pride in being a Baptist. Merely confessional at first, the word assumed significant connectional dimensions only three decades earlier. A denominational consciousness still rooted in the Protestant Reformation, being a Baptist reflected many of the complex drives and conflicts that emerged from the Reformation.

Second, these convening Baptists were also driven by a consuming missionary conviction birthed in England in 1792 with the courage of William Carey and indigenous to these shores in the convictions of Burma-bound Adoniram Judson. In May of 1814 that missionary conviction led to formation of a national denominational body which they called the General Missionary Convention of the Baptist Denomination in the United States for Foreign Missions. Known as the Triennial Convention for meeting every three years and focused on foreign missions, it was soon joined by two other societies—one for publications (1824) and a second for home missions (1832). Painful consideration of separation from at least two of those connectional ventures had brought these southern Baptists to Augusta.

Their passion for missions had been sharpened against a rock of dissent in their ranks from hyper-Calvinistic, anti-mission positions to the still young missionary impulse. Isaac McCoy and the churches that he represented from Kentucky were still reeling from conflicts with Alexander Campbell and the followers of Barton Stone, who among other things denied the legitimacy of extra church organizations. They had seen Daniel Parker's passionate anti-mission oratory reap a divisive harvest.

Third, these two influences, however, increasingly mingled with an entrenched sectionalism that reflected not only the geography of the South and its economy, but also its tragic "peculiar" institution of slavery. Baptists in the south felt a growing sense of estrangement from a northern-dominated national government, and the galling condemnation of the South's Baptist churches and leaders by northern-based abolitionism further inflamed their sectional partisanship. The Baptists gathering in Augusta, however low-keyed and genteel they were when they spoke to the matter, felt keenly the sting of rejection in this sectional estrangement.

Thus, though the story's crucial event took place in Augusta, Georgia, in 1845, that event constituted the interaction of a growing Baptist confessional and connectional consciousness, a passionate missionary conviction, and a visceral sectional spirit. These forces brought the founders of the Southern Baptist Convention together in a city founded over a century before and named in honor of Princess Augusta, the mother of King George III of England, whose reactions had triggered the founding of the same young nation now rent by these forces.

The confessional and connectional consciousness which these Baptist believers represented as they came to Augusta was both testified to and tested by their gathering. William Bullein Johnson and his mentor, Richard Furman, led in the organization of the Triennial Baptist Convention in Philadelphia in 1814 to create a Foreign Mission Society to undergird the missionary adventures of Adoniram Judson and his colleagues in far-off Burma. The Triennial Convention was joined by a Tract Society in 1824 and a Home Mission Society in 1832. The Tract Society sent a representative to the Augusta gathering, hoping that the conflicts between the southerners and the Foreign and Home Mission Societies would not include them. While those gathered at the Convention felt betrayed by the leaders of the Triennial Convention, they were quick to point out that the betrayal was structural and organizational and did not take issue with their common Baptist confession. That confession and its subsequent connections can best be understood by examining its beginnings.

The Baptist Tradition in America

The first Baptist church in the region represented at Augusta during those days in May appeared in Charleston, South Carolina, in 1696. It owed its origins to both a common and an uncommon Baptist experience up and down the coast of the new American republic. What was common was that some of its members had been in Charleston for a while. They were immigrants from Baptist life in England where persecution had been consistent and bitter until 1689 when the Act of Toleration had been signed.[6] What was uncommon was the fact that these immigrant Baptists joined a church that migrated into their midst from Kittery, Maine. In fact, an examination of the roots of the first Baptist church in the South reveals that it came by way of Kittery, Maine, which came by way of Boston, which came by way of England.

Baptist immigrants fleeing intolerance in England and influenced by Baptist beginnings in nearby Rhode Island had founded a church in Boston in 1665. The Boston church in 1682 officially affiliated with a group of Baptists in Kittery and helped them organize into a church a short time later. By 1696 this church moved "lock, stock, and barrel" to the more religiously favorable climate of Charleston, a city whose founders had decided that they would need religious toleration to attract settlers. Of course, their move may have been helped along by the opportunity for cheaper land and available timber, because many of the Kittery church members were shipbuilders.[7] Gathering timber in Maine was taking them farther into Indian territory where hostile reaction increased.

Their pastor, William Screven, typified many early Baptist ministers. He had been converted in England and was said to have there signed one of the early confessions of faith called the Somerset Confession.[8] In England he associated with a Baptist leader who was later discredited, which may explain why the Boston church asked him to be rebaptized when he migrated to the New World. But they recognized his gifts, and though he was an aggressive entrepreneur, he was ordained to the ministry in 1682 and became the pastor of the Kittery congregation. Capable and energetic, Screven was the leader of the southern exodus. Thus, he and his followers and their descendants were a significant part of the early development of southern Baptist life. Only ten years before the Augusta gathering, Basil Manly helped the First Baptist Church at Charleston, of which he was then pastor, celebrate its founding. He lauded the faith of that "persecuted flock" who had fled to the religious freedom of South Carolina.[9]

If the first Baptist church in the South was gathered at Charleston, South Carolina, where was the first Baptist church established in America? It was not the Boston church which spawned the Kittery congregation. Historians have given that honor more often than not to a congregation gathered in what became Rhode Island by the indomitable father of religious liberty, Roger Williams.[10]

Just as William Screven fled England to escape persecution, so Williams journeyed with his bride to the New World. They arrived in Boston on a wintery February 5, 1631. Though not a Baptist at the time, he had already made the increasingly common journey from the Anglican Church to its Puritan wing to a Separatist body. As a Separatist, Williams' path to the New World was well established. It had been pioneered by the Mayflower's pilgrim fathers who had connections with the group that turned out to be history's first Baptist congregation.

A bright man who was educated under the patronage of a famous English jurist at Cambridge before taking Anglican orders, Williams was also a very independent thinker. His thoughts found support first in Salem and later in Plymouth, where he was a leader among latter-day pilgrims. His winsome, yet compelling witness attracted a strong following much as history's pioneer Baptist, John Smyth, had thirty years before in England. Williams returned to Salem as an elder in 1634, despite the objections of his followers in Plymouth. They decided to endorse his going only after William Bradford, who had known John Smyth, detected some disturbing parallels between Smyth's pilgrimage and that of Williams.[11]

While still in England, Williams had undoubtedly known of Smyth and his celebrated flight to Amsterdam and probably his subsequent development. But he does not cite Smyth at any point to support his own progress.

In Salem Roger Williams' preaching took an even bolder turn as he argued for absolute separation of church and state and for freedom of conscience. The leading advocate for a theocratic state based upon Puritan principles, John Cotton, countered with a call for civil penalties for "armianism, papism, familism or other heresies." His agitation helped bring about Williams' banishment in October, 1635. Williams, hoping for a reprieve, withdrew from the Bay churches and, holding services in his own home, quietly began preparations for a new settlement guaranteeing religious liberty. But in January of 1636, the Court of Boston, hearing of his activities, ordered his immediate deportation to England. Only a friendly warning from the colony's Governor Winthrop allowed him to escape.

Roger Williams' flight that winter of 1636 took him into the wilderness of the Narraganset Bay, where he took shelter among the Indians. He had an affinity for America's original citizens and made efforts to learn their language and to understand their culture. He acknowledged and championed their prior rights to the land—part of the reason he was at first suspect and then banished.

Here Williams pursued his dream of a colony where people could be free from religious persecution. At the mouth of the Mohassuck River he set up the town of Providence on land he purchased from the Indians. He intended it to be a place for all "distressed for conscience." Soon Williams was joined by dissidents from Salem and possibly Plymouth, and in a replay of John Smyth's refugee group thirty years before, the little congregation began to question their baptism.

Evidently, a woman, the wife of Richard Scott and one of the group that had joined Williams, played a key role in convincing Williams to act on his developing convictions. Governor Winthrop's journal, reflecting on news from the Narragansett dissidents, claimed in a kind of "the woman made him do it" scenario that Catherine Scott "being infected with anabaptistry emboldened" Williams to take the big step.[12]

Catherine Scott came by her boldness honestly, for her sister, Ann Hutchison, was considered to be the first woman preacher in America. Like her sister, Hutchison and her family would later flee the oppressive Massachusetts colony for what is now New York. There they died in a Indian massacre.[13]

In March, 1639, Williams, the Scotts, and others decided to renounce their infant experience and take up believer's baptism. Aware of the storm that had followed Smyth's self-baptism, Williams convinced a fellow member, Ezekiel Holliman, to baptize him, and then he baptized Holliman and ten others.

Williams, ever the seeker, did not remain a Baptist long but continued his pilgrimage. In part, he was troubled by the way he was baptized. His concern was not the mode (historians differ on whether it was by effusion or immersion), but the authority. Williams fell victim to the same hunger that troubled John Smyth before him, a hunger that took root more strongly two hundred years later in Baptist life. He believed that somehow there needed to be a succession in place all the way back to Jesus, and he left the Baptist group to become a "seeker."[14]

Thomas Olney took over as pastor but, reflecting the Calvinist-Arminian fault line that dogged Baptists through the years, the church split in 1652. The Calvinist group died out in 1720, but the remaining congregation was again won to a Calvinist Confession in 1771.[15] Richard Scott later became a Quaker, and Catherine Scott disappeared into history.[16]

This shaky Baptist beginning in the New World found a more substantive start through the labors of a physician named John Clarke. Born to well-to-do parents in Suffolk, England, in 1609, the same year John Smyth's separatist group fled to Amsterdam and nine years after Williams fled, Clarke emigrated to New England at the age of twenty-eight with proficiencies in medicine, theology, and law. He arrived in Boston to find religious persecution in full swing. Identifying with the dissidents, he was soon a leader. After an aborted effort to go to New Hampshire, Clarke and a group of dissidents sought out Williams, who helped them purchase a tract of land from the Indians in what is now Rhode Island.

When Clarke became a Baptist is not known. Because of the presence of a John Clarke at the University of Leyden in Holland, some have speculated about early Baptist influences, but the church he helped establish and began to lead in the new colony was clearly Baptist by 1648 and possibly had adopted Baptist principles as early as 1639 or 1640. Tradition has held that the Newport group embraced immersion as the correct mode of baptism even before the Providence church. More recently, the case has been made that both the Williams group and the Clarke group immersed from the beginning, which if true would predate English Baptist immersion.[17] Arguments over just when that practice took hold in English Baptist life were later to cause William Whitsitt, president of Southern Baptist Theological Seminary, to resign under fire.

The more stable Clarke, a physician, not only continued to play a leading role in the new colony, but also to lead what turned out to be the stronger Baptist church in Newport. Yet Clarke too faced the bitterness of persecution when he, a man named Crandall, and one Obadiah Holmes made a visit to Massachusetts in 1651. They were arrested and fined, and Holmes was put to the lash. This incident is reported to have influenced the recently established Harvard University's president, Henry Dunster, to become a Baptist. That move cost him his job in 1654.[18]

Shortly after the persecution incident, the young colony sent Williams and Clarke to England to protect its interests, which were being threatened by William Coddington who had become governor. The two Baptist pioneers had collaborated to secure a charter which brought religious freedom to these shores. Reassured that their cause would prevail, Williams returned to the colony, but not before writing the second of a pair of historic tracts. "The Bloudy Tenent of Persecution," published in 1644, challenged Massachusetts' Congregational giant, John Cotton, on the subjects of religious liberty and the separation of church and state. In 1652, Williams published a follow-up, "The Bloudy Tenent Yet More Bloudy."

Catching the spirit of tractarian battle, John Clarke penned his own contribution, "Ill Newes from New England or a Narrative of New England Persecution." He recounted his own firsthand experience and made an impassioned plea for liberty of conscience. Preaching and practicing as a physician, Clarke was able to stay in England until he received an expanded charter for the colony from Charles II in 1663. It provided "that no person within the colony, at any time hereafter shall be in anywise molested, punished, disquieted or called in question for any differences in opinions in matters of religion."[19]

When Clarke returned to the colony the next year, he resumed his place of leadership, later serving as deputy governor. Although Williams, now calling himself a seeker, did not again become a Baptist, both he and Clarke lived long enough to see a Baptist church established in Boston in 1665. It was in that church that William Screven and his wife were baptized sixteen years later.[20]

The First Baptists

Yet the Baptists who gathered in Augusta looked further back into time and beyond their own shores for their true beginnings. As presaged, these beginnings, just as in the South and in the New World, were also developed around the search for religious liberty.

Baptists have long been divided among three historical roots: some think that the first Baptist church was organized in 1609 in Amsterdam out of a Puritan-Separatist tradition that had embraced a general atonement; others hold to the first Baptist church really being formed in London, England, in 1641 from another Puritan-Separatist tradition with a Particular or Calvinist theory of atonement; and still others believe that Baptist life really began with the continental Anabaptist reformation in 1525. In recent years, most historians have conceded the honor to the little group of believers that surrounded John Smyth in Amsterdam in 1609.

Given Baptists' appeal to common people through the centuries that would follow, Smyth is an appropriate latter-day John the Baptist.

Smyth was educated at Cambridge University where he, like Roger Williams, served as a fellow for a time following his graduation. He, too, was ordained an Anglican priest but soon embraced the Puritan hope that the reformation which separated the Anglican Church from Roman Catholicism nearly a century before would move on to new purity. Like many other Puritans he, too, soon became a Separatist.

Separatists were basically Puritans who despaired of change within the Church of England. Defying authorities at varying times and in different places, they set up Separatist churches based on Puritan tenets. Robert Browne's congregation in 1581 was the first such church, and Separatists for years after would derisively be called Brownists.

One of the best known of the Separatist churches was the Ancient Church of English Separatists established in London in 1587. Elizabethan persecution drove this congregation to the Netherlands in 1593. When King James ascended to the English throne in 1603, high initial hopes for improvement were quickly dashed, and by 1604 a number of stringent canons required allegiance to the Church of England. These created new tensions and, ultimately, acts of persecution against Puritan and Separatist clergy; however, these also created new Separatist churches.

By 1606 Smyth was associated with what some historians describe as a Puritan conventicle in the Gainsborough area; there his talents and spiritual gifts led him to be included as one of their ministers. This group included some of the people who would soon journey to America on the Mayflower.[21]

The leader of that group writing years later recorded their decision to covenant together as a separate church: "as the Lord's free people joined themselves (by a covenant of the Lord) into a Church estate, in the fellowship of the gospel, to walk in all his ways made know, or to be made known to unto them, according to their best endeavors, whatsoever it should cost them, the Lord assisting them."[22] As it turned out, it would cost much.

For years historians assumed that this congregation divided for safety's sake into groups in Gainsborough and Scrooby. Recent research suggests that at this time they might still have been one congregation which, drawing membership from a wide area, met in both locations under the leadership of several ministers, including the increasingly influential Smyth.[23]

Another minister in the group, John Robinson, later led a portion of this fellowship to break with the Smyth group. It was this group that would later become the pilgrim fathers. Because of that, many historians have traditionally assumed two distinct congregations, one at Gainsborough and one at Scrooby.

This Gainsborough group met at Broxtowe Hall by 1607, and its young master, Thomas Helwys, was a staunch supporter and admirer of John Smyth. Helwys, from an old Nottingshire family, had secured a good education before marrying Jane Ashmore in 1595; the first of their seven children was born the next year. Helwys' devotion to Smyth increased as their Separatist convictions deepened and he became Smyth's soul mate in his incessant efforts to find new truth. When they later split, Helwys said of Smyth, "All our love was too little for him and not worthy of him."[24]

As King James's crackdown on nonconformists continued, the embattled congregation looked increasingly toward the religiously tolerant Netherlands. The seaport of Amsterdam was the financial and trade center of the western world at the beginning of the seventeenth century. To further enhance their crossroads business reputation, the Dutch declared religious tolerance, making the Netherlands a virtual island of freedom in a religiously divided post-reform Europe. Besides freedom of worship they allowed a free press and provided universal education.

By 1607, Amsterdam's confines included many groups seeking relief from religious persecution in both England and the continent. Among them were the Mennonites, followers of Menno Simons and successors to the Anabaptists. Prominent among the groups from England was the

Ancient Church led by Smyth's old friend and mentor, Francis Johnson.[25] Smyth's group, aware of the imprisonment that awaited those who did not attend the Anglican church, decided to join them.

It has been suggested that Thomas Helwys financed the considerable adventure, but for Helwys the cost was more than money. His wife Jane and their seven children, evidently planning to join him later, stayed at Broxtowe hoping women would be spared. She was wrong. Arrested almost immediately after her husband's flight, she spent nearly a year in prison before she was able to join the exiles.

Smyth and Helwys and their followers accomplished the crossing in late 1607 or early 1608. They did not unite with the Ancient Church, as some have maintained, but established their own identity and discovered that they were among many such groups.

Trying to define differences between these groups caused Smyth to publish a book in 1608 called *The Differences of the Churches of the Separation*. In this writing Smyth and his fellow believers spelled out their view of Scripture: "The Holy Scriptures, viz., the Originals, Hebrew and Greek, are given by Divine inspiration, and in their first donation were without error, most perfect, and therefore Canonical."[26]

Some years later, one of Smyth's and Helwys's supporters, John Murton, in his "Supplication" would add: "The rule of faith is the doctrine of the Holy Ghost contained in the sacred scripture, and not any church, council, prince, or potentate, nor any mortal man whatsoever." He added, "That the Spirit of God to understand and interpret the scripture is given to all and every particular person that fear and obey God, of what degree soever they be."[27]

A constant search for truth and a commitment to change their position as rapidly as they could discern a better way (or "further light" as they called it) launched the Smyth group on the path that identified them as history's first clear-cut Baptist church.[28] However, their efforts also precipitated two significant splits.

One of their first steps was to modify the Calvinistic concept of grace that had been their Puritan heritage. They began to espouse a concept of salvation advocated by Netherlands theologian Jacobus Arminius. Arminius taught that salvation was meant for all who would believe, or a general atonement, rather than just the elect, or a particular atonement as advocated by John Calvin. While they were following the growing influence of Arminius, they were also undoubtedly impressed by similar Mennonite-held views. Smyth's embracing of Arminian views is one of the reasons that many later historians tie Baptist beginnings to continental Anabaptists from whom the Mennonites sprang.

Smyth's followers also moved to a congregational form of church authority rather than an eldership or presbytery. According to historian William Henry Brackney, "For Smyth, church leaders were altogether accountable to the congregational body and for this reason, Smyth is rightly remembered as the first egalitarian among the Separatists."[29]

Additional changes were made "in the treasury" where they claimed only the saved should give. They also believed that one could "fall away."

One or all of these steps precipitated a break with the John Robinson wing of the fellowship sometimes called the Scrooby group. Robinson's group petitioned the city of Leyden to let them migrate there in early 1609. It was from Leyden that many from their ranks, led by William Bradford, began the journey that culminated with the Mayflower's arrival in the New World.

The big move of the Smyth group's "further light" commitment came two years after taking up their stay in Amsterdam's more religiously hospitable climate. They became convinced that only believers should be baptized. A church, therefore, was to be formed not by covenant but by baptism.

In contrast to what Williams did later, Smyth did not have himself baptized by someone like Helwys and then return the favor; Smyth baptized himself. Called se-baptism for self-baptism, this act came in for much criticism. Smyth then baptized Helwys and the rest of the group.[30] Consensus thinking among historians points to this baptism by pouring or affusion.

But once again, anticipating moves that Roger Williams would make three decades later in the New World, Smyth became dissatisfied with his actions and attempted to lead his new fellowship to seek ties with the Mennonite's Waterlander congregation. This is another reason some historians believe that early Baptists drew significant inspiration from continental Anabaptists.[31] Though Smyth later denied a belief in successionism, it was obvious at this time that he longed for its security.[32]

Smyth's uncertainties and his hunger for apostolic succession soon caused a break between him and his most ardent disciple, Thomas Helwys.[33] In the early days of the Reformation, positions were so fragile that as reforming thinkers continued to define their positions through study of the Bible and the searching of hearts and minds, they often divided, sometimes amiably, more often bitterly. About a dozen of the exiles, led by Thomas

Helwys and John Murton, refused to join Smyth's efforts to unite with the Mennonite congregation. They considered themselves the original church and stewards of the truth that Smyth and the others were abandoning.

Smyth's efforts to clarify his position for this move provide early understanding of the initial Baptist position, but he died shortly after the break with Helwys and before the Mennonites cautiously agreed to accept the group. They did not require a new baptism, however.

In addition to his antipathy to Smyth's successionism, Helwys felt that the little fellowship of believers had no right to be refugees from their own land; that, despite the danger, they needed to return to England, their homeland, to bear witness there to their new faith.

In anticipation of their return, Thomas Helwys wrote a powerful work entitled "A Short Declaration of the Mystery of Iniquity." The document was a passionate call for religious liberty. Published upon their return to the Spitalsfield area near London in 1612, one copy was even addressed to the King in Helwys's own hand.

In response, Helwys was seized shortly after his return to England and imprisoned for his advocacy. Just months before, Bartholomew Legate, who had ties to the Mennonites, was burned to death on order of King James; a month later Edward Wightman suffered the same fate for Separatist views. Fortunately for Helwys, these were the last public burnings of "heretics." Instead, dissidents were silently and privately left to waste away in prison. Helwys, suffering "silently and privately," died in the infamous Newgate Prison in 1616.[34]

His widow, Jane Helwys, returned to Amsterdam and joined the Mennonite church that now included the deceased Smyth's group. Given her support of her husband, her imprisonment for her faith, and her persistent pursuit of her convictions, Jane Helwys deserves a place in the largely untold story of women's contributions to Baptists.

The little Baptist congregation fell to the leadership of John Murton. Despite Helwys's experience, the church under Murton published a treatise Murton wrote while also imprisoned. The document was supposedly written on paper smuggled as a stopper in a milk bottle, and the text was written with milk. Held before a fire, the otherwise invisible text could then be read and reproduced. "A Most Humble Supplication" addressed to the king and an impending new parliament argued passionately against persecution for the cause of conscience. It was this document that came to Salem's John Cotton twenty years later. His answer occasioned Roger Williams's famous "The Bloody Tenent of Persecution, for cause of Conscience discussed in a conference between Truth and Peace."

Because their concept of salvation was anchored in a doctrine of free grace to all who would receive it, a position in conflict with the prevailing Calvinistic concepts, these early Baptists were called General Baptists. At this point, they were at odds with many Congregationalists and Separatists and even with non-separatist churches that, despite disputes with the Church of England, remained strongly Calvinistic. A group of Baptists, however, was soon to surface that, unlike the Smyth-Helwys-Murton group, continued in their Calvinism.

Particular Baptists

The General Baptist group that began in Amsterdam and returned to England to become the first Baptist church on English soil shares history's spotlight with a second genesis of Baptists developed from an independent church founded by Henry Jacob. This group's Calvinism, though mild, caused them to be called Particular Baptists.

Jacob had attended Oxford University while Smyth was at Cambridge. Jacob also became an Anglican clergyman but soon became a part of the reform movement within that church. It cost him a stint in jail because of a treatise he wrote on the subject. Jacob, however, refused to join the Separatists and tried to establish what he called the true church of England. The church was independent, but Jacob did not consider it a separated church. His followers, first John Lathrup and later Henry Jessey, continued to lead the church, but in 1633 it divided.

Somewhere between 1633 and 1638 the group led by Jessey began advocating believer's baptism. Hearing of the practice of immersion in Holland, one of their members, Richard Blunt, went to the Netherlands in 1641 to visit a Mennonite group, the Collegiants, who practiced immersion. Blunt supposedly received baptism by immersion there, then returned and baptized another member; between them they baptized fifty-one members of what was now two congregations.

A group led by John Spilsbury, a cobbler by trade, held that baptismal succession was "neither possible nor necessary." Claiming that when beginning, someone must be first, he began baptizing without any worry about historic succession.[35]

Baptist beginnings had witnessed se-baptism in Smyth, reciprocal baptism in Williams, acquired baptism in Blunt, and incipient baptism in Spilsbury. The latter two if not three were by immersion, however, and this historic act uniquely set the fledgling Baptists apart from other Separatist groups. General Baptists quickly adopted immersion. The contention that the American Baptist churches immersed from the beginning is based on the lack of any document citing a change in mode after the beginning.

Though the Mennonites were not Calvinists, the Spilsbury-Blunt group maintained the modified Calvinism that had been a part of their founding. Believing in Particular atonement, they were known as Particular Baptists.

Particular Baptists numbered seven congregations by 1644 and developed a confession of faith clearly identifying baptism as immersion, with which they later sought toleration from Parliament. Known as the First London Confession of Faith, this partially borrowed document strongly influenced Baptists in America.[36] The confession defined the church as both visible as the local church and invisible as the church of all the redeemed.

Not surprisingly, in an environment where the Bible was being constantly searched for "further light," a third stream of Baptists emerged on the basis of literal Sabbath-keeping in contrast to first-day practices by both General and Particular Baptists. Seventh-day Baptists delineated themselves in the 1650s and have had an unbroken though less visible history since.[37] American Baptist historian William Brackney says Seventh-day Baptists "seem to have sustained more intense persecution in troubled times and enjoyed less toleration in permissive periods than their General or Particular brethren."[38]

The Anabaptists

Were these fellowships the true fountain head of Baptist life? Although controversy over successionism was not to flower until over two centuries later, many more, like Smyth and Roger Williams would want a far more expansive genealogy undergirding their faith. Aware of the involvement of Mennonites in both General and Particular Baptist beginnings, they would look beyond the English cradle to the Anabaptists and their forebears for their real beginnings.

Most historians classify Anabaptists as a distinct part of the Protestant Reformation and generally date their emergence to around 1525, eight years after Luther launched the Reformation.

Followers of Ulrich Zwingli in Switzerland began to press that reformer to go beyond his limited reform to true restitution of New Testament practices and especially to reject infant baptism. Leaders such as Conrad Grebel and Felix Manz originally supported Zwingli but broke with him to become early leaders of reformation Anabaptists. The Anabaptist movement spread rapidly and varieties developed not only in Switzerland but also in southern Germany, Austria, middle and northern Germany, Holland, and even England.

Most Anabaptists were generally grouped into what is called "the left wing of the Reformation," because many versions of them organized small communal groups and held everything in common.[39]

The name *Anabaptist* was not nomenclature they chose, but a term given to them by those who advocated severe repression. The origin of the word Anabaptist goes back to A. D. 529 when the Code of Justinian made rebaptism (that is, anabaptism) one of two heresies punishable by death. It was applied to sixth-century dissidents, who protested the validity of the baptism practiced by certain priests and rebaptized as a result. This was a part of the Donatist Controversy that followed the severe persecutions of Christians in the fourth and fifth centuries. On the strength of Justinian's sixth-century code, authorities in 1528 moved against Reformation Anabaptists by reaffirming the ancient legislation at the Council of Speier, although the sixteenth-century Anabaptists had no relationship to the Donatists except that they too were called "Anabaptists."

In their most radical Reformation version, a group of Anabaptists mounted a short-lived, eschatologically-driven revolt in Münster, Germany which was cruelly put down by Luther's followers. The excesses of this group were so notorious that Anabaptists everywhere were tainted with their reputation. David Benedict, an early Baptist historian, would even deny that the radicals were Anabaptists.[40]

Heroes of mainstream Anabaptists commended themselves to later Baptists, however, who admired the terrible price they paid for their beliefs. Anabaptist martyrs include Michael Sattler, who was executed in southern Germany in May of 1527; Jacob Hutter, whose followers were known as Hutterites in Austria and Moravia; and Balthasar Hubmaier of Nicholsburg, who was burned at the stake in Vienna in May 1528 and whose wife was drowned. Hubmaier rejected infant baptism, advocating baptism only following a confession of faith. He believed in the separation of church and state and taught that a local church was "a particular, external congregation" of a universal church made up of the totality of the redeemed.[41]

The Münster rebellion brought widespread persecution to all varieties of continental Anabaptists. Those survived best who fled to Holland and its religious toleration. Leaders there included Melchior Hoffman and the well-known Menno Simons. The Mennonites, as they came to be called, were one of the largest Protestant groups in Holland before they were supplanted by reform movements in the seventeenth century.

John Smyth and members of his Separatist group of refugee Christians came in contact with this group when they organized the first Baptist church in Holland in 1609. And Richard Blunt and the Particular Baptists approached a related group in 1638–41 to secure baptism by immersion. These contacts and doctrinal similarities are cited by a small group of historians who feel Baptists cannot and should not deny their Anabaptist ties.[42] They continue to be a minority, however, when compared to those who feel only an English Separatist cradle can legitimately claim Baptist beginnings.

Yet, underlining the persistence of those who affirm Anabaptist roots is the fact that as late as 1991, the president of Southern Baptists' Southeastern Seminary would speak warmly of "our Anabaptist fathers" while commending their style of church discipline.[43]

Successionism

As mentioned earlier, hunger for a specific genealogy for faith haunted early Baptist pioneers like Smyth and later Williams, but not nearly so much as it later fired Baptist passions on America's frontier to identify a continuity in the face of competing visions of the Christian church. Robert G. Torbet said Baptist beginnings have rested on three theories: (1) the English Puritan Separatist beginnings of 1609 and 1638–41; (2) the Anabaptist spiritual kinship theories that expand on the contacts and influence of continental Anabaptists with English reformers; and (3) the successionist historians who have sought to trace Baptists through a succession of churches from the ministry of John the Baptist and New Testament beginnings.

Successionism in this sense emerged early in Baptist life with the efforts of some of its pioneering historians. It gained its primary momentum, however, during the Landmark controversy in Southern Baptist life in the nineteenth century, which in turn may have been fueled by the Campbell controversies that preceded it. Campbell's "reformers" talked of restoring New Testament churches. Landmark Baptists responded that there had always been Baptists and that their unbroken history make them the only true church. Southern Baptists came together in the "seam" between the beginning of these two movements and outside of both traditions.

The earliest Baptist historian, Thomas Crosby, is grouped with successionists by Robert G. Torbet but is better known for trying to disassociate Baptists from Anabaptists because of the radicals of Münster.

David Benedict's Baptist history in 1813 featured a successionist attitude by claiming Baptists included John the Baptist, Augustine of Canterbury, and John Wycliffe. But Benedict really built his case on Christian dissenters through the ages such as the Waldenses, the Moravian Brethren, Swiss and Dutch Anabaptists, and like groups. As mentioned earlier he denied that Münsterites were Anabaptists.[44]

A book by G. H. Orchard, an English Baptist writer, first published in England in 1838, became the standard of Landmark successionism. Reprinted in America under the aegis of James R. Graves in 1849, this book helped fire the imagination of frontier Baptists yearning for historical validity and authority. Later successionists such as Richard B. Cook, W. A. Jarrell, and John T. Christian added such names to a Baptist family tree as Montanists, Novationists, Donatists, Paulicians, Albigenses, Patarenes, Petrobucians, Henricians, Arnoldists, Waldenses, and finally Anabaptists. Many stressed a continuity of principles rather than a succession of churches.

A series of lectures by J. M. Carroll of Texas were copied and published in a booklet called "The Trail of Blood," which may have received the widest circulation of all successionist literature.

As late as 1962, R. G. Lee, former Southern Baptist Convention president and pastor of Bellevue Baptist Church of Memphis, wrote in a preface to a successionist tract, "all Christians today should believe that Baptists began their denominational life under the ministry of Jesus."[45]

Developing Connections

Baptist traditions that began in the South in Charleston, in America in Rhode Island, in England and in Amsterdam, and possibly in spirit in Anabaptist struggles and the long history of dissent in Christian history constitute the confessional background of the gathering in Augusta in 1845. But the true denominational consciousness of these churches developed through a halting but significant connectionalism. Connectionalism refers to church-relatedness or affiliations of churches. Apart from the Smyth-Helwys beginnings, all of Baptists' definitive confessions would emerge through connectional entities.

Associations in England

After returning to England the General Baptists, successors to the Smyth-Helwys-Murton efforts, faced persistent persecution as the Church of England's Archbishop Laud continued his efforts to limit dissent. During this period, Roger Williams, John Clarke, and others were forced to migrate to New England. When the civil wars that brought Oliver Cromwell to power began, General Baptists and Particular Baptists both began to prosper. Cromwell's Commonwealth period (1640–60) was called Baptists' golden age.

When Oliver Cromwell led his New Model Army against Britain's monarchy, he was heavily dependent upon Baptists at all levels. In contrast to the pacifism of Anabaptists, General and Particular Baptists were quick to take up arms. Perhaps it was their quest for religious liberty, but they made their way into the decision-making structures of Cromwell's efforts and were eager to use their offices for evangelism. Strong Welsh Baptist life owed its growth to Baptist opportunism during this period.

At the height of the Commonwealth in 1655, Baptist congregations had grown from five in 1625 to seventy-nine among General Baptists, and Particular Baptists numbered ninety-six congregations. At least ten Seventh-day Baptist fellowships had also emerged.[46]

Like other Arminian bodies, General Baptists quickly became connectional. As early as 1624 they manifested the beginnings of a denominational body, though it was 1654 before they actually had an annual national assembly. This trend among General Baptists reached its zenith in 1679, when they developed "An Orthodox Creed," elevating the assembly as a divinely ordained structure with authority over local churches.[47] They also formed associations derived from models developed in the army during Cromwell's days. One historian, Slayden Yarbrough, believes the true impetus for such connectionalism goes back to the Dutch Reformed "classis," a voluntary association of churches.[48]

Particular Baptists were more reluctant to connect, though some did come together to issue a confession of faith in 1644. However, they also began to organize associations of churches during the Cromwell period.

The purpose of such connections among both General and Particular Baptist churches was "to steady one another in doctrine and explain themselves unitedly to the world, to aid one another in time of need, and especially to propagate their views."[49] A tacit recognition of the church as both universal and local was involved, as well as practical implications and such

Scriptures as Jesus' prayer in John 17:21 "that they may all be one," the Jerusalem Council described in Acts 15, and Romans 12:5 with Paul's assertion that "we, being many, are one body in Christ."

Following the English Restoration in 1660, Baptists in England again came under heavy restrictions until the Act of Toleration in 1689. Major migrations of Baptists to the colonies ensued, including South Carolina's Welsh Tract group that provided support for the Kittery Church when it came from Maine.

General Baptists declined rapidly during this period and later; many became Quakers and Universalists. Particular Baptists grew and in 1689 convened their first council or national assembly to endorse the Second London Confession of 1677. Whitley claimed the Second London Confession stressed the duty of every member to preach if gifted and called by the church, and the need for real connectionalism between churches.[50] From this time on Particular Baptists would be dominant in English Baptist life. Surviving General Baptists united with the Particular Baptist's Baptist Union in 1891.

Connectionalism in America

Most English Baptist experience necessary to understand the American Baptist version was in place by 1700. Particular Baptist sentiments, with their orthodox Calvinism and reluctance to develop extra-church bodies, held primary sway, but General Baptists' tendencies toward modified Calvinism and connectionalism surfaced soon. Many of the conflicts between General and Particular Baptist thinking would reemerge again and again in Baptist development in America and especially in Southern Baptist life. The tendency for General Baptists to be more sectarian with a more radical separation of church and state, and Particular Baptists to support the civil concerns of Calvinism, can be seen in contemporary Southern Baptist conflicts.

Connectionalism[51] in American Baptist life finally took hold in the middle colonies in 1707 when five churches in the Philadelphia area organized an association. Their Particular bent was evident in 1742 with the issuance of a Confession of Faith, reflecting direct influence from the Second London Confession of Particular Baptists.

Baptists developed rapidly in the middle colonies after the founding of the first church there at Pennepeck. In 1682 Pennsylvania passed its "Great Law" which provided that no person "shall in any case be molested or prejudiced for his or her conscientious persuasion or practice."[52] Baptist Elias Keach took advantage of this opening to establish a church at Old Pennepek in 1688.

Keach, the son of an English Baptist minister, was a colorful person who had come to the colonies pretending to be a minister even though he had never been converted. It is said that he was converted during his own sermon and confessed his deception; this met with such favor among his hearers that after his baptism they ordained him.[53]

By 1701 there were five Baptist churches in the Philadelphia area, and in 1707 they organized their association. Initially designed to "consult" with each other and "order" things, the association sent out missionaries even before the Revolutionary War. Its influence in the South was to be considerable.

The Great Awakening

The real growth of Baptists in the New World awaited what history has called The Great Awakening. Beginning in New England in the mid 1700s among Congregationalists, this remarkable revival of religious fervor soon spread south and west in dramatic proportions. Many churches enlivened by the Great Awakening were called "New Light" or "Separate" churches; when they found resistance from older churches they became Baptist churches, which caused a famed Great Awakening evangelist, George Whitefield, to complain that his chicks had become ducks.

During this period older Baptist churches were called Regular Baptist churches and the newer churches emerging out of the revival were known as Separate Baptist churches. The most famous of the Separate churches grew up around the preaching of a man named Shubal Stearns.

Originally from Connecticut, Stearns was converted in the Great Awakening and became a Baptist in 1751. He and several friends, including a colleague named Daniel Marshall, migrated with numerous followers to North Carolina and settled at a place called Sandy Creek. They organized a Separate Baptist church there in 1755. This church grew rapidly and was credited with the establishment of forty-two additional churches.

Unique to this Baptist growth was an openness to women as preachers. Stearn's sister, Martha, married Daniel Marshall and became an outstanding preacher in Separate Baptist churches. It was a practice forbidden in the more established Regular churches.[54]

While both the Regular Baptists from the Philadelphia tradition and the Separate Baptists affirmed Calvinistic doctrine, the Separate Baptists brought a lively evangelistic element that soon modified the Calvinism of both groups of Baptists. The result was that while subsequent Baptist Confessions of Faith would reflect a Calvinistic theology, their enthusiastic evangelism would be emotionally akin to General Baptists' free grace. Extremes, however, gave Baptist history such terms as "hardshell" and "free will."

According to Baptist historian Walter Shurden, Southern Baptists were at this time developing two traditions, the Charleston tradition and the Sandy Creek tradition. While the Sandy Creek tradition was a direct outcome of the Great Awakening, the Charleston tradition was also affected by the pervasive revival. George Whitefield, perhaps the most influential evangelist of the Great Awakening, was said to have had his greatest success in Charleston, where he began preaching in 1740.[55]

A young preacher attending the Philadelphia Association meeting in 1749 heard of a pastoral vacancy in Charleston and offered himself. Oliver Hart from Warminster, Pennsylvania, converted in 1740 during the early days of the Great Awakening, was just twenty-six when he took over the Charleston pastorate. He began a thirty-year tenure there in 1750 and with the Philadelphia model in mind, led in the organization of the Charleston Baptist Association in 1751. Not surprisingly, the Charleston Baptist Association adopted a confession of faith in 1767 based upon the Philadelphia Confession.

The Charleston Confession represented the triumph of Particular Baptists over General Baptists who had enjoyed a strong role in coastal Baptist life earlier, but General Baptist propensities toward centralized connectionalism would become evident.

Hart, a Revolutionary War resistance leader, was driven from Charleston during the conflict and finished his ministry in New Jersey. In 1787 the Charleston Baptist congregation secured a pastor who was even more influential in the development of Baptists in the South. Richard Furman, also a product of the Great Awakening, in that the one instrumental in his conversion was only once removed from the evangelistically modified Calvinism of Shubal Stearns, was also a Revolutionary War hero. Furman became the epitome of post-revolution Baptist unity. His experience included the best of both the Sandy Creek tradition and the Charleston tradition, though he became better known for the latter. Because of this and his concepts of Baptist connectionalism, Richard Furman would beome the spiritual father of the Southern Baptist Convention, the ardent advocate for an educated ministry, and the mentor of W. B. Johnson.

Religious Freedom

An amazing breakthrough for Baptists came in the patriotic arena. After years of persecution and an undeserved reputation for anarchy and libertinism which was attached to Anabaptists after the Münster Rebellion, Baptists in America earned a well-deserved reputation for support of the colonies in their battles with England. They were as quick to take up arms in the battle for independence as their forebears had been to fight the crown under Cromwell during the Commonwealth era. They wed their support with an unrelenting commitment to civil and religious liberties.

Baptists like Isaac Backus and John Leland influenced later Presidents Thomas Jefferson and James Madison in critical issues of religious liberty. As early as 1776 their efforts paid off when Virginia guaranteed religious liberty in its constitution and achieved full fruition when an amendment forbidding the establishment of religion was ratified by the states of the young nation. Baptists had not only won the battle for their most cherished principle but in the process secured a new degree of social acceptability and respect.[56]

When it is recalled how the search for religious freedom led to the first Baptist church in Amsterdam and the role it played in the establishment of the first Baptist church in America and in the first Baptist church in the South, it is only fitting that religious liberty be a cornerstone of the Baptist conscience.

These were the traditions budding among Baptist churches throughout the nation at the close of the eighteenth century. One more tradition would bring them to flower as a denomination.

A Passion for Missions

Baptists' confessionalism and incipient connectionalism awaited a catalyst for full realization in the American Baptist experience. The missionary movement was that catalyst.

The leading reformers in the Protestant Reformation showed little missionary zeal until Pietists in the northern countries of Europe organized early missionary efforts to St. Thomas, Greenland, Lapland, and Surinam.[57] A modest missionary commitment of sorts emerged through a society facilitating the ministry of the Church of England among its colonists and they in turn among the Indians in the New World.

Baptists gave the world a strong missionary consciousness in Protestant Christianity through a Baptist pastor named Andrew Fuller and one of his mentees, a bivocational minister named William Carey. The product of Particular Baptists, Fuller took the church in Kettering in 1782; his reputation for a moderate Calvinism had been revealed in 1781 in his book, *The Gospel Worthy of All Acceptation.*[58] It went against the grain of the hyper-Calvinism that had been the legacy only two decades earlier of John Gill who, ironically, was born in Kettering.

Fuller's influence on Carey began in Kettering and a year later, in 1783, Carey was baptized. He soon commenced a bivocational ministry as preacher and cobbler. Both Fuller and Carey believed that Christians had a responsibility to share the gospel with all people everywhere. Carey's convictions were nurtured by reading *The Voyages of Captain Cook,* images from the map he kept over his cobbler's bench, and his own Bible study. They sharpened his beliefs and helped shape a dream.

Carey tried to outline his ideas to a group of fellow clergymen as early as 1786, but he was sternly rebuked. Yet with Fuller's support, Carey persisted and wrote a tract on the subject in 1792 entitled "An Enquiry into the Obligations of Christians to Use Means for the Conversion of the Heathen."[59] Carey aggressively suggested a pooling of resources to support an overseas venture, but the breakthrough came when, taking a text from Isaiah 54:2, he exhorted his congregation to "Expect great things. Attempt great things." He told Fuller he would "go down if Fuller would hold the rope." The English Particular Baptist Society for the Propagation of the Gospel among the Heathen, to be known simply as the Baptist Missionary Society, was the result.

Societies did not constrain churches to undertake the support of missionaries. They were simply gatherings of like-minded individuals who pooled their resources for that purpose. This form of denominationalism was different from that inherent in associations, but under the excitement of missions it flourished. Thus, the society model took its place alongside associationalism and became a compelling connectionalism by which Baptists could fulfill their missionary vision without encountering the growing opposition to extra-congregational connections. Hundreds of such societies followed this initial effort, many with "interlocking directorates" which "gave a cohesiveness to Baptist church life which otherwise autonomous sentiments militated against." Brackney holds that "virtually all of the major twentieth-century Baptist organizations have their origin in organized missionary endeavor."[60]

William Carey departed for India with his reluctant wife in 1793. Her reluctance may have been prescient, since her relatively short life in India was dominated by disease and depression. Leon McBeth notes that "a word of compassion should be written for Dorothy Carey, who paid a high price for Baptist missions and never knew why."[61] Despite pain, loss, and incredible hardship, Carey's forty-year missionary venture became a model to be emulated in the escalating enterprise that followed his lead.[62]

With few publications of their own, American Baptists depended upon "The Baptist Registry," a publication among Baptists in England by John Rippon. News of Carey's departure for India and his missionary adventure, and the use of a societal structure to undergird it, spread like wildfire among American Baptist churches.

Societies for religious causes were not new in American Baptist life. One had been formed in Charleston in 1755 to raise funds for an educational venture.[63] They found a unique acceptance among American Baptists, otherwise wary of extra-congregational ventures despite the presence of associations.

But it took a handicapped Baptist woman in Boston to lead the way in establishing a societal response in America to the new Baptist missionary initiative. Born in 1779 to a Congregationalist family and severely disabled by disease at the age of five, Mary Webb became a Baptist through the influence of a neighbor, Thomas Baldwin, pastor of Second Baptist Church in Boston in 1798. Her heart responded to the Carey mission, and she began to raise funds and then helped organize the Boston Female Society for Missionary Purposes in 1800 to do the same. She helped Baldwin organize the Massachusetts Baptist Missionary Society in 1802, which focused on the American frontier as well. Skillfully guiding the female organization in a manner calculated to avoid confrontation with male leaders of other societies, Webb's ministry stretched over sixty years, and she became a role model for a host of other mission-minded women who would significantly impact Baptist history, though for long years historians neglected their role.[64]

The Judsons and Luther Rice

Meanwhile, another great revival was breaking out in New England, which historians call the Second Great Awakening. It, too, influenced Baptist life, but in a quite different way. Under the influence of this new religious quickening, several Congregationalist students, led by Adoniram Judson and Luther Rice, came to the conviction that they should be missionaries and join Carey in India. The Congregationalists formed a missionary board called the American Board of Commissioners for Foreign Missions in Boston to support them.

A strange thing happened to Judson, his wife Ann Hasseltine, and Rice on the voyage. While studying the New Testament, Judson became convinced of the Baptist position and offered himself to Carey and his colleagues for baptism when they arrived in India. Rice, who sailed on a different ship, was told upon arrival about his colleague's reorientation. He sought to understand Judson's reasoning and three months later was himself baptized.

Ann Judson, who at first had been reluctant to make the move because of the pain involved, finally joined her husband in seeking baptism by immersion. She wrote her parents, "We are both confirmed Baptists, not because we wished to be, but because truth compelled us to be."[65]

Feeling that they should notify the Congregationalists about what had happened to their beliefs, they also notified the Baptists that they hoped support would be forthcoming from their new community of faith. Judson and Rice decided that it would be best for Rice to return to the United States to try to develop that support. When Rice returned, he found some of his warmest supporters in the South, including Richard Furman from Charleston, South Carolina, and the promising W. B. Johnson of Savannah, Georgia, whom Furman had so faithfully mentored.

A National Body

Many historians think that W. B. Johnson suggested that the Philadelphia Association host a meeting to form a denominational organization to sponsor the missionaries who dropped into their laps from heaven.[66]

This call for a national organization of Baptists was not the first. In his Centennial history, W. W. Barnes said early Baptist historian Morgan Edwards had proposed expanding the Philadelphia Association into such a body as early as 1771, and that the Warren Association in Virginia had tried to convene a "Continental Association" in 1776 in the spirit of the Continental Congress. Troubled times prevented this meeting, but the call helped Regular and Separate Baptists to began coming together. Barnes also points to a 1799 call for a General Conference by the Philadelphia

Association.[67] Yet it cannot be overlooked that it was the missionary impulse that finally made it happen.

Both Furman and Johnson strongly advocated a much broader form of organization than the mission societies already developed. By the time the meeting came about in 1814, their plans helped bring about the Triennial Baptist Convention, called the General Missionary Convention of the Baptist Denomination in the United States for Foreign Missions. It was called the Triennial Convention because it was to meet every three years. It is clear that Furman and Johnson wanted a stronger organization to cover a broader range of concerns—more on the associational model—but the newer society concept prevailed. However, Furman was elected the first president of this convention, and Johnson was asked to lead the group that drafted the constitution.

The denominationalism, inspired by the missionary spirit, continued to escalate and brought Baptists together in a way that "faith and order" had not been able to do. As mentioned earlier, many of the same people and churches organized a Tract Society which became a Publication Society in 1824; many also helped found a Home Mission Society in 1832. This growing denominationalism, increasingly connectional, helped Baptists resist the divisiveness and defections of anti-missionists and Alexander Campbell's reformers in the western part of the new country.

State Conventions

Given this new openness to a missions-motivated connectionalism, state conventions in the South rapidly followed the national organization, though the model was the association rather than the society. Not surprisingly, given the influence of Furman and Johnson, the concept was pioneered by South Carolina, which through the efforts of three associations organized a state convention in 1821.[68]

Georgia Baptists followed a year later with their own state convention. Only ninety years earlier the first colonists had arrived there under the leadership of James Oglethorpe, an English philanthropist. The first Baptist congregation was gathered at New Savannah in 1773. The first association had emerged in 1784.

Virginia Baptists and Alabama Baptists both organized state conventions the following year (1823), though the work in Virginia was older and more established. A Baptist meeting in Virginia can be documented as early as 1699. The three main streams that fed Virginia Baptist life began with General Baptists from England in 1714, followed by Regular Baptists from Maryland in 1743, and most significantly Separate Baptists from New England during the Great Awakening in 1755. A General Meeting of Correspondence, organized in 1800, gave way in June of 1823 to the General Association of Baptists in Virginia.[69]

Alabama was settled later and grew little before the war of 1812; nevertheless it had Baptist churches as early as 1808 and an association, Flint River, by 1814. Much of their cooperation issued from the missionary zeal of supporters of Judson and Rice and the Triennial Convention. By the time the Baptist State Convention of Alabama was constituted in October of 1823, missionary societies and associations dotted the state, still really a frontier.[70]

North Carolina Baptists, primarily through the Sandy Creek Association, served as a fountainhead of many Baptist churches to the south but did not organize their own state convention until 1830. Although Baptists were probably among the earliest settlers in 1660, their first church was established under the ministry of Paul Palmer at Chowan in 1727.[71]

Thirteen associations were already in existence when what would become the Missouri Baptist Convention was formed in 1834. This was remarkable, considering that the first Baptist church was organized in the state in 1807, just two years after the Louisiana Purchase brought it into the Union. Despite rumors that Daniel Boone was of Baptist sentiments, a missionary, John Mason Peck of the Triennial Convention, was the prime mover behind the organization of the first Baptist Church in St. Louis.[72]

When Maryland Baptists formed their state organization in October of 1836, Baptist churches had been in existence since 1742. Although Maryland was settled by Roman Catholics, Baptists were not persecuted there as their brothers were across the Chesapeake Bay in Virginia.

Baptists in Mississippi were among the settlers who invaded Choctaw, Chickasaw, Natchez, and Pascagoula Indian territories in the late eighteenth century. The first Baptist church was established near Natchez in 1791. In December of 1836 Baptists formed a "Convention of the Baptist Denomination in the State of Mississippi for missionary purposes, and other objects connected with the Redeemer's Kingdom on earth."[73]

The ninth state Baptist body represented when the Southern Baptist Convention was formed in 1845 was in Kentucky. Baptists were prominent there even as the new territory was being carved out of wilderness. As elsewhere in the South, strong missionary support followed the formation of the Triennial Convention, but it ran into fierce resistance in Kentucky before the ministries of John Taylor, Daniel Parker, and Alexander Campbell.

Campbell and his father Thomas, both Presbyterian preachers, migrated to America in 1807 and 1809 and were baptized into a Baptist church in 1813. Alexander Campbell developed a loyal following as the publisher of *The Christian Baptist,* later called *The Millenial Harbinger.* Rejecting all creeds and calling for the Bible alone, Campbell opposed all organizations other than the church. As early as 1830 he began to dispute with other Baptists over the true meaning of baptism. By 1827 the movement was splitting associations and taking over whole churches. Campbell's followers were known as Reformers, and between 1830 and 1832, ten thousand Baptists joined Campbell's movement. Later called Disciples, they united with the followers of Barton Stone who called themselves Christians. Before it was over the movement even split anti-mission forces.

Among most Kentucky Baptists, however, mission support continued and mission societies flourished. Georgetown College was founded in 1829. After a number of failed efforts, the General Association of Kentucky Baptists was organized in Louisville in October of 1837.[74]

The Conflict over Slavery

The excitement of denominational consciousness with its expanded connectionalism riding a passion for missions was soon overshadowed by the dark cloud of sectional conflict. As historian Robert A. Baker noted, sectionalism was nothing new in American life in the years that led up to the Augusta meeting. Different interests were certainly involved in the commercial and shipbuilding centers of New England and the agricultural economy of the South, and still other issues devolved from the expanding frontier.[75]

That sectionalism washed over into the Baptist denominational experience early on can be amply demonstrated as early as 1837. Kentucky Baptists complained about the appointment and deployment of missionaries by the Home Mission Society. Several Baptist papers began to editorialize about eastern dominance.

But it was the issue of slavery that galvanized this sectionalism for both Baptists and the nation as a whole. Nonslaveholding states and slaveholding states began to fight over the conditions under which new states would be admitted, each always with an eye on the balance of power.

England abolished slavery in the 1830s. Baptists were among the leaders of the abolition effort there and wrote the Triennial Convention in 1833 urging their Baptist brethren to do the same thing in America. Baptists reacted in two ways. One group indicated that while they were sympathetic with the point of view that deplored slavery, they would not make it a test of faith. A second group said they would have no more to do with those who operated with the "taint of blood" on their hands.[76]

Baptist abolitionists pressed the question until several annual meetings were forced to address it and reiterate that neither the appointment of missionaries nor participation in the denominational enterprise was based on any such tests. But the abolitionists were persistent and kept forcing the issue. Southerners were on the defensive and began to defend the institution of slavery, whether or not they were slaveholders.

In 1822 Richard Furman made a famous rationale for the practice, and in 1835 the Charleston Baptist Association went on record in defense of slavery.[77] Influential ministers like Richard Fuller engaged in an elaborate scriptural defense of the practice; then Georgia Baptists challenged the Home Mission Society with a slaveholding candidate. When the Society's board rejected the candidate, Alabama tested the Foreign Mission Society with a direct inquiry. The Board of Managers, bowing to the pressure of the abolitionists, abrogated the neutrality embraced by the 1841 meeting of the Triennial Convention to say they would not appoint a slaveholder.[78]

In the immediate aftermath of this, the Virginia Baptist Convention called for the Augusta meeting and made hurried preparation to gather in Augusta in a consultative convention. Sentiment ran strong that the South needed a Foreign Mission Society and a Home Mission Society that would not discriminate against their missionary candidates or accuse their funds of being tainted.

Thus, the Southern Baptist Convention walked on the stage of history burdened by its defense of a practice which subsequent history would condemn and which Southern Baptists themselves would one day condemn. Worse, it would take years to overcome the segregational aftermath of the abolishment of slavery. Sectionalism and slavery would become the fault lines of the forthcoming national schism. Sectionalism and segregation would be lashed to the residual pride of a defeated South and work out its negative heritage for years afterward.

A New Connection

All of this was beyond the vision of the delegates who gathered in Augusta that spring. They were Baptists. They were proud of their confessionalism, and at this point they saw no difference between themselves and the Baptists from whom they were thinking about separating. Missions had finally coalesced Baptists into a denomination, but problems related to the appointment and deployment of missionaries constrained Baptists in the South to develop their own denominational structures.

Denominationalism, missions, and the heat of sectionalism were birthing a new connection when W. B. Johnson gaveled the consultation to order on Thursday, May 8, 1845.

2

A New Connection
1845–1865

Regardless of the roots and reasons that led to Augusta, the Southern Baptist Convention became a new connection of people and churches led and sustained by dedicated and pious men and women. In the beginning, however, it was uniquely the work of William Bullein Johnson, guided by the ideas of his deceased mentor, Richard Furman.

Furman and Johnson

While it is always risky to highlight the determinative role of particular individuals in large movements, few can argue with the assertion that behind Johnson's leadership and convictions lay the shaping role of Richard Furman. More accurately, Furman's influence and ideas converged with opportunity in the person of Johnson. Thus, though he had died nearly twenty years earlier, Richard Furman was a compelling presence at Augusta in 1845.

Viewed as the classic southern gentleman, Furman was actually born in New York in 1755. His father, Wood Furman, was an Anglican, though his mother, the former Rachel Brodman, had been introduced to evangelicalism through George Whitefield during the Great Awakening. Furman's parents moved to South Carolina's seaport of Charleston shortly after his birth, and he never thought of himself as other than a southerner.[1]

Although his formal education was limited, Furman was a lifelong student of language, the classics, and even medicine, along with his theological pursuits. His own labors to secure an education made him a forceful advocate of formal education, and he set up a pioneering program to educate young ministers.

Uniquely influenced by the southern plantation experience, Furman became the patriarch of a large, influential progeny. His first wife, Elizabeth, whom he married in 1774, the year he was ordained, bore him a daughter and a son. She died in 1788 and months later Furman married fifteen-year-old Dorothea Maria Burn, who was the same age as Furman's daughter. This faithful child-woman bore his offspring every other year, thirteen in all, until she died of exhaustion. One of his grandchildren later wrote, "Of course, Grandfather was no doubt thinking of biblical heroes, but my heart has always gone out to the pretty child whose life was one of pain and service until the tired body found rest in God."[2]

Furman was at the peak of his powers and influence when the Triennial Convention was organized in Philadelphia in 1814. With the assistance of his protégé, W. B. Johnson, Furman tried to influence the polity of that missionary-driven body toward a more comprehensive denominational type organization. They were up against the cautions of Brown University's Francis Wayland, however, who felt that the autonomy of the local church argued for a society-type structure and against a convention-type structure. Wayland's position prevailed, and the General Convention was organized as a society. A curious compromise allowed the term "convention" to remain.

Although Johnson and Furman did not achieve their connectional goals, Furman was elected the first president, a position Johnson would later hold, and his call for an educational program resulted in steps that would lead to the formation of Columbian College, forerunner of George Washington University.[3]

Furman, like many southern aristocrats, was a thoroughgoing Federalist in his politics; therefore, it is not surprising that his religious polity reflected the same bent. The fact that his centralized ecclesiology did not succeed at Philadelphia in 1814 made the posthumous triumph of his ideas under W. B. Johnson at Augusta in 1845 all the more poignant. W. B. Johnson, twenty-seven years Furman's junior, was himself sixty-three when he stood poised to realize the dream nurtured by his mentor.

As a boy of nine, Johnson had joined his parents in a reception line in Georgetown, South Carolina, to meet George Washington. The founding father of the United States of America made a lasting impression on the youngster, but is doubtful that he was prescient enough to see himself becoming a founder of a different kind of body.[4]

Johnson, who was converted in 1804 and called to the ministry the next year, moved to Columbia to pursue his education at South Carolina College (later to become the University of South Carolina) and to serve as its chaplain. While there he again became a founder of a church. Moreover, he became the first pastor of the First Baptist Church of Columbia. In 1811 he accepted the pastorate of the Baptist church in Savannah, where his distinctive role as a denominational architect began to develop.

As mentioned earlier, the remarkable experience of Adoniram and Ann Hasseltine Judson and Luther Rice gave American Baptists a missionary opportunity as they responded through a plethora of societies to support William Carey and the English Baptist venture in India. Rice had returned to the States to develop mission support and was traveling the South in 1813 when he arrived in Savannah. His goal was to organize as many missionary societies as he could and then try to gather their delegates in Philadelphia the following year to organize a Baptist foreign mission society for the United States. According to Rice, the idea of the Philadelphia meeting did not occur until he met William Bullein Johnson in Savannah. Rice always claimed that it was Johnson's idea.[5]

Johnson, of course, was deeply indebted to Rice for broadening his own vision about what the denomination could do. Together they organized the Savannah Society for Foreign Missions, and Johnson was elected president.

Spurred on by Furman, his friend and mentor, Johnson sent a message to the Baptists of Georgia and South Carolina, outlining his plan to "convene in some central situation of the United States for the purpose of organizing an efficient and practical plan, on which the energies of the whole Baptist denomination, throughout America, may be elicited, combined and directed in one sacred effort for sending the word of life." The words "elicit, combine, direct" appeared in the constitution of the Triennial Convention when it was organized in 1814, and these prominent words were also in the plans which William Bullein Johnson brought to Augusta and which occasioned the Southern Baptist Convention.[6]

With his experience in forming the Savannah Society for Foreign Missions, helping to organize the Triennial Convention, and in 1821 organizing the South Carolina State Baptist Convention—and having served as president of all three—Johnson's views were fully matured. This was not to be a Triennial Convention-type society gathered for a single task, but a comprehensive organization of churches for all the tasks that might commend themselves to that body in the years ahead. Although he had been deeply influenced by first Furman and then Rice, it was now his dream to realize.

Call for a Consultative Convention

Though Johnson had a clear vision of what needed to take place, he worked hard to avoid a schism in the ranks of the denomination that he had helped to bring together. In fact, in 1844 when the Triennial Convention met in Philadelphia, W. B. Johnson was serving as president and was sure to be reelected, but he declined "for health reasons." Close friends indicated that he moved aside in an effort to bring about some conciliation between abolitionists and slaveholders. Francis Wayland was elected in his stead in hopes of effecting a compromise. Wayland's opposition to slavery had been clearly expressed in his celebrated debate with Richard Fuller of South Carolina. But while Wayland led the Triennial Convention to agree to stay neutral regarding slavery, the Board itself, as noted earlier, changed its mind when the test case came the next spring at Providence.

Johnson was not at the Providence meeting, but he was quickly aware of it and moved in concert with Jeter and Taylor and the Virginia contingent to call the Augusta meeting. In turn he issued his own call for a South Carolina Baptist Convention meeting, which he served as president. There he first broached his ideas for a southern organization and then turned to Augusta with their backing.

Augusta

Augusta was clearly Johnson's platform. He knew his colleagues and knew that the groundwork had already been done. Historians through the years have enjoyed saying that Johnson arrived at the consultative meeting in Augusta with a constitution already drafted and tucked away in his coat pocket. Furthermore, Johnson knew that Wayland and other leaders in the North would understand and would probably even acquiesce to the move. Many northerners saw the impending split only in the terms of Foreign Mission and Home Mission Societies. The Publication Society would not be affected and would even send representatives to Augusta.

The delegates arrived in Augusta on Wednesday evening, May 8. Pastor W. T. Brantly of the Augusta church had prepared diligently for their gathering including a registration point at the church. Many of the Virginia contingent stayed in the mansion of Dr. W. H. Turpin that first night before reporting to the red brick church on Green Street for the first meeting the next day.[7] As mentioned earlier, no women and no blacks were among the delegates, despite their majority status in the southern Baptist churches being represented.

On Thursday, May 9, 1845, W. T. Brantley, as host pastor, called the meeting to order. J. B. Taylor of Richmond moved that Governor Wilson Lumpkin of Georgia be asked to chair the initial stages. Lumpkin, who represented Georgia in Congress and had finished a stint as governor, took the chair through the phases of recognizing the delegates and electing W. B. Johnson to preside. Lumpkin and Taylor were elected vice-presidents of the consultative session, with J. C. Hartwell of Alabama and J. Crane of Virginia elected as secretaries.

Behind the scenes the leaders were working hard to move it with some degree of order and directness to its logical but largely prearranged conclusion. Before the day was out, Richard Fuller had moved the appointment of a committee to prepare a preamble and resolutions for the body to consider. Johnson then appointed the group with Fuller as chair. The representative group included most of the influential persons in attendance.

On Friday, Fuller stood to reiterate their findings and the reason for considering a southern organization. The resolution was "resolved unanimously, that for the peace and harmony, and in order to accomplish the greatest amount of good, and the maintenance of the Scriptural principles on which the General Missionary Convention of the Baptist denomination in the United States was originally formed, it is proper that this convention at once proceed to organize a society for the propagation of the gospel."[8]

Although it was adopted unanimously, the word "society" would quickly give way to "convention," a move which was far more than just semantics. No Philadelphia compromise would emerge.

In light of subsequent Baptist battles over "scriptural principles," many people have wondered at the founding fathers' lack of concern over such matters. "No creed but the Bible" had been a battle cry for the followers of Alexander Campbell, and 140 years later people defending the role of a creed in Baptist life would argue that such anti-confessionalism was Campbell's bitter legacy to Baptists.[9] It could also be argued that opposition to creeds was Baptists' contribution to Campbell during his sojourn among them.

Some have held that there was such uniform acceptance of the Philadelphia Confession of 1742 and an increasingly popular, more moderate, and succinct New Hampshire Confession, that no one felt the need for further delineation. As their history unfolded, however, Southern Baptists' lack of a clear-cut confessional consensus constituted an ambiguous area that consumed Southern Baptists' energies over and over again.

The irrepressible Jeter from Virginia took the floor to speak to the resolution and quoted from a letter he had received from Francis Wayland: "You will separate, of course. I could not ask otherwise. Your rights have been infringed. I will take the liberty of offering one or two suggestions. We have shown how Christians ought not to act, it remains for you to show us how they ought to act. Put away all violence, act with dignity and firmness and the world will approve your course."[10]

The debate proceeded, though generally supportive of acting positively on the resolution. There was some concern as to whether Baptists in Tennessee and Kentucky would go along; R. B. C. Howell, pastor of the First Baptist Church in Nashville and editor of *The Tennessee Baptist,* was conspicuously absent and had sent a letter to the meeting urging caution. Isaac McCoy of Kentucky, representing the Indian Missionary Association, however, said Kentucky would follow. The delegates adopted the resolution and moved to expand the committee to present a constitution.

When the delegates reassembled on Saturday morning, the preamble and a constitution were ready for them to consider. J. B. Jeter in his biography said the constitution had already been prepared by Dr. Johnson and referred to the committee which Fuller chaired.[11] It seemed to take very little work to get it ready to report out, since there was general agreement between Johnson and Fuller going in.

The only significant change from Johnson's draft was in Article I, where the name, the Southern and Southwestern Baptist Convention, was changed to the Southern Baptist Convention, reflecting the sectionalism that had been evident in Baptist life for several years. Some had wondered whether the split would be east and west rather than north and south. With Tennessee and Kentucky and Missouri Baptists in mind, Johnson had first thought to include them in the Southwestern Convention. With some assurance that they would be in line anyway, the body chose the clearer name reflecting the most obvious fracture-line, north and south.

The fifth article stated that the convention "shall elect . . . as many Boards of Managers, as in its judgement will be necessary for carrying out the benevolent objects it may determine to promote."[12] These brief words ensured that Johnson's Furman-nurtured concept of a broad-based denominational effort to "elicit, combine and direct the resources of the churches" was in place, even though the convention organized initially just the two Boards for Foreign Missions and Domestic Missions. Thus, in contrast to the Triennial structure with separate, autonomous, and independent societies for each benevolence, the Southern Baptist Convention provided for one body that would promote all benevolences that commended themselves to it, with an emphasis on denominational unity rather than any single benevolence.

Proving the power of precedence, however, was the inclusion in the new structure of three patterns more endemic to society-type operations than a convention style. One emerged from the initial, limited focus on missions that indicated a benevolent centrality rather than denominational solidarity. Another was the financing of such efforts by designated giving. The third was representation based upon financial gifts. Robert Baker was later to call these anomalies "congenital tensions" that would plague the new body for the better part of a century.[13]

Baker, the late dean of Southern Baptist historians, cited three reasons it would take so long to rectify the first of these tensions. First, he said, was the expectation that a reunion might take place at some future date and the resulting resistance to any new work that might further alienate the two bodies. Second, the Landmark controversy caused opposition to the work of any nonlocal body. Third, many of the constituents of the new organization doubted their financial ability to promote the array of benevolences that already commended themselves to many Southern Baptists.[14]

Time would take care of those three concerns. The Sunday School Board of 1891 would provide the impetus to become a real convention-type entity, while the Cooperative Program of 1925 and a representational change in 1931 would ameliorate the other two tensions.

By the time the delegates retired on Saturday, provisional boards had been elected for the Foreign Mission Board to be located at Richmond, Virginia with J. B. Jeter as president, and for a Domestic Board to be located at Marion, Alabama, with Basil Manly as president.

The Convention, not surprisingly, elected W. B. Johnson as president, Wilson Lumpkin as vice-president, J. B. Taylor as second vice-president, A. Dockery as third vice-president, the absent R. B. C. Howell as fourth vice-president, J. Hartwell and J. C. Crane as secretaries and physician, and M. T. Mendenhall as treasurer.

Each one was tapped to ensure the broadest possible support for the Convention. One that deserves some explanation is the choice of Tennessee's R. B. C. Howell as one of the vice-presidents. He was not there and he had urged the delegates to be cautious in considering a split, that is, to give it more time.

But Howell was a highly influential man who had served as president of the Western Baptist Association, occupied an influential pulpit in the west in Nashville, and exerted enormous influence through his paper, *The Tennessee Baptist*. Howell was not to be taken lightly, and it was hoped that by including him as a vice-president, his support would be in place from the beginning. Howell was a compelling personality with a very strong ego. In 1837, he received an honorary doctorate at Columbian College with no less than the president of the United States, Martin Van Buren, in attendance. Though much of his life was to be embroiled in battles with J. R. Graves and the Landmark Movement, Howell never lost his place of eminence. He served as either vice-president or president of the Southern Baptist Convention every year of his life after 1845.[15]

Howell was born in 1801 in rather humble circumstances in North Carolina, though he later referred to his farmer father as a "planter." He was named Robert Boyte Crawford Howell. The Crawford was obviously from his mother, Jane Crawford Howell. They were initially Episcopalians, but at the age of nineteen, young Howell became a Baptist through conviction and soon entered Columbian College, one of the educational dreams of Furman and Luther Rice. Located in the nation's capital, Columbian College was increasingly the educational opportunity of choice for aspiring southerners.

Following his experience at Columbian, Howell became a pastor in Norfolk, Virginia, where he married Mary Ann Morton Toy. The name of Crawford was passed on in the Toy family when Howell's brother-in-law named his son, Crawford Howell Toy. Young Toy would figure in Southern Baptist life in ways that R. B. C. Howell could never have imagined when he first learned of his namesake.

Those who had gambled that naming Howell as a vice-president would help in gaining Tennessee church support for the new convention guessed right. Howell accepted the post. Even though two Baptist papers questioned the appropriateness of his election, he was an ardent supporter of the convention from then on.

Sunday was not a day for business. Worship services were held during the day with Johnson preaching in connection with the communion service that afternoon. This popular practice in society and associational meetings fell victim to the Landmark controversy in later years because of insistence that the ordinance was the sole prerogative of a local church and should be closed or limited to the membership of that church.

The fifth and final day of the "crucial event" was Monday the twelfth. Tired but heady with what had been accomplished and excited over what it could mean in the years ahead, the group moved to a precedence-setting consideration of resolutions. Some of these were housekeeping items, such as the decision to affiliate with auxiliary societies, to forward funds to the appropriate boards, and to make application for a charter of incorporation.

Governor Lumpkin was charged with seeking the charter of incorporation for the convention, which he accomplished before the end of the year. Nearly one hundred and fifty years later, Texas Baptists' Baylor University changed its charter and triggered a major controversy in that body. Only then would the full implications of a corporate charter for a religious entity be understood by the rank and file of Southern Baptists.

Other resolutions were more directive, such as one to take "all prudent measures for their religious instruction of our colored population" and instructions to the Domestic Board to "direct their effective attention to aid the present effort to establish the Baptist cause in New Orleans." One resolution gave fruition to the hopes of Isaac McCoy, who had journeyed all the way from Kentucky, when it urged the churches to sustain the "Indian Mission Association with zeal and liberality."[16]

The new work commenced immediately. Johnson moved quickly to interpret the new convention to related groups. Jeter and Manly called the first meetings of the new mission boards. The convention, despite the controversies of its beginning and the taint of slavery hovering over its separation from the North—a taint that understandably would cause it to be defensive for years—was decisively launched on a journey that would accomplish more than even its most optimistic participant could imagine.

Little note was taken when the Triennial Convention later that year reiterated its polity and restated its focus as it changed its name to the American Baptist Missionary Union.

The Foreign Mission Board

Before J. B. Jeter left Augusta he pressed William Bullein Johnson to represent the Foreign Mission Board. Johnson resisted. His work in Edgefield at the church and the academy continued, and he was due almost immediately at the Indian Baptist Missionary Association meeting and had already agreed to attend the North Carolina Baptist meeting later in the fall. Too, his doctors had advised him that his recurring health problems would be aggravated if he spent much time in the harsh winters of northern climates. Compared to South Carolina, Virginia was a good distance north, not to mention other areas in which he would have to travel. He declined, but he did agree at Jeter's insistence to be an agent for the Foreign Mission Board and raise funds during the course of his travels. Not surprisingly, he did it well.

Jeter called the newly appointed members of the Foreign Mission Board together in Richmond just eight days after the conclusion of the convention in Augusta. The major challenge was not in organization, however, but in full-time leadership. After their aborted efforts to draft Johnson, five other persons were elected corresponding secretary and each in turn declined. This included James B. Taylor who declined in December. Finally, Taylor offered to serve part time while continuing his pastorate at the Second Church in Richmond.

In frustration, Jeter and his fellow board members accepted Taylor's offer which in itself had been elicited by unusual circumstances. During the time Taylor was struggling with what to do about the board's offer and his responsibilities at the Second Baptist Church in Richmond, Adoniram Judson himself visited Richmond to speak on the missionary challenge facing all Baptists. Taylor missed Judson's presentation because of illness, only to have the great man visit him.

It was Judson whose life-changing experience with Rice enroute to India had presented Baptists with ready-made missionaries and brought about the Triennial Convention. Judson's heroic sacrifices in Burma had cost him his health and the life of his wife, the much-admired Ann Hasseltine Judson, and even children. His heroism caught the imagination of Baptists in the South and gave them a passionate missionary conviction that steadfastly resisted the radical anti-missions sentiments still plaguing many churches.

Now Judson, though firmly allied with the Triennial Convention, encouraged the fledgling Foreign Mission Board of the Southern Baptist Convention and painted for Taylor a firsthand glimpse of the need of the peoples of foreign lands to hear the gospel of Jesus Christ. Taylor, who much later wrote the biography of Luther Rice, was awed by Judson. In fact, when he wrote Luther Rice's story, he came in to possession of letters written by Judson and his sacrificing wife, as well as other colleagues in the Burma mission, which reflected conflict and acrimony. Taylor carefully separated those letters from the ones he used in his biography. They did not come to light again until 1963, when this author discovered them in the files of the Foreign Mission Board and realized Taylor's idolization of Judson and Rice had constrained their exclusion from his writing.[17]

James B. Taylor

Jeremiah Bell Jeter, with Judson's inspiring help, convinced Taylor not only to take the part-time task, but later convinced the gentle Virginia pastor to assume the role of corresponding secretary of Southern Baptists' foreign mission enterprise full time.

Jeter had known Taylor since his early years as a minister, when he served as a missionary for Virginia Baptists. Jeter and Taylor had served together on numerous committees and helped establish the University of Richmond. As fellow pastors in Richmond they drew on a long background of camaraderie and appreciation, though it was obvious that Taylor depended heavily on the elder Jeter's wisdom and energy.

Taylor was born in England in 1804, where his mother had him christened in the Church of England. While he was still an infant his father, George, and his mother decided to immigrate to America. Enroute, their merchant ship was seized by a British man-of-war and the little family was rudely taken prisoner so James B. Taylor's father could serve as a conscript.

The wife's illness and the baby's needs kept the father nursing rather than sailoring, however, and soon the contrite British leadership hailed an American-bound vessel and transferred them back.

When they arrived in New York they found yellow fever raging and anything but the promise that they imagined while in England. Only after the father was converted and baptized in the First Baptist Church of New York did his American dream begin to unfold. Young James B. Taylor was spiritually precocious and became the youngest person to be baptized in that church before he and his family moved to Virginia, where Taylor began to preach as early as age twenty. He met Jeter soon after that.

The First Missionaries

The Foreign Mission Board's initial actions were to contact existing missionaries. Three of them, I. J. Roberts, J. Lewis Shuck and his wife Henrietta Hall Shuck, southerners under appointment to China with the Triennial Convention, agreed to transfer their support to the new Board. The first appointees of the Foreign Mission Board were the S. C. Cloptons, who went to China in the fall of 1845. Later that fall George Pearcy followed the Cloptons. Shuck and Roberts were appointed in March of 1846. Shuck himself appeared at a meeting of the Foreign Mission Board. He had come home the previous winter, bringing five motherless children following Henrietta Shuck's death.

I. J. Roberts, whose support had been ensured by his own estate through the China Missions Society of Kentucky, was affiliated with the Board later in the year.

At the second meeting of the Southern Baptist Convention, held in Richmond in 1846, J. Lewis Shuck and a Chinese convert who was now Shuck's colleague appeared on the platform and both gave testimonies. In a pattern that would persist for some years, the Southern Baptist Convention entered directly into the work of its Foreign Mission Board, advising it on strategy and direction.[18] It recommended work in Mexico, South America, and Palestine, and suggested that American Negro ministers would make the best missionaries to Africa. Following the pattern of the Triennial Convention, the Foreign Mission Board scheduled its next meeting three years hence in Nashville in 1849. Meanwhile, under James B. Taylor's leadership and Jeter's energetic guidance, the foreign mission enterprise continued to expand its China beachhead. W. B. Johnson's own son, Francis Cleveland Johnson, and a medical doctor, J. Sexton James, went out in the fall of 1846.

A year later the Foreign Mission Board leaders learned just how costly their China beachhead might be. Clopton died of fever during his first year. Dr. and Mrs. James never set foot on Chinese soil but were drowned in a storm in Hong Kong harbor.

Southern Baptists' first, and for a long time only, single woman missionary sailed for China in 1850. Harriet A. Baker from Powhatan, Virginia, received a reluctant appointment the year before to "establish a school for female children." The goal was to ensure that young men emerging from the existing missionary schools should find suitable mates. Baker immediately found I. J. Roberts so hostile to her presence that she moved from Canton to Shanghai. The Board broke ties with the difficult Roberts in 1851, but Harriet Baker became ill and resigned in 1853, terminating a pioneering role that was all but forgotten for many years.[19]

Another notable woman, appointed in 1849, was the wife of B. J. Whilden. Though his testimony claimed he had volunteered in response to the "long-continued prayers" of his wife for their missionary service, her first name is not mentioned. Her illness required him to bring her home the next year. Two Whilden daughters returned to China in 1872, when once again the door of service cracked for women, though one was single and was granted permission to go only because she could accompany her married sister and husband.[20]

Also in 1847, an American Negro missionary, John Day, serving in Liberia under the Triennial Convention, agreed to work under the new convention. And in 1848 another black American, B. J. Drayton of the First African Baptist Church in Richmond, sailed for Liberia to join him.[21] Liberian work had been established in 1821 by a freed slave, Lott Carey, backed by Baptists in Richmond.

Given the absence of either women or blacks in Southern Baptist deliberations in those early days, the roles of these women and black missionaries are all the more remarkable.

The Board formally committed itself to another African field when Thomas J. Bowen was sent to what is now Nigeria in 1849. Africa was even harder on missionaries than was China, however, and in not many years a missionary graveyard was more populated than the missionary roster. Bowen returned within a few years, though not before distinguishing himself with a book, *Yoruba Land*, published by the Massachusetts Institute of Technology and recognized as a significant anthropological contribution. He later tried to develop a mission in Rio de Janeiro in 1859, but again his health collapsed, and he spent his final years in a mental institution in Georgia.[22]

A measure of just how committed Southern Baptists were to the missionary task is evident in the fact that receipts to the Foreign Mission Board doubled between 1846 and 1849 and almost doubled again by 1853. They reached their high-water mark in 1859, after which the war devastated support.

Domestic Mission Board

The Domestic Mission Board's beginning in Marion, Alabama, was less auspicious, and the reason was the same as the Foreign Board had initially encountered: leadership. The Board, which had been located at Marion because of the strong contingent of able representation from Marion at the organizational meeting in Augusta, found that representation did not translate into board leadership. Basil Manly, the president, and several corresponding secretarial prospects came and went before Russell Holman from New Orleans took over in 1846. Holman was already a veteran with one of the major Home Mission Society fields in New Orleans. Holman and I. T. Hinton had traveled together to the organizational meeting in Augusta. Upon their return home a yellow fever epidemic took Hinton's life.

Holman had identified with Southern Baptists after only seven years in the South, including two years as a publication representative and three years as a pastor in Kentucky. Bothered by poor health, he had accepted his Home Mission Society appointment to New Orleans only two years before Augusta. One would think that his Massachusetts birth in 1812, his New England upbringing, and his brief Brown University education would have turned his allegiance more to Northern Baptists. Not so. He even joined the Confederate army as an evangelist in 1862.

Holman endeavored to get the Domestic Board underway despite significant obstacles. Most significant was the fact that in 1846 the Home Mission Society was still involved in Arkansas, Florida, Kentucky, Missouri, North Carolina, Texas, and Virginia. They did begin withdrawing shortly after that in reluctant recognition of the Southern Board's existence.

Holman led the Board to identify work with Negroes, Indians, Chinese in California, and Germans in Missouri and Maryland, plus the white population in places like New Orleans and frontier areas. While the withdrawal of the Home Mission Society did not last long, the Domestic Mission Board's primary conflict during this period was with existing associations and state conventions that had developed their own missionary projects and followed their missionary impulse in ways that seemed to conflict with the Domestic Mission Board's ambitions. Receipts were significantly less than those of the Foreign Board during the same period with only a little over eighteen hundred dollars given in 1846. Though the amount had increased to ten thousand dollars by 1850, that was less than one fourth of what was given the Foreign Mission Board. The gap closed somewhat by 1860, and the Domestic Mission Board received nearly forty-nine thousand dollars compared to a little over eighty thousand dollars by the Foreign Mission Board.[23]

Holman resigned in 1851, frustrated with the competition and the lesser degree of acceptance by the constituents of the sponsoring convention. The task was taken over by T. F. Curtis, also a founding member of the Alabama delegation in Augusta, but Curtis stayed only two years before deferring to Joseph Walker. Walker, in turn, put in three years before the post was again vacant and the Board in desperation talked Russell Holman, who had been serving as a professor of mathematics at Alabama's Howard College, into returning.[24]

In 1853, the Domestic Board sent former missionary to China, J. Lewis Shuck, to California. Shuck, who left the Foreign Mission Board under a cloud when some of his colleagues in China accused him of moral laxity, developed a promising work among the Chinese and established an anglo-American church in Oakland. This western effort appealed to Southern Baptists and was strongly supported as late as 1861 before it fell victim to the Civil War.[25]

At its 1855 meeting in Montgomery, Alabama, the Southern Baptist Convention asked the Domestic Board to take over the Indian Mission Association, whose cause had brought Isaac McCoy to the organizing session. The Board's name was changed to the Domestic and Indian Mission Board, but the new Board learned belatedly that it had inherited more debt in the process.

Collections for both of the boards, domestic and foreign, during this period were generally in the hands of agents whose role was like the one W. B. Johnson played for the Foreign Mission Board for a few years. Johnson, with an eye to the broader convention goals of his founding dream, also raised money for the Domestic Mission Board and Furman University. Individual missionaries often raised additional funds, though most of these were dutifully transferred to the sponsoring boards. The loosely woven organizations allowed some of these funds to go directly to individual projects.

New State Conventions

In 1848 new state conventions were formed in Arkansas, Louisiana, and Texas. In each case the work was a combination of migrations from other states and missionary efforts by the Home Mission Society of the North. Florida formed a state convention in 1854, with work begun there in much the same way as in the other new states. Especially in Arkansas and Florida, anti-mission elements caused major rifts in the churches and associations, but in each case the state conventions led their cooperating churches in the missionary task and were soon allied with the churches of the nine original states.

The Baptist beginnings that led to a state convention in Arkansas go back to 1814 at least and to a Baptist preacher named George Gill. In 1817 a Missouri association sent missionary James Phillip Edwards into northeastern Arkansas to preach among settlements in the wake of a southwestern migration only slightly deterred by the threat of Indian retaliation.

Despite this missionary activity, Arkansas Baptist life was torn again and again by anti-mission sentiments and other Baptist controversy. Alexander Campbell's followers made their impact along with the anti-mission or Hardshell Baptists. And within a few short years Arkansas was strongly influenced by J. R. Graves and Landmarkism, which was initially seen as a way of dealing with the Campbell movement.[26]

The dominance of the missionary motif was evident when Arkansas Baptists organized the Arkansas Baptist State Convention on September 21, 1848 in what is now Tulip, Arkansas. The organization of the Southern Baptist Convention only three years earlier and the example of other state conventions undoubtedly influenced this decision. Similar organizations were later formed, primarily for geographical reasons, but were later subsumed by this initial group.

While the Arkansas state convention was organized a number of weeks before that of Louisiana, Baptist work in Louisiana predated that in Arkansas. The first Baptist church in the state was organized in 1812 in east Louisiana only nine years after the Louisiana Purchase and three years before Andrew Jackson's historic victory at New Orleans. An association of Baptist churches was in place by 1818. After two aborted efforts, a convention was formed in Mt. Lebanon on December 2, 1848, and named the Baptist State

Convention of North Louisiana. The term "North" was dropped in 1853 and the name The Louisiana Baptist Convention was adopted in 1886.

Texas, like Louisiana, faced Roman Catholic opposition in its incipiency. Stephen Austin's first settlement in 1821 had come under such restrictions, though eleven Baptist families were supposed to have accompanied the original anglo-settlement. Ironically, the first Baptist church in Texas, which met in 1834 in Austin's colony, was led by the anti-mission leader Daniel Parker. It had been organized in Illinois as "The Pilgrim Church of Predestinarian Regular Baptists" and with Parker as pastor began its move to Texas in 1833. The church later moved to Houston County.[27]

Because Baptists in Texas trace their roots through Missionary Baptist churches, they give credit for the pioneer efforts to Z. N. Morrell from Tennessee, who organized a Baptist church in Washington, Texas, in 1837. Baptists in this group had helped petition the Home Mission Society to send missionaries to Texas.[28] Texas Baptists' first association was organized in 1840 though one man, T. W. Cox, was pastor of all three churches represented. This association, the Union Association, authorized the educational society whose efforts eventually created Baylor University, which secured its charter from the Republic of Texas in 1845.

The first state convention in Texas was organized on September 8, 1848, in Anderson, with fifty-five messengers from twenty-three churches.[29] A rival body was formed in 1853, and the two combined in Waco in 1886 as the Baptist General Convention of Texas under the organizing powers of B. H. Carroll and S. A. Hayden. Unfortunately, these two men became bitter foes years later.

The first Baptist church in Florida was organized on January 7, 1821 in Nassau County. Affiliated with the Piedmont Association in Georgia, Baptists there faced Spanish opposition for several months before the United States took over the territory in July of 1821. This removed the threat of Catholic proscription which Baptists faced in Louisiana and Texas.

By the time Florida became a state in 1845, Baptists there were seeking support from Baptists in neighboring states. The West Florida Baptist Association, formed in 1847, affiliated with the Alabama Baptist Convention. This association took the lead in 1854 in organizing the Florida Baptist Convention on November 20, 1854, with delegates from three associations.[30]

Southern Baptists now included churches from thirteen states.

Landmarkism

By the time the Southern Baptist Convention met for its triennial meeting in 1849 its work was underway, but events that year foreshadowed new difficulties. The national scene continued to be polarized politically between the North and the South, while the West loomed as a prize to be won by political maneuvering between advocates from the North and the South. Southern Baptist life, on the other hand, was facing a different challenge.

In 1849 the convention was supposed to meet under R.B.C. Howell's hospitality in Nashville, but a cholera epidemic caused most would-be messengers to cancel their travel plans. Only twenty-eight persons were there when Howell as vice-president called the meeting to order.[31] Because of the epidemic, Howell adjourned the session. Later that same month in Charleston, with Johnson presiding, the convention was reconvened. They decided to begin meeting biennially and to return to Nashville in 1851. There Howell was elected president, the first other than the respected W. B. Johnson to lead the new convention.

But Howell was no longer in Nashville. He had been called to Second Baptist church in Richmond, Virginia, to succeed James B. Taylor. Proving that his popularity was more personal than power-based, Howell was reelected president of the Southern Baptist Convention in 1853, 1855, and 1857, at which time he declined, but that is a part of a larger story developing among Southern Baptists during this period.

That story is called Landmarkism. Leon McBeth voices the convictions of many Baptist historians when he says, "It is impossible to understand Southern Baptists apart from Landmarkism."[32]

The beginnings of the Landmark controversy surfaced in Nashville under Howell's very nose and almost before he realized it. In 1845 a young schoolteacher-preacher named James Robinson Graves moved to Nashville and set up a school.[33] He soon joined the First Baptist Church. Howell was genuinely impressed with him and not only sent his son, Morton, to his school, but helped Graves secure the pastorate of the Second Baptist Church. The next year, 1846, he asked the bright and energetic Graves to be his associate in publishing *The Tennessee Baptist*. That same year Howell deeded the paper to the General Association and helped Graves become its general agent.

Graves, born in Vermont in 1820, was gifted and self-taught. He moved to Nashville from a teaching post in Kentucky. One letter would suggest that during his Kentucky sojourn Graves became involved in the Campbell controversy and at first may have supported Campbell's followers.[34]

His vehement opposition to Campbell's doctrine in later years when he was leading the Landmark contingent would seemingly belie any such affection, but obviously Graves learned a lot in the Campbell controversy, which had rocked Baptists from 1810 to 1830. It cost Baptists countless churches and members before the fellowships that would become the Disciples of Christ and the Churches of Christ took their own identity.

Graves bore striking similarities in style and power to Campbell. Like Campbell, he could destroy the opposition in a debate with a combination of reasoned dialogue, cutting sarcasm, and ridicule.[35] Like Campbell, he was a presence to be reckoned with in any group.

Almost immediately after joining *The Tennessee Baptist,* Graves began to attack some Baptists' practice of sharing their pulpits with non-Baptist ministers. Opposition to pulpit affiliation was the first plank in what became Graves' Landmark system. In 1849, Howell, increasingly less involved in the paper in the face of Graves' aggressiveness, resigned *The Tennessee Baptist* and allowed Graves to take over. This became the platform Graves needed. Perhaps his growing influence and his charismatic, controversial style may have motivated Howell, nearly twenty years his senior, to move on.

Howell was a sensitive man. He had accepted the church in Nashville after eighteen of nearly four hundred members at his church in Virginia had voted against his annual call. This sensitivity may also have led him to leave Nashville in 1850 to take over as pastor of the Second Baptist Church in Richmond, Virginia.

With Howell out of the way, Graves launched what was later to be called the Landmark Movement (based upon the use of the word in Prov. 22:28) in an historic meeting in Cotton Grove, Tennessee, on June 24, 1851. Posing five queries, Graves led those gathered to respond with the Cotton Grove Resolutions.

Essentially, the Resolutions and J. R. Graves' approach to Baptist life were ecclesiological. He felt that the local church was the only church and, contrary to early confessional statements in Baptist life, that there was no such thing as a universal church. Furthermore, he felt that the Baptist church was the only legitimate local church. This he based upon Baptist successionism, the belief that Baptist churches could be traced all the way back to the time of Christ. (In later years in a written defense of his actions called "Old Landmarkism: What Is It?" Graves insisted that he taught New Testament church successionism and denied that he taught Baptist successionism.) This view met a need similar to the one that had lured John Smyth from his early Baptist moorings and later had intrigued Roger Williams. Succession-ism was at the heart of Graves' scheme of things, and he even found some support for this position from his aborted mentor, Howell.

Given this conviction, Graves taught that only Baptist churches were authorized to baptize and to serve the Lord's Supper. Thus, Landmarkers railed out at what they called "alien immersion" and insisted upon a "closed communion."[36] The frontier environment was ripe for Graves. Robert A. Baker cites the hunger for religious authority, the confusion of religious pluralism, and the role of religious debate as factors favoring the Landmark movement.[37]

The full development of Graves' system awaited two colleagues: J. M. Pendleton and A. C. Dayton. Pendleton had been pastor in Bowling Green, Kentucky, before he heard Graves preach in 1852; he found himself attracted to Graves' teachings denying the validity of any immersion other than that done by a Baptist and forbidding any non-Baptist preacher to be in a Baptist pulpit.[38]

In 1854 Pendleton penned four articles addressing the exclusive ecclesiology of Graves, and Graves published them in a pamplet entitled "An Old Landmark Re-set." This pamphlet effectively named the movement. In 1855 Pendleton supported Graves' publication of the English historian G. H. Orchard's book, *A Concise History of Foreign Baptists*. This book became the centerpiece of the Landmark approach. It presented "irrefutable" proof that Baptist churches had survived from the days of Jesus in unbroken succession, therefore Baptists were the only true Christian church.[39]

Landmarkism spread rapidly in the fertile soil of the fierce competition that consumed frontier churches and what some historians called an ongoing identity crisis. Graves and Pendleton provided key answers. Graves helped Pendleton secure a teaching position at Union University in Murfreesboro in 1857 by helping endow a chair of theology there. Pendleton's ideas caught on quickly with professors and students, though one of his students, young William Whitsitt, later became one of Graves' followers' most significant targets.

The third member of the Landmark triumvirate was A. C. Dayton. Amos Cooper Dayton had come to the South as a young man from his native New Jersey and became a dentist. After practicing in Mississippi, where he was also a Presbyterian layman, Dayton was converted to Baptist life in 1852.

Almost immediately he became acquainted with Landmark views and became a contributor to Graves's *The Tennessee Baptist* before Graves secured his placement on the Bible Board and later in the Southern Baptist Sunday School Union. When later Dayton was displaced from the Bible Board, he served as an associate editor for a time, beginning in May 1858. In the 1860s he established a Landmark paper in Atlanta, Georgia, called *The Baptist Banner.*

Dayton's major contribution to the Landmark movement, however, was a two-volume novel entitled, *Theodosia Ernest.* The novel was first serialized in Graves's paper in 1855 and then published in book form in 1857. Its success helped popularize Landmark tenents. A second book called *Pedo-Baptist and Campbellite Immersions* followed in 1858 and provided—along with Graves' editorializing, Pendleton's tract, and Orchard's history— vehicles for the rapid spread of Landmark ideas.[40]

W. W. Barnes has characterized the triumvirate as the warrior (Graves), the prophet (Pendleton), and the sword-bearer (Dayton).

Graves used *The Tennessee Baptist* to battle other Baptist editors who did not join him, though he had the support of papers in Arkansas and Texas and the *Biblical Recorder* of North Carolina. He also had strong support among Mississippi Baptists and *The Baptist Record,* where J.B. Gambrell was getting his start.

In addition to his efforts among Baptists, Graves continued to pursue an aggressive attack on other denominations, including one on Methodists with a book in 1856 entitled *The Great Iron Wheel* and another in 1857 called *The Little Iron Wheel.* In 1858 he published a fairly accurate history called *Trials and Sufferings for Religious Liberty in New England.* A book called *The Trilemma* emerged in 1860, castigating Presbyterianism.[41]

Challenging the Convention

Graves and his followers were politically adroit, but their most dependable weapon was a publishing company that Graves organized in Nashville. Through it he was able to secure significant financial support and mount efforts to influence churches everywhere with Landmark-oriented literature produced by this enterprise. His efforts constituted a direct challenge to the Southern Baptist Publication Society. Unlike the Mission Boards, the Society, organized in 1847 and operated out of Charleston, was only "endorsed" by the Southern Baptist Convention.

When Southern Baptists began a Bible Board in 1851, it was located in Nashville despite growing fears of Graves' influence. Justifying those fears was Graves' successful efforts the next year to get A. C. Dayton elected to head the Bible Board. At this point there was some question whether Graves could be stopped from becoming the dominant force in Southern Baptist life. Graves believed he was calling Baptists back to their historic and distinctive principles; he billed his position and efforts as a defense of Southern Baptists.[42] The same argument would resurface in Southern Baptist affairs under a different agenda in 1920 and again in 1979.

Robert Boyte Crawford Howell returned to Nashville in 1857 to resume the pastorate of the First Baptist Church. Two men had served in the six years since he had left, and both felt that Graves had speeded their departure. Howell had just been reelected as president of the Southern Baptist Convention for the fourth time at its meeting in Louisville. As president he was an ex-officio member of the Bible Board, although he had given it little attention from Virginia. When Howell returned to Nashville, however, he began participating and quickly became aware of Dayton's efforts to use the Board for Landmark purposes. So, early in 1858 he led a successful challenge of Dayton's leadership.

That same year Howell managed to get together a Southern Baptist Sunday School Convention. At its meeting on October 3, 1857, in Nashville, the Convention organized a Southern Baptist Sunday School Union. Graves, however, managed to place key Landmark leadership on the board and immediately seized control. Once again, Dayton was made president and Graves became secretary.

In a new confrontation with the Southern Baptist Publishing Society, the Landmarkers again endeavored to channel Landmark literature published by Graves' company through this new enterprise.

Howell was now in a position of having to oppose his own creation. Ever popular in Nashville, he rallied his supporters and succeeded in removing Dayton, but then Graves turned his full attack on his old mentor. Howell responded vigorously. The focus of their celebrated battle was the First Baptist Church of Nashville, where Howell's supporters preferred charges against Graves for his attacks on their pastor. After a church trial, which ruled for Howell, Graves and about twenty-five supporters withdrew and established what they considered the first true Baptist church. A threatened suit blocked their use of the name, but churches and associations divided over the battle. The extent of Landmark influence was evident, but the presence of R. B. C. Howell prevented victory.[43]

In 1859 Graves challenged both the Foreign Mission Board and Howell at the Southern Baptist Convention. Like the earlier anti-mission and Campbell positions, Graves also battled extra-church efforts. The local church was to be the authority for everything. He wanted the Convention to have a church-based representation rather than the contribution-based representation with which the Convention began. The latter was a holdover from the society method as previously mentioned, but Southern Baptists were reluctant to give up the idea that whoever pays the bill ought to have direction of the enterprise. Graves felt that only the local church had any authority, and he constantly disparaged those who led from Convention posts.[44]

Graves, Dayton, and Pendleton went to the Southern Baptist Convention meeting in Richmond in 1859 determined to have the Foreign Mission Board abolished. Richmond was not the place he would have chosen, for Virginia was the bastion of anti-Landmarkism. The messenger count was over twice as large as any other Southern Baptist Convention. When the votes were counted, Graves had been soundly defeated. A measure of the passion inspired by the battle can be seen in the fact that only after twenty-four years that messenger total would be eclipsed, and again Landmark issues enlivened the agenda.[45]

Graves next endeavored to oppose Howell's reelection as president. His efforts forced two ballots before Howell received a plurality. Howell's sensitivity again came to the fore and he declined. It took four more ballots before Richard Fuller was elected, though he accepted as readily as if it had been a landslide.[46]

Landmark Decline

In 1861 the Landmark leadership team was separated by the same forces that divided the young nation. Pendleton held strong antislavery views, which drew enough fire to cause him to abandon his Union University post. His position cut to the heart of his own family when his son, John Malcolm, joined the Confederate army. Pendleton returned north to Ohio, where in 1862 he learned that his son had died in battle representing the cause that Pendleton so deplored.[47] Later, in 1867, the "prophet" of Landmarkism as W. W. Barnes called him, published his *Church Manual* which, with its Land-mark ecclesiology, was widely circulated and exerted a pervasive influence.

As mentioned earlier, after Dayton was forced from his post in 1858, Graves took him in at *The Tennessee Baptist* for a time before Dayton moved to Georgia. There he edited a Landmark paper called *The Baptist Banner* until his death in 1865. Strangely, Graves made no mention of Dayton's death.

Graves and his followers failed to accomplish their goal, but their opposition and the Civil War contributed to the collapse of both the Bible Board and the Southern Baptist Publication Society in 1863.[48]

What Baptist leaders failed to do, the Civil War accomplished. When Nashville fell, Graves lost his publishing empire and never again found the platform he needed to mount the vigorous attacks of the 1850s when Pendleton and Dayton were by his side. He survived the war, however, and from a new base in Memphis enjoyed a latter-day renaissance of influence, especially among followers in Mississippi, Arkansas, and Texas. His platform ability continued unabated, and witnesses reported that he could keep an audience spellbound for two or three hours at a time. He would debate opponents whether they were there or not, and when he concluded, it was as if they had been there and had been thoroughly discredited.

Graves' self-confidence, single-mindedness, and passionate convictions drove him. And even in later years, when confined to a wheelchair and handicapped from a stroke, J. R. Graves could still move people.

There are many, however, who credit R. B. C. Howell for defeating Graves in the crucial votes that, had Graves won, would have drastically weakened the Convention. When Nashville fell to Union forces in 1862, Howell was imprisoned for refusing to sign a loyalty pledge. His health rapidly declined after his release, and the sensitive old warrior died in 1868.

Education

Despite the educational level and commitment of the founders of the Southern Baptist Convention, members of its preponderance of rural churches were often ambivalent about education. For many of them religion was so much a matter of the heart "that many Baptists came to look upon the ability to preach as the gift of the Holy Spirit that required neither special training nor prolonged preparation." Too often, these people were able to prejudice the masses against educated or "head-made preachers."[49]

However, Southern Baptist leaders consistently supported an educated ministry. Colleges in South Carolina (Furman), Virginia (Richmond),

Georgia (Mercer), and a number of other states were already offering a quality education in Southern Baptist ranks when the convention was organized. Most of these institutions included theological departments that actively trained ministers. Many Southern Baptist leaders, however, envisioned a seminary dedicated to the professional training of ministers. Basil Manly, Sr., as president of the University of Alabama, had made the first known call for a seminary in the South in 1835. His son, Basil Manly, Jr., joined the faculty at Furman, where he continued his father's advocacy for a seminary for the graduate training of ministers.[50]

Several efforts were made to realize Manly's dream. An ill-fated venture in Cincinnati opened its doors as Western Baptist Theological Institute the same year that Southern Baptists organized in Augusta. A similar idea was discussed among some at Augusta but was not pursued at that time. R. B. C. Howell's support was evident in an Indian Mission Association meeting in Nashville as early as 1847, and a committee was formed to look into the matter with a view to reporting to the 1849 Convention. Some significant planning took place, but the growing presence of Graves' Landmark followers and their opposition to the idea kept it at bay.

Under the leadership of the Baptist Education Society of Virginia, "friends of theological education" gathered at the SBC meeting in Montgomery in 1855 and held another meeting in Augusta in 1856. But it took the passionate commitment of James P. Boyce of South Carolina to bring the Manlys' vision to reality.

Boyce dreamed of a seminary with a difference. As early as July 1856, he had outlined his thoughts in an address at Furman. He wanted a seminary that admitted noncollege men to theological studies. He also wanted advanced or graduate work to prepare college men to teach in Baptist colleges and to include an abstract of principles to which each professor would subscribe and therefore prevent aberrations. He feared Campbellism and Arminianism and noted that "heresy usually becomes articulate first in an individual of strong influence and ability."[51] The abstract would guard against that possibility in his scheme of things.

Boyce convinced South Carolina Baptists to dedicate the funds of Furman's theological program to the founding of a seminary, with the agreement that South Carolina Baptists and the other Baptist state conventions would provide matching funds. An educational convention meeting in May 1857 launched the effort. And with Boyce's almost single-handed efforts, the Southern Baptist Theological Seminary opened its doors in rent-free quarters in Greenville, South Carolina, in the fall of 1859, with James P. Boyce as president (then called chairman of the faculty) and John A. Broadus, William Williams, and Basil Manly, Jr., as faculty. Boyce and Broadus, especially, would be the founders of this pioneering institution which again and again became the focus of controversy, both from those who were essentially anti-institutional and anti-intellectual and those who felt violated by theological or historical positions advocated by its professors.[52]

War Breaks Out

While the Southern Baptist Convention's young mission boards struggled to establish viable ministries and credibility with their constituents, and while its leadership battled with the Landmarkers, the United States of America was moving toward an unprecedented cataclysm. The Missouri Compromise had further defined the sectional antagonisms of the country. The 1857 Dred Scott case and memories of the 1831 Nat Turner rebellion dramatized the worst nightmare of the slaveholding South and hardened opinions. Though Lincoln was elected on a platform of giving the South the right to maintain its "peculiar institution," the die was cast. When South Carolina seceded, war to preserve the Union was inevitable.

Though war actually began on April 9, 1861, when southern troops in South Carolina tried to take the federal fortress at Fort Sumter, the formal declaration was not until a week later.

All of the Southern Baptist Convention enterprises were affected. When the convention gathered in Savannah, Georgia, in 1861, with Fuller again as president despite a new pastorate in Maryland, it went on record as supporting the Confederacy and urging prayer on its behalf. It moved to sustain its foreign enterprise through agents in Maryland and Kentucky, which had not seceded.[53]

Feelings ran strong, as the rhetoric in the report of a special committee reveals: "With astonishment and grief, we find churches and pastors of the North breathing out slaughter and clamoring for sanguinary hostilities with a fierceness which we have supposed impossible among the disciples of the Prince of Peace."[54] A resolution urged prayer for their foes and another urged them to keep the "spirit of Jesus in the face of the North's lawless reign."

Throughout the South individual Baptists and ministers were caught up in the passions of war. Young William Whitsitt graduated from Union University in Murfreesboro, Tennessee, with an M.A. in 1861, and immediately joined the Confederate Infantry. Before the year was out, however, his education and his ministerial experience caused him to be promoted to the chaplaincy. For three years he was in the middle of the worst fighting. Twice captured, he spent twelve months in a Confederate prison camp before being exchanged.[55]

Across the Alleghenys and the Blue Ridge in Virginia, Crawford Howell Toy, the nephew and namesake of R. B. C. Howell, was coping with the disappointment of a lack of funds that prevented his sailing to Japan with two new missionary families.

Toy had completed his education at the University of Virginia with great promise and began teaching at the nearby Albemarle Female Academy. He was convinced, however, that God wanted him to follow his boyhood idols to the mission field. At Albemarle, which was located adjacent to the University of Virginia, he had been attracted to an aggressive and bright student named Charlotte Moon. According to Moon's first biographer, Toy proposed to her, only to be rejected. If true, it was not because of missions, however, for he was the volunteer and she was a relatively new convert to the Christian faith. Her missionary interest had yet to flower, and her attraction to Toy was purely intellectual. Their paths would cross again as would those of Toy and Whitsitt.[56]

Like Whitsitt, Toy joined the infantry and was soon promoted to the chaplaincy. Usually attached to hospital units in battle, though he preached to front-line troops on Sundays, Toy chose to remain at Gettsyburg with a group of wounded Confederates after Lee's forces retreated in devastating defeat following the death of Stonewall Jackson.[57]

Union troops quickly surrounded them, and Toy, with his compatriots, spent several years in a Union prison before being repatriated. He immediately joined up again, and the end of the war found him serving as a chaplain but anxious to get back to his studies.

James P. Boyce followed a different course. An anti-secessionist, he ran for the South Carolina legislature in hopes of heading off a split. Overwhelmingly defeated, he became a chaplain when secession came and war followed. Finally, he was elected to the state legislature, though he later lost a bid for the Confederate Congress. He finished the war as aide-de-camp to the governor. Boyce returned to his well-appointed home near Greenville after the city was abandoned, just in time to be held at pistol point as his home was ransacked by Union troops.

Robert A. Baker notes that Southern Baptist enterprises at the beginning of the war included the Foreign Mission Board, the Domestic Mission Board which since 1855 had included the Indian Mission enterprise, the Bible Board at Nashville, the Southern Baptist Publication Society at Charleston, and the Southern Baptist Seminary at Greenville. The Bible Board was shut down in 1863 after the fall of Nashville, and the Southern Baptist Publication Society ceased even before that. The fledgling seminary completed only three sessions before it too shut down, and the Domestic Mission Board was badly crippled as its missionaries either joined Confederate forces or served as both official and unofficial chaplains.[58]

A Sunday School Board was formed in 1863, following the failure of the Southern Baptist Publishing Society and the Bible Board, to provide literature for the churches. Headed by the talented John A. Broadus and Basil Manly Jr. during the time the seminary was shut down, the Board began a remarkable little publication for children. Later known as *Kind Words,* the venture enjoyed dramatic success. The Board's successor, the present-day Baptist Sunday School Board, recognized the contribution of Broadus and Manly by naming its book publishing arm Broadman Press after the two enterprising professors.

The Domestic and Indian Mission Board

The Domestic Mission Board at Marion, which had been augmented by its merger with the Indian Mission Board in 1855, had approximately 150 missionaries deployed at the outbreak of the war. Indian Missions were the first to go under, because they had been heavily subsidized by government appropriations. As indicated, many of the missionaries and ministers either joined the army or began to minister in its camps. Despite the travails involved, their efforts met with astounding revival among the displaced forces.[59]

While gifts dropped initially to less than $15,000 in 1862 from a high of $37,000 in 1860, they soon rebounded. But even the record gifts of $156,000 in 1865 only masked the problem, because by then Confederacy currency had little or no value.[60]

The biggest problem for the Domestic Board developed in 1863 when the Home Mission Society, which had initially backed off and ceded southern territory to the Board, resumed work in the South. They did so by asking the War Department to allow them to take over all houses of worship belonging to the Baptist churches in the South "in which a loyal minister of said church does not officiate."[61] The Home Mission Society's official reason was its desire to protect these facilities. Not surprisingly, the leadership of the Domestic Mission Board saw it otherwise, but their protests fell unheeded and Home Mission Society personnel followed victorious northern armies deep into the South. Soon they had relocated missionaries in Kentucky, Louisiana, Tennessee, Virginia, Missouri, and South Carolina. Northern Baptists felt that this was consistent with the whole underlying moral theme of the Civil War, that is to free the slaves, and most of their work was done among freed slaves.

Russell Holman, who had done much to keep the Board from floundering in its early days, stepped aside in 1862 and was succeeded by M. T. Sumner. Sumner faced a bleak task as the war spread across the South.[62]

Foreign Mission Board

The Foreign Mission Board came to the war years with a strong program concentrated in China despite small beachheads in West Africa and Brazil. The Board planned to open work in Japan and appointed two couples, the J. Q. Rohrers and the J. L. Johnsons along with Crawford Howell Toy. Mrs. Johnson was Toy's sister. With the looming specter of war, only the Rohrers sailed along with a new China appointee, A. L. Bond. Had Toy gone with them, he would have met a different fate, for they were all lost at sea and the opening of work in Japan was delayed.[63]

James B. Taylor exerted sacrificial leadership in behalf of the foreign effort, though it took its toll on his health. He depended on Southern Baptists in Kentucky and Maryland as well as friendly agents in New York to help him move his increasingly meager funds to the struggling China missions and missionaries, including R. H. Graves, a preacher with medical skills from Baltimore. Graves had been appointed to China in 1856 and was already seen in heroic proportions by his prayerful supporters, thanks to the organizing abilities of his dedicated mother in Baltimore.

Graves's father had befriended James P. Taylor when Taylor was a boy in New York, and Taylor had always felt a warm place in his heart for the father and took special pride in the doctor son when he sent him to China. Graves himself had joined Matthew T. Yates in Shanghai, along with J. L. Holmes, though Holmes and an Episcopalian named Fulhart were murdered by rebellious Chinese bandits.[64]

The J. B. Hartwells and the T. P. Crawfords were in northern China and stayed on throughout the war, despite the uncertainty of funds and support.

The Crawfords, who were appointed in 1852 and about whom much more will emerge, had moved to the North after he came into conflict with missionaries in the south. In the North, he became convinced that missionaries ought to eat and dress like the Chinese and, strongly influenced by J. R. Graves's Landmark views, he argued that missionaries would be more appropriately supported by local churches than by mission boards. But these views were not to become divisive for a number of years.[65]

When the Southern Baptist Convention met in Augusta in 1863, Richard Fuller, who was serving his second term as president, was north of Union lines in Maryland. P. H. Mell of Georgia was elected to succeed Fuller, since there was no assurance Fuller could make the next session.[66]

Taylor continued to travel throughout the devastated South often going into occupied territories or behind lines trying to raise money. In addition, to help defray his salary, Taylor worked as a chaplain and colporteur in hospitals and as an employee of the Virginia Sunday School and Publication Board. Nevertheless, when the war was over and despite the faithful support of the churches in Kentucky and Maryland, the Foreign Mission Board faced a staggering $10,000 debt.

On April 2, 1865, Taylor wrote in his diary as his train approached Richmond: "About nine o'clock I took the cars for Richmond. Long before reaching the city, the dark, rolling clouds of smoke and the sound of bursting shells too fearfully told of the destruction that was going on. On reaching the suburbs, as the train slowly approached, we saw the blue uniforms of the soldiers already posted in the fields, showing that the city had fallen. But deep was my grief to find my beautiful city in flames, and all over her streets advancing troops, and excited crowds telling the sad story of the ruin which had overtaken us"[67]

The following Sunday General Robert E. Lee met the victorious Union commander, General Ulysses Grant, in Appomattox, Virginia, and formally surrendered the Confederate forces. The war was over.

William Bullein Johnson, the architect, the tireless agent, the advocate of the Southern position that became the Southern Baptist Convention, was not there at the end. The founder passed away on October, 2, 1862, at the height of the fratricide. The Convention had adopted a memorial honoring him at its 1863 meeting. It was crafted by Richard Furman's son, James C. Furman, who in curious understatement did not mention Johnson's Convention role.[68]

3

Reconstruction and Survival

1865–1900

With its people and territory devastated emotionally and economically by the bloody and costly Civil War, the Southern Baptist Convention's leadership regrouped and started again. Historians call the period following the Confederate surrender "Reconstruction," but some things could not be reconstructed. The bitter strife cost both armies 617,000 American lives.[1] Not even subsequent American losses in two world wars, Korea, and Vietnam approached that total.

Some analysts concluded that a Southern trilogy of aristocracy, decentralization, and agriculture had fallen to a Northern trilogy of democracy, nationalism, and industrialism. Such analysis notwithstanding, the pressing reality was the need to reconcile two bitter foes and harmonize two rival societies.[2]

The magnanimity natural to the American spirit floundered in the face of arrogance in victory and stubborn bitterness in defeat. This magnanimity all but disappeared after the assassination of Abraham Lincoln. The malignancy of slavery had been banished, but the plight of the previously enslaved and the newly disenfranchised lingered and left unresolved and, for the most part, unaddressed a whole new set of problems for African-Americans that retarded their assimilation into a resistant culture.

While Reconstruction technically ended in 1877 when Union troops finally left the South, it was a de facto reality until the end of the century when a transcendent nationalism emerged with the Spanish-American War.

Since organized religion furnished one of the initial rents in the national fabric preceding the acrimonious conflict, many northern churches assumed that the triumph of Federal armies meant not only the end of southern political independence but also the end of separate church organizations. Presbyterians and Methodists had followed the same course of division as Baptists.

For Southern Baptists, however, Reconstruction was not a time of reunion but of a second start. While many Northern Baptists thought a reunion with their southern brethren was just a matter of time, most Southern Baptists thought their separate denominationalism was more important than ever before.[3]

Reopening the Seminary

The turmoil of war's end caused the Southern Baptist Convention to cancel its 1865 meeting, and it did not begin biennial meetings again until 1866. The symbol of Southern Baptists' second start, therefore, was the reopening of Southern Baptist Theological Seminary in Greenville, South Carolina, in the fall of 1865.

James P. Boyce, John A. Broadus, Basil Manly, Jr., and William Williams gathered almost immediately after Appomattox to plan the reopening. Boyce as the initiator pledged the remainder of his once considerable wealth to get it started. In correspondence begun by Broadus, Manly betrayed his pessimism and confided that Williams was dispirited about the whole thing. But they did agree to meet, and in that meeting they laid their trepidations aside. Broadus is believed to have said, "Suppose we quietly agree that the seminary may die, but we'll die first."[4] That statement later became a rallying cry for the seminary faculty whenever it was under fire theologically or financially.

Only seven students were enrolled, but the four professors who had made the initial efforts resolutely returned to the task. They reflected the Charleston tradition, as it was later called, from which Southern Baptist leadership was drawn for many years.

James Petigru Boyce was born in Charleston, South Carolina, in 1827 with the proverbial silver spoon. Wealth and position provided superb educational opportunities including Charleston College and Brown University, where he pursued a law degree. However, the preaching of Francis Wayland in chapel engaged him while he was there, and in the spring of 1846, during a return trip to Charleston, he made a Christian profession during a revival meeting in which Richard Fuller was preaching.[5]

Boyce completed one more year at Brown University before he became convinced that he had been called to Christian ministry. His wealthy and ambitious father did not approve, but Boyce persisted and continued his education at Princeton. After a stint editing a new weekly paper called *The Southern Baptist* from 1848–49, Boyce was called to be pastor of the First Baptist Church in Columbia, South Carolina. Despite the success inherent in such an influential position, his real desire was to be a theological professor, and in 1855 he assumed a post at Furman University.

In 1857 an education convention, called to consider the matter of establishing a seminary, appointed Boyce as agent to raise the funds for the effort, and in 1859 Boyce, at thirty-two years of age, became the founding president or "Chairman of the Faculty" and enlisted the rest of the initial faculty of the Southern Baptist Theological Seminary. Boyce, who at different times taught theology, homiletics, New Testament, and church history, was also treasurer; and his personal wealth enabled the institution to stay afloat through the years when funds were insufficient for operations.[6]

John A. Broadus was Boyce's soulmate in the task. Broadus, a Virginian, came from an educated and religious background, but not necessarily one of wealth. Receiving his M.A. degree from the University of Virginia in 1850, he was ordained to the ministry and married the same year. He married the daughter of a professor at the University of Virginia and began teaching Latin and Greek there while serving as pastor of the Baptist church at Charlottesville.

There he became the mentor of young Crawford Howell Toy, the brightest student Broadus, by his own testimony, ever had. Toy was later his colleague at the seminary. In Charlottesville, also, the bright and feisty Lottie

Moon dropped her initial cynicism to become a Christian under Broadus' preaching.

Broadus was approached in 1858 to be a part of the new seminary faculty and, though he struggled with the decision, he was there when it opened in 1859. His skills in New Testament interpretation and homiletics were foundational to the seminary and his influence was such that he gave the Yale lectures in preaching at Yale University in 1889.

Basil Manly, Jr., was the son of a former president of the University of Alabama and is credited with sounding the first note for the need for a seminary. He was born in South Carolina and raised in Charleston, where his father was pastor before taking the post in Tuscaloosa. Converted at fifteen, Manly was preaching by age nineteen. He studied at Newton Theological Institution in Massachusetts and was there at the time the Southern Baptist Convention was organized in 1845. Later he went to Princeton, graduating in 1847. Early pastorates followed, before he came into his own as a person of influence as pastor of the First Baptist Church in Richmond, Virginia beginning in 1850. His intellectual skills and educational background made him a natural for the presidency of the newly established Richmond Female Institute in 1854.

Invited to join the faculty of the new seminary, he accepted Boyce's invitation to take the post of professor of Biblical Introduction in Old Testament Interpretation. Manly was also asked to draw up the articles of faith that each professor was required to sign. The "Abstract of Principles" was a masterful document that survived decades of Southern Baptist controversy.[7]

The fourth member in the group of founding fathers of Southern Seminary was William Williams, a native of Georgia. Williams received an impressive education at the University of Georgia and Harvard Law School before he abandoned law for the ministry. He was pastor in Auburn, Alabama, for a time before becoming a professor at Mercer University, which was at that time still in Penfield, Georgia. Boyce enlisted Williams to become professor of ecclesiastical history, church government, and pastoral duties.

Williams became the focus of one of the seminary's first controversies in 1872 when his teachings on alien immersion conflicted with pervasive Landmark ideas. Boyce solved the problem simply by taking that course over from Williams.[8] Boyce's tact and finesse on theological issues caused all sides to claim his allegiance.

The four men were joined by a long stream of colleagues, but none eclipsed their ability or dedication. Yet theirs was to be a stormy ride, predicted by Broadus in a letter to Boyce when he agreed to join the venture: "As to pleasing everybody, I suppose it must be our lot, the balance of our lives, to have various persons all the time finding fault with us."[9] It turned out to be an understatement.

Post-War Trials

Along with all the other Southern institutions, the struggling seminary and the mission boards faced desperate conditions in the war's aftermath. Robert A. Baker did an exhaustive study of the statistics and demographics of the South during the reconstruction period. His numbers reflect how deeply damaged were the economies and social structures of the seven southern states that along with Kentucky and Maryland organized the Southern Baptist Convention.

The college at Richmond had been gutted of books and equipment, and its endowment was totally worthless at the end of the war. The Virginia Baptist paper, *The Religious Herald,* had seen its entire plant destroyed by Union troops. Wherever Union troops marched, this destruction was often repeated. Where it was not, the depletion of workers who made the economy go, disarray among freed Negroes not sure where to turn with their freedom, and lack of capital resources took their toll.[10]

Southern Baptists were led at this time by Patrick Hues Mell, a Georgian who was elected presiding officer at the 1863 meeting in Augusta, replacing Richard Fuller. Fuller, who was serving in Maryland, surrendered his position when the war made it increasingly difficult to relate to the majority of Southern Baptists, though he continued to be a key agent for the Baptist foreign mission enterprise.

P. H. Mell trained at Amherst College in Massachusetts and then taught at Mercer University and at the University of Georgia. At the time of his election as president of the Southern Baptist Convention, he was vice-chancellor of the University of Georgia and preached in churches throughout that area. In fact, he was so well-known and so effective that country churches in that area were known as "Mell's Kingdom."

Mell presided over sessions of the Convention until his death in early 1872. James P. Boyce, still president of Southern Baptist Theological Seminary at that time, was elected president.

While the question of reunion with the North was in the air, most Southern Baptists continued to be committed to the separate institutions that they had begun twenty years earlier. Their resolve faced strong opposition from the North and especially from its Home Mission Society and some southern leaders who had broader national ties. J. S. Backus of the Home Mission Society stated the Northern Baptists' problem: "If it is politically and morally wrong to support the Southern Confederacy, how can it be religiously right to support the Southern Baptist Convention?"[11]

But while the institution of slavery no longer existed and political tensions eased after the affirmation of the Union through force of arms, sectional bitterness and division had, if anything, deepened. The question of reunion with Northern Baptists lingered among Southern Baptists until the end of the next decade.

The aggressiveness and the effectiveness of the Home Mission Society was one of the main reasons it took so long to resolve the question. At the close of 1865 Northern Baptists had sixty missionaries in twelve southern states. Just two years later the Home Mission Society listed over a hundred missionaries in those states.

Robert A. Baker's analysis of Baptists' growth in the period following the Civil War attests to one thing beyond all else. Despite the Convention's initial striking of the word Southwestern from the name of the new organization in 1845, the center of gravity for Southern Baptists was moving in that direction, due in part to the devastation wrought in the old South and in part to the inherent promise in new lands. Family after family reinforced the obvious: reconstruction reality included the relocation of multitudes of families and individuals toward the west.[12] In this sense, history was being determined by a future that had been called manifest destiny, as surely as it was being constrained by a past that included a lost cause and a persistent southern culture.

Baptist churches in states of the Old South struggled. First, the numbers in churches dwindled because of the withdrawal of former slaves to form their own churches. Second, church totals suffered statistically with the separation of West Virginia from Virginia. And finally, they lost membership in the migration to the southwest.

In turn, this migration resulted in significant growth of membership in churches organized just before the war in the southwestern states of Texas, Arkansas, and Louisiana.

The suffering in the South during this period, dramatized graphically by the book and motion picture, "Gone with the Wind," was broad and pervasive. Widowed or displaced women bore unaccustomed burdens in the Old South and took on new burdens in the march west. Newly freed blacks found it difficult to make their way outside the system so deeply entrenched throughout the economic structure of the South. They struggled to adapt to being tenant farmers and day laborers. Many Christians from all persuasions endeavored to give them a new start with educational opportunities, and the Home Mission Society of the Northern Baptist Convention was one of the leading groups in this effort.

The Southern Baptist Convention's efforts following Appomattox were focused in its churches and associations, its meetings, the work of its Domestic Mission Board, its Foreign Mission Board, its struggling Sunday School Board in Greenville, and the newly reopened Southern Baptist Theological Seminary, also in Greenville.

Domestic Mission Board

The Domestic Mission Board's fortunes during this period reflected the larger environment better than anything else. The Home Mission Society was aggressively pursuing work in the South and challenging the very existence of their Southern Baptist counterpart. With followers on both sides of the Mason-Dixon line, the Home Mission Society sought to serve both conventions.

Led by J. S. Backus, the Society had followed the victorious Union armies into the South. Two years after the war the Home Mission Society claimed one hundred missionaries in twelve states. Many of them were teachers working with small schools and often with both black and white constituents.

At its convention in 1867, Southern Baptists urged the Society to work with the Domestic Mission Board which, since absorbing the Indian Mission Society in 1855, had been officially the Domestic and Indian Mission Board. In 1868 the Society responded by sending a group to confer with the Southern Baptist Convention, and at that meeting a committee was appointed to meet with them. The committee, chaired by J. B. Jeter, recommended the Convention develop ties with the Home Mission Society, but their recommendation was rejected in 1869. The very next year a John Broadus-penned motion rejected any connection with the Society.[13]

The Home Mission Society of the North was next led by H. L. More-house. He refused to recognize the Southern Baptist Convention as having any supervisory responsibility for the work south of the Mason-Dixon line. The graciousness of the reports on the part of both groups veil the differences that continued to divide them. The North was organized for a particular benevolence and could focus directly on it, while the South was in a convention structure sponsoring numerous benevolences through individual boards. Thus, the northern group was less conscious of denominationalism, while the southern group was uniquely conscious of it.

Since its inception in 1832, the Home Mission Society had considered all of North America as its jurisdiction, but the Southern Baptist Convention's vision stood in the way. Its survival-mode led the Domestic Mission Board during this period to settle for defining the South and near by Southwest as its territory.

The Home Mission Society's Backus and Morehouse, aided by a few southern leaders, wanted to see a unified Northern and Southern Baptist Convention. They worked with state conventions, associations, and individual churches in the South during all of this period. By 1869, one-third of the Society's missionary force was at work in the South.[14]

Domestic Mission Board secretaries, one after the other, complained bitterly about these undermining alliances with the Northern Society. Their finances, however, limited them, and they were unable to match the sums of money that the northern group's supporters were contributing for their work among Negroes and Indians as well as for frontier opportunities.

M. T. Sumner, who followed Russell Holman in 1862 as secretary of the Domestic Board, labored through the difficult time. In 1873, Southern Baptists closed down their first Sunday School Board after ten years of operation and transferred its remaining publications, including the highly successful children's publication, *Kind Words*, to the Board along with some debt. If it seemed like déjà vu, it was, because the Domestic Mission Board had inherited the Indian Mission Board in the same condition in 1855. Then in 1874, the Convention voted to change the name of the Domestic and Indian Mission Board to the Home Mission Board; one year was enough with the unwieldy title of "Domestic Mission Board and Indian Mission Board and Sunday School Board."

The Board's headquarters location in Marion, Alabama, became a drawback. Local Baptist pastors criticized M. T. Sumner's salary level, though it was much less than that of the pastor serving the Marion Baptist Church.

While in many ways he had done well, Sumner came under additional criticism with new debts that accompanied a severe national financial crisis in 1873. Overexpansion and overlending in the still-fragile Union led to a paralyzing panic, aggravated by battles between advocates of paper money and hard money in President Grant's second administration. The post-war expansion that Mark Twain sarcastically called the Gilded Age collapsed. The South was still so close to the bottom that it didn't have far to fall, but by 1877 Domestic Board receipts had dropped from a high of $38,000 to just under $17,000.

In 1875, Sumner declined to be renominated and was elected president of Judson Female College in Marion. He left there after one year to serve as an agent for Southern Baptist Theological Seminary and then, to the chagrin of his fellow Southern Baptists, became an agent for the American Baptist Publication Society. At the end of this checkered career he was again a pastor in Alabama.[15]

The Domestic Mission Board endeavored to replace Sumner with one of its proven leaders, Basil Manly, Jr., still on the faculty at Southern Baptist Theological Seminary. Manly, who had made the first Sunday School Board so successful and had been one of the progenitors of *Kind Words*, declined, however, and a Marion pastor, W. B. McIntosh, was given the task.

McIntosh previously served as one of the Board's missionaries to the Negro people, having been appointed in 1848 in cooperation with the Georgia Baptist Convention, and in 1861 he preached the annual sermon for the Southern Baptist Convention. With a mandate to retire the debt, he jumped into his new role energetically, although retiring debt meant reducing the Domestic Board's missionary activities. McIntosh eliminated the debt in 1871, but the retrenchment left the Home Mission Board with only twenty-two missionaries, whereas it had as many as a hundred during the Civil War.[16]

Having been burned by debt, caution constrained the Board's leadership. On several occasions the Convention had to urge it to attempt new work. McIntosh even struck an agreement with the American Baptist Home Mission Society in the late 1870s to conduct institutes for Negro ministers. He did lead the Board to open work with Great Plains Indians and even revived the previously attempted mission among Chinese people in California. The publication of *Kind Words* was the Home Mission Board's most prosperous venture.

New State Conventions

During the period of reconstruction, only two new state conventions were organized despite the great westward migration. In part this was because much of that flow went to Arkansas, Louisiana, Texas, and Florida which had already seen state Baptist organizations established in the previous period.

Tennessee, despite having much older work in place, did not organize a permanent state convention until 1875, twenty-one years after Florida Baptists accomplished their union. Baptist churches were probably planted in Tennessee as early as 1765, only to disappear during the fierce Indian wars fought in the area in 1774. By 1781, however, a Baptist Association was formed in the Holston Valley in East Tennessee, the result of a large migration of Baptists from North Carolina and the missionary labors of the Sandy Creek churches.

Though numerous efforts were made to form a statewide organization, this goal was impeded by geography and controversy. Natural barriers tended to divide Tennessee into three areas, and for years there were three regional groups. In addition, the Campbell controversies, anti-mission sentiments, and Landmarkism kept Tennessee Baptists at odds.

An early effort was attempted by James Whitsitt of Mill Creek church near Nashville. He was the father of William Whitsitt, who was dogged in later years by a reprise of Tennessee's bitter Landmark fights. Finally, in 1874, leaders from the three areas organized a state convention in Murfreesboro. The first effort was motivated by missions, the second by education.

Two years later the District of Columbia, despite its size, delineated itself from Baptists in Maryland and Virginia by establishing a state convention. Cecil and Susan Ray later referred to these fifteen state organizations as the "foundation states" of Southern Baptist life.[17]

Later Landmarkism

James Tull, in his extensive studies on Landmarkism, points out that after the Civil War, J. R. Graves, without his publishing empire and with neither Pendleton nor Dayton at his side, was relatively quiet in his Memphis pastorate, though he was continuously sought after as an inspirational speaker. He toned down his divisiveness, but he never relinquished his hold on the people who had embraced Landmark views.

The Landmark cause was far from abandoned, however, and its individual tenets continued to be championed by independent and state Baptist papers. Foremost among these were *The Baptist Record* in Mississippi, under the editorship of J. B. Gambrell, and *The Baptist,* which Graves had taken over from Howell in Tennessee. *The Baptist* later became *The Baptist and Reflector* and was accorded the role of state paper for Arkansas and Louisiana for some years before *The Arkansas Evangel* and its successor, *The Arkansas Baptist,* took over in 1880.

D. B. Ray of Missouri touted Landmark views with *The Battle Flag* and *Church Historian.* Kentucky's *The Western Recorder,* at first sympathetic to Landmark views, switched under the editorship of A. C. Caperton and then again became a strong Landmark voice in the late 1880s when T. T. Eaton took over its editorship. The *Texas Baptist and Herald* in the 1880s became a Landmark publication, though the *Baptist Standard,* under the leadership of J. B. Cranfill, opposed the radical Landmarkism of S. A. Hayden, despite Cranfill's Landmark opinions.

Graves's own assessment of Landmarkism was far from modest. "At this writing, January, 1880—and I record it with profound gratitude—there is only one Baptist paper in the South of the sixteen weeklies, that approves of alien immersion and pulpit affiliation, while already two papers in the Northern states avow and advocate Landmark principles and practice."[18]

In opposition, *The Religious Herald* of Virginia was the staunchest and most consistent anti-Landmark paper and the one to which Graves referred above. According to Tull and despite Graves's assertions, the Virginia paper also enjoyed support from *The Biblical Recorder* of North Carolina and *The Baptist Courier* of South Carolina. *The Christian Index* of Georgia and *The Alabama Baptist* espoused anti-Landmark views, as did the *Florida Baptist Witness* which began publishing in the late 1880s.

In contrast, the publications of the first Sunday School Board and later the Home Mission Board, as well as the Foreign Mission Board, shied away from the persistent ecclesiological battles swirling around Landmark views. They focused instead on denominational programs and biblical studies, leaving the battle to independent and state Baptist papers, a pattern that has persisted until recent times.

Not only did these publications relish the role, but they were also in many cases probably dependent on such controversy for survival. At one time there were over two hundred of these publications, according to Tull, who claims that over half of them may have supported strong Landmark views.

Landmarkism in the late 1880s became less evident on the floors of the Southern Baptist Convention and more evident in state convention battles. An exception emerged toward the close of the century when the conflict engulfed Southern Baptist Seminary.

Tull called it a chronic element in the bloodstream from this point on and, as shall be seen over and over again, that "chronic element" or what W. W. Barnes, Southern Baptist historian, was later to call "a deposit" would be in the background of many future conflicts.[19]

Foreign Missions

Under the almost Herculean efforts of James B. Taylor, the Foreign Mission Board maintained its fragile beachheads throughout the Civil War. With strong support from Kentucky and Maryland outside the embattled Confederacy, the able work of Baltimore pastor Richard B. Fuller who handled much of the transfer of funds, the efforts of the Board's agent in New York, and the ingenuity of missionaries, the flame of foreign missions was kept burning.

The three stations in China dominated by the figures of R. H. Graves, Matthew Yates, and T. P. Crawford persisted despite losses and hardships. In West Africa, where Negro missionaries in Liberia and Sierra Leone had to cope with their own civil war, the work continued even though some of the missionaries had to provide for their own living. In contrast, the fledgling effort in Brazil collapsed as T. J. Bowen returned home broken physically and emotionally by his efforts to begin a mission in the Catholic-dominated country.

Yet, as James B. Taylor informed the Board in a series of poignant statements, survival had not been without cost. He reported that the Rohrer family and A. L. Bond had perished at sea on the boat that Crawford Toy would have taken had funds been available. J. L. Holmes was murdered trying to negotiate with rebels in China, and Robert Gaillard died in Canton when a typhoon slammed through that city collapsing the roof of his house. R. H. Graves, who had earlier lost his wife, married Mrs. Gaillard and adopted her infant son.[20] Toward the end of the war, John Shillings lost his wife, and Taylor reported that the bereaved missionary was returning with his small children.

At the end of the war Taylor struggled doggedly to cope with the problems. He shipped cotton out of Charleston to England to be converted to funds and sent to the missionaries. He and the Board planned to send J. B. Jeter to London to raise funds there and operate as their agent. Though approved, the plan was never implemented. The collapse of the Confederacy came too rapidly to expedite it.

After the war several mission volunteers who had been ready to go before the war were no longer available. Either the battlefields and privations of war had decimated their ranks or, like Crawford Howell Toy, they changed their plans. Early in 1866 Toy sailed for Germany with a family named Sanders from Charleston. The Sanders were going to run a girls' school in Berlin and Toy was to room with them. He made the journey with the strong support of John A. Broadus, his long-time mentor, who dreamed of Toy's joining the faculty of Southern Seminary with the advanced scholarship that German study would allow him. Toy's romance with Lottie Moon seems to have faded into the background during the war.

Lottie Moon, following her graduation from Albemarle Female Institute, spent much of the war helping her widowed mother manage their plantation, teach her younger sister Edmonia, and giving help in the war effort, including nursing the wounded. When the war was over and Lottie Moon felt free to leave, she took a teaching position in Danville, Kentucky. There she met Anna Cunningham Safford, a fellow teacher and strong Presbyterian. There also she and A. C. (as she called her soulmate and life-long friend) were introduced to several missionaries from China. Both Moon and Safford were deeply impressed and confessed to each other their interest in missionary service, but both were aware of their respective denominations' resistance to unmarried women as missionaries.[21]

Though Moon was pushing women's roles, as evidenced by a thesis on "Women's Rights" during her school years and a later series commending deaconesses for the Religious Herald, she was not considered radical.[22]

But the expectations of women were still very clear in Southern Baptist churches. Moon was primarily expected to be a homemaker and mother. She was also expected to be subordinate to her husband and to church and society. Preachers reinforced these expectations by lauding women in their domestic roles. In addition, they were careful to point out that the scriptures taught they were neither to address public assemblies nor have power or authority over men.[23]

Though women had achieved a modicum of acceptance in teaching roles, Moon and Safford were still going against the grain when they seized an opportunity in 1871 to open a female school in Cartersville, Georgia. On the way, Moon visited Richmond, where she was delighted by the religious fervor and interest in missions of her younger sister Edmonia, now at the Richmond Female Academy.

Taylor's own health was one of the costs of beginning and sustaining the Southern Baptist foreign mission enterprise. In 1869, poor health prompted him to suggest to the Board that he resign from his post, but they asked him to stay. In 1871 his health worsened and he again offered to resign. Thinking that they were affirming his great contribution, the Board still refused his resignation. On December 22, 1871, the missions pioneer died at his home in Richmond, Virginia.

Taylor left as a legacy a mission enterprise that would prevail against great odds, though none greater than he had confronted. Eighty-one missionaries had been appointed and served in China, Liberia, Sierra Leone, Nigeria, and Italy, where Taylor's own son, George B. Taylor, was part of a pioneering effort.

J. B. Jeter, who had been both mentor and colleague to Taylor and had fought many battles with him at his side, said, "Of all the men I've ever known intimately, his qualities, intellectual and moral, were the most perfectly proportioned and rounded."[24]

Jeter, who still chaired the Foreign Mission Board, and his colleagues began a search for Taylor's successor. In 1872 they elected Henry Allen Tupper of South Carolina as corresponding secretary. Tupper had business experience as well as pastoral experience. The committee also liked to point out that Tupper had once expressed an interest in being a foreign missionary himself.

One of Tupper's first moves was to convince the Foreign Mission Board to appoint single women for missionary service, and he had a ready volunteer in Lottie Moon's younger sister, Edmonia. The bright and energetic Edmonia Moon had found enthusiastic support in Richmond from a society organized for that purpose. Edmonia Moon, her eyes bright with the excitement of her venture and barely twenty-one, became a pioneer for her gender in Baptist life. She sailed for China with South Carolina's Lula Whilden who, having been approved earlier, is listed as the first single woman in the missionary service.

At this point, Edmonia's lifelong dependence on her sister began to assert itself. Her letters from China evidently revealed emotional difficulty almost from the beginning and stirred in Lottie Moon a desire to join her sister as a needed helper as well as missionary. In 1873 she completed correspondence on the matter with Tupper and received notice of appointment to China's Shantung province where the T. P. Crawfords and the Hartwells were stationed. It would place her near Edmonia and also near her friend A. C. Safford, who had secured a similar appointment from the Presbyterians. The women at Cartersville Baptist Church near the school where Moon and Safford taught organized a mission society the same year for "the elevation of woman in heathen lands."[25]

In retrospect, these women were breaking ground of historic proportions. Gregory Vickers would later note that the opportunity to do mission work either by going or by support through giving and proliferating organizations filled a void of religious expression for women. Vickers observed: "These two vocations provided Baptist women the opportunity to serve their God in an extraordinary fashion." He went on to say, "But as examples of Christian womanhood, they helped change Baptist women's understanding of themselves."[26]

Tupper also attempted to strengthen the work in Nigeria and Italy, opened work in Mexico and Japan, and reopened efforts in Brazil. Hard hit by disease in its early days, the missions effort in Nigeria was kept alive by Sarah Harden, the widow of a black missionary from Liberia, for a number of years. Taylor's son, George Boardman Taylor, was the director of the Baptist work in Italy.

Southern Baptist efforts in Mexico followed the martyrdom of a Texas Baptist missionary, John Westrup, in December 1880. The thirty-three-year old native of London, England, and former agent of the American Bible Society was appointed by Texas Baptists earlier that year and accepted by the Foreign Mission Board, but he fell victim to hostile Indians. William Powell, who had gone to Mexico to find out what happened to Westrup, then wrote the Foreign Mission Board to offer to continue his work. The Board accepted his offer in 1882, the year after the William Bagbys sailed for Brazil in a second effort to start mission work in that country.[27]

The ill-fated prewar efforts to begin work in Japan finally came to fruition in 1889, when the John McCollums located in Fukuoka. Tupper urged them to "lay the foundations of an eternal work." He said, "Look a hundred years ahead."[28]

The Foreign Mission Board began publishing the *Foreign Mission Journal* in 1876 after earlier efforts with first its own publication and later a publication with the Domestic Mission Board, a cost-saving approach that would be tried once again. By 1882 it reached more and more Southern Baptists, but the Foreign Mission Board's real support lay among women and women's prayer groups. The women were especially effective in circulating letters from missionaries as R. H. Graves's mother, Ann Baker Graves, often did in Baltimore and as the friends of Lottie Moon soon began to do with her moving correspondence from China. As in Cartersville, women's missionary societies sprang up throughout the South.[29]

Lottie Moon's initial years were difficult not only from concern about the declining emotional health of her sister, but also because of an ongoing feud between Crawford and Hartwell. In 1876 she returned with Edmonia, whose mental health could no longer handle the situation. If Lottie Moon's main motivation had been Edmonia, one could excuse her from returning. But China now had a hold on her and she was eager to go back. The problem was that her return home with Edmonia had eroded confidence in their mission in the eyes of those who had been reluctant to send single women, and funds were not available for her transportation back.

Tupper worked hard to rebuild confidence, and the Richmond women again got on the bandwagon and allowed a "Moon House Fund" to be used for transportation. Lottie Moon sailed on her return trip to China in late 1877.[30]

She arrived back in China to the aftermath of the first General Conference of Protestant Missionaries in China held in Shanghai. A Woman's Missionary Association had been organized during the conference and Moon's close friend, A. C. Safford, had been elected vice-president and editor of a new publication, *Woman's Work in China.* Safford wanted Lottie Moon to be a contributing editor and Moon readily consented.[31] Safford was winning renown as a fierce business woman and "something of a man-hater," and as a journalist who "never made a mistake and never forgot anything."[32] For Moon, however, A. C. Safford was a confidant and release valve until Safford's death from cancer some years later.

Moon's brief stay in the United States may have included a reunion with Crawford Howell Toy, now a member of the faculty at Southern Baptist Theological Seminary. It is certain that by the time of her return she was corresponding once more with the now-beleaguered professor.

The Toy Incident

Crawford Howell Toy, the namesake of R. B. C. Howell of Tennessee and the prize protégé of John A. Broadus, completed two years at the University of Berlin while living withthe Sanders family. When he returned to the United States in 1868, he was immediately offered a post at Furman University in Greenville. He was extremely well qualified for the university's chair of Greek Languages and Literature, but it was already known that John A. Broadus and James P. Boyce coveted Toy for the faculty of the seminary. Thus, to no one's surprise, in the summer of 1869, Virginia's *Religious Herald* announced Toy's appointment to the seminary faculty and said he was "deemed by competent judges, to be one of the best linguists of his age, in this or any other country." The article then predicted, "He will, at no distant day, rank among the foremost Biblical scholars of the world."[33] Their prediction was to be realized, but in a way far different from these enthusiastic expectations.

Toy's scholarship and abilities were evident in his inaugural address entitled "The Claims of Biblical Interpretation on Baptists," which was published in 1869 without eliciting any opposition. In it Toy said, "The Bible, its real assertions being known, is in every iota of its substance absolutely and infallibly true."[34] He was obviously a very popular addition to the seminary's faculty, and his classes often outnumbered those of his colleagues, even when he was teaching the same courses as they did.

Basil Manly, Jr., who had been one of the beginning faculty members as well as a guiding light in the Sunday School Board during the war days, took a pastorate in 1871. He was replaced in 1872 by William Seth Whitsitt who had, at Broadus's advice, also gone to Germany to study because of the tremendous impact such an adventure had on Toy. Whitsitt had evidently laid aside his foreign mission plans, also.

The Seminary was now located in Louisville, Kentucky. The decision, made in the summer of 1872 with the hope of a more favorable economic climate in Kentucky and the potential of a broader-based constituency, came to fruition in 1877 when the exhaustive fundraising efforts of Boyce made the move possible. William Williams left the faculty the same year, leaving only Boyce and Broadus of the founding faculty along with Toy and William Whitsitt.

In 1879 Toy became involved in a major crisis at Southern Seminary, the first other than the perennial financial ones, since Landmark forces had attacked William Williams over his theories on the administration of baptism. Boyce had finessed that problem by substituting himself in the classes where Williams had been questioned, and with Boyce there was no question. But Toy wrote articles concerning the authorship of the Old Testament book of Isaiah that brought criticism from both Landmark and anti-Landmark sources. This brought his whole teaching bias under scrutiny.

And it was soon obvious that Crawford Howell Toy's German sojourn had led him to embrace not only the higher critical approaches of Germany's Julius Wellhausen to the authorship and interpretation of the Old Testament, but the Darwinian evolutionary theories that were associated with the increasingly maligned "modernists" in American education. A Southern Seminary professor a century later said, "It shoved him beyond the comfort range on the principles laid down by Boyce."[35]

Darwin's *Origin of the Species* had been published in 1859, but the 1879 publication of his *Descent of Man* left no doubt about the implications of his evolutionary theory for the development of humankind. It put him in direct conflict with biblical creationists.

As the conflict progressed, Toy felt it necessary to write an explanation of his point of view and a letter of resignation for the trustees. There is some question whether Toy expected his resignation to be accepted or whether he just felt it was the proper thing to do while the Board considered his position. Friends thought he fully expected to be vindicated and was genuinely surprised when he was not. Over a century later, Paige Patterson, leading opposition to Toy's successors over many of the same issues, would offer surprising praise for Toy for "openly preaching and writing his perspectives."[36] But his resignation was accepted and, though Boyce and especially Broadus were disheartened, they backed the Board's decision.[37]

In a letter to his wife, Broadus wrote, "Poor bereaved three; we have lost our jewell of learning, our beloved and noble brother, the pride of the Seminary. God bless the Seminary, God bless Toy, and God help us, sadly but steadfastly to do our providential duty."[38]

Those who had wanted Toy's teaching to be evaluated and judged were disappointed when his resignation was accepted because he had diverged from traditional views. It was not so much his belief in inspiration as his concept of what went into a doctrine of inspiration with which Baptists, and even his colleagues, disagreed.

His new colleague, William Whitsitt, defended him in foretaste of what he himself would experience. Several students of whom Toy was a favorite were vocal and active in his defense, and it caused at least two of them, T. P. Bell and John Stout, to be rejected for missionary service. In Bell's case the stigma did not remain long, for he later served on the staff of the Foreign Mission Board and still later headed up the Sunday School Board. Stout gave his wife strong support in the founding of the Woman's Missionary Union. Their rejection was still another blow for Moon and her colleagues, however, since it was their badly undermanned station that Bell and Stout were to have joined.[39]

Basil Manly was asked to return to the faculty as Toy left for his home in Richmond in time to be at his dying father's bedside. Toy's anguish deepened as he realized that his scholar-father's heart had been broken by the whole episode.[40]

Toy was reportedly offered a presidency and a professorship, but he declined both, since he was waiting for John A. Broadus to try to negotiate a place for him at Johns Hopkins University in Baltimore. In the interim he edited a small religious periodical called *The Independent*. The Broadus initiative did not work out, and when Harvard University offered him a position the next year, he accepted and spent the remainder of his days there.

Lottie Moon, monitoring the controversy through Toy's letters and the letters of others, may have planned at one point to accompany Toy to Harvard. T. P. Crawford thought she would. Yet she finally backed off and broke the engagement, though several versions of the incident indicate that she sincerely struggled to understand Toy's views before she did. The next few years she focused on language study and began an itinerate ministry in the surrounding countryside. Gradually, the old dream gave way to a new one of rural missions in and around Pingtu, carving out new dimensions of what a woman could accomplish in direct missions.

Toy did not marry for many years. Then, at age 52, he married the youngest daughter of the Sanders family, Nancy, who had been six years of age when he lived with that family in Germany.

True to the *Religious Herald's* prediction, Toy did become an acclaimed scholar at Harvard and, with Nancy's expert social skills, served as host and friend of such people as Woodrow Wilson, who would later become president of the United States. The fact that Toy subsequently became a Unitarian caused many original supporters to back off and his critics to feel vindicated.

The issues related to Toy's resignation and departure from Southern Seminary reappeared eighty years later and triggered fears that again involved Southern Baptists in a major conflict. Manly, who had served as president of Georgetown College after leaving Southern Seminary, voiced those fears years in advance in his introductory lecture upon returning: "From the doubt or denial of God's book, the road is short to doubt and denial of God; and after that comes the abyss, where all knowledge is not only lost but scoffed at except that which the brute might enjoy as well."[41]

The Home Mission Board

By the time Southern Baptists gathered in Atlanta for their convention in 1879 the issue was not Toy, but the continued conflict between the northern Home Mission Society and their own Home Mission Board. Henry Morehouse's leadership of the Society was geared to replace the Southern Board.[42] Hopes of merging the two institutions persisted and precipitated a lengthy debate.

As mentioned earlier, a resolution framed by John A. Broadus urged cooperation with northern Baptists but firmly resolved to maintain separate institutions.[43] In passing it, Southern Baptists clearly reaffirmed their commitment to their own Board. This temporarily energized McIntosh, and the Home Mission Board began to increase missionary appointments once again. Work among Indians, almost abandoned during and after the war, received attention. Particularly significant was the growth of the Board's Sunday School efforts when the publication of *Kind Words* was expanded to include weekly, semi-monthly, monthly, and quarterly editions, plus other age-level publications.[44]

However, the Home Mission Board continued to suffer by comparison with its foreign counterpart, its gifts continued to lag, and it remained vulnerable to its enemies. The issue again came to a head in 1882. The Convention adopted a report that effectively changed the makeup of the Home Mission Board and its location, thanked McIntosh and colleagues, and authorized the search for a new secretary. This headed off efforts to combine the Home Mission Board with the Foreign Mission Board. The Board was moved from Alabama to the more bustling Atlanta, Georgia, and in short order flamboyant Isaac Taylor Tichenor was tapped to replace stolid William McIntosh.[45]

Seldom has a leadership change achieved such a dramatic turn-around as did that which brought the former president of what is now Auburn University to the helm of the Home Mission Board. Tall, forceful, commanding in voice and in presence, Tichenor, with his well-developed social and political skills and mesmerizing platform abilities, was just what the Home Mission Board needed.

He had been a pastor in Birmingham when the war broke out and joined the Confederate forces as a chaplain. However, he made his reputation as a sharpshooter and by rallying the troops to victory in one notable battle that unfolded on a Sunday. Tichenor, responding to the challenge and ignoring the danger, ran to the forefront of the Confederate line and exhorted the soldiers to remember that the people back home were in church and praying for them. He promised them that God would help them carry the day. After the war in a speech to the Alabama legislature, Tichenor moved that group with his eloquence and told this story the first of many times. He always modestly omitted that he was the soldier involved, much as John A. Broadus would do on the occasions he would tell about his own challenge to the young seminary faculty to resolve to die themselves before letting the seminary die.[46]

The energetic Tichenor traveled extensively, urging state conventions, associations, and churches to prove their loyalty to the Southern Baptist Convention through cooperation with the Home Mission Board. He hacked away at their ties with the North's Publication Society and with the Home Mission Society. He sold them on the Sunday School literature of the Home Mission Board and developed cooperative ventures in missions to replace Society-sponsored efforts.

By 1887 every southern state was in cooperation with the Home Mission Board and all missionaries to the whites in the South were related to the Home Mission Board. Dedicated and persistent efforts among the freed slaves by the Home Mission Society were seldom challenged, though advisory roles were sought. Later Tichenor hired his predecessor, William McIntire, to work with Negroes. Still later Tichenor led the Board to begin appointing Negro missionaries.[47]

Tichenor was especially adroit in stirring the denominational consciousness to which the convention-type polity developed by W. B. Johnson lent itself. Tichenor made it clear that the Home Mission Board and the Southern Baptist Convention were one entity. If a person was for one, he was for the other.

In 1884 he started a church loan fund, and in 1886 he led the Board to begin work in Cuba. A program of mountain missions in the southern Appalachians was especially successful. Under Tichenor the missionary force doubled in just two years, tripled in five years, and quadrupled by the eighth year. He even anticipated the need to minister to ethnic groups appearing in large American cities.[48]

It is hard to overestimate the progress Southern Baptists made during Tichenor's tenure or to overstate his contribution. His role in revitalizing the Home Mission Board is matched by his success in heightening denominational pride and commitment. But his role in developing Sunday School literature and, as shall be seen later, his statesmanship in the formation of the Sunday School Board in 1891 may be an even more significant achievement. Nor can his role in encouraging the work of women's missionary societies and their subsequent organization be overlooked.

Declining health finally slowed the remarkable Tichenor, and he retired in 1899 at the age of seventy-four. His tenure had changed the face of the Southern Baptist Convention. Besides the accomplishments already mentioned, it was said that he saved the Southern Baptist Convention by saving the Home Mission Board and that he led Southern Baptists to envision the South as a base for world missions. It was even said that his emphasis on systematic giving laid the foundation for the Cooperative Program.[49]

Woman's Missionary Union

At its convention in 1878 a Southern Baptist Convention committee on women's work recommended to the two mission boards that they organize central committees of women in each state to promote the organization of societies throughout those states. By this time women's societies for the promotion of missions had a long and distinguished record.

As previously noted, a wheelchair-bound twenty-one-year-old woman named Mary Webb is credited with organizing the first such organization in America, the Boston Female Society in 1800. Webb found strong support from her pastor, Thomas Baldwin, who maintained correspondence with Baptists' first missionary, William Carey.

By 1819 there was evidence of 210 similar societies. Such a society can be documented as early as 1812 in South Carolina and another in North Carolina around the same time.[50] The Female Missionary Society of Richmond, organized in 1813, and another formed in Baltimore the same year were among the strongest. Despite fears by some pastors, these societies flourished, and state organizations appeared in Georgia in 1817, Kentucky in 1822, Alabama in 1823, Arkansas in 1828, and Texas in 1832.

Such activity undoubtedly helped state Baptist groups to organize in the wake of the Triennial Convention, before the focus switched with Southern

Baptist beginnings in 1845. A women's meeting in conjunction with the Southern Baptist Convention meeting in Baltimore in 1868 was led by Ann Baker Graves, whose son continued his missionary labors in China.

National women's organizations were increasingly evident, with the Women's Christian Temperance Union, organized in 1874, becoming a compelling model. Representatives of various women's missionary societies began to meet as early as 1883 with the support of the hard-pressed mission boards. In 1888, in Richmond, Virginia, the Woman's Missionary Union was organized as an auxiliary to the Southern Baptist Convention. Key players leading up to this historic beginning included Martha McIntosh of South Carolina, Mrs. W. E. Hatcher and Mrs. Theodore Whitfield of Virginia, Mrs. John Stout also of South Carolina, and the singularly influential Annie Armstrong of Maryland.

South Carolina's Stout read a paper entitled "Shall the Baptist Women of the South Organize for Mission Work?" Annie Armstrong, opposed to any further delay, pressed the issue. On Monday, May 14, 1888, the executive committee of Woman's Missionary Societies, auxiliary to the Southern Baptist Convention, was formally organized with offices to be located in Baltimore. Armstrong was elected the first corresponding secretary.[51]

As will be discussed later, action by the Southern Baptist Convention in 1885 barring women messengers may have given the women new impetus for their own organization. Nor can the growing national woman's suffrage movement be discounted as an influence. In turn, many men supported the new organization, convinced that it would keep the women from pressing for a convention role.

It is doubtful that Southern Baptist missions would have made as much progress had not the powerful women's organization come into being. Its leaders, including its first executive, Annie Armstrong, seemed to have an instinct for keeping the organization free from the politics that dominated the men's sessions, though its own would occasionally be fierce. It was 1992 before it finally became embroiled in Convention conflict.

Woman's Missionary Union also had a passion for calling the churches back to what it felt was Baptists' fundamental task: missions. The preamble to its constitution reflects an awareness of male sensitivities with the words "disclaiming all intention of independent action."[52] The statement meant the WMU did not intend to send missionaries itself; but it would be independent. In fact, WMU leadership soon dropped from the document what WMU historian Catherine Allen would call "that defensive statement thrown in at the last minute to comfort the fearful" as a detractor, citing the original language over a hundred years later would discover to his chagrin.[53]

H. A. Tupper, who had been instrumental in the appointment of Virginia's Lottie Moon to China, maintained a lively correspondence with her. His correspondence, which elicited from her a frankness not always present in her letters elsewhere, was encouragement to her and revealed his admiration for her.[54]

In 1888, following the organization of WMU, Tupper discussed with Annie Armstrong the possibility of a special offering to send a missionary to relieve Lottie Moon for one year. She had been back on the field eleven years. An offering in response to a letter brought in $3,315.26.[55] The effort became an annual affair, and in 1918 was named the Lottie Moon Christmas offering.

In 1895 an effort to help the Home Mission Board with a debt prompted the promotion of a "week of self-denial," and an annual offering for Home Missions began, which in 1934 was named for Annie Armstrong.[56]

Leadership Style

As the Southern Baptist Convention gathered in Richmond, Virginia, in 1888, for its thirty-third session, a record 835 delegates were registered. Scant attention was paid to the women's meeting and their new organization being structured in the basement of the adjacent Broad Street Methodist Church. Yet it was by far the most significant event for Southern Baptists during the Richmond gathering.

For the fourth time, the Convention was held in the old capital of the Confederacy, and few places constituted more hospitable surroundings. For twenty-five years only two men had served as president of the Convention, P. H. Mell (1863–71 and 1880–87) and James P. Boyce (1872–79). With Mell's death earlier that year, the Convention had the previous year decided to call its old leader, Boyce, still the president of Southern Seminary, back for one more stint. But this was to be Boyce's "last hurrah." Already ill, he took a leave of absence following the convention and journeyed to Europe to recover. That recovery eluded the sixty-one-year-old patrician and he died in southern France that December.

The Seminary leadership naturally fell to Boyce's old comrade, John A. Broadus, but the Convention took a new step. It handed Boyce's Convention gavel to a layman, Judge Jonathan Haralson of Birmingham, Alabama, who had for many years served in the same capacity for Alabama Baptists. During his tenure as convention president, he was named a justice on Alabama's Supreme Court. The son of a wealthy planter, Judge Haralson was regarded as a connecting link between the old and new South.

Southern Baptists continued to turn to lay leadership when, in 1898 the Convention, meeting in Louisville, elected W. J. Northen, a former governor of Georgia and even then president of the Georgia Baptist Convention. Governor Northen was presiding as the Convention completed the nineteenth century in 1900 and met for the first time in Arkansas.

The New Sunday School Board

The statesmanship of I. T. Tichenor, who had rescued the Home Mission Board from its almost fatal collision with the North's Home Mission Society, was never more evident than in 1885 when he called for Southern Baptists to appoint a committee to study the best way to provide Sunday School literature to its constituent churches.

The report that followed launched the Home Mission Board deeper into the Sunday School literature business and gave Southern Baptists' growing denominational consciousness more reason to turn away from previous sources, including the Baptist Publication Society. In 1886 the Home Mission Board obtained a new publishing contract for *Kind Words* and began to print quarterlies and teachers' magazines.

When the Southern Baptist Convention met in Richmond in 1888, the Home Mission Board's Sunday School publication effort received a special commendation and was urged to push its periodicals even more vigorously. However, A. J. Roland, then head of the American Baptist Publication Society in Philadelphia and, as usual, in attendance at the Memphis Convention, urged the messengers to reject those recommendations. But I. T. Tichenor's oratory carried the day, and the report was adopted.

The northern Society's opposition can be understood. The Society had long served the South and C. C. Bitting, the head of Southern Baptists' first Sunday School Board, which perished after its transfer to Memphis, was working now for the northern Society. Though it took three more years for the Southern Baptist Convention to organize a new Sunday School Board, historian Leon McBeth says "the die was cast in 1888."

When the publishing contract initiated in 1886 expired, Southern Baptists were ready to consider a separate Sunday School Board. Realizing that *Kind Words* and related publications were the most successful efforts of the

Home Mission Board from a financial point of view, Tichenor's ability to recognize that they were divergent ministries was remarkable. At its meeting in Fort Worth in 1890, the Southern Baptist Convention overcame its final hurdle. It was raised by J. B. Gambrell, whose objectivity was compromised by the fact that he was being paid by the American Baptist Publication Society while also serving Southern Baptists as editor of the *Baptist Record* of Mississippi.[57]

James Bruton Gambrell was born in South Carolina just four years before the Southern Baptist Convention began in Augusta, Georgia. He grew up in Mississippi, however, as his parents moved there when he was still very young. A scout for Robert E. Lee, Gambrell saw action at Gettysburg and was commissioned a captain before the war was over. After his marriage, he enrolled at the University of Mississippi and while there answered a call to the ministry and served as pastor for several years at Oxford, Mississippi, where the university was located. His initial fame came as editor of the *Baptist Record* in Mississippi (1877–93), where his Landmark views were often in evidence. Later he served three years as president of Georgia's Mercer University before going to Texas for the rest of his highly influential ministry.[58]

Gambrell, with his ties to the American Baptist Publication Society, strongly opposed any effort to create a Southern Baptist counterpart, and despite his compromised position, his opposition was significant. The Southern Baptist Convention was meeting in Texas, however, and that was B. H. Carroll's territory. Carroll came to the aid of the Sunday School Board plan.

Benajah Harvey Carroll was formidable in any setting. Approximately six feet, four inches tall with a flowing beard and a commanding voice, he had served as pastor of Waco's First Baptist Church since 1870. Texas Baptists had learned to listen to him. Under his leadership they had just stood down S. A. Hayden and a radical Landmarkism. Carroll was no stranger to Southern Baptist life: He had preached the convention sermon in 1878; his church hosted the convention in 1883; and he made a strong speech in behalf of the Home Mission Board in 1888.

His support neutralized Gambrell's opposition. Then J. B. Hawthorne, a pastor in Atlanta and a most eloquent preacher, supported the Sunday School Board idea. With the backing of J. M. Frost, a Virginia pastor, such broad-based support overwhelmed any remaining opposition. A committee headed by Frost was authorized to bring final plans to the next Convention meeting. But Gambrell was put on the committee.

Frost grew up in Kentucky and graduated from Georgetown College in that state. He was not a man to push himself forward, but he had strong convictions about the need for Southern Baptists to expand their publishing efforts. The committee appointed to study the matter reported at the Southern Baptist Convention's meeting in Birmingham in 1891 after a report was jointly drafted by J. M. Frost and J. B. Gambrell. Gambrell agreed to let Frost write the report if Frost would let him write the closing paragraph. Frost agreed, but only if he could write the last sentence.[59]

Strongly influenced by the Landmark point of view, Gambrell wanted to reiterate the autonomy of churches in Baptist life. But he also wanted to hold the door open for the Publication Society in the South. It was Frost's words, however, that carried the day. The decision to create the Sunday School Board was made. With this action taken, not surprisingly I. T. Tichenor, whose statesmanship had set up Frost's efforts, felt free to lay down his task at the Home Mission Board the next year.

The Southern Baptist Convention's 1891 decision to create a Sunday School Board completed the schism with its northern counterparts. The Triennial Convention created in 1814 had subsequently led to three societies: the Publication Society of 1824 and the Home Mission Society of 1832, in addition to the original foreign society. Southern Baptists were now totally independent of the North.

When the Sunday School Board met for the first time, Gambrell, who had been elected to the new Board, graciously proposed that Frost be elected secretary. Frost declined, but the next candidate they turned to declined also. Then the Board once again approached Frost and this time convinced him. Since the Board would be located in Nashville, Tennessee, Frost reluctantly resigned his pastorate at the Leigh Street Church in Richmond and made his move.[60]

Frost served only eighteen months before he accepted the pastorate at Nashville, unable to lay aside that tender but demanding calling. T. P. Bell, evidently unencumbered by his rejection for foreign missions, took over for Frost, and Frost continued to work with the Sunday School Board as one of its trustees. Bell did not stay long, however, and at the Board's insistence, Frost burned his bridges to the pastorate in 1896 and gave himself fully to the Sunday School Board for the next twenty years.

At Home and Abroad

At this point the Southern Baptist Convention had strong leadership in place and a clear sense of direction. The revitalized Home Mission Board continued to prosper in the last decade of the nineteenth century. With the creation of the Southern Baptist Sunday School Board under J. M. Frost's leadership, the Board could focus clearly on its mission task, especially in the expanding Southwest.

Only three years before, in 1888, the Convention had to confront efforts by some messengers to unite the Boards or to phase out the Home Mission Board. As mentioned earlier, the champion who emerged for the Board's autonomy and course was from Texas, an area that was a focus of much of the Board's activity. B. H. Carroll, who not only led the First Baptist Church in Waco but served as chairman of Baylor University's Theological Department, stepped to the fore at the 1888 Southern Baptist Convention in Richmond, Virginia, to make the case for the Home Mission Board's role. He used its work in Texas as a compelling example. It was vintage Carroll: "From . . . the most western territory of the Southern Baptist Convention, I come tonight for the first time in life to stand upon the soil of the other, the most eastern in our bounds, to plead the cause of the Home Mission Board and to vindicate the wisdom of its missionary operations."[61]

While the claim that this address was singularly responsible for saving the Home Mission Board is disputable, especially in light of Tichenor's successes, it did establish Carroll as the Convention's most influential Texan. Carroll had earlier led Texas Baptists to reject a dual alignment with the Home Mission Society. In doing so Carroll contended that the southwestern part of the Convention territory deserved more attention and respect. That his point was a two-edged sword and that the Convention would soon feel the other side, was not yet obvious.

In 1894 T. T. Eaton offered a resolution at the Southern Baptist Convention, calling for new understandings with the North's Home Mission Society. It was not lost on the northern leadership that in contrast to earlier years, Southern Baptists were now dealing from strength and as peers. The committee that met with northern leadership at Fortress Monroe, Virginia, that September recognized the North's ownership of Negro schools in the South but called for local advisory committees and appealed for local financial support. Other cooperative work among Negroes was approved at the same time. But one proposition from the southern contingent gave the northern representatives pause: the call for a plan to resolve differences when working in the same field. At stake was a Texas Baptist desire to enter New Mexico as a mission field.[62] The whole conference reflected the Home Mission Board's new strength.

When I. T. Tichenor stepped down from the Home Mission Board in 1899, six hundred and seventy-one missionaries were supported by the Board in conjunction with state Boards throughout the Southern Baptist Convention, including strong contingents in Texas and the Oklahoma territory.

Gospel Missionism

The Foreign Mission Board's steady advance was clouded by a nagging controversy called Gospel Missionism that erupted in China under the leadership of missionary T. P. Crawford. Crawford's militant personality had long been a thorn in the sides of fellow missionaries and stateside administrators. During the Civil War, when other missionaries had sent back letters of concern and prayerful longing for peace in their homeland, Crawford had written strongly worded Confederate statements. When the war was over, his correspondence still reflected a defiant Confederate mentality, but now he transferred some of his militancy to conflicts with his fellow missionaries and board leadership.

T. P. Crawford, born in 1821 in Kentucky, graduated at the head of his class in 1851 at Union College in Tennessee where Landmarker T. T. Eaton was president and where J. M. Pendleton had taught. When he was appointed as a missionary later in the same year, Crawford was sponsored by the Big Hatchie Association of Kentucky, a storied center of Landmark influence.[63]

At the time Crawford was appointed, officials were concerned about his single status and put him in contact with Martha Foster, a single woman candidate. Their courtship was little more than an introduction, and their marriage focused on their common missionary aspirations.[64] The Crawfords served in Shanghai from 1852 until 1863 and in North China in Tengchow from 1863 until 1893.

Crawford was a natural battler. He grew up in the middle of the Campbell controversy and was influenced as a young adult by J. R. Graves. Once, he faced down disgruntled Chinese with a drawn revolver.[65] During a trip back to the States in 1859 he heard Graves's challenge to the Mission Board at the Southern Baptist Convention when Graves was at the height of his controversy with R. B. C. Howell. Like Graves, Crawford felt strongly that churches rather than mission boards should be the ones sending out foreign missionaries. And this feeling often erupted into conflict with the Board leadership.

Crawford believed that missionaries ought to live off the land. During the Civil War, he made several beneficial investments in Chinese real estate and became financially independent. Years later the Board forbade its missionaries to engage in such commerce overseas, but it probably helped sustain Crawford and others during the war years.

Even more galvanizing than his Landmark influence was Crawford's fascination with Presbyterian missionary John Nevius's philosophy of missionary methods. Believing direct evangelism was the only justification for missions, Nevius opposed institutional efforts such as schools and any support of Chinese workers. Crawford initially embraced these views and may have influenced his wife, Martha, and Lottie Moon to close their schools, which had been to that time among the most successful ventures in the north China field.[66]

As more is known of Martha Crawford's contribution, she is representative of the significant missionary labor of wives whom the culture of the time all but ignored. She had a strong influence on women's missionary movements through correspondence and her infrequent trips home, and she made solid contributions despite her husbands rancorous and disruptive career.

Crawford returned to the States in the late 1880s and tried to get the Foreign Mission Board's policies changed in the direction of Landmark polity and Nevius methods. When he was rejected he returned to the field and in 1892 severed his connections with the Board. His wife had no choice but to stand stoically with him. The Foreign Mission Board's H. A. Tupper felt strongly that the policies that lent themselves to a Convention approach to the Foreign Mission endeavor were at stake. Crawford's defection, which included several other missionaries, did not change Tupper's convictions. 67 In contrast, John Nevius's principles would strongly influence Mission Strategies including those of Southern Baptists in later years.

While Gospel Missionism, the name Crawford and his colleagues took for their separate venture, stirred the pot in the long simmering Landmark controversy in the Southern Baptist Convention, it did no significant damage to a foreign mission enterprise that continued to make progress, especially with the help of the aggressive new women's organization.

Foreign Mission Leadership

In 1893 Henry Allen Tupper stepped aside at the Foreign Mission Board. Under Tupper, the Board had opened work in Mexico, Brazil, and Japan and appointed 147 missionaries.[68] He led in the decision to include single women, gave critical support in the organization of Woman's Missionary Union, and fought off the Crawford challenge. But the shadow of a growing debt clouded his closing years.

The Foreign Mission Board gave the reins to R. J. Willingham, also a native of South Carolina, but a graduate of the University of Georgia and Southern Baptist Theological Seminary from its new location in Louisville. At the time of his selection, Willingham was pastor of the First Baptist Church in Memphis in the shadow of J. R. Graves and a Tennessee board member, serving as a vice-president of the Foreign Mission Board.

The debt hanging over the Board became Willingham's first concern. Initially successful, he announced with great pride in 1898 that "all debts had been paid." That condition, which would not last long, was a source of encouragement to everyone and owed much to the efforts of Woman's Missionary Union, which took an extra offering in 1894 to help the Foreign Mission Board's debt and another in 1895 for the Home Mission Board.

It was ample motivation for both Willingham and his Home Mission Board counterpart, I. T. Tichenor, to step into a sticky situation involving WMU leadership. The stickiness involved conflict between WMU's two most powerful women, Fannie Heck, president, and the indomitable Annie Armstrong, corresponding secretary.

The issue was joined when Armstrong began supporting a Sunday School Board Bible Fund without a WMU vote. Heck objected, not just because of Armstrong's unauthorized initiatives, but because she believed it would sap strength from the two mission boards. According to WMU historian Catherine Allen, Heck's decision to stand for reelection in 1897 was motivated by a determination to address both the issue and Armstrong's leadership. Heck courted Willingham while Armstrong appealed to the Sunday School Board's Frost and the Home Mission Board's Tichenor.

As the matter heated up , T. P. Bell, who was at this time editor of Georgia's *Christian Index*, suggested "Annie Armstrong's powers had met their match."[69]

Armstrong appealed to Convention president, Jonathan Haralson, to resolve the question of which woman was right. Though Haralson was at first supportive of Armstrong, he agreed to meet in Montgomery with

Tichenor and Frost at Willingham's suggestion. They convinced him of the need to get the two strong minded but alienated women to a conference table, which was accomplished in Norfolk. Allen described Heck as "cool, calculating and focused" while Armstrong was "tense, emotional, bitter." To the men's credit, they negotiated a settlement which both women signed to keep their differences private. The next year Heck stepped down and stayed out of WMU matters until Armstrong resigned in a later public dispute over the proposed WMU Training School in Louisville. The lengths that Tichenor and Willingham were willing to go indicated their growing awareness of the women's organization's importance to missions.[70]

Two years after taking over leadership at the Foreign Mission Board and committing himself to retiring the Board's debt, the aggressive Willingham hired a young Texan to join him at the Foreign Mission Board as his associate. Edgar Young Mullins, who was born in Mississippi in 1860 but migrated with his parents to Texas shortly after the Civil War, graduated from Texas A & M College and Southern Baptist Theological Seminary. He was pastor of the Lee Street Baptist Church in Baltimore. He was touted as one of the bright young comers in Southern Baptist life when Willingham convinced him to move to Richmond in 1895. Mullins' tenure there lasted less than a year. He discovered that despite his love for foreign missions, he was unable to work with the demanding Willingham, so he accepted the pastorate at Newton Center in Massachusetts. That proved to be a fortuitous move.

Willingham became the first secretary to visit overseas fields during the course of his administration with trips to Mexico, Japan, China, and Italy.

The Whitsitt Controversy

Southern Baptists celebrated their fiftieth anniversary when they met in Washington, D.C., in May 1895. With Jonathan Haralson of Alabama presiding over his seventh session, the Convention felt a sense of permanence it had not known before. With three vigorous boards at work and an increasingly reputable seminary training new leaders, the speeches of George B. Eager of Alabama and W. H. Whitsitt of Kentucky soared with confidence. For Whitsitt, that sense of well-being was short-lived, however.

William Seth Whitsitt, who joined the faculty at Southern Baptist Theological Seminary three years after Crawford Toy began his ill-fated tenure, was a Tennessean educated at Union University during Pendleton's era, but untouched by the Landmark influence there. He distinguished himself in the Civil War and was twice captured. Following the war he completed his education at the University of Virginia before enrolling at Southern Baptist Theological Seminary while it was still in Greenville.

Shortly after going to the seminary, Whitsitt seriously considered foreign missions and an appointment to Rome, Italy. Boyce and Broadus both persuaded him to remain at the seminary. Perhaps his missions commitment was part of a larger crisis, when he found himself questioning whether he should remain in the Southern Baptist Convention because of his strong opposition to the still pervasive Landmark influence. In September, 1874, however, he wrote in his diary that he was "set in his Southern Baptist relations."[71]

While Whitsitt was a student at Southern Seminary, John Broadus recognized his scholarly abilities and, noting the beneficial effect German studies had on others, urged Whitsitt to continue his studies in Germany also. For two years, from 1870 to 1872, Whitsitt studied first at the University of Berlin and then at Leipzig. When he completed his studies, he became pastor of a church in Albany, Georgia, while Broadus and Boyce cleared the way for him to join the faculty at Southern Seminary. He was elected professor of Biblical Introduction and Polemic Theology and assistant professor of New Testament Greek. He added church history in 1879, at the height of the Toy controversy.

The dedicated and well-trained faculty at Southern Seminary faced a continuing Landmarkism and anti-intellectualism that distrusted institutions and education. It was obvious during the Toy controversy, though it is doubtful that Whitsitt, despite his support of Toy, was in sympathy with Toy's views. After the passing of Boyce in 1888 and then of John A. Broadus in 1895, Whitsitt, with the support of the faculty, students, and alumni of Southern Seminary, was elected president over the candidacies of the *Western Recorder* editor, T. T. Eaton, and a Southern Seminary professor, F. H. Kerfoot. Eaton, when he realized that Whitsitt had the votes, tried to get the search continued, but he was voted down.

Whitsitt's first year was uneventful, but by 1896 he landed in the center of what turned out to be one of the final great Landmark controversies. According to Rosalie Beck, fewer than 6 percent of all Southern Baptist preachers had earned seminary degrees in 1899, and almost 60 percent had no college training. Many of them were truly frontier preachers who distrusted their educated brethren. From their point of view, evolutionary thought and criticism of the Bible went hand in hand with education.[72]

The strong denominationalism that flourished in the latter part of the nineteenth century sustained the Landmark idea of church successionism that was planted in so many Baptist hearts and minds a half century earlier. Although J. R. Graves died in 1893, Landmark strength on the growing edge of Southern Baptists' advance in the Southwest conflicted with the increasing centralization of Southern Baptist life as reflected in its surging agencies. The continuing strength of those convictions pulled Whitsitt into the center of controversy.

Utilizing carefully honed tools of historical investigation, Whitsitt published an article in *Johnson's Universal Cyclopedia* in 1886 suggesting that immersion was first practiced by Baptists in the year 1641. He denied that English Baptists had immersed believers before that date, doubted it was a practice that Roger Williams had known, and suggested it was introduced at the Newport church after the founding of both churches. Since successionists took their lineage through Clarke, the Williams statement drew little fire. But the English immersion question was quickly challenged by Baptist editors of a Landmark stripe since one of the Landmark concepts of successionism was that there had been both legitimate Baptist churches and valid Baptist baptisms back through the ages.

A certain poignancy surrounds the whole ensuing affair in light of Whitsitt's lifelong friendship with J. R. Graves. Not surprisingly, Whitsitt had even sided with Graves in his battles with Howell, given the fact Graves had been a family friend, had often been a guest in Whitsitt's father's home, and had preached Whitsitt's ordination sermon. Graves had, however, questioned Whitsitt on his successionist position as early as 1893. Yet, Graves, who died in 1896, was to be a factor only through his disciples.[73]

Throughout 1896 and 1897 associations and state conventions demanded Whitsitt's resignation from Southern Baptist Seminary. Landmark historian John T. Christian, who wrote one of the more widely circulated Baptist successionist histories published during the last half of the nineteenth century, said Whitsitt had used questionable sources and attacked the seminary president's scholarship. Baptist papers and Baptist leaders were drawn into the controversy and, though pro-Whitsitt writers were also in evidence, the incident became a lightning rod for Landmark hostility toward the Southern Baptist Convention and a field day for vocal pockets of anti-institutionalism and anti-intellectualism.[74]

The trustees made a defensive report to the Southern Baptist Convention meeting in Wilmington in 1897. They stated that Whitsitt had not broken any seminary principles, but they did not attempt to defend his position. Their action alienated one of their own trustees, however. The powerful B. H. Carroll of Texas felt that they had dodged the issue. Equally vocal in their opposition were the candidates Whitsitt defeated for the job. Kerfoot, a faculty member, tried to neutralize the support of John Sampey and W. O. Carver by warning that they, too, could fall. T. T. Eaton, editor of the Kentucky paper, was given credit for encouraging B. H. Carroll's opposition.[75]

Initially a Whitsitt supporter, though of selective Landmark views himself, Carroll as a denominationalist thought the trustees had shirked their duty. When the trustees reconfirmed their defense of Whitsitt at the Southern Baptist Convention in 1898 in the face of strong opposition, Carroll, carefully skirting the issue himself, let it be known that he would introduce a motion the following year to cut Southern Seminary free from the Convention to avoid any kind of a split.[76] The Carroll threat had the force of a drawn gun to the heads of Whitsitt's supporters.

Upon adjournment of the Convention, A. T. Robertson, Southern Baptist Seminary professor of New Testament, wrote Whitsitt ten reasons he should resign. And within days Whitsitt did so, the resignation to be effective at the end of the next school year. Whitsitt thought his resignation was critical for the well-being of both the seminary and the Convention. Almost a year later, at the trustees' annual meeting in Louisville in May 1899, the seminary accepted his resignation.

Edgar Young Mullins

As soon as the Louisville convention meeting was over, the Southern Seminary trustees quickly moved to recover the Convention's confidence in the seminary by securing a new president. Feeling that they had to find somebody who had not chosen sides during the three rancorous years of the Whitsitt controversy, they quickly settled on Edgar Young Mullins, in his fifth year at Newton Center, Massachusetts, following his brief stint at the Foreign Mission Board. The distant but respected church was safely removed from the conflict. It turned out to be an adroit and effective move, not only helping Baptists cope with their internal Landmark squabbles, but helping them deal with the next major battlefield, which was developing around the same suspicions that Crawford Howell Toy had elicited.

Years later, Albert McClellan, a veteran denominationalist, said that Mullins "burst into Southern Baptist life like a comet, to burn brightly for twenty-eight years."[77]Mullins's family had moved from his Mississippi birthplace to Texas with his farmer-preacher father, who established what became the First Baptist Church of Corsicana. Industrious and bright, young Mullins worked as a telegraph operator to help educate his sisters before enrolling as a cadet at Texas A & M in 1879 to prepare for a career in law. An adult conversion at age twenty changed his plans, however, as he acknowledged a call to Christian ministry and went to Southern Seminary in Louisville to prepare himself. His unusual maturity, six-foot-two-inch height, and A & M-bred military bearing quickly placed him in student leadership roles.

After completing his studies at Southern Baptist Seminary he became pastor of a church in Kentucky, married Isla May Hawley, and then served as a pastor for seven years in Baltimore. It was from there that he began his short-lived association with Willingham at the Foreign Mission Board in Richmond, Virginia. When the Baptist church at Newton Centre, Massachusetts, approached Mullins, he was receptive and moved there after only one year in Richmond. Five years later he was ready for the challenging position at Louisville.

Almost unknown to Southern Baptists when elected, Mullins preached the Convention sermon in 1901 and from that time on was never far from the center of Convention activities. During the first three decades of the new century, few matched his influence in the defining of the denomination.

Closing a Century

When the nineteenth century closed, the Southern Baptist Convention was fifty-five years old, with strong home mission programs in the South and Southwest and a growing missions presence abroad. Its grassroots mission support was galvanized by an aggressive woman's organization. Its new publishing venture, the Sunday School Board, was gaining strength and circulation rapidly, and its cherished seminary had weathered another major storm. Riding the tide of westward expansion and a surging national consciousness, it was truly time to define itself as a unique Christian body. A cadre of gifted leaders and an infrastructure of state convention-sponsored educational institutions were ready to lead it into the twentieth century.

4

Defining a Denomination

1900–1927

The regionalism inherited from the Confederacy broke down rapidly as Southern Baptists entered the twentieth century. Reconstruction had been left behind, and the western movement of the United States' population broadened its frontiers. The Spanish-American war, fought in 1898, gave America possession of Cuba, Hawaii, the Philippines, and Guam. It also opened up new possibilities for Southern Baptists who, though still struggling in comparison to other Protestant denominations attempting similar ventures, were enjoying the challenges they faced.

Southern Baptist organizations—the Home and Foreign Mission Boards, the Sunday School Board, Southern Seminary, and the auxillary Woman's Missionary Union—though continually buffeted by economic reverses and controversy, were increasing their viability and their vision. To a large

109

extent, the Southern Baptist Convention still mirrored the Northern group from which it had withdrawn. Yet the convention-style potential, over against the society-style, was in place and awaiting further definition. The new century brought that definition and also brought dramatic growth.

Southern Baptist growth, which according to an analysis by Robert Baker, averaged an annual 4.79 percent from 1845 to 1860, dropped sharply to 2.25 percent following the Civil War. Then during the period beginning in 1877 and continuing until the beginning of the first World War, it jumped dramatically to an annual 5.22 percent compared to a general population increase during the same period of 3.27 percent.[1]

Westward Movement

Significant to this growth and to Southern Baptists as a denomination was its move to the west and especially to Arkansas and Texas. Arkansas hosted its first Southern Baptist Convention in 1900. The southwestern look was further enhanced when the convention met in Louisiana in 1901.

James P. Eagle, governor of Arkansas and president of the Arkansas Baptist Convention, succeeded W. J. Northen at the next meeting, continuing the trend to elect high-profile lay leadership. Eagle presided when the Convention met in 1902 in the beautiful mountain resort of Asheville, North Carolina, and registered over one thousand messengers for the first time.[2]

That pattern prevailed, both in terms of the lay leadership theme and the westward movement, when Eagle was followed by E. W. Stephens, a highly respected journalist from Missouri. The lay theme persisted in 1907 when Joshua Levering of Maryland assumed the gavel the year after he had been instrumental in the beginning of the Baptist Layman's Movement, forerunner of the Brotherhood organization.

George W. Truett, born in the mountains of North Carolina, followed his family to Whitewright, Texas, in 1888, after recognition by Georgia Baptists as an outstanding young educator because of his work in founding that state's Hiawassee Academy. Recognizing Truett as a gifted speaker and promising leader, they tried to persuade him to go to Mercer University. But Truett and his brother felt the same westward pull that had attracted his family. In Whitewright, Truett had a unique experience: a Baptist congregation told him he had a call to preach and persuaded him that God had called him through them.

In 1890 he was enlisted by Baylor's B. H. Carroll to head a debt-eradicating drive for that Texas Baptist institution. Despite his youth and his lack of state connections, young Truett was successful, and he celebrated by enrolling in Baylor University. When he completed Baylor, he was set to go to Southern Baptist Seminary, as all of his contemporaries who were preparing for Christian ministry were doing. But in 1897 the First Baptist Church of Dallas called him as pastor. Beginning at thirty years of age, he served that body over a period of forty-six years, one of the great records to be found in Christian ministry.[3]

In 1888 the family of eleven-year-old J. Frank Norris left Alabama for Hubbard, Texas, where he became a Christian and soon responded to a call to preach. At the turn of the century he enrolled in Baylor University and from there went to Southern Baptist Seminary in 1903. Following his course at Southern he accepted a brief pastorate in Dallas, then he bought a controlling interest in the *Baptist Standard* and began to make a name for himself. In 1909, with B. H. Carroll's support, he was called to the pastorate of the First Baptist Church in Fort Worth.[4]

Another example of Southern Baptists' westward movement was Lee Rutland Scarborough. His father, George Scarborough, born in Mississippi, married Martha Rutland of Tennessee and moved to Louisiana. George served in the Civil War and then, with the six surviving children of the nine born to them, moved to Texas in 1874. Lee was four years old at the time. Lee's father was ordained to the ministry in a small church west of Waco, with B. H. Carroll serving on the ordination council. But in 1878, in an effort to improve his wife's health, he moved his family to west Texas and took up ranching and preaching. Thus, Lee R. Scarborough, who was to have a dramatic influence on Southern Baptists, grew up as a hard-riding west Texas cowboy.[5]

But the elder Scarborough's experience with Carroll had convinced him of the importance of an education. He made Lee hang up his chaps and enroll at Baylor in 1888. There Scarborough settled a spiritual question that had haunted him. He asked B. H. Carroll to baptize him, fully convinced that his conversion had come after an earlier baptism. Carroll, after extensive counselling, agreed, and thus began a new mentoring task for Carroll that influenced not only both men, but Southern Baptist history as well.[6]

Benajah Harvey Carroll was the common thread between Truett, Norris, and Scarborough. Born in Mississippi in 1843, Carroll moved with his preacher father, who made his living farming, first to Arkansas in 1848 and then to Burleson County, Texas, in 1858. Young Carroll was at Baylor University when the Civil War began and joined the Texas Rangers before he could be mustered into the Confederate forces. He was an anti-secessionist, but the Confederacy's need grew and the Ranger became a gray-clad rebel. Before being inducted into the army, Carroll, then eighteen, married a fifteen-year-old neighbor—not all that unusual for the time. While in service, word from home and later his own investigations caused him to authorize his brother to file for divorce on the grounds of adultery. It was granted and became a painful and embarrassing memory for Carroll the rest of his days.[7]

Carroll distinguished himself in battle during the bitter days of the Civil War. He was credited with leading an heroic charge before a Minie ball in the thigh felled him. His brother, Laban, carried him from the battlefield and a long convalescence followed, for Carroll was well aware that wounds by such large projectiles usually led to death.

Despite his father's influence, a baptism that he felt was not valid at age thirteen, and his days at Baylor, Carroll did not consider himself converted until his recovery at war's end. Five years later he began a twenty-nine-year pastorate at the First Baptist Church in Waco.[8]

Carroll's influence in Southern Baptist life and the growth of Baylor accounted for the Convention's first meeting in Waco in 1883. It was not the SBC's first trip to Texas; that had been accomplished in 1874 in Jefferson, Texas. And, as mentioned in the previous chapter, Carroll preached the Convention sermon in 1878 when the Convention met in Nashville, the first Texan to be so honored.

That moment was not the triumph for Carroll one might have expected, however, for it triggered the revelation by unknown sources of his divorce. With Carroll's support, a friend did "an investigation" and published his findings that Carroll's first wife had committed adultery, and thus, Carroll's divorce and remarriage was scriptural.[9]

Carroll began teaching theology and Bible at Baylor in 1872 while pastoring the Waco church. In 1905, he organized the Baylor Theological Department, which in 1908 separated to become Southwestern Baptist Theological Seminary.[10]

Carroll, Truett, Norris, and Scarborough thus became not only examples of the Baptist move west, but their lives illustrate both the energy and the conflict that accompanied Southern Baptists' westward movement.

New State Conventions

Three new state Baptist conventions organized during this period reflect this westward move. The first, Oklahoma, organized in 1906. The second,

Illinois, was a break in 1910 from a long-standing Baptist organization in that state. The third, New Mexico, was an outgrowth of a long feud between the North's Home Mission Society and the Southern Baptist Home Mission Board.

In the nineteenth century, Oklahoma was populated largely by Indians, a few of whom were also slaveholders. Then in 1830 the federal government began resettling there Indian tribes displaced from their original locations by a rash of treaties being imposed upon them. Soon, large groups of Cherokees, Choctaws, Chickasaws, Creeks, and even Seminoles from Florida had been forced into the Oklahoma territories.[11]

The first Baptist church was organized among Creeks by Isaac McCoy in September, 1832.[12] A church among the Cherokees began two months later. The first association was organized in 1848 in what was known as the Indian Territory, but in the postwar period, the area became a battleground between the conflicting northern and southern mission agencies. Their work in turn was complicated by a flood of white immigration after 1889 when the territory was officially opened for settlement. Though an Oklahoma Baptist convention was organized in 1895, it was not until November, 1906 that all of the competing state organizations in both the Indian Territory and Oklahoma Territory came together. The new body initially aligned with both Northern and Southern Conventions until 1914, when they committed themselves to the Southern Baptist Convention.[13]

Baptists entered New Mexico soon after it became a territory of the United States in 1846. The Home Mission Society had a missionary, Hiram W. Read, working in Santa Fe by 1849. The first Baptist church was organized, however, in Albuquerque in 1852, called the Baptist Church of Christ.[14] By 1868, Roman Catholic pressure caused the Society to withdraw, and it was 1880 before its missionaries reentered.

By 1888 the Lincoln County Missionary Baptist Association had been formed in the territory. And in 1900, six years after the Home Mission Society and Southern Baptists discussed the matter at their Fortress Monroe Conference, a territorial-wide convention was organized.[15]

Soon afterwards, this organization divided into two groups, one northern-related and the other, southern. In 1912, they came together in Clovis to dissolve the separate groups and organize the Baptist Convention of New Mexico. They began reporting to the Southern Baptist Convention that same year, showing six associations, 166 churches, and 6,323 members.[16]

Baptist work in Illinois was much older than that of Oklahoma and New Mexico. Settled by soldiers of the revolution after independence in 1781, Illinois Baptists organized their first church there in 1789.

The first Baptist association formed in 1807 and aligned itself with Baptists' new mission efforts as early as 1818. But despite brief periods of unity, Baptists in Illinois were emotionally and often organizationally divided roughly north and south. In 1906, a controversy over the seating of Unitarian congregations and the practice of open communion (communion open to all in attendance rather than limited to members of the church) provoked a split. The more conservative churches formed the Illinois Baptist State Association in Pinkneyville in January, 1907. It voted in 1909 to cooperate with the Southern Baptist Convention in home and foreign missions, and its first messengers were seated in 1910.[17]

By 1917, 13.49 percent of all Southern Baptists lived in Texas alone. In the seventeen states where Southern Baptists were located, population grew by an annual 3.27 percent from 1880 to 1920. Southern Baptist membership increased by 5.22 percent. Southern Baptists, led by work in the southwest, were outdistancing most other major denominations in their growth.[18]

Landmark Separation

In the initial part of the twentieth century, neither Carroll, Truett, nor Norris gathered the attention gravitating toward Ben M. Bogard of Arkansas and S. M. Hayden of Texas. Bogard and Hayden were the last fiery leaders of the Landmark movement whose founder, J. R. Graves, died in Memphis in 1893.

Yet even before Graves's death, Arkansas and Texas succeeded Tennessee as Landmark's stronghold. As late as 1919, *Baptist Standard* editor J. B. Gambrell wrote, "Baptists antedate the Reformation by many long centuries. Spurgeon said with a good view of truth: 'Baptists sprang directly from the loins of Christ and his Apostles.' "[19]

But despite such sentiment, neither state organization was ready for the anti-conventionism that Bogard and Hayden espoused. Hayden's base was a rival Baptist paper to the *Baptist Standard,* and his strident rhetoric alienated even mild-mannered George Truett. Hayden and his Texas followers organized the Baptist Missionary Association in 1900 and joined with Bogard's Arkansas group in 1905 after the rejection of a petition to the SBC meeting in Kansas City. Among other things, the Landmarkers demanded an end to the financial and associational basis of membership in favor of a church basis.[20]

Landmarkism continued to be found in Southern Baptist life and especially in Tennessee, Arkansas, Texas, and the westward movement for years. Landmarkism's tenets had a remarkable persistency, and their pervasiveness was obvious in state Baptist convention and Southern Baptist Convention proceedings for years.

In 1991, a Foreign Mission Board executive, sensitive to this residue of Landmark feelings wrote, "There is no Bible reference to any kind of foreign mission agency other than the churches. Therefore, the means by which we have ministered to the world has been the creation of a mission board whose trustees are elected by the churches, whose missionaries are members of the churches, whose support comes from the churches, and whose responsibility is to report back to the churches."[21] The fact that trustees are elected by messengers seated at the convention might mitigate his statement, but the sentiment he was addressing reflected Landmark ecclesiology's deep roots.

Historian Walter Shurden called Landmarkism one of the four great traditions that molded Southern Baptist life. One of his students, John Franklin Loftis claimed a fifth tradition, evangelical-denominationalism, which was at this very time taking its place on stage under the direction of Carroll, Scarborough, and Gambrell.[22]

Southwestern Seminary

This new tradition took its most visible form in a single institution when in 1908 B. H. Carroll almost singlehandedly brought about the founding of Southwestern Baptist Theological Seminary.

The need for a seminary in the burgeoning Southwest was hard to refute; it boasted a natural constituency in Texas, Arkansas, and Oklahoma. But some felt Carroll's reaction to Southern Baptist Seminary and the Whitsitt Controversy, which left even Texas' more moderate Landmark points of view disaffected, motivated the move. Carroll, as mentioned in the previous chapter, served on the Southern Baptist Seminary board of trustees that accepted Whitsitt's resignation. Moreover, Carroll, who tended toward Landmarkism himself, may have played the decisive role.

This point of view was fueled by a 1903 editorial in the *Christian Index* of Georgia, subsequently quoted in the *Biblical Recorder* of North Carolina. The editorial had claimed "Baylor University has been bidding for a place as rival of the Louisville Seminary with the Whitsitt controversy as a basis." Carroll responded by denying the statement and added, "Whenever I regard Baylor University's theological department as a rival of the Seminary, then I will resign as Seminary Trustee and quit influencing Texas preachers to attend the Seminary."[23]

No one could deny, however, that training preachers was in Carroll's blood. During his pastorate in Waco he attracted and significantly molded dozens of young ministers destined to play definitive roles in Southern Baptist life. He held classes in his church for Baylor "preacher-students." Carroll joined hands with J. S. Tanner, a faculty member at Baylor, in the late 1880s to hold summer Bible schools to train ministers. The success of these schools probably brought enough reaction from Southern Seminary supporters that President Samuel Palmer Brooks of Baylor published this statement: "It must be understood that the summer Bible School . . . in no sense is, or expects to be, a rival of our own Seminary in Louisville."[24]

Carroll was by 1899 willing to accept this as his primary calling in life and resigned his long pastorate at Waco's First Baptist Church to devote his full time to his "theological department." Carroll was formally named dean in 1901 by then President O. H. Cooper. Carroll's reputation and persuasiveness brought a number of outstanding colleagues, including famed Baptist historian Albert Henry Newman.

In the summer of 1905 while President Brooks was in Europe, Carroll, still chairman of the Baylor board, led the trustees to authorize a major expansion of the theological department. He assumed responsibility for raising the money. Two years later pressures to separate the department into a full-fledged seminary were such that Brooks, who had strongly opposed separation from the university and was offended by Carroll's action, relented. Brooks's discomfort because of Carroll's role on his Board probably made this move attractive.[25]

In an irony of history, one of Brooks's successors, Herbert J. Reynolds, instituted action in 1991 to create a seminary at Baylor as a rival to Southwestern because of the Southern Baptist moderate-conservative controversy. It was named for George W. Truett.[26]

The Baptist General Convention of Texas agreed in 1907 to take responsibility for electing trustees for what was already called Southwestern Baptist Theological Seminary. Its charter was granted May 14, 1908.[27] The Texas Convention invited other states to participate. The state organizations of Arkansas, Florida, Illinois, Kentucky, Louisiana, Mississippi, Missouri, New

Mexico, Oklahoma, and Tennessee accepted and began to appoint members to the board. This broad support paved the way for Southwestern to be officially assumed by the Southern Baptist Convention in 1925.[28]

John Franklin Loftis later claimed to have found evidence of a movement to split the southwestern area from the Southern Baptist Convention and form a new convention around Southwestern Seminary.[29] There was certainly an abundance of suspicion that this was so, and Carroll's enlisting of other state-convention participants probably fed this fear.

As early as 1906, B. H. Carroll tried to enlist his young protégé, Lee R. Scarborough, for the seminary project. Scarborough was among the one hundred persons who had pledged money for the expansion of the theological department at Baylor in 1905. The highly successful young pastor of First Baptist Church, Abilene, was also asked to take the secretaryship of the Education Commission, but Carroll's persistent appeal bore fruit. In 1908 Scarborough agreed to teach evangelism in what Carroll chose to call the Chair of Fire. Carroll soon made the young professor his right-hand man.

It is possible that Carroll wanted to move the seminary to Dallas, but that President Brooks's friendship with George Truett kept it from happening. Truett was named to the first board of trustees, which held its initial meeting in Dallas on May 8, 1908. Truett was the one who conveyed to Carroll a Dallas offer of a location and support which was obviously inadequate. Despite Dallas's usual rivalry with Fort Worth, no better offer ever came from Dallas leadership. Truett's friendship with Brooks and with R. C. Buckner and possible competition between the Seminary and Buckner's orphans' home and Baylor Hospital, a major Truett project, may have discouraged serious efforts by Dallas to land the Seminary.

In contrast, Fort Worth's Baptists and business leaders went all out. In 1909, with J. Frank Norris's support as editor of the *Baptist Standard* and with Scarborough organizing the financial efforts, the new seminary's board agreed to locate south of the city of Fort Worth on an elevated area to be known as Seminary Hill. A building campaign led by Scarborough was launched to raise money for the first building, Fort Worth Hall, which would allow the new institution to open in October of 1910.

Fort Worth was founded just four years after the Southern Baptist Convention's organization. It was one of a line of forts built west of Dallas as a defense against marauding Indians. After the Civil War it became the center of cattle drives moving north and was known as "Cowtown." Rough and rowdy, its gambling parlors and houses of prostitution attracted such notorious outlaws as Butch Cassidy and the Sundance Kid.

By 1910 Fort Worth's population had grown to seventy-five thousand and Baptists, with about fourteen churches, constituted the strongest denomination. Fiercely competitive with Dallas, just thirty miles east, Fort Worth had hosted a Southern Baptist Convention in 1890, four years before Dallas landed one. Unaware that Dallas Baptists may have conceded the issue, Fort Worth's Baptists considered the seminary a real coup.

As this scenario was unfolding, B. H. Carroll kept a wary eye on Southern Seminary, where he was still a trustee. In a letter to E. Y. Mullins he requested that Southern Seminary fundraisers stay out of Texas. At the end of one such letter he even reminded Mullins that he differed from the Southern faculty on the definition of a church and on alien immersion. Carroll also led the new seminary to adopt the New Hampshire Confession of Faith, which was more supportive of evangelism and of a Landmark view of the church than was Southern Semimary's Abstract of Principles. It is possible that the old warrior sought a Landmark edge for the new institution. One thing is certain: a competitive tradition was in place from the beginning.[30]

Scarborough was successful; the building was completed and the seminary opened as planned. J. Frank Norris wrote in the *Baptist Standard*, "Scarborough stands forth among his fellows like Saul among his brethren—a born leader of men."[31] Norris, with the support of his old mentor, Carroll, assumed the pastorate of Fort Worth's First Baptist Church in the fall of 1909.

Thus, in moving the Seminary to Fort Worth in 1910, all three of Carroll's distinguished protégés played a role. That the relationship of these three men would change so drastically in the years ahead is a part of the continuing story of Southern Baptists and a story all by itself.

Carroll had aggresively involved women in his efforts and soon made a previously begun (1904) Woman's Training School a department of the Seminary. Shortly after Scarborough succeeded him, Texas women agreed to raise fifty thousand dollars to build a building for that program.[32]

On the other hand, Scarborough, even more than Carroll, was sensitive to resistance to women's roles and noted that young women were being trained, not as pastors, "but as teachers, soul-winners, missionaries, nurses, helpmeet to preachers, and as leaders among women."[33]

Illustrative of the ongoing influence that Carroll's dream had over the years is the fact that one member of the first Fort Worth class at Southwestern Seminary was L. M. Keeling, who took degrees there in 1913 and again in 1914. In 1936, Keeling's daughter and son-in-law, James T. Draper, moved to Seminary Hill with their eighteen-month-old son. That son, James Draper, Jr. himself enrolled there in 1957 and served as president of the Southern Baptist Convention from 1982–84. He was elected president of the Sunday School Board in 1991.

Southwestern pioneered four areas in theological training among Southern Baptists. First, it "opened its doors, its courses of study, and its degrees to women on exactly the same terms as men."[34] It was a coed institution and twenty-six women were enrolled during its first full year. Second, it accepted a role in training laity for Christian service. Third, it pioneered a religious education department when in 1915 J. M. Price began his tenure with Southwestern; and in 1921 this department became the School of Religious Education. Fourth, Southwestern pioneered the field of church music which also began in 1915 under I. E. Reynolds and became a School of Gospel Music in 1920.

Southwestern's founder, B. H. Carroll, died in November, 1914, having expressed to several people his conviction that Scarborough should succeed him. Within months the trustees did name Scarborough president to the reported bitterness of J. Frank Norris who may have once hoped to succeed his old mentor. In fact, the break between J. Frank Norris and the seminary community was aleady well along.[35]

L. R. Scarborough was inaugurated as the second president of the seminary on May 28, 1915. In his address, he noted that the seminary was founded on the same principles that James Boyce had sounded in the founding of Southern Seminary. Scarborough said that Southwestern had a threefold foundation: denominationally anchored; its teachings based upon the Word of God; magnifying both scholarship and spiritual life and practical efficiency in church and kingdom service.

J. Frank Norris

Norris's support as a trustee from 1909 until 1915 when Scarborough took over as president was relatively free of acrimony, but radical changes in Norris personally began in 1911 following a revival meeting he preached in Owensboro, Kentucky. He is reported to have called his wife to tell her, "You have a new husband. He has been saved tonight. He is starting home, and we are going to start life over again and lick the tar out of that crowd and build the biggest church in the world."[36]

Already a gifted orator, Norris added an unbridled sensationalism. Crowds increased at Fort Worth's First Baptist Church as his latest accusations and rhetorical excesses were widely reported. But so did controversy. "Shots were fired at Norris in his study. Someone set fire to the church, causing damage to the amount of eight thousand dollars. Twice attempts were made to burn the pastor's home. Then, on the night of February 4, 1912, the church building was entirely destroyed by fire."[37] Norris was tried for arson and, though he was acquitted, the event started an exodus of his most influential members. Carroll and Scarborough were among those who departed.

A major concern was Norris's tendency to suppress any internal organization, committee, or member who might challenge his authority. He accomplished this by conferring all church authority to an inner circle of deacons completely committed to him. Charles E. Matthews, who later distinguished himself as secretary of evangelism for the Home Mission Board, was converted under Norris's preaching. Later, when Norris was away, the church ordained Matthews and he entered Southwestern, which so angered Norris that he had the church rescind the ordination and refuse to grant him and his family a church letter. When the First Baptist Church of Breckenridge, Texas, learned of the action they accepted Matthews, who had been supplying the pulpit for them as a member and ordained him.

In 1914, the Fort Worth Pastors' Conference expelled Norris for calling a fellow pastor a "long, lean, lank, yellow suck-egging dog."[38] That was to be only the beginning.

Internationalization

Southern Baptists were still insulated from much of what went on in the world, but in missions they kept a window open especially eastward to China. There, in 1900, the Boxer Rebellion brought horror stories as the lives of well over a hundred Christian missionaries were lost to an indigenous Chinese reaction to foreign intruders. Southern Baptist missionaries were spared because they were not as deeply entrenched in the interior of China where the Rebellion took place.

Yet, as their missionary program expanded, Southern Baptists' openness to internationalization began to broaden. They were part of a Baptist World Alliance organized in London in 1905, and the first known call for that may have come from a Kentucky Baptist editor, J. N. Prestridge. Southern Baptists played a significant part in the Baptist World Alliance, with Southern Seminary's E. Y. Mullins and Dallas's George W. Truett offering statesmanlike leadership in the early years, and Theodore Adams of Richmond, Virginia, and Kentucky's Duke McCall serving as president in later years.

In 1910, Foreign Mission Board administrators and several Southern Baptist missionaries participated in an international missionary conference held in Edinburgh, Scotland. That conference was part of a larger ecumenical movement that began a strong courtship of the Southern Baptist Convention. But Southern Baptists were not ready for anything that might hinder their freedom to pursue their objectives in their own way. Too, the Landmark bias against "pulpit affiliation" made Baptists leery of all union efforts.

Southern Baptists generally took a dim view of their northern counterpart's tendency to support such movements. On the other hand, the society-style organization in the North gave way in 1908 to efficiency and coordination calls that united the three societies into a Northern Baptist Convention. It moved those churches in the direction the Southern Baptist Convention had taken in 1845.[39]

The Southern Baptist Convention meeting in Nashville in 1914 adopted a definitive statement urging Baptist independence "by preserving a complete autonomy at home and abroad, unembarrassed by entangling alliances with other bodies holding to different standards of doctrine and different views of church order."[40] It was part of the "Pronouncement of Christian Union and Denominational Efficiency," a document that James E. Carter later called "the first doctrinal statement adopted by the Southern Baptist Convention."[41] Primarily the work of E. Y. Mullins, the "Pronouncement" was considered the forerunner of his "Fraternal Address" of 1919, the Foreign Mission "Board's Statement of Belief" of 1920, and the Mullins-led "Baptist Faith and Message" of 1925.[42]

By 1916 both the Home and Foreign Mission Boards adopted policy statements opposing church-union views, though the Foreign Mission Board continued for some years to participate in mission-related meetings of the ecumenical groups.

Laymen Organize

Under the leadership of Joshua Levering of Maryland and W. J. Northen of Georgia, the Laymen's Missionary Movement of the Southern Baptist

Convention was organized in 1907 at the annual meeting in Richmond. Its purpose, promoted by future executive secretary J. T. Henderson, was to enlist men for inspiration and instruction of the world mission task of the Convention. This gave the men a counterpart of sorts to the Woman's Missionary Union, which was continuing to build its state-by-state structure and garnering dedicated, even sacrificial support for the missionary cause.

Levering, who was elected president of the SBC that year, and Henderson tried to set up state organizations in the years that followed, though success came slowly. In 1927 the organization's name was changed to the Baptist Brotherhood of the South.

That they encountered some sensitivity from pastors along the way is evident in a statement in their report to the Convention in Richmond in 1919: "The General Secretary never loses an opportunity to magnify the leadership of the pastor and to stress the importance of loyalty among the laymen in support of his policies."[43]

Higher Education

Early Baptists acknowledged that the task of higher education was a legitimate Baptist concern, but until the nineteenth century only Rhode Island College offered a Baptist education. After the Triennial Convention was organized, however, Columbian College was begun as a denominationally supported institution. What became Furman University in South Carolina was originally promoted as a Georgia-South Carolina effort before the South Carolina Convention actually established it. After Georgia established Mercer University and Virginia began Richmond College, the matter rested with the states, with the Southern Convention taking responsibility for the seminary level.

In the latter days of Reconstruction, other educational institutions began to arise throughout the South. By that time, however, secular, state-supported institutions rivaled the private institutions that had carried the burden for a long time. These public institutions opened up a new area of ministry, and in 1914 the Home Mission Board launched the Baptist Student Missionary Movement in Fort Worth, Texas.

The student movement probably owed its origin to an interdenominational organization, the Student Volunteer Movement created in 1888, which by the turn of the century had achieved enormous popularity, and had adopted as a goal the winning of the world in its generation. Southern

Baptists' aloofness from ecumenical organizations, however, made their own effort necessary.

By 1921, the Baptist Student movement was conventionwide and received offical status from the SBC under an Inter-Board Commisssion. Its work was soon transferred to the Sunday School Board. Under the leadership of Frank H. Leavell, it achieved broad acceptance in Southern Baptist life in every state.

Despite their heavy commitment to higher education, the rank and file of Baptists remained suspicious of such an institutional role. In an article in the *Baptist Standard* in 1920, the Foreign Mission Board's J. F. Love articulated that ambivalence when he said, "It is perfectly plain . . . that education above everything else will at last prove to be either the most important ally, or the most dangerous foe, of evangelical religion and its missionary propagation."[44]

Sunday School

One reason the student program was entrusted to the Sunday School Board was that agency's rapid rise in Southern Baptist life. In 1900 only about one-half of Southern Baptist churches had Sunday Schools, but by 1926 Sunday Schools were in eighty-four percent of churches cooperating with the SBC.

James Frost's appointment of Bernard Spilman in 1901 as a "field worker" was one reason. Another was the work of Arthur Flake and his book, *Building a Standard Sunday School,* which was published in 1919. Flake took a systematic approach: discover prospects, organize to reach people, enlist and train workers, provide space, and visit and enlist the prospects. Flake's system provided Baptists with a methodology that fit the times. The Sunday School demonstrated that it facilitated evangelism as not even the tried and true "revival meeting" had done. The Board recommended adult classes as early as 1909, though that took a while to be implemented. When Sunday School did catch on, church growth rapidly followed.

When Frost died in 1916, the trustees turned to a staff member, I. J. Van Ness. A native of New Jersey, Van Ness was baptized by Adoniram Judson's son, Edward. After surrendering to the ministry, he attended Southern Baptist Seminary and became a pastor in Nashville. Soon he was elected to the Sunday School Board and in 1900 joined the staff as editorial secretary. He was a natural to succeed Frost when the latter passed away. At that time the Board had fifty-eight employees, but by 1927, about 210 men and women were producing literature that was more and more in demand.

One of Van Ness's great shocks came when Arthur Flake joined the staff of J. Frank Norris in Fort Worth in 1919, just as the Seventy-five-Million Campaign was getting underway. Fortunately for Van Ness and the Sunday School Board, Flake returned to Nashville within a few months.

Van Ness also believed in Baptist Young People's Union (BYPU), and after it came under the guidance of the Sunday School Board it flourished. In 1917, BYPU had enrolled 180,000 young people in Southern Baptist churches, and by 1927 that number had reached nearly half a million.

Missions Expansion

In the few years before the outbreak of World War I, Southern Baptists attempted on many occasions to clarify their relationships with Northern Baptists and especially the Home Mission Society. A conference similar to the Fortress Monroe conference of 1894 was held in Washington in 1909. Another was convened at Old Point Comfort and later at Hot Springs, Virginia, in 1911. Efforts continued in these conferences to clarify Baptist responsibilities in New Mexico as well as other comity agreements that would allow the revitalized Home Mission Board and the old Home Mission Society to work more harmoniously. The latter had its hands full with tremendous immigration and urban growth in the Northeast which probably led it to make more concessions than it would have earlier.[45]

Foreign Missions support continued to grow with the help of Woman's Missionary Union, which in 1907 established its own school alongside Southern Baptist Theological Seminary in Louisville. WMU and others helped to organize a fund-raising campaign in 1912 commemorating the one-hundred years since Adoniram Judson had committed himself to missions and started the journey that brought Baptists into the missionary task.

Lottie Moon's Death

On Christmas Eve, 1912, Lottie Moon, the venerable China missionary who had spurned the advances of Crawford Toy, survived the turmoil of T. P. Crawford, and inspired Southern Baptist women to organize their support for missions, died on board a ship anchored in Kobe harbor, Japan. She literally starved herself to death in sympathy for her beloved Chinese, who once again were being decimated by a severe famine. Within a few years WMU named its annual Christmas offering for the woman who inspired the first one, and it grew beyond anyone's wildest predictions.

While to many Southern Baptists, Lottie Moon is almost a caricature as well as a call to give, her life grows in meaning and respect with time and the unfolding of history. Though she labored for years in the shadows of the controversial and larger-than-life dimensions of T. P. Crawford, her life has so completely eclipsed his as to leave the careful reader nonplussed. It is as if Crawford made his mark trying to hold on to the past, while she made hers anticipating the future. A non-Southern Baptist writer, Irwin T. Hyatt said, "She has in fact become a genuine culture heroine, to a degree seemingly unapproached by any other missionary—or for that matter any American of any sort—who ever went to China."[46]

Hyatt, in reviewing Moon's life, claimed Lottie Moon was from her beginnings prepared for something dramatic: "Her ancestry included English royal favorites, Quaker scholars, colonial governors, heroes of duels and of the American Revolution, and a Lady Gordon known as 'The White Rose of Scotland.'"[47]

In an effort to explain her unique contributions to redefining women's roles, he points out that her plantation home, Viewmont, functioned as a matriarchy and produced children both independent and idealistic. A physician brother died from yellow fever, treating patients no one else would. Her sister, Orianna, a genuine rebel, went north for her education, became a feminist, an abolitionist, and the first woman "south of the Mason-Dixon line to earn an M.D. degree." Orianna worked in the Holy Land, served as a medical officer in the war, and bore twelve children. Cousins were heroes of the Confederacy and included female spies who "cut a swath among Yankee officers."

For a time Lottie Moon was trapped by responsibilities—the war, her mother, her sister, Edmonia—and for a longer time, by roles such as tutoring and teaching. Even in China she fell into such restraints before she found a way to break out into a singular and archetypical ministry for women. Hyatt concluded that Lottie Moon represents "a wistful dream that lies somewhere, probably, in all of us."[48]

Even in death Lottie Moon bucked the system, her remains returning to the States as ashes as required by Japan where she perished. The burial of cremated remains, very unusual in the South in those days, was accomplished at Crewe, Virginia, not far from what had been Viewmont. The *For-*

eign Mission Journal called the tiny four-foot-three-inch woman, "the best man among our missionaries."[49]

Women on the Move

Lottie Moon's remarkable story and influence might not have escaped the layering effects of history had it not been for Woman's Missionary Union. More, the continued growth and support of Southern Baptists' missionary program was in no small part due to the work of Woman's Missionary Union, which was still being led at the turn of the century by Annie Armstrong of Baltimore.

By 1900, WMU had begun weeks of prayer and special offerings for both foreign and home missions as well as noteworthy efforts to help the Boards retire their debilitating debts. In 1900, the organization funded the Home Mission Board's first Church Loan Fund and the same year sponsored their first churchwide event, a stewardship emphasis.

In conjunction with WMU's first president, Martha McIntosh, and then the remarkable Fannie E. S. Heck, the volatile and brilliant Armstrong led the women's organization from strength to strength.

A WMU historian later characterized Armstrong as quick to anger and quick to forgive, and Heck as slow to anger and slow to forgive.[50] Not surprisingly, given the events described in the previous chapter, their relationship was often uneven, though their common, uncommon committment to missions saw them through again and again.

Heck was born in Virginia during the Civil War in a place her father had taken the family for safety. Because of this, the mother named the girl Fannie Exile Heck, to keep the memory of their odyssey alive. The girl later added Scudder to her name as a sign of her missionary commitment nurtured by a grandmother with that name. She came to the fore of the womans movement in North Carolina where she was serving that states woman's organization at the time she was tapped for the southwide office. She served three different times; 1892–94, 1895–99, after which she stepped aside in the wake of her conflict with Armstrong over the Bible Fund, and again in 1906–15, after Armstrong gave up her post.

Heck's last stint was in the aftermath of a series of conflicts among the women over a training school in Louisville. Besides the promotion of missions through its organization, materials, and special offerings, WMU began operating the Margaret Home of Missionary Children for education they could not get on the fields where their parents served. It later became a fund for missionary children's educational needs in the States. But in 1902, Southern Baptist Theological Seminary began enrolling women in its classes. A group of women in Louisville, led by John A. Broadus's daughter, Eliza, and the young wife of a Texas physician, Mrs. S. E. Woody, set up a Board of Managers to provide a home for women students at the seminary in 1904. It was a short distance from this reality to a demand for a Woman's Missionary Training school, an idea broached as early as 1895 but effectively killed by Annie Armstrong every time it arose. The Louisville women, however, stayed with idea and when they finally carried the day in Chattanooga in 1906, Armstrong decided to step down. This issue had so energized the women whose meeting was held in connection with the annual Southern Baptist Convention that the messenger count for the convention that year reached a record 1451, up from the previous year's 816 and over 300 more than the previous record. And the women couldn't even be messengers at the convention. They made sure their husbands, who would register, brought them.

The result was that the home for young women attending Southern Seminary became the Woman's Missionary Union Training School. The Sunday School Board provided them a building in 1907, and in 1918 the women completed their own building. "In a chapel of their own, women could plan and women could speak."[51]

Armstrong who, despite the painful erosion of her own finances, never took a salary during her eighteen year stint lest it limit her cherished independence, was forgiven her imperiousness and was deeply appreciated by the women who followed in her train.

The first of those successors was Edith Campbell Crane. Though a Baptist from Baltimore, Crane was an executive with the YWCA in New York City when hired. Despite her lack of involvement with the WMU before accepting the corresponding secretary's role, her missions credentials in the Student Volunteer Movement gave her a creditable role for four years before ill health forced her aside. Her successor, Kathleen Mallory, led WMU for 36 years.

Kathleen Mallory was born in Summerfield, Alabama, on January 24, 1879, a few months before Crawford Howell Toy left Southern Seminary. Her father, a lawyer and Baptist layman, moved his family into a well-appointed Victorian home in Selma. One of six children, she went to Goucher College in Baltimore. There, a romance with a young medical student blossomed into a formal engagement. Janney Lupton finished medical school and entered his internship. Exhausted from his efforts, he contracted tuberculosis and, lacking resistance, soon succumbed.

Mallory channeled her heartbreak into church service and became Alabama's WMU secretary in 1909. When Crane's health forced her aside, she recommended Mallory as her successor. At the annual WMU meeting in connection with the Southern Baptist Convention in 1912 in Oklahoma City, Kathleen Mallory formally took over the leadership of the Union and moved back to Baltimore with its painful memories of her lost love.

In 1914, the Mallory-led WMU changed its quarterly publication *Our Mission Fields* to a monthly magazine entitled *Royal Service*. It was the beginning of a significant new chapter in the women's organization.

The added impact may have been one reason the Home Mission Board's B. D. Gray decided to tackle a sixty-five-year tradition when the convention met in Asheville, North Carolina, in 1916 by giving to WMU the first thirty minutes of the time allowed the Home Mission Board for its report. Kathleen Mallory and Maude McClure not only broke a sixty-five-year tradition, they became the first women ever to address the Southern Baptist Convention. The report from WMU was traditionally read by a man. In fact, it was 1929 before a woman was again invited to speak to the convention, and it was 1938 before the WMU gave its own report to the convention,[52] and then some men elected to walk out in protest. The messenger count of the convention presided over by Lansing Burrows climbed above two thousand for the first time in the history of the SBC.

In 1921, the president of Woman's Missionary Union, Mrs. W. C. James, reminded WMU that the "woman's movement has moved with amazing momentum and irresistable power, and the time has come when we must widen yet further the work of our WMU." Born Minnie Kennedy in Palestine, Texas, James had been a schoolteacher and married a schoolteacher. When he was called to preach, she accompanied him to Louisville and there became active in WMU. He was a pastor in Richmond, Virginia, when she took the gavel of the missionary support group in 1916 in time to join Mallory in her precedent-breaking appearance on the convention rostrum.[53]

James called on the Southern Baptist Convention's executive committee to put nine members of WMU on its committeee and twelve on each of the convention's boards. It was years before her call was even partially answered.[54]

Growth and Leadership

By 1915 Southern Baptist churches passed the 24,000 mark and membership climbed beyond 2,600,000. Southern Baptists' offering plates and envelopes yielded over $12 million to all causes that year, including nearly $3 million to the cause of missions. Yet, nearly half of Southern Baptist churches failed to give anything to causes beyond the local church, and less than 10 percent of Southern Baptists were in cities of over 2,500 in population. They were still largely a rural people which made their growing world vision and outreach even more remarkable.

After twenty-two years of electing prominent laymen as president, Southern Baptists again turned to the ranks of their ministry with the election of Edwin C. Dargan of Georgia at their 1910 convention in Baltimore. Dargan, pastor of the First Baptist Church of Macon, where Georgia's Mercer University was now located, had previously served as professor of homiletics at Southern Seminary.

Dargan, in turn, was followed by another Georgia pastor, Lansing Burrows of Americus, who became president and first presided in the 1914 convention in Nashville, Tennessee, where he had earlier been pastor of the First Baptist Church for ten years. As mentioned in connection with the tradition-breaking Mallory speech, Burrows was presiding when the Convention returned to Asheville, North Carolina, and broke the registration record it had set in its last gathering in Asheville in 1902. Over 2,100 registered for the the 1915 meeting.

Burrows was followed in 1917 by J. B. Gambrell, who became the first Texas Baptist to be elected president of the Southern Baptist Convention. He presided over the Convention during the years of 1917–18 while America was enmeshed in World War I, which had the unique effect of healing some of the old scars that dated back to the Civil War. Southern Baptists found themselves wearing the same uniform as Northern Baptists, and their Confederate legacy began to recede, though it reflected itself for years in their culture and their attitude toward the descendants of slavery.

Baptist Bible Institute

In 1914, P. I. Lipsey, editor of the Mississippi *Baptist Record* suggested the need for a training school for ministers in New Orleans. The idea had surfaced before, but now that Southwestern Seminary had broken the Southern hegemony, it received action. A pre-session meeting at the Southern

Baptist Convention in Houston in 1915 set up the passage of a resolution asking the conventions of Louisana and Mississippi, along with the Home Mission Board, to appoint a feasibility committee. In 1917, following a mass meeting of Baptists in New Orleans, a memorial was prepared which M. E. Dodd presented to the Southern Baptist Convention meeting in New Orleans that year. The memorial was adopted and the Convention instructed its Home Mission and Sunday School Boards to cooperate with the groups interested in establishing "a Baptist missionary training school" in New Orleans.

Thus, while Southern Seminary had been established for the cause of an educated ministry, and Southwestern Seminary had been brought into being to train preachers, the Bible Institute was given a missions motif. The institution was actually birthed in a meeting at Coliseum Place Baptist Church on July 10, 1917, where it was named the Baptist Bible Institute and given a president in the person of B. H. DeMent, pastor of First Baptist Church of Greenville, S. C.

DeMent penned a ten article confession of faith for the new institution called the "Articles of Religious Belief." It reflected the New Hampshire Confession with its approach to inspiration, atonement, and the local church.

That fall a campaign was held to secure funds to buy the old campus of Sophie Newcomb College and classes began on October 1, 1918. The school, later to become the New Orleans Baptist Theological Seminary (1946), came under the formal aegis of the Southern Baptist Convention in 1925, the same year Texas Baptists surrendered Southwestern Seminary to the SBC.[55]

Relief and Annuity Board

In 1918, with the Germans on the offensive in the Marne, the Southern Baptist Convention, meeting in Hot Springs, Arkansas, established the Board of Ministerial Relief and Annuities of the Southern Baptist Convention. Southern Baptists were the tenth national denomination to take such an action, though numerous state programs existed, beginning with The Widows and Superannuated Ministers Fund in Maryland in 1893.

Credit for the idea is given to William Lunsford, a Nashville pastor, who presented it to the Nashville Pastors' Conference. Since he and several other pastors in the group served on the Sunday School Board, they secured a hearing for the idea there. The Sunday School Board set aside

$100,000 for such an enterprise and requested the next Southern Baptist Convention to appoint a commission to consider the matter. It was done, and when the group reported at Hot Springs, they recommended: "a Board of Ministerial Relief and Annuities be established" to be located in Birmingham, Alabama. The Southern Baptist Convention approved the report on May 20, 1918, with one change: it would be located in Dallas, Texas. This probably reflected the presence of the Education Board in Birmingham and continued agitation from the southwest for the need to put an agency headquarters in the area west of the Mississippi.

Appropriately, William Lunsford was elected the first secretary of the Board, and a charter was obtained in July which two years later was changed to call the agency the Relief and Annuity Board of the Southern Baptist Convention. As early as 1923, the Board had assets of $1,490,193.59.

Women as Messengers

Despite the heroics of numerous women in Southern Baptist life in its first seventy-five years, their roles continued to be limited and genuine aspirations opposed by even such stalwarts as John A. Broadus, despite the talents of his daughter, Eliza. Henrietta Hall Shuck, Ann Graves, Annie Armstrong, and Lottie Moon found their way into Baptist histories, but few others did. Impressive work in education, medicine, publications, and pioneer efforts in social work have only recently been documented, which means that little note was taken at the time. C. Anne Davis, writing seven decades later referred to their contributions as being "lived and made on the backside of the world's main agenda."[56] A 1987 Baptist history mentioned women on only 66 of its 850 pages despite the fact that the author was a strong believer in women's contributions.[57] In a *Baptist History and Heritage* article, the same author concluded, "If you men want to get away from women, here is one way you can do it: just get into the pages of Baptist history."[58]

Though not coming as messengers, women attended the Southern Baptist Convention as early as 1868. Only in 1872 did the Convention's Committee on Women's Work endorse the appointment of unmarried women as missionaries. But ten years later only ten women had been appointed by the Foreign Mission Board, including Lottie Moon. Further underscoring their conviction that women should be denied leadership roles in religious life, Southern Baptists changed Article III of their constitution from the word "messengers" to "brethren" in 1885. The change was precipitated by the arrival of messengers from Arkansas including two women. The women were not seated, and Article III was changed to make sure the men were not embarrassed again. The frustration engendered may have, according to historian Leon McBeth, helped bring about the organization of Woman's Missionary Union just three years later.[59]

Aggressive moves by women were still happening elsewhere when women were quietly allowed on the convention floor again in 1913. At that convention George Truett's colleague, R. H. Coleman, shocked them and the body by announcing that he intended to bring action for a constitutional change at the next convention in 1914 to allow women messenger status. It didn't happen. In 1914 Southern Baptists joined the celebration of the Judson Centennial, and women were among those helping to raise a significant Judson Memorial offering for foreign missions.

The fact that Coleman took such a lead is not so remarkable, given the place women already enjoyed in the Baptist General Convention of Texas. Following the state convention meeting in Ft. Worth in November, 1901, the *Baptist Standard* editor commented, "We are bigger than the Southern Baptist Convention in numbers, but that is not as distinguishing as the fact that we are bigger than our great Southern Baptist Convention on the woman question. Our women are messengers to our conventions—to all of them. This is as it ought to be."[60]

The straightforward Cranfill prophesied later in the same article, "Some day the Southern Baptist Convention will get ashamed of itself on this point, and will annihilate their old mossback regulation against the admission of women delegates."

In 1917, the year after B. D. Gray broke the gender barrier on the convention's platform by allowing WMU's Mallory part of his time, Coleman made good on his promise. The vote to change Article III failed, however, 324 to 242. A committee was appointed to study the matter, and the next year the resolution was passed.

Five years later, Margaret Lackey would write, "From this date on Baptist women have been regarded as people."[61]

By 1919, the president of the Southern Baptist Convention, J. B. Gambrell, was lauding the victory of women's suffrage and the successful passage of prohibition. While some historians suggested that it was the preachers' consuming desire to accomplish prohibition that swung their support to women's suffrage since they needed the women's vote, Texas' position and Cranfill's 1901 article argues for less compromised motives.

A Social Gospel

While women's suffrage and prohibition could be considered social issues, Southern Baptists resisted the societal meaning of the gospel that moved to the center of many Christian group agendas in the early years of the twentieth century. While Southern Baptists from their earliest years stressed religious liberty, temperance, marital fidelity, acts of compassion, and good citizenship, they were leery of the social gospel. They saw it as the resort of Christians liberalized by modernism. They believed God's grace in the human heart was the starting place for Southern Baptists, and A. J. Barton, the first chairman of the Convention's Social Service Comission, said all social and civic responsibilities began there.

Studies suggest that racial justice was not on the agenda of Baptists north or south in this period.[62]

Robert Baker defends Southern Baptists by pointing out that in 1907 and again in 1913, Southern Baptists responded to calls in their own ranks for attention to social ills. The Social Service Committee was one result.

Critics of the Convention, on the other hand, said it was a culturally bound institution "sanctifying a secular order devoted to state's rights, white surpremacy, laissez faire economics, and property rights." John Lee Eighmy pointed to three aspects of Southern Baptist life that inhibited social thought and action. He cited an ecclesiastical system of independent churches focused on missions, revivalism that emphasized the spiritual welfare of individuals rather than the social problems of society, and social pressure that caused the churches to acquiese to if not embrace the attitudes of the secular society around them.[63]

Nevertheless, as numerous studies subsequently pointed out, many Baptists in the South had a sharp social conscience and worked hard to act it out in the face of stern opposition in their own churches. The denomination entered the fray only in terms of occasional, highly circumspect resolutions.

Seventy-Five Years and Seventy-Five Million

Toward the end of the year that women won their messenger status, the United States emerged from World War I. Before the expeditionary forces returned from France, however, the homeland was devastated by a major outbreak of influenza that was as mortal as war. A physician in Knoxville, Tennessee, William Wallace, lost his wife to the epidemic and had to raise his young son, Bill Wallace, with the help of an older daughter. The boy grew up to write a dramatic chapter in Southern Baptist foreign missions.

Baptisms fell to a major low under the impact of the war and the epidemic, and expanding debt incurred by the Mission Boards again became a threat to operations.

While the "war to end all wars" involved American doughboys less than two years before the gas and gangrene ridden spectacle came to an end, it marked a profound change among American people and Southern Baptists. Even as the United States became aware of its might and potential as never before, so Southern Baptists began to flex their own muscles.

Reflecting this and the euphoria of the armistice in Europe, Southern Baptists meeting in Atlanta, Georgia, in 1919, launched their most dramatic denominational endeavor. They authorized a financial campaign to raise seventy-five million dollars for their various organizations in celebration of the Convention's upcoming seventy-fifth anniversary. The ambitious plan was designed to get the Convention's agencies out of debt and launch a bold post-war outreach. The Convention planned to have the endeavor well underway when they celebrated their anniversary event in the nation's capital in 1920.

A committee of eighteen representing each of the states embraced by the Southern Baptist Convention asked George W. Truett to chair the effort, and in a significantly propitious move, tapped Southwestern's Lee Scarborough to lead the actual campaign.

Scarborough had proven his abilities in this kind of endeavor. In Abilene, he had led a major campaign on behalf of Simmons College, later Hardin-Simmons University, and he had chaired a successful Texas Baptist educational campaign in 1917. He and George Truett had conducted a "Conquest Campaign" to pay all State Convention debts the next year. He had been B. H. Carroll's prime fund raiser in the opening of Southwestern Seminary in Fort Worth.

Possibly because of this experience, Scarborough let the committee know that he thought felt the amount should be 100 million and that a five-year pledge was too long. However, the seventy-five number matched the anniversary, and it stood, as did the five-year pledge plan. To his credit, even after the final collections reached only $58,591,713, Scarborough was never heard to say "I told you so."[64] Given the larger financial environment impacting Southern Baptists, the miracle may have been the record shattering amount actually realized.

Inter-church Response

Perplexing in light of the way history would focus on the campaign and its implications, the Convention meeting in Atlanta itself was far more concerned with J. B. Gambrell's presidential address and reactions to it. The reason is that though controversy always holds the floor and takes most of the immediate press, history reserves judgment for residual effects and their subsequent meaning.

The controversy Gambrell highlighted was the heated interest in mainline denominations for church union and especially for post-war cooperation in fund raising, missions, and ministry. A number of Baptist leaders strongly supported such efforts and thought the time was ripe for Baptists to get involved. The Federal Council of Churches was planning a huge financial ingathering to fund their plans. Southern Baptists, however, resisted such moves, feeling that Baptist distinctives and religious freedom were at stake. In retrospect, the Seventy-Five Million Campaign may have been fueled by a competitive position with the inter-church effort and with the Northern Baptist Convention which mounted a 100-million-dollar campaign in what they called the New World Movement the same year.

Gambrell, at the height of his influence and powers at age seventy-eight, gave their battle cry. In his address, Gambrell excoriated War Department actions that forced Baptist chaplains into general Protestant categories while protecting Roman Catholic prerogatives. Though Landmarkers had traditionally denied Baptists were in any sense Protestants, even non-Landmarkers tended to support the idea that Baptists were a category apart. Gambrell's stirring speech quoted England's David Lloyd George as claiming that the war was at bottom for Baptist principles. Gambrell explained that by that George meant the common rights of man. Gambrell concluded by calling for the word to go out as to who and what Baptists really were. "We ought to send out to our fellow Baptists everywhere, a rallying cry to unite."[65]

The electric response stirred old fires of Baptist pride reminiscent of Landmarkism. A special committee, Committee on the President's Address and Questions Raised By It, was set up to handle the interest. The most unique response was J. F. Love's call for a committee of five to prepare a fraternal address to people of "like precious faith with us." To be chaired by E. Y. Mullins, the committee included L. R. Scarborough, already inundated with the campaign planning, J. B. Gambrell, Z. T. Cody, and William Ellyson. The Fraternal Address was finished in a few months but never adopted by the Convention. Love and the Foreign Mission Board published it and followed it in 1920 with their own Statement of Beliefs which was adopted only as a part of the Foreign Mission Board's report. Little more was heard from either the Fraternal Address or the Foreign Mission Board's Statement of Belief.[66]

During the Convention, J. C. White, a delegate from the Inter-Church Movement was allowed to bring a message from that group to Southern Baptists. They heard it politely, but nervously, because of the strong feelings attendant to it. When J. C. White finished his presentation on the union movement, J. B. Gambrell took him by the hand at the podium and said, "Baptists do not have popes. They never put anybody where they can't put him down . . . and another thing: Baptists never ride a horse without a bridle." Reports indicated that a storm of laughter and amens greeted Gambrell's statement.[67]

E. C. Routh was elated with the Convention. He called it the "greatest convention of all," and he cited as reasons: "greatest in number, greatest in spirit, greatest in vision and the response to a world challenge, greatest in defining the relations which should subsist between religious bodies and civil government."[68] As it turned out, the 1920 gathering in Washington celebrating Southern Baptists' seventy-fifth anniversary would challenge his penchant for superlatives.

Victory in Washington

By the fall of 1919 the Seventy-Five Million Campaign was ready to go. It began with an October "Calling Out the Called" day in which Scarborough's previously published "Recruits for World Conquest" played a prominent role. On November 30, pledging was begun. Fifty-four million dollars had been pledged by nightfall and seventy-six million by the evening of December 7th. When Scarborough turned over direction to the Campaign Commission headed by George Truett, $92,630,923 had been pledged.

The overwhelming success of the effort fueled another record setting convention as 8,359 messengers registered for Southern Baptists' Seventy-Fifth Anniversary meeting in 1920 in Washington, D. C., where J. B. Gambrell handed the gavel over to Southern Seminary's E. Y. Mullins.

A great outdoor service on the steps of the capital on Sunday highlighted many's memories of the Jubilee. Dallas's R. H. Coleman led an estimated ten thousand in such hymns as "My Country 'Tis of Thee," "Battle Hymn of the Republic," "Rescue the Perishing," and "My Faith Looks Up To Thee."

Then George W. Truett, in his finest hour, spoke on the subject "Baptists and Religious Liberty;" it was Southern Baptists' most exhilarating gathering to that time.[69]

In 1920, Southern Baptist membership exceeded 3,000,000 for the first time, with over 27,000 churches. Total gifts reached $34 million almost three times what they had been only five years before.

But this was to be Southern Baptists' high water mark for many years. It was twenty-seven years before that many messengers again registered for a convention gathering, and felt the same confidence and power.

Ironic in light of the anti-ecumenicalism of the previous year was the fact that a number of Foreign Mission Board officials went directly from the Washington meeting to participate in a conference in London which would draw them into new work in Palestine, Spain, and Hungary as a result of agreements reached there.

In 1921 as E. Y. Mullins, president of Southern Baptist Seminary, presided, the promise of the Seventy-five Million Campaign was already beginning to tarnish. Pledge payments came more slowly than predicted. Despite the warnings, agencies participating in the distributions of campaign proceeds moved ahead on the basis of the pledge total rather than on the actual collections. Thus, the Boards, for whose debt eradication the campaign had been launched, began to struggle with an even more crushing liability.

Prohibition

Sharing the limelight with the post-war planning and excitement of the Seventy-five Million Campaign was the approaching victory of those who had fought so long for prohibition of the sale of alcoholic beverages. The constitutional amendment that would trigger prohibition had been ratified by the required number of states and was scheduled to take effect in a matter of months.

From the late 1880s on, abstinence regarding alcohol was the method of choice to battle the "saloon forces," which especially on the frontier had been destructive to Christian values. In 1886, the Southern Baptist Convention adopted a report that called for total abstinence and for state and national prohibition. Two years later, however, James Boyce, presiding over his last Convention and within months of his death, ruled out of order a resolution on alcohol. He explained that it was not germane to the purpose of the convention. Despite the almost saintly role the founder of Southern

Seminary was accorded, the ruling was challenged. Perhaps out of deference for Boyce the ruling was sustained, though narrowly.[70]

After 1890 the Convention supported prohibition at every meeting, and in 1910 appointed a permanent Committee on Temperance. "As the North led the nation against slavery," the committee believed,"the South should lead the nation" against liquor.[71]

Women, denied leadership in other matters, did not hesitate on this issue. Most WMU leaders were also active in Women's Christian Temperance Union chapters. As mentioned earlier, many believed that women's support of prohibition is what drew the preachers to their side on the suffrage issue. They needed women's votes.

Certainly, Baptist leaders did not leave them in the field alone. Gambrell, Truett, Mullins, Carroll, and a host of others joined them with all the powers of oratory at their command, and in Gambrell's case, they had the increasing influence of Texas's *Baptist Standard*.

B. H. Carroll was especially committed to the crusade and joined the fray in speech, sermon, and debate. Once he was accused of hypocrisy when an opponent in a debate claimed to have a receipt for whiskey signed by Carroll. The Texas giant vehemently denied it and his opponent backed off. Information by his brother in posthumous biography indicated that it might have been true, for Carroll's father raised his sons with the strange habit of starting a day with a swig of whiskey. If so, his early initiation served only to increase his enmity against the use of alcohol.[72]

While Baptists did not include such convictions in their Statements of Faith, many widely circulated Baptist church covenants required abstinence pledges.

Fundamentalism

J. Frank Norris, who had led his church to pledge $100,000 to the Seventy-five-Million Campaign, announced that it would not pay its pledge, and he urged other churches not to pay theirs because of what he charged was rampant liberalism and corruption among Southern Baptist teachers and officials. Norris consistently failed to substantiate such charges, but that did not deter him. His actions were the thunder and lightning of the next storm approaching Southern Baptists.

This new divisiveness appeared as a reaction to the continued inroads of continental liberalism and the impact of Darwinian evolution on theological thinking in the North. Several Christian laymen funded a series of tracts in 1910 called *The Fundamentals.* Focusing on the inspiration of the Scriptures, the virgin birth, the bodily resurrection of Christ, the atonement, and the eminent return of Christ, the tracts were widely disseminated. They included the work of seven Baptist authors including the highly respected E. Y. Mullins.

In 1984, successors to the Norris-led Fundamentalist Movement would say it had six watermarks: fidelity to Biblical and Baptistic doctrines, emphasis on heritage and succession, fervent evangelism, Bible preaching, militant opposition to error, and separation, not inclusivism.[73] Members of this group pointed to James R. Graves, the father of Landmarkism, as one of their progenitors because of his exclusivism and dispensational theology. They would also credit B. H. Carroll, J. M. Carroll, and above all, J. Frank Norris as helping define and advance Fundamentalism.[74]

On the surface of things, Southern Baptist life did not seem to be fertile ground for Fundamentalist charges. Liberals and evolutionists were hard to come by, the Toy controversy not withstanding.

However, Southern Baptists were not spared the storms that rent the fellowship of a number of denominational groups in the North. J. Frank Norris began not only to join hands with northern fundamentalists, but to mount attacks on perceived liberals at Baylor University and Southwestern Seminary. After the death of B. H. Carroll, there seemed to be no restraint to Norris' actions. First he opposed a Texas Baptist program of missions and then started a Bible school with slaps at Southwestern and Baylor. By 1919, when he cancelled his Seventy-five-Million Campaign pledge, he was a leader of the World's Christian Fundamentals Conference.

In 1920, he cancelled Southern Baptist literature and attacked Baylor University for "evolution and infidelity." The Fort Worth firebrand found an ally in a pastor, Dale Crowley, who was also a student at Baylor and who had accused a Professor Fothergill of supporting Darwin's theories of evolution. Crowley was suspended by Baylor's President Brooks before threats to bring his case and his charges before the Convention yielded a quiet reinstatement that Crowley never accepted. He later represented conservative causes on the east coast, and his son, Robert Crowley, played a significant role in the "conservative resurgence" of the 70s and 80s.[75]

Norris, who had sold *The Baptist Standard* to Texas Baptists in 1909 when Carroll helped him secure the call to Fort Worth's First Baptist Church, continued to use his writing and publishing skills through a church publication called *The Searchlight,* later *The Fundamentalist.*

His attacks, more and more shrill, included his old Carroll-sponsored cohorts, George W. Truett and Lee R. Scarborough. Just how bitter the feelings between them became is evident in the fact that neither Truett's nor Scarborough's official biographers were allowed to refer to Norris.

Norris later sent deprecating telegrams to Truett just as he was preparing to preach. In turn, Scarborough wrote a pamphlet entitled "The Fruits of Norrism" and said, "It thrives on sensationalism, misrepresentation, and false accusations of good men and true causes. It masquerades under the cloak of anti-evolution, anti-modernism, anti-catholicism in order to ride into public favor and cast poisonous suspicion on the leadership of constructive Christianity."[76]

In 1922, Norris was expelled from the Tarrant County Baptist Association. Txhe Baptist General Convention of Texas censured him in the same year and refused to seat him the next. Energized by both attention and rejection, Norris helped found the Baptist Bible Union of America in 1923. American Baptist historian William Brackney called the Baptist Bible Union one of the three identity shaping events in Baptist life, along with the London Confession of 1644 and the Baptist Missionary Society of 1792.[77] Calling it the coalescence of several streams of theological conservatism in Great Britain and the United States, "including the legacy of Charles Haddon Spurgeon," Brackney claimed it not only sought to redefine Baptist identity, but to legitimize fragmentation.[78]

In 1926, Norris, who had earlier been indicted for arson, shot a man to death in his study. He was acquitted in both cases, but his influence among the ranks of Southern Baptists was greatly diminished.

A Confession of Faith

In 1920 the Foreign Mission Board presented a Statement of Beliefs to the Convention in its report that it asked all missionaries to affirm. Claiming to be an expanded version of the E. Y. Mullins's Committee's Fraternal Address produced in response to the J. F. Love motion in 1919, it included confidence in the New Testament as the sole authority for faith and practice in all matters religious and a strictly local church interpretation of the Bible. As such, the document seemed to be related more to the union or ecumenical movement than either Landmarkism or Fundamentalism, since it included a long disclaimer for any agreements with other Christian bodies regarding missionary work.[79]

The statement from this distance leaves some ambiguity, for the Board announced in the same report that it was sending Love and George Truett to a missionary conference in London. At that conference, as mentioned earlier, the Board accepted assignment in several European areas in a seemingly comity-type agreement. In addition, the doctrinal statement was introduced with assurance that no one would be required to sign it, though the document itself said missionaries would be required to subscribe to it.[80] Futhermore, the claim to have been inspired by Mullins's Fraternal Address was patently false since a letter by Mullins to Love in the fall of 1919 referred to a copy of the Foreign Board's statement and indicated that the Fraternal Address had not yet been prepared.[81] The statement also included language that referenced the kind of work done overseas to basic patterns at home. When such guidelines were considered by the Foreign Mission Board in 1991, no awareness of the 1920 experience was in evidence.

A joint "consultative" meeting between representatives from both the Northern and Southern Conventions convened in 1922 to give serious consideration to issuing a joint confession of faith.[82] Despite growing pressures facing both groups, the idea was rejected. As it turned out, the anti-creed convictions of the North's majority were more pronounced that those of the South.

Evolution and the perceived threat of scientific teachings pushed concerns with the inter-church movement off the front burner of Southern Baptist gatherings in the period that followed. Norris's followers were not the only ones raising questions about what Baptist institutions were teaching. Enough questions and charges appeared in Baptist state papers and from platforms large and small that in 1922 the Education Board's report asked the Convention to beware of "innuendo and nebulous criticism."

President E. Y. Mullins tried to steer for middle ground in 1923 when he called for "firm faith and free research" from and for Southern Baptist scholars. That the battle continued to heat up, however, was obvious as the Convention met in Atlanta in 1924, and Mullins called on those same persons to "protect the supernatural elements in the faith." J. Frank Norris in his widely circulated literature demanded that evolution be "extracted root and branch" even if a schism resulted.

A Mississippi leader proposed that the Convention divide after the Education Association denied that the Bible could be taken literally. The controversy swelled the ranks of messengers from 4,193 in 1923, to 5,622 in 1924, and 5,600 in 1925.

The Atlanta meeting in 1924 rejected a call for a binding doctrinal statement, but it put a committee in place to consider a statement related to the Baptist Faith and Message. Mullins chaired the committee. Strangely, he ignored Southern Seminary's own Abstract of Principles and the work he had done on the Fraternal Address. The committee began its work with the Foreign Mission Board's 1919 Statement of Beliefs.[83] However, when the committee reported its findings in 1925, they were in the form of a Confession of Faith taken from the 1833 New Hampshire Confession with additions.

Mullins said, "Southern Baptists have on two or three occasions in recent years adopted some form of doctrinal statement, but the menace of materialism justifies us in reaffirming some such document as the New Hampshire Confession of Faith."

The New Hampshire Confession of Faith was developed by Baptists in New England as their Calvinist beliefs came under pressure from the youthful free-will movement. While it did not depart radically from the prevailing Philadelphia Confession of 1742, it did modify the Calvinist language. In addition it was much shorter and simpler. It quickly became the document of choice of the American Baptist Publication Society and, as Charles De weese points out, forms of this confession appeared in a variety of church covenants circulated widely in Southern Baptist life. It was the confession adopted by Southwestern Seminary at its founding in 1908 and seems to have influenced the Bible Institute's articles. This growing acceptance in the South and Southwest probably explains why Mullins eschewed the better known Philadelphia Confession of 1742 that in an earlier form had been accepted by the Charleston Association and other Southern groups. Its roots went back to the Second London Confession of 1677.

Mullins was by this time the undisputed theological authority among Southern Baptists. In fact, recent studies give him a more definitive role, yet he realized that the real issue was the Bible and its perceived battle with science. Mullins stated that "religion and science should not invade each others territory." But he did not pass up the opportunity to present a more modified Calvinism and to broaden the church definition so limited by Landmarkism. Both adjustments reflected the prevailing practice of Southern Baptists.

Mullins and other leaders hoped the passage of the document would calm Baptist passions. A minority report by C. P. Stealey, editor of Oklahoma's *Baptist Messenger,* called for an addition to the article on the fall of man (and insured that it would not). Stealey wanted to add "and not by evolution." Reports indicate Stealey's defense of his motion did not help, and Mullins's reply did. Mullins noted that since they were not saying how God did create man, they need not say how He didn't.[84] The amendment lost 2,013 to 950.[85]

The 1925 Confession was introduced by a number of denials that it was in any form a step toward creedalism. It stated, "Confessions are only guides in interpretation, having no authority over the conscience." It went on to explain that it was not "to be used to hamper freedom of thought or investigation in other realms of life."[86]

Herschel Hobbs, who filled Mullins's role when next the question of confessions became an issue, said, "The Baptist Faith and Message served to hold Southern Baptists to their position of progressive conservativism. It anchored their faith for thirty-seven years, but left them free of a creed."[87]

One reason most conservatives were generally mollified by Mullins's actions is that fundamentalist leader, W. B. Riley, of the Northern Baptist Convention, had tried to get that group to adopt the New Hampshire Confession of Faith three years before. He failed, but Mullins succeeded in the Southern Baptist Convention.[88]

In a wrap-up of the Convention in the next *Baptist Standard*, E. C. Routh complained, "There was a considerable element in the Convention opposed to the adoption of any Confession of Faith whatever, and this group had no opportunity to be heard."[89]

However, that same summer a Tennessee science teacher named Scopes was indicted for teaching evolution contrary to a Tennessee law passed earlier that year. To say the highly publicized trial further inflamed the issue is understatement.

When the Convention met in Houston in 1926, George McDaniel, pastor of First Baptist Church, Richmond, Virginia, took the step many felt was lacking in the Confession of Faith and rejected "evolution" in his presidential address. Interestingly, McDaniel was a Texan who had attended Baylor and was also one of B. H. Carroll's "preachers." M. E. Dodd moved this be the sentiment of the Convention and that Baptists then get on with the task of missions and evangelism. Fundementalist elements led by Oklahoma's C. P. Stealey and Arkansas's S. E. Tull stayed with the matter, however, and secured passage of a resolution that called for the McDaniel statement to be binding on all employees of Southern Baptist institutions or agencies.

J. Frank Norris was elated and headlined the "victory" for fundamentalism in his paper. Many agreed that the 1925 Confession of Faith was a clearcut victory for fundamentalism since that movement held strongly to creeds as a way to ensure orthodoxy in denominational structures. When teachers or writers were suspected of heretical views, they could only be challenged if some standard was in place.

Since it quieted the storm and financial exigencies were more pressing, the whole thing soon went on the back burner.

Cooperative Program

Lost in the passion of the battle over evolution in 1925 and the resulting acceptance of the Convention's first Confession of Faith was the adoption of a whole new way of financing the Southern Baptist Convention. It became known as the Cooperative Program and was so foundational to Southern Baptist life that it was called a "golden calf" in a later controversy. With the confessionalism that had nurtured Baptists as a people and the connectionalism that had made them a denomination, cooperation gave them a way to bond the two in an equilateral foundation that would define them as few other actions had done.

Debt that plagued agencies when the Seventy-five Million Campaign was launched had deepened dramatically when collections fell far short of the pledges. As already noted, the final total was roughly fifty-eight million of the ninety-two million pledged. But the cooperative approaches pioneered in that effort promised a better way to fund Southern Baptist enterprises, and that better way was introduced in 1925.

The Cooperative Program was basically an agreement between the state conventions cooperating with the Southern Baptist Convention to receive funds from the churches and forward an agreed-upon percentage of those funds to south-wide causes. It eliminated the need for agents and competitive fund-raising efforts in the churches and let the pastors promote the broader view of the denominational program. It was a natural to bring the organizing vision of the convention concept to full fruition. But it needed consensus, and the Confession of Faith and other actions in the 1925 and 1926 annual meetings gave that sense of consensus.

Executive Committee

In many ways Southern Baptists were following the broader culture of the country where the entrepreneurial and independent spirit gave way to corporate structures, financial models, and efficiency.

The Southern Baptist Convention in 1913 had authorized a study for its own affairs. Its first report in 1914 called for a Convention budget and apportioning throughout Baptist life. It stressed agency cooperation and Convention coordination but accomplished little until 1917, when a follow-up recommended an Executive Committee and led the Convention to adopt an annual budget.[90] This Executive Committee did not fully come into its own for a few years, but it was a necessary step toward an organizational efficiency that Southern Baptists needed. Though the Convention was still subject to the attacks of those proponents of the old anti-missions and Campbell controversies in Kentucky and the Landmark controversies of the 1800s, there was a growing openness toward seeing itself as a progressive and cohesive denominational organization.

In 1927, George W. Truett of Dallas took over as president of the Southern Baptist Convention when it met in Louisville, Kentucky. At this meeting a report by the Committee on Business Efficiency enlarged the responsibilities of the Executive Committee. Besides budget responsibilities and interim roles, the enlarged committee was given responsibility for promoting the new Cooperative Program.[91]

Along with its Cooperative Program and its Executive Committee, Southern Baptists adopted a process for the election of trustees of institutions and agencies and their rotation that was more representative than even that for their meetings. According to Nancy Ammerman, they thus balanced the pure democracy of their annual gatherings with a more Republican arrangement for interim operations.[92]

Between the structure the Executive Committee offered and the financial plan that the Cooperative Program provided, Southern Baptists seemed poised for growth with the broadest consensus of support among its constituents it had yet known.

Definition

In the twenty-seven short years of the twentieth century, the denomination had not only survived, but it had come of age. It had at last begun to define itself in terms of the potential inherent in the convention system that first Richard Furman and then W. B. Johnson had so fervently sought. The four key boards managing missions at home and overseas, developing literature and religious education, and supervising relief and retirements were alive and flourishing. Three seminaries trained a new generation of leadership and a student movement, a laymen's movement, and a vibrant Woman's Missionary Union organized a broad base of support for Southern Baptists' total program.

In addition, the Southern Baptist Convention had survived its second major controversy, further defined its confessionalism, reaffirmed its connectionalism, and discovered a new basis of cooperation. It had developed a financial plan and a coordinating management structure. It had expanded its representative approach to decision making and to the management of its collective endeavors.

Not surprising then was the unabashed triumphalism abroad in Southern Baptist life as illustrated by J. M. Dawson's Home Mission report in 1919. Dawson said, "America is in fact God's new Israel for the races of men." He said it was imperative that Southern Baptists "make the southland the base for a world capturing religion." He claimed that "a Christianized world waits on a Christianized America. The South is America's best hope."[93] Seventy-three years later Memphis pastor, Adrian Rogers, voiced similar thoughts, but in a less affirming climate.[94]

If Dawson saw the cloud on the horizon, he did not mention it. The rural post-World War I recession was expanding into something far broader and more devastating. The debt problems that had come following the failure of the pledges of the Seventy-five Million Campaign to be paid continued to grow.

5

Adversity and Change

1927–1945

By 1927, Southern Baptists' chronic preoccupation with financial matters became acute. The chronic aspect was evident, both in the business efficiency studies that culminated in an expanded Executive Committee and in fund-raising concerns that brought the Cooperative Program into being. The acute aspect came to the fore first not in institutional terms but in highly personal terms.

Severe financial disasters rocked American agriculture throughout the twenties during a period when the farmer was still the mainstay of Southern Baptists' economic base. Despite the flapper age and the giddiness that was sending the stock market to new heights, most Southern Baptists' plight only worsened. For every story of someone getting wealthy overnight in stocks and bonds, there were dozens of stories of families displaced through inability to meet their obligations at the banks and seeing their family farms foreclosed.[1]

This financial problem throughout Southern Baptist territory was one of the reasons that the seemingly successful Seventy-five-Million Campaign launched in 1919 and reporting over ninety million pledged by 1920 turned into a disaster. As mentioned earlier, only fifty-eight million dollars was finally collected. While that in itself constituted a dramatic new height for Baptists' giving, it fell so far below the expectations upon which Southern Baptist agencies had planned and spent that the worrisome debts the campaign had tried to address now compounded to alarming proportions.[2]

Critics like Fort Worth's J. Frank Norris used the failure to realize the promise of the Seventy-five-Million Campaign and the escalating agency debts to lash Southern Baptists unmercifully.

Embezzlement

These open financial wounds in Southern Baptist life were worsened by two events that took place in 1927 and 1928. At the Convention meeting in 1927, the Foreign Mission Board reported as quietly as it could that for the first time in its history an embezzlement had incurred. Auditors had turned up a shortfall of a little over $103,000. G. N. Sanders, treasurer, was relieved of his duties and the Board's new treasurer, E. P. Buxton, reported that the Board had recovered from the fidelity bond that had been required for such an office and other assets of Sanders approximately one-half of the loss. They also reported that friends of the Foreign Mission Board were rallying to provide more help. But for a Board already in debt and with the larger enterprise struggling with accumulated debt that would reach over six million early in the next decade, great damage had been done.

Secretary J. F. Love, who had led the Board since 1915 and had seen the missionary force grow from 298 in nine fields to 489 in fifteen countries, now had to struggle with debt and retrenchment. He died under the burden in May of 1928, and the Board turned to a long time staff member, T. B. Ray, to take over.[3]

If lightning does not strike in the same place twice, it certainly struck close when the very next year the Home Mission Board revealed its own case of embezzlement. Clinton S. Carnes had become treasurer of the Home Mission Board the same year that Sanders had taken that post at the Foreign Mission Board. Carnes, an experienced accountant, brought strong business credentials and recommendations from church sources when he joined the Board; he received a great deal of authority from Board officials to carry on his business in the several states where the Home Mission Board was at work. This included the power to borrow money from banks in different states.

The bookkeeping theft of just under a million dollars was revealed in August of 1928. With the revelation of the defalcation, information also came to light that Carnes had a criminal record which had been carefully shielded from Board officials. The bond proceeds and Carnes' assets restored roughly a third of the loss, but when the remainder was added to the already growing debt of the agency, the total approached $2,500,000.[4]

The embarrassment and overwhelming debt left the Home Mission Board in disarray. Southern Baptists' newly organized Executive Committee was about to receive its baptism by fire.

Convention Response

The Home Mission Board asked the Executive Committee for help in a special meeting in Atlanta on September 4, 1928. Its new executive secretary, Austin Crouch, assembled the committee and moved to the task.[5]

Crouch, a native Missourian, was fifty-eight years old when he came to Atlanta for this special session. He graduated from Baylor University the year after George Truett and then took a master's degree at Howard College before attending Southern Seminary the year that Whitsitt left. He served churches throughout Texas as well as Mississippi, Alabama, Arkansas, and Tennessee. He had also served as superintendent of church extension for the Home Mission Board.

Crouch, at the 1925 Convention, had called for a Business Efficiency Committee to bring chaos out of Southern Baptists' financial problems. As often happens when people make such motions, he was appointed chairman of the committee to develop a business and financial plan and reorganize the Executive Committee. He was elected its first executive secretary-treasurer in 1927, and his leadership skills soon became apparent.[6]

Crouch and his committee were aware of the task that faced them and knew it required a leadership change. The venerable leader of the Home Mission Board, B. D. Gray, knew it too; he stepped down after twenty-five years of leading the Home Mission effort. In a pattern similar to the one the Foreign Mission Board's Love had experienced, Gray's first eighteen years brought outstanding success, but his last seven years had been marked by the increasingly dark clouds of depression and retrenchment. The Carnes defalcation was a final blow.

The Executive Committee called on Southern Baptists to respond positively to the problem by declaring Sunday, November 11, 1928 as Baptist Honor Day. Under Crouch's leadership communication was hurriedly developed through every channel available. Southern Baptist churches in varying degrees raised just under $400,000 to apply on the Board's debt. That one offering probably saved the Home Mission Board from bankruptcy and preserved the Southern Baptist Convention's agency record of never defaulting on debt.[7]

Under the Executive Committee's leadership, the Home Mission Board was reorganized, and John Benjamin Lawrence was persuaded to accept the charge. Lawrence had not wanted the position and any reasonable awareness of what he faced when he took over in early 1929 made his reluctance thoroughly understandable.[8]

Mississippian J. B. Lawrence was an experienced pastor and denominational official. He had served as a state executive secretary, a former university president, and state paper editor. Crouch and the other members of the Board and the Executive Committee realized that the breadth of his experience was desperately needed.

Under Lawrence's leadership the climb back was to be resolute if uneven. He served nearly twenty-five years as chief executive of the Home Mission Board.

Change in Representation

The adversity of financial difficulty all but overshadowed a significant change in Southern Baptist life, and that had to do with the way its constituency was represented in its annual conventions. In the 1845 meeting, W. B. Johnson's convention concept had been compromised in Article III of its constitution by a financial base of representation reflecting the earlier society model. It provided that the convention would be constituted by members who contributed funds or were delegated by religious bodies contributing funds. Three hundred dollars within the three year period between meetings was the basis. Six hundred dollars during the same period allowed two representatives to be seated. This proportion operated up to a maximum of five representatives. While this basis applied to both individuals and organizations (primarily local churches), larger entities, termed "great collateral societies," faced a thousand dollar test per year for three years for each representative and were also subject to the five representative limit.

Nothing limited one individual from representing more than one entity, however, and a single person representing larger donations could cast more than one vote.

Not surprisingly, this financial basis was challenged early and often in Southern Baptists' deliberations. This first effort came in 1859 with a proposed amendment limiting "messengers" to "members in good standing of a regular Baptist church." The heated Landmark issue clouded this effort, and it never emerged from the committee to which it was referred.

The next effort, in 1869, tried to limit representation to churches. The existing rules allowed for representatives from "churches, Sunday schools, woman's missionary societies, ladies of the church, African missionary society, ministers' conference, associations, foreign missionary society of a state, woman's missionary society (state body), colleges, young men's or young women's missionary societies (college organization), legacy to the convention, periodicals, (and) business firms."[9] But this move to develop a strict ecclesiastical basis instead of financial also failed, and again the Landmark movement was probably in the background of much of the resistance.

Efforts to move to a church basis or some version of it were thought to limit the perceived freedom of the financial base of representation. Besides those who clung to a method adopted in the original Triennial Convention and those who resisted anything that smacked of Landmarkism, undoubtedly some did not want to do anything that might limit the already uneven funding of Southern Baptists' struggling institutions.

An effort to challenge the financial basis occurred again in 1874. It was first tabled and then referred to the credentials committee. This committee's report reflected many Southern Baptists' continuing suspicion of Convention power, when it said the Convention had "no right to dictate to the states or their instructed delegates as to who shall represent them in this body, provided the applicant be within the requirements of the Constitution."[10]

As already noted, the Convention did tamper with Article III in 1885 when it changed the word "members" to read "brethren" to formally exclude women. This was not a change of heart as much as it was a formal statement of something they had always taken for granted until women asked to be seated.

In 1905, Landmark groups from Arkansas and Texas challenged the Convention to abandon the financial basis and move to a church basis tied to membership. Their request asserted that the missionary commission was given to churches and that any church, regardless of size or wealth or contribution, should be able to have a messenger seated. As before, the financial basis was reaffirmed, though the convention did increase the financial benchmark from $100 per year to $250. This caused the two Landmark organizations in Texas and Arkansas to break away from the Southern Baptist Convention to form their own organization, but it certainly did not eliminate Landmark convictions among Southern Baptists, especially in the Southwest. A similar petition from Florida Baptists in 1906 met the same fate.

And yet in 1924, a committee took on the question again under the broader concern of dealing with the problem of increased attendance. The heated evolution controversy put the committee's work on the back burner until 1926, when its report included a reinforcement of the financial basis of representation, terming it "sound and scriptural."

This report put nothing to rest, however, and in 1929 Washington, D. C.'s Columbia Association called for a constitutional convention in a memorial that focused on the representation issue. A committee of five reported out in favor of such a convention in 1930, and in 1931 a Committee on Changes in the Constitution brought recommendations that Article III be changed at several points. But a financial basis was still at the heart of it.[11]

Essentially, the Committee reported in favor of the original principle of representation based on gifts or on the notion that the people who give the money ought to have the most to say about how it was to be dispersed. This argument was resuscitated fifty years later in a new controversy.

On the other hand, the depression era was producing a different mentality. Rural churches, still in predominance in the South, felt keenly that the financial basis of representation was going to throw the clout of the Convention to the relatively few well-to-do churches, most of which were in urban centers. A spirit of egalitarianism, a part of the common bonds of hardship and adversity, argued that the church principle seemed to more nearly approximate the Baptist democratic ideal.

When the recommendation was brought before the Convention, E. C. Routh, who had succeeded C. P. Stealey as editor of the *Oklahoma Baptist* paper, offered a substitute. The plan recommended that the Convention consist of "messengers" who were members of missionary Baptist churches, cooperating with the Southern Baptist Convention, on the basis of one messenger for every church contributing to the work of the Convention and one additional messenger for every $250 actually paid to the work of the Convention during the calendar year, with the limit of three messengers.[12] The substitute motion triumphed over the committee recommendation, and it would not be the last time messengers would flex their democratic muscles.

In 1933 the limit of three was raised to ten which remained in place with only a small change in 1946, when efforts to head off fundamentalist schismatics caused the inclusion of the words "in friendly cooperation with this Convention and sympathetic with its purposes and work and has during the fiscal year preceding been a bonafide contributor to the Convention's work."[13]

Another 1931 action recognized the dual decision-making structure of the Convention by putting new procedures in place for its agency and institutional trustees. Interestingly enough, this was also refined in 1946.[14]

The 1931 representation change completed a rapid reorientation of Southern Baptist organized life that began with the first Executive Committee's formation in 1917. Robert A. Baker noted that the society-type holdovers when the Southern Baptist Convention was founded had left "congenital tensions" that had dogged the Convention for years. One of these was benevolent centrality rather than denominational solidarity. A second was a corollary financing of this benevolent work by designated giving rather than denominational support, and the third was representation based on financial gifts. The denominational approach to ministry, though helped by the founding of the Sunday School Board in 1891 and the Relief and Annuity Board in 1918, really began to solidify with the development of an Executive Committee between 1916–27. The undesignated giving was facilitated by the Cooperative Program of 1925, and the representation change from financial to church messengers broadened the denominational base and consensus needed to fully realize the convention method.[15]

Thus, 1931 constituted a watershed year in the development of the Convention and its constituency and became a very important factor not only in terms of dramatic later growth but in the battles that developed in Southern Baptist life, beginning in the late 1970s.

Landmark Influence

Was the change in representation a triumph for Landmarkism? Robert A. Baker, in his 1972 history of Southern Baptists, denied that it was. He noted that Landmark concepts favored a delegated church representation, while the 1931 amendment called for a designated church representation. In a telling point, he said, "Landmarkers asserted that the Great Commission was given to churches only; the 1931 amendment says that the Great Commission was given to individuals, and no authority is needed from the churches to legitimize its perceivings."[16]

Baker felt that the tenor of the times, as mentioned earlier, and the failure of the society method to deliver the funds necessary for a far-reaching Convention program were much more significant than the Landmark concept. Others think that this new representation plan more nearly fit the potential of the Cooperative Program and the way funds were actually collected through the Cooperative Program than had the previous one.

Undoubtedly what W. W. Barnes referred to as a "deposit" in the minds of Southern Baptists, i.e., the Landmark focus on the primacy of the local church, aided the move. Hugh Wamble said the whole move was compatible with Landmark views.[17] It did probably represent a triumph of western Southern Baptists' convictions over deep south Southern Baptists' traditions, however.

The Depression

Less than a year after Baptist Honor Day and the double devastation of the two defalcations, Baptists' recovery efforts received a serious setback with the stock market crash of October 1929. It would be history's benchmark for the beginning of what has since been called the Great Depression.

While the two boards were struggling with defalcation and debt in 1928, stock prices were going up, up, up. Urbanization, fed by immigration and the failure of the small farm, was a phenomenon and a problem. Consumerism was led by automobiles and the radio.[18]

Despite the fact that from 1921 to 1929 industrial output had nearly doubled in the United States with the mechanization of much of its industry led by auto assembly lines, some noted nervously that one-third of the booming income was going to just 5 percent of the population and 87 percent of the nation was still getting by on less than $2500 a year.[19]

Some complained that society was moving to a place where status was determined by "styles of leisure and comsumption" and the work ethic and moral fiber of rural America was being lost. Preachers blamed much of the degradation on the modernism of Darwin and the moral impact of Freud.[20]

The Eighteenth Amendment, ratified in 1919 to prohibit the manufacture, selling, or transport of alcoholic beverages, had been a triumph for Baptist leadership, but it had spawned a massive, illegal venture which seemed to have fallen largely into the hands of gangsters by the late 1920s. When Herbert Hoover took office in early 1929, America's hopes were running high, but all of that was shattered in October.

In the next three years the economy went through a disastrous free fall. By 1932, American industry had dropped to less than half of its 1929 volume. New investments had gone from $10 billion a year to $1 billion a year.[21]

On a single day in April of 1932, in the heart of Southern Baptist territory, it was said that one-fourth of the state of Mississippi "fell under the auctioneer's hammer."[22]

National income was cut in half during these three years and the unemployed numbers soared to over fifteen million. Stories of beggars and people freezing to death and children being sold in desperation began to appear in the newspapers.

Southern Baptists, unlike that portion of the country which had been prospering before the collapse, had for some years been under pressed conditions. While gifts to state conventions had risen from $3.5 million in 1925 to $5.5 million in 1929, the Cooperative Program had gotten off to a dismal start as gifts to SBC causes dropped from $4.6 million to $2.2 million.[23]

By late 1932, as the nation faced a presidential election, the country was in a near state of anarchy and demanding change. New York's governor, Franklin D. Roosevelt, was the political answer. He took over as president in March of 1933 at a time when banks were failing everywhere, and the stock market had closed. With his bank holiday, his first New Deal measures, and his first fireside chat of March 12, 1933, Roosevelt took steps to stabilize the country. By the end of the year, the Twenty-first Amendment was ratified, repealing prohibition.

A. J. Barton, who had led Southern Baptists in their temperance pursuits, called it "the greatest backward step in economic sanity and moral welfare legislation ever taken by a great people." He urged that Southern Baptists "buy dry and say why."[24]

Struggle to Survive

These were the conditions with which Austin Crouch had to cope in his new leadership role at the Executive Committee. Its seriousness was driven home in September 1930, when a litany of dismal reports was capped off by a report from L. R. Scarborough of Southwestern Seminary.

"Brethren, we are through at Southwestern." Choking with emotion according to the reports, he told of faculty salaries unpaid and nothing with which to pay expenses. "Here is my resignation and I turn over to you the seminary property. You'll have to sell it to pay our debts, and Southwestern will go out of existence."

A stunned silence followed before, in dramatic fashion, Southern Seminary president, John R. Sampey, said, "I may lose my job for what I am about to say. Southern Seminary has some income from endowment on which we can live. I move that Southern Seminary's apportionment be cut and the difference given to Southwestern."[25] The generous act helped, but the problems persisted.

That the situation was worldwide in scope was equally evident at the Foreign Mission Board. After the Foreign Mission Board's J. F. Love died from exhaustion on May 3, 1928, and as the Board still struggled with debt and their defalcation experience, the critical search for leadership was undertaken. When efforts to secure George W. Truett and several others failed, the Board turned to one of Love's associates, T. B. Ray.

Ray took over in 1929 at the most difficult period since the Civil War. In the previous three years, eighty-two missionaries had resigned from overseas appointment and nine had died in service. Only twelve new missionaries had been appointed. The Foreign Mission Board had no choice but to retrench, yet it could not do so fast enough. The Board continued to incur more debt, record fewer gifts, and face a more and more uncertain future.[26]

In October 1931, Ray was asked to take a staff position again, and a committee was appointed to nominate a new executive secretary. It took them nearly a year to convince Charles E. Maddry to accept. Maddry, who had graduated from Southern Baptist Theological Seminary and served as pastor of churches in North Carolina and Texas, had been serving as executive secretary of a specially constituted promotion committee to help with the Cooperative Program. He had served earlier as the general secretary of North Carolina Baptists.[27]

Maddry was fifty-six years old when he took over in January of 1933. His position was analogous to that of Franklin Roosevelt—he first had to deal with the Richmond banks to which the Board owed over $1 million and who were demanding immediate payment. Maddry and L. Howard Jenkins, a Richmond layman who had been elected as chairman of the Foreign Mission Board, finally convinced the banks to give them additional time. They promised that they would repay every cent if given the opportunity to continue to operate.[28]

The bankers agreed to the critical concession. The Board had reported to the Southern Baptist Convention in 1932 the loss of nearly a quarter of its force in the previous six years. It had been able to appoint only three missionaries in 1931, one in 1932, and had to detain thirty from returning to the fields in 1932 until funds were available. When Maddry took over, 397 missionaries were under appointment, but many of those were at home.[29]

After the Richmond banks agreed to work with the Foreign Mission Board, Maddry began to return missionaries to the field. In 1933 the Board reappointed eight missionaries and appointed nineteen new ones.

By 1936, more normal operations emboldened Maddry to reorganize the operations of the Foreign Mission Board. He set up area offices for the Orient, for Latin America, and for Africa and named M. T. Rankin, W. C. Taylor, and George Greene respectively to head those positions.[30]

The story was much the same at the Home Mission Board, where J. B. Lawrence renegotiated the Board's debt with the banks and then began some adroit retrenchment. Lawrence led the Board to turn over the El Paso Sanitarium to a local physician and later traded the property to the Foreign Mission Board, which began to use it as a publishing house. Lawrence terminated the Board's mountain school program, turning such efforts over to local groups where possible.[31]

The Home Mission Board had always been more in jeopardy in difficult times than had its sister board, first because of the aggressiveness of the North's Home Mission Society and later because of overlapping roles with state conventions' mission efforts. Following the disclosures in 1927 and 1928, again some thought that the Home Board should be abolished or at least combined with the Foreign Mission Board. George W. Truett, president of the Southern Baptist Convention when news of the embezzlement broke in 1928, and other Convention leaders, argued persuasively, however, that the original wisdom was right and that the Convention should hold its course.[32]

The Home Mission Board's missionary force dipped to a low of 106 in 1930 before Lawrence and his colleagues were able to stabilize operations and begin the long, slow recovery. Even as Maddry reorganized the Foreign

Mission Board, Lawrence readjusted the ministry of the Home Mission Board to the new realities, and a Department of Evangelism, reestablished in 1936, found special favor in evangelistical minded Southern Baptists' ranks.

Hundred Thousand Club

Nothing burdened Baptist leaders, however, quite so much as the awesome debt their agencies carried. Debt service took the heart out of giving and the Executive Committee, meeting in April 1933, struggled with solutions. Of all the ideas advanced, the one that found the most favor was the brainchild of a thirty-nine-year-old pastor from St. Joseph, Missouri, Frank Edward Tripp. Called the Baptist Hundred Thousand Club, its unabashed goal was "the liquidation of the present debt of all the agencies of the Southern Baptist Convention."[33]

At once simple and comprehensive, Tripp's plan envisioned a membership of one hundred thousand persons paying one dollar per month over and above their regular subscription to the church budget. For the more prosperous, a Luther Rice Memorial Membership at ten dollars per month was available.

To facilitate the plan, Tripp proposed a general leader, a state leader in each state, an associational leader in each association, and naturally, a leader in each church. W. B. Johnson would have been delighted with the comprehensive denominational look of the effort.

Tripp's church members, backing their pastor, gave him a leave of absence to lead the ambitious enterprise while continuing his salary. This, plus the pledge of the Sunday School Board to bear all promotional expenses, meant that every penny raised would find its way to debt retirement.[34]

The Baptist Hundred Thousand Club produced $37,588.28 its first year. Within three years it forwarded $191,296.88 to convention agencies for debt retirement and, before the task was accomplished in 1943, had given $2,627,822.36. Its success bred concern among state Baptist convention officials also struggling with debt in both their state efforts and the many institutions within their borders. This led to a memorial presented to the Southern Baptist Convention at its meeting in Memphis in 1935 to allow the Baptist Hundred Thousand Club to help state causes also. South Carolina Baptists joined by several other states opposed the broader purpose, but the club was enlarged in 1937 to allow six states to participate.[35]

After three years, Tripp declined to serve longer and returned fulltime to his generous and patient congregation. Recognizing the enormity of the club's role in Southern Baptist life, the Executive Committee, in 1936, expressed "undying gratitude" to Tripp and the St. Joseph church for the service and sacrifice "which to a large extent saved our mission causes." No small credit for the Convention's final emergence from debt was due to Frank Tripp and his far-sighted church.[36]

When Tripp could not be enticed to leave his pastorate for a permanent position, the Executive Committee elected its own president, J. E. Dillard, pastor of Southside Baptist Church in Birmingham, Alabama, as Director of Promotion for the Cooperative Program and the Baptist Hundred Thousand Club. The Cooperative Program, which struggled throughout this period to take hold in Baptist life, undoubtedly inherited the momentum of the Baptist Hundred Thousand Club after its final victory.

Migration

As Southern Baptist Convention agencies struggled with debt and retrenchment, Baptist state conventions and a host of institutions sponsored by them also struggled. Many colleges begun earlier perished. Those that survived did so on the strength of dedicated sacrifice.

Faculty members at Hardin-Simmons University in Abilene, Texas, gave up their salaries to help that institution as it struggled with debt and shortfalls during the hard times.[37]

And hard times were everywhere. Farmers who lost their farms in Mississippi and Alabama moved west only to find farmers there leaving a dust bowl for the orchards and crops of Arizona, Colorado, and California.

In 1935 most Southern Baptist churches were still rural churches. The depression had worked a special hardship on many of them and their struggling members. The famed Oklahoma and Arkansas displacement to the West Coast fictionalized in John Steinbeck's *Grapes of Wrath* included many, many Baptists. These Baptists, many of them espousing strong Landmark positions, often felt uncomfortable in the Northern Baptist churches they found in the West. Consequently, Southern Baptist churches soon developed there.[38]

Arizona Baptists

Under the leadership of the North's Home Mission Society, Baptist work began in the Arizona territory during the Civil War. But Southern Baptists had their eye on the western regions as early as 1909, when a report included sentiment that "the time will soon come when Arizona and Southern California will be recognized as belonging to the Southern Baptist Convention."[39]

Seventy-two members from the Calvary Baptist Church in Phoenix formed the First Southern Baptist Church in 1921 after a dispute over comity restrictions agreed to by the Arizona Baptist Convention, which was affiliated with Northern Baptists. The Calvary Church had itself split from the First Baptist Church of Phoenix over perceived liberalism. Its pastor was C. M. Rock, a North Carolinian. Also in 1921, Calvary Baptist Church sent messengers to the Southern Baptist Convention in Memphis where they were welcomed warmly by presiding officer George Truett. The next year they joined the Southwestern Baptist Association of New Mexico. Ten other Arizona Baptist churches followed suit. When distance became a limiting factor, these churches formed the Gambrell Memorial Association and affiliated with the New Mexico Baptist Convention.[40]

This same group of churches organized the Baptist General Convention of Arizona on September 21, 1928, and petitioned immediately for affiliation with the Southern Baptist Convention. Despite conflict with Northern Baptists over this and despite old-line Southern Baptist leadership opposition, the Southern Baptist Convention in 1929, with George Truett presiding, voted to receive the churches from the Arizona Convention. That they did so was due in no small part to a report from a committee that included such notables as E. Y. Mullins, I. J. Van Ness, and B. D. Gray.[41] At this point ten churches were affiliated with the state convention cooperating with the Southern Baptists, and thirty-six churches in the original state convention were still cooperating with the Northern Baptist Convention. In 1929, they were given representation on the Home Mission Board, the Sunday School Board, and the Executive Committee.

Stability among Arizona's southern-oriented Baptists was hard to come by until S. S. Bussell, New Mexico Baptists' Sunday School secretary, agreed to take over in 1931. In 1932 they began publishing what quickly became the Arizona Baptist Beacon.

Both the Southern Baptist Convention's Sunday School Board and its Home Mission Board gave financial assistance to the Arizona group.[42] Like the New Mexico Baptist Convention, and indeed much of the developing western work, new church subsidies represented a problem as stewardship committments lagged. A reducing contribution strategy worked to offset this early ailment.

Baptist life in the West had a strong Landmark tinge through the years as evidenced by the famous "Apostle to the West," Willis J. Ray. Ray headed the Arizona Convention beginning in 1944. Because Arizona became the initiator and sheltering arms for new work all over the West and Northwest, at one point Ray presided over Convention activities stretching from Mexico to Canada and including ten states.[43]

Hard Times Persist

While this expansion should have helped Southern Baptists' giving, the Cooperative Program, though bolstered by the 1931 change of representation which more nearly fit its style, could not stem the tide of recession and displacement. Total gifts in 1930 reached $32,000,600, but by 1935 they had fallen to $29,000,188, reflecting the widespread economic difficulty. The effects of the depression are seen even more clearly when these figures are compared to the $39 million given in 1925.[44]

On the other hand, Southern Baptist churches numbered over 24,000 by 1935 with a membership of 4.3 million compared to 3.6 million ten years earlier with approximately the same number of churches. Such numbers may have reflected the beginning of Baptist membership inflation, however, because Baptist churches tended not to drop members who had moved unless their letters were formally requested by some other church. Often, in Baptist frontier areas in the West, such formalities were neglected. It may have also reflected the demise of many rural churches while urban churches continued to grow.

In the meantime, the democratic New Deal under President Roosevelt struggled with the nation's depression. Much of it, like the Tennesee Valley Authority created in 1938 and the Rural Electrification Administration set up in 1935, affected Baptist life. Within twenty years these programs meant that nine out of ten American farms which had started the period without electricity gave way to nine out of ten farms with electric power.

Soil conservation programs followed the great drought that brought about the dust bowl of the early 1930s, and the Civilian Conservation Corps (CCC) employed displaced youths and in so doing moved many young Baptists to new areas. The Works Progress Administration (WPA) and many other federal projects, including the National Youth Administration, followed on the heels of a Federal Housing Administration.

These programs gave jobs to massive ranks of the unemployed. One report claimed that by the beginning of 1935 one out of every six persons in the nation was receiving some kind of public assistance.[45]

As Southern Baptist workers displaced by agricutural failures moved north to find work in industry, they encountered the rapid growth of unions and saw the nation respond with a National Labor Relations Board.

By 1935 the depression seemed to be yielding a bit to all of these efforts, and in the spring of 1937 production for the first time rose above the 1929 levels. But in that same fall another recession struck, and as late as 1939 ten million Americans were still unemployed.[46]

Holcomb and BSSB

Tough times inevitably spawn strong leaders and call them to the helm of societies and institutions. Southern Baptists were fortunate during these trying periods to have outstanding leaders such as Austin Crouch with the Executive Committee, J. B. Lawrence at the Home Mission Board, and Charles E. Maddry at the Foreign Mission Board. Beginning in 1935 T. L. Holcomb joined this impressive group as he took over from I. J. Van Ness at the Sunday School Board.

Unlike the mission boards, the Sunday School Board managed to remain financially in the black during Van Ness's era and was stronger than ever when Holcomb took it over in 1935. However, Van Ness's latter years were marred by a power struggle with the chairman of the elected Board, W. F. Powell, pastor of Nashville's First Baptist Church.[47]

The solid financial condition of the Sunday School Board stood out as quite a counterpoint to the debt and discouragment everywhere else. As early as 1907, the Sunday School Board's J. M. Frost had given a $20,000 check for the founding of the Woman's Missionary Training School. That same financial stability enabled the Sunday School Board under Van Ness to take over the Baptist Young People's Union, assume the retreat property of Ridgecrest, and help innumerable times with Home and Foreign Mission Board needs.[48]

In almost comic contrast to the towering C. E. Maddry, Thomas Luther Holcomb stood just over five feet. He was pastor of a big church, the First Baptist Church of Oklahoma City and a member of the Sunday School Board representing Oklahoma at the time he was elected leader.

Holcomb initially dealt with the question of who was in charge by leaving no doubt that he was. But he was equally adroit at enlisting top lieutenants, including J. N. Barnette, Jerry Lambdin, and Frank Leavell. Even as Maddry would do at the Foreign Mission Board and Lawrence had done at the Home Mission Board, Holcomb set about to reorganize the forty-four-year-old institution.

Holcomb was above all a promoter. While Van Ness had largely been an editor most comfortable in operations, Holcomb hit the road. No secretary had done so since J. M. Frost's initial year of service. In short order, Holcomb set out a five-year plan to culminate in 1941 on the Board's fiftieth anniversary. The genius of Holcomb's plan centered on a broad-based promotional organization utilizing associations and volunteer workers.

By 1941 the effort had added 1,839 Sunday Schools with nearly half a million new scholars. The number of training unions jumped by two thousand and registered a quarter of a million new participants.[49] Though it was seldom trumpeted, this development had significant impact on the publishing revenues of the Sunday School Board. Even in the midst of the depression era, the Sunday School Board achieved dramatic results.

Women in the Gap

Less obvious as one reads history, but increasingly significant with the passage of time, was the evolving role of women in the nation's experience and in Southern Baptist life. The strong and pivotal leader of early Woman's Missionary Union, Fannie E. S. Heck, appointed a personal-service committee of WMU's Executive Committee in 1910 designed to help women focus on the needs of the poor, neglected, and outcast of their own neighborhoods.[50]

Even before the depression, personal service work reported included mission Sunday Schools, hospital and prisoner visitation, relief work, sewing schools, day nurseries, work with Jews, rescue work, immigrant work, clubs for boys and girls, cooking schools, and service to mill workers. Many of the latter were women in very poor working conditions.

The concept of personal service motivated WMU Training School to espouse settlement houses in 1912 which were the forerunners of the Good Will Centers that by 1929 numbered twenty-six. While such women's leaders as Mrs. W. C. James stressed the relationship of personal service to soul-winning, the pressing social needs of people in the lower stratas of southern communities during the 1930s found the women organized and motivated to react. Mrs. W. J. Cox, WMU president in 1930, appointed Una Roberts Lawrence, a native of Arkansas, as southwide personal service chairman.

Lawrence, born Una Roberts to schoolteachers in 1893, graduated from the Training School in 1919 and the next year became young people's secretary of WMU in Arkansas. She married Irvin Lawrence, a railroad man, in 1921 and spent almost three decades with the organization. A prolific writer on human needs, Lawrence helped women learn how to conduct community surveys and how to link the churches with community agencies. She was Lottie Moon's first biographer.

Mrs. P. B. Lowrance of Tennessee and Eureka Whitaker of Kentucky also took part in this key ministry to open up new vistas for women with heretofore restricted visions of ministry. Lowrance promoted black ministries with "Open Doors" and reached out to Jews through "Friends of Israel."[51]

These efforts led to a professional position with WMU in 1941 as Mary Christian of Georgia led the women to change the program from personal service to community missions. She also stressed soul-winning as an integral part of all that was done.

The term "missions" continued to highlight the women's first love and not only enlisted the support of women but, however quietly, the number of women under appointment in both home and foreign missions increased signficantly.

Presiding

At the beginning of this period the beloved and broadly acclaimed George W. Truett of First Baptist Church, Dallas, was presiding over the Southern Baptist Convention. His poise and reputation undoubtedly helped the Convention cope with the hammer blows of defalcation, debt and depression. In 1934 Truett was elected president of the Baptist World Alliance, a position that Southern Baptist E. Y. Mullins had held in the early 1920s.

W. J. McGlothlin of South Carolina followed Truett as president of the Convention. A native of Tennessee, McGlothlin graduated from Bethel College in Kentucky and Southern Baptist Theological Seminary. Like Crawford Howell Toy and William Whitsitt, he studied in the University of Berlin where he secured his Ph.D. degree in 1901. He was already on the faculty at Southern Seminary in the Church History department at the time of the Whitsitt controversy, though involved in his studies abroad. In 1919 he became president of Furman University, where he was serving at the time he was elected president of the Southern Baptist Convention in 1930.

McGlothlin died during the convention year in 1933 and was replaced by much-appreciated Fred Brown of Knoxville, Tennessee's First Baptist Church. Brown's health, however, permitted him to serve only one year, though he helped birth the Hundred Thousand Club.

Reflecting the times, Southern Baptist Convention attendance, which hit a record 8,359 in its 1920 meeting in Washington, D.C., began a steep decline in 1926, falling below 5,000. It dropped below 4,000 at the 1928 meeting in Chattanooga and below 3,000 in 1932 in St. Petersburg, Florida, where a registration of 2,178 marked the lowest point since 1917. It may have been the excitement of the Baptist Hundred Thousand Club or the fiery presence of J. Frank Norris that caused a sharp jump to 4,435 in 1934 when the convention met in Fort Worth.[52]

Leadership continued to move about the developing Southern Baptist Convention as M. E. Dodd of Louisiana succeeded Tennessee's Fred Brown in 1934. Dodd, a native of Tennessee, had been serving the First Baptist Church of Shreveport since 1912. He had been president of the Louisiana Baptist Convention and had been influential in founding what later became New Orleans Baptist Theological Seminary and in launching the Cooperative Program.

Dodd, in turn, handed the gavel to John R. Sampey, who was by then president of Southern Seminary, having succeeded E. Y. Mullins who died in 1928. It was Sampey who had opposed Whitsitt's remaining as president on the basis of the financial harm it was doing the seminary.[53]

Sampey had been committed to Foreign Mission service as had Toy and Whitsitt before him, and even as they had been convinced by John A. Broadus to stay at the seminary, so had Sampey. He was already sixty-six years old when he became president of Southern Seminary and was seventy-three when he was elected president of the Southern Baptist Convention. He demonstrated financial adroitness as well as denominational skills in handling Southern Seminary's debt during the 1930s.

In 1938 Sampey handed the gavel to Lee R. Scarborough, who had been president of Southwestern Baptist Theological Seminary since 1914. Whether this represented further evidence of the rivalry that had been in place between these two institutions since the days of its founding by B. H. Carroll is not clear. It was a matter of taking turns by then, however, since Scarborough yielded the gavel to Baptist Bible Institute's president, W. W. Hamilton, who served that institution from 1928 to 1942 and presided over the Southern Baptist Convention in 1941 and 1942 when it met in Birmingham and San Antonio respectively.

Fundamentalism

J. Frank Norris lost a lot of his following after he shot and killed a Fort Worth citizen named Chipps in 1926. Another questionable fire destroyed his church in 1929, and he was again suspected of arson. Though he was acquitted in both cases, these episodes turned aside many more reasonable people from Norris's form of fundamentalism. For the next dozen years, he continued to attack George W. Truett and Southern Baptist causes, especially Baylor and Southwestern Seminary.

With the demise of the Baptist Bible Union, Norris in 1931, organized the Premillennial Fundamental Missionary Fellowship, later called the Premillennial Baptist Missionary Fellowship. The same group still later took the more expansive nomenclature of World Fundamentalist Baptist Mission Fellowship, and in 1939 a Fundamentalist Baptist Bible Institute was developed in connection with his church.

After 1935, Norris was pastor of two churches, commuting between the Temple Baptist Church of Detroit, Michigan, and the First Baptist Church of Fort Worth, Texas. In part, this was the result of financial difficulties caused by the depression and his effort to broaden his leadership in fundamentalism.

But a fundamentalist spirit was not wholly a western phenomena in Southern Baptist life as a 1939 incident at Mercer University, now located at Macon, Georgia, later revealed. There a group of fundamentalist-minded students brought charges against professor John D. Freeman, one of the more popular Bible teachers on the faculty. Essentially he was charged with espousing higher criticism theories of the Bible and Darwinism resulting in questions about the literalness of Scripture and the validity of miracles. The student body was sharply divided in the debate that followed. A student named Chauncey Daley led those supporting the professor while a young man named John Birch led the fundamentalist students seeking Freeman's ouster. The trustees cleared the professor, but then let him go as a way to appease all sides.[54]

John Birch later attended J. Frank Norris's school in Fort Worth before becoming an independent missionary to China and a possible intelligence officer. He was an early victim of communist insurgents in China and an anti-communist society was named for him two decades later. Daley later became the outspoken editor of the Kentucky state paper and a central figure in the controversy that broke out in 1979.[55]

Foreign Missions

Under Charles Maddry, the Foreign Mission Board began slow but definite progress in the late 1930s. After his 1936 reorganization of the Board's overseas administration into three areas, a needed sense of stability began to grow. Much of the attention focused on China, however, where M. T. Rankin was area secretary when the Japanese-Chinese war broke out in 1937.

Baptist work in China peaked in 1924 when Southern Baptists had 287 missionaries stationed there. The Great Depression started for Baptists in the South a lot earlier than it did for the rest of the country. The murder of Southern Baptist missionaries in China dropped that number to 196 in 1933, though strong efforts were made to strengthen it from 1936 on. One such addition was a young physician named William Wallace of Knoxville, Tennessee. Bill Wallace was assigned to South China's Wuchow Hospital, 220 miles inland from a strong Baptist center in Canton. His fifteen-year career ended in martyrdom at the hands of Chinese Communists and was an island of compassion in a sea of the tragic uncertainty that flooded China during those years.[56]

In 1931, a dramatic revival broke out in the Shantung province, which had been the scene of such distressing Baptist experiences during the days of Crawford, Hartwell, and Moon. While portions of it had strong charismatic dimensions, many Baptists who participated in it said it was one of the life-changing religious revivals in history.[57]

When the Japanese attacked China in 1937 they struck quickly in the coastal areas where many Baptists' efforts were located, and Baptist mission work was divided by Japanese occupation. The president of the Baptist University of Shanghai was assassinated in 1938, and the all-China Seminary that began in 1939 at Kaifeng managed only one session before the war closed it.

M. Theron Rankin was forced to move eight new missionaries to the Philippines for Chinese language study in 1940.[58]

A pair of prize additions to the missionary force in China went out in 1939 in the persons of Baker James Cauthen and his wife, Eloise Glass Cauthen. Cauthen, a popular speaker throughout the Southwest, served as pastor of a strong church in Fort Worth and was professor of missions at

Southwestern Baptist Theological Seminary. His wife, Eloise, the daughter of missionaries, W. B. and Eunice Glass, had always wanted to return to China. Cauthen, much like those whom John Broadus had convinced to stay at Southern Seminary, was talked into staying at Southwestern Seminary. In 1939, however, he experienced what he felt was an unmistakable sense of God's leadership, sought appointment with the Foreign Mission Board, and soon sailed with his wife and two small children toward war-torn China.[59]

He told a friend before leaving, "Do not worry. This is God's will for us. If we die in Hong Kong harbor and never set foot on Chinese soil, it was still God's will for us."[60] Cauthen was perhaps alluding to an experience that a pair of early Baptist missionaries going to China had experienced when they perished on their ship during a storm in Hong Kong harbor before they could begin work there.

While the Cauthens studied the language in North China, Bill Wallace and colleagues at the Wuchow Hospital in South China were forced to flee Japanese advances and move the whole hospital on river rafts farther west into free China in an effort of heroism and sacrifice that was later retold in a commercial motion picture.

Missionaries in Japan during this period experienced more and more government interference. All Christian work was forced into a United Church of Japan in 1940, but throughout the months that followed, growing tensions and pressures caused a number of missionaries to withdraw until Maxfield Garrott was the only Southern Baptist missionary in Japan in 1941.[61]

The war in Europe broke out in 1939, interrupting Baptist missions not only in those countries, but also in Africa. When Secretary Maddry visited Nigeria in 1938, a mission of approximately forty missionaries was working among nearly 21,000 national Baptists in over two hundred churches.

Upon returning to the States in 1939, Maddry recommended that the Foreign Mission Board elect George W. Sadler as Secretary for Africa, Europe, and the Middle East. Sadler, who had served as a missionary from 1914, had to return home in 1931 and held a pastorate in Liberty, Missouri, before taking on the task at Maddry's request. The desired expansion in that part of the world had to await the conclusion of the exploding turmoil of World War II.

Breaching Regionality

The Home Mission Board, which reported 833 missionaries in 1925, saw that number attenuated to 174 by financial woes and the depression that followed by 1935. Baptisms, which numbered over 1,900 in 1925, were reported at just over 3,800 ten years later.[62]

J. B. Lawrence was able to rebuild from that point, however, and by the close of World War II had more than six hundred missionaries at work.

Home Mission efforts included work among Indians, Baptist centers in certain urban areas such as New Orleans, major projects with various state conventions, continued efforts in the Appalachians though no longer involving schools, and more and more emphasis in the West. A number of missionaries followed the major migration of Baptists into Arizona and California.

Southern Baptist work in California dated as far back as 1855, when a former missionary to China, J. Lewis Shuck, began work in San Francisco's Chinese community. This was the same year that Mexico ceded the state to the United States and one year before the famed gold rush with its "forty niners." The glitter of that promise helped that state's admission to the Union the next year.

Shuck's major success, however, was an anglo church in Sacramento. When he returned east to North Carolina five years later, little was left of this early effort and what there was was affiliated with the North's Home Mission Society. Subsequent Baptist efforts in California were largely affiliated with Northern Baptists.

The first Baptist church in California related to Southern Baptists was established at Shafter, near Bakersfield in 1936. Every charter member had been a Southern Baptist elsewhere, revealing the impact of migration during the depression years.[63] Three years later, a small association was organized with churches in the San Joaquin Valley. In the aggressive style of Arizona a decade earlier, fourteen churches, sympathetic with the Southern Baptist Convention and led by Sam Wilcoxon, who was then pastor of the Shafter church, organized a state convention in 1940 and began to press for affiliation with the Southern Baptist Convention in 1941 in anticipation of the Convention's meeting that year in Birmingham, Alabama. In typical Southern Baptist style, a committee was appointed to "study the question." One of the members of that committee, J. B. Rounds of Oklahoma, went to California that spring for two and a half months of revival meetings.

When the Southern Baptist Convention met in 1942 in war-time San Antonio, it was dominated by messengers from the Southwest. The committee could not make a solid recommendation and asked for an extension of their study. Oklahoma was once again the source of an alternate plan. J. B. Rounds, fresh from his California evangelistic efforts, brought a minority report from the committee urging that California Baptists be immediately accepted. A number of messengers protested vigorously, pointing out that this would be a major break with agreements that had been worked out in the previous comity sessions at Fortress Monroe, Old Point Comfort, and Hot Springs between 1894 and 1912. The Convention, however, overwhelmingly approved admission of California Baptists.[64]

The action was almost as far-reaching as the representative change of 1931 and also as much a product of the times. Meeting in San Antonio undoubtedly helped win the California vote, as messengers from Texas, Arkansas, Oklahoma, and Louisiana dominated. These were also the prime feeder states for the new western Baptist constituency. The Kentucky Baptist paper suggested shortly afterwards that all boundaries be abandoned.[65]

California Southern Baptists in 1942 numbered approximately three thousand members, worshiping in thirty churches in seventeen counties. But with so many Southern Baptists in California following the depression and now with the war effort, these churches were strategically located for thousands of homesick and transplanted southerners. By 1944 California led every state in the Southern Baptist Convention in organizing new Sunday Schools.[66]

That same year Golden Gate Baptist Theological Seminary was founded and began classes with sixty-five students. By 1949 it required 30 percent of California Baptists' budget and began looking toward the Southern Baptist Convention for help.

Rejecting Ecumenism

Baptists, with their Landmark background, had fought being called "Protestants" by government in both the First World War and the Second World War. Though missionary executives had participated in international missionary conferences held throughout the early part of the twentieth century, the Convention had declined to send delegates to a World Conference on Faith and Order in 1932. Although John R. Sampey, while president of the Southern Baptist Convention, attended a conference on Faith and Order sponsored by the World Council of Churches at Edinburgh in

1937, he refused to address the group, in recognition of Southern Baptist sensibilities.

All of this came to a head in 1940 when the World Council of Churches issued Southern Baptists a direct invitation to join them. A committee headed by George W. Truett tactfully declined, pointing out that the ecclesiological basis of the Convention did not permit it to become a member, as the Convention could not authoritatively speak or act for the churches affiliated with it.[67]

A minority report was also filed that urged Southern Baptists to open avenues of cooperation with the world Christian community through the Council. It was signed by such Baptists as Ryland Knight of Georgia, Theodore Adams of Virginia, and Blake Smith of Texas.[68]

The minority position toward ecumenicity continued to ferment among some Southern Baptist leaders, who wanted to define further their role in relation to other Christian bodies and the task ahead.

World War II

Though the war in Europe had raged since 1939 between the axis powers led by Hitler's Germany and the allied powers led by England and France and continued in Asia between Japan and China, the United States fought hard to maintain neutrality despite clear cut sentiments of support.

A strong isolation spirit had developed following World War I and rejection of the League of Nations that Woodrow Wilson had helped fashion. At least one Baptist leader had fought for Wilson's dream. In 1920, J. B. Gambrell had decried efforts of "sordid, self-centered souls throughout the nation to discredit the present administration and play the American people down into a policy of selfish isolation, while the world bleeds and starves."[69]

But the Gambrells of that era did not prevail and the resulting isolationist spirit may have contributed to the intensity of the economic depression that racked the United States in subsequent years. America First forces tried to keep the United States out of another European war and saw little reason to be concerned about what was going on in China, other than how it might affect America's interests, missionary or otherwise.

That attitude changed when the Japanese attacked Pearl Harbor on Sunday morning, December 7, 1941. The stealth and suddenness of the attack united America as nothing else had been able to do. Stunnned and outraged, the nation reacted dramatically. The depression was gone overnight as the United States surged into an industrial mobilization undreamed of before. Young Americans lined up at recruiting stations everywhere to fight the "Germans and the Japs." In America, itself, everybody went to work, including women in unprecedented numbers. The war changed social structures and population patterns and broke down cultural walls. Soon bombers and fighter planes and ships and equipment of all kinds were rolling off the assembly lines toward war fronts across two oceans.

Just as America's entrance in World War I had turned the tide, so America's entrance into World War II turned the fortunes of the embattled allies. Britain, which had held out dramatically against German bombers, became a base of American operations, along with North Africa and Australia. Soon the might of the West that had been awakened so suddenly began to overwhelm the Axis powers.

Historians and sociologists are still studying the impact of the war. Great advances in technology, including medicine and science, transportation and communication, ripple through the years. They also analyze the cold war that followed and the collapse of one whole section of the world order when that was over.

Baptists were very much a part of this total experience. Ministers became chaplains, even as college and, despite deferments, seminary students became soldiers, sailors, marines, and airmen. On their mission fields, Southern Baptists coped even as they had learned to do during the Civil War and, with the kind of leadership that was in place, managed to keep their work going in China and Africa and in Latin America, though the work in Europe and the Middle East went on the back burner. War encouraged religious feelings and church attendance grew dramatically. New churches sprang up with the displacement of Southern Baptists around the country.

By 1943 Charles E. Maddry announced that the Foreign Mission Board was debt free and by 1944 the Convention was debt free.[70]

Of course, the war did not leave Southern Baptists unscarred. Rufus Gray, one of the missionaries studying Chinese in the Philippines, perished in a Japanese labor camp. Other missionaries in China were imprisoned by the Japanese, and many of them spent much of the war in such places as the famous Shantung Compound. Some were repatriated early and made their way back to the States to assist churches in ministry opportunities here.[71]

Edwin Dozier, of the pioneering missionary family in Japan, and his wife Mary Ellen and family were evacuated to Hawaii to work with Japanese there. Quietly, he was pressed into military intelligence service to help unravel Japanese codes; some give him credit for the clue that allowed American intelligence to break a key Japanese code.[72]

Women

Women's roles in Southern Baptist life continued to focus in home and church roles as war came. Missions offered their main ministry opportunity, but war time mobilization would change prevailing mores dramatically on many fronts. Woman's Missionary Union continued to be Baptist women's most active arena.

The year after the Convention granted women messenger status, the women pledged $15 million to the Seventy-five Million Campaign and became self-supporting through the sales of their periodicals. In 1920 they began an offering for Ministerial Relief and Annuity in support of Southern Baptists' newest agency, and in 1925 they threw their weight behind the new Cooperative Program.

When the depression hit in 1929, WMU membership passed a half million and the dedication of women in the next decade was a significant factor in the Convention's agencies fortunes. WMU adopted a plan in 1933 to help the Foreign Mission Board retire its debts and by 1940 had pledged one million dollars to help retire all SBC debt. In 1945 women raised the first million-dollar Lottie Moon Christmas offering.

Yet Southern Baptist women remained sensitive to male concerns about their strength and role, and this may have fueled another internal conflict in 1944. A survey committee commissioned by the auxiliary that year was charged with a plan for post-war advance. When the report came before the organization's leadership in 1945, its recommendations so alarmed Kathleen Mallory that she sealed it in a vault. Its sticking points seemed to be a call for more churchwide involvement, stronger foreign roles, ties with women's schools in the seminaries, and a challenge to confront race relations. While the report did not become public, time did see the implementation of many of its recommendations. Kathleen Mallory may have seen it both as a threat to the auxiliary's ties with the SBC and as a leadership challenge, and she stepped down three years later after thirty-six years.[73]

Centennial

The Southern Baptist Convention had begun anticipating its centennial as early as 1939 when a Centennial Session Program Committee was formed. The plan was to celebrate the event in Atlanta on May 8–13, 1945. Despite the lingering depression and war in Europe and Asia, Southern Baptists were looking ahead, and in the 1939 session in Oklahoma City they also adopted a business and financial plan to guide the Convention and its agencies and institutions developed by the Executive Committee. They also tipped their hat to modernity by naming a radio committee to develop a ministry in radio broadcasting.

As Southern Baptists approached their centennial in 1945, they were rapidly fashioning a new worldview. At the Convention meeting in San Antonio in 1942, they elected Baylor University's Pat Neff as president, continuing the pattern of electing educators that had already given the gavel to Southern Seminary's Sampey, Southwestern's Scarborough, and the Bible Institute's Hamilton. Messengers also heard a report from the Social Service Commission calling for a statement to the world of "the great Baptist principles which we believe constitute the best expression of the true teachings of Jesus and New Testament Christianity." Subsequent to this report, a motion was made to appoint a committee to prepare "a declaration of faith and principles." Chaired by Southern Seminary's Ellis Fuller, the committee was a Southern Baptist Who's Who.[74]

Due to the war, the Convention did not convene in 1943, but did gather in 1944 in Atlanta, Georgia, with 4,301 messengers. The Statement of Principles report called for in the 1942 session was continued to the Centennial planned for 1945.

But this convention in Atlanta was a celebration despite the ongoing world conflict: Southern Baptists were out of debt. It had taken a war that put everyone to work and an inflationary environment to achieve it, but many people credit the sacrifices of the Hundred Thousand Club and new commitment to the Cooperative Program as the true facilitators.

The centerpiece of the Centennial was an evangelistic crusade, paired with a new stewardship effort to help Southern Baptists address the wreckage of war and the pressing needs of humanity. M. E. Dodd directed the Centennial Evangelistic Crusade, and as the First Baptist Church of Shreveport continued his pay, the Convention did not have to divert funds for the project. The ambitious goal of the crusade was one million converts. State, association, and church crusade committees were organized, and bands of personal soul-winners joined as prayer partners were hastily trained for their task and went forth in a biblical two-by-two fashion. Although the goal of one million was not reached, five hundred thousand converts were claimed in the biggest effort of its kind yet seen.

Giving took an equally giant step forward when church contributions for 1945 reached $98,458,425, a nearly $22,000,000 increase over the previous year.

But the war effort denied Southern Baptists their planned centennial celebration in 1945. Due to a government ban on large group meetings, they cancelled their annual session once again. A Baptist Hour program, aired on May 6, 1945, originated from the site of the Convention's founding at the historic First Baptist Church of Augusta. Its impressive evangelistic and stewardship numbers took a backseat to the celebration that summer of victory in Europe in June and over Japan in August.

Such momentous events may have taken the edge off the anniversary when it was finally celebrated in Miami, Florida, in 1946. The Sunday School Board had produced a film called "The Romance of a Century," which was shown in an evening celebration at the convention session. An address by Louie D. Newton of Atlanta, Georgia, on the 1946 occasion made such a good impression that he was handed the gavel by a majority of the 7,973 messengers gathered.[75]

A two-part Boyce Memorial history celebrating the Centennial had been commissioned in 1939 and funded by gifts from the daughters of Southern Seminary's founding president. The vision was for a first volume, encompassing Baptist history in America up to 1845, to be written by Rufus Weaver of the District of Columbia and for a second volume, focusing on Southern Baptists' first century, to be written by Southwestern Seminary's William W. Barnes; however, the ambitious project did not materialize. Chairman W. O. Carver reported in 1942 that Weaver had to abandon his project. In 1946 he reported that Barnes's work was "far-advanced" but had not been completed due to the illness and death of Barnes's wife. Infighting in the supervising committee, possibly reflecting old Southern-Southwestern rivalries, further delayed the project until 1954, when Porter Routh completed Barnes's manuscript.[76]

Yet Southern Baptists were not looking back. They were looking at the United States and the world with new eyes. One reason was that more of them than ever before had seen it firsthand through the armed services and the mobilization for war. Also, many of them had been forever dislodged from their traditional bases, and the California decision of 1942 had removed the last barriers to embracing the whole nation. The evangelistic and missionary spirit inherent in Southern Baptist life developed strongly during the nearly four years of war and waited for a chance to break forth.

Statement of Principles

The Committee on Statement of Baptist Principles, chaired by Southern Seminary's Ellis Fuller, published its statement in a 1945 annual report even though the Convention itself did not meet. Finally reported at the 1946 Convention, it claimed to state Baptist beliefs in place "at its Centennial meeting."[77]

Despite its potential significance, the Statement took a backseat to the centennial celebration and other business, including the adoption of a Capital Needs Budget, the creation of the Baptist Foundation, and a revised constitution that among other things set up a rotating plan for boards of trustees and a two-term limit. The constitutional change promised to broaden the tent of leadership participation for the task ahead.

The Statement's preamble explained that the document was meant "to state afresh the basic principles that we must proclaim to the world in our day." Clearly the writers intended a sincere effort to state who Southern Baptists were and what they hoped to do in the post-war world.

The report, taking a different approach from any prior confession, held that the doctrine of man was the true distinctive among Southern Baptists. It held that Baptists believed in (1) the value of the individual, (2) the competence of each man to deal with God and his fellowmen, (3) the rights and privileges of the individual, and (4) man's responsibility to receive fellowship with God and fulfill the purposes of God.[78]

The five doctrines that followed, "concerning all aspects of religious experience and life," were a distillation of dominant Southern Baptist thought and attracted no opposition at all. The first doctrine called for the experience of regeneration and a regenerate church membership. The second defined the church as local, "a voluntary fellowship of baptized believers," directly responsible to Christ. The church was to be a democratic body and its ministry was to be chosen by the church as the Holy Spirit led. It would be 1963 before a Southern Baptist doctrinal statement would acknowledge the larger concept of church. The third doctrinal principle focused on the New Testament as "the one and only authority in faith and practice" and defined it as the "divinely inspired record and interpretation of the supreme revelation of God through Jesus Christ." The fourth principle called for the separation of church and state as demanded by the above.

The final principle insisted on religious liberty as a basic right under God, including the right of individual worship and propaganda without the interference of the state.

Why these doctrinal statements were not referenced to the 1925 Statement of Faith, which was itself a restatement of the New Hampshire Confession of Faith of 1833, is not clear. Most likely the 1925 statement was aimed at the evolution controversy, while this document was aimed at the ecumenical movement and a postwar agenda. Without controversy to highlight it, Baptist state papers took little note of it, and neither the Barnes history nor subsequent efforts by Robert A. Baker or Leon McBeth referred to it. James Carter, in a Ph.D. dissertation at Southwestern Seminary, did ponder some of these questions, but he agreed that the 1946 Statement of Principles was a succinct and purely original Southern Baptist statement.

In the statement's application section, possibly the noblest ever produced by the body, the developing Southern Baptist agenda was most clear and, in retrospect, was its marching orders for the next three decades. It stressed four areas: (1) spiritual unity rather than ecclesiastical overlordship; (2) a world based upon the rights of all men, the ideas of brotherhood, justice and truth, and opposition to "principles of materialism, selfish nationalism, arrogant imperialism and power politics"; (3) the necessity of opposing inequities of basic rights and privileges in church and society which arise out of racial prides and prejudices, economic greed, and class distinctives; (4) the repudiation of "all forms of exploitation, manipulation or neglect and indifference on the part of any section of our human race by any other section on any and every pretext whatever."[79]

Into a Second Century

The end of World War II and the celebration of its centennial foretold the abandonment of any remaining isolationism among the Southern Baptist Convention. Ahead loomed a missionary and social program that would be a challenge for years to come.

This watershed and a concurrent changing of the guard was reflected in uniquely human terms in the 1946 meeting when memorials were presented for both George W. Truett, who had died on July 7, 1944, and Lee R. Scarborough, who passed away on April 10, 1945. Since there was no meeting in 1945, the Truett memorial was delayed until the 1946 Convention. Both men's old nemesis, J. Frank Norris, had written Scarborough as he lay dying in the hospital that they would meet in heaven.[80] At the same meeting

President Pat Neff presented Truett's young successor, W. A. Criswell, who preached his first convention sermon.[81]

Southern Baptists had seen Cooperative Program gifts of $7.8 million in 1941 grow to $21 million by 1946. Membership had gone from 5.2 million to over 6 million.

The Statement of Principles may have been the way Southern Baptist leaders envisioned themselves rather than the perceptions of the average church member. If so, the vision was an outgrowth of the denominational pride that had been nurtured partly by the successionism of early Landmarkism and partly by the triumphalism of the 1920s. But it also represented a coming of age on the part of Southern Baptists in the larger world of human affairs and was definitely focused in a new American pride as the preeminent world power.

The adversity of defalcation, debt, and depression and the change in representation, abandonment of regionality, and expanded worldview had somehow been interwoven. The Statement of Principles, however taken for granted, revealed Southern Baptists' belief, at least among the leadership, that they had come into being for a unique purpose that would unfold in the second century.

6

The Great Advance

1945–1964

When American planes dropped atomic bombs on Hiroshima and Nagasaki on August 6 and August 9 of 1945, the unprecedented destruction made it obvious the war was all but over. The carnage of the war, as the world rapidly discovered, had been terrible. Images of bombed cities and maimed, diseased, and displaced persons were prelude to the unfolding horror of the Jewish holocaust. America, its territory neither violated nor its cities destroyed, stood in sharp contrast to most of the other nations involved. It was a rare home, however, that was not touched by the war, and gold stars hanging in the windows of both rich and poor mutely testified to the loss of loved ones in every community throughout the land.

America emerged from the war as the world's great power with its industrial might fully developed, its citizens scattered to every corner of the

179

globe, and its commercial interests poised to expand rather than to rebuild as much of the world would have to do. However, through the Marshall Plan, America helped Europe and Japan rebuild.

The United Nations was organized in London on January 7, 1946, and then moved to New York City for its permanent headquarters.

As the men and women who had made up the armed forces flooded back to the country, they moved, almost en masse, to college and university campuses. By 1947 more than one million war veterans were enrolled in college under the G.I. Bill of Rights.[1]

Southern Baptists were part and parcel of this whole experience, but the war marked the beginning of a series of rapid changes for this previously regionally concentrated people as they marked their centennial. When, as previously noted, Southern Baptists finally observed their centennial in 1946, there was much to commemorate and to celebrate. There was even more to assimilate. A new urban South had emerged, and the thriving city church emerged with it.

Resurgence of Religion

Many veterans like Buckner Fanning of Dallas, Texas, came back from the war committed to Christian ministry. Fanning was a part of the great religious resurgence among the young men and women who had been abroad. He enrolled at Baylor University following his stint in the Marines, which included landing in Japan and being assigned to help assess the devastation in Nagasaki.[2]

Fanning was a member of the church made famous by George W. Truett, First Baptist Church of Dallas, its pastor now a rising young star in the person of W. A. Criswell. As previously mentioned, the most highly visible and best-known Southern Baptist, George W. Truett passed away on July 7, 1944 while the country was still at war. Criswell was called on September 27 of the same year from the pastorate of First Baptist Church, Muskogee, Oklahoma.[3]

Wally Amos Criswell, flamboyant and popular, recognized the promise of young Fanning and often featured him in his pulpit. Fanning joined other young men on the Baylor campus preaching in youth revivals all over the United States.

Following seminary training, Fanning, like many of the talented and charismatic of this new breed, went into evangelism and was part of the revivalistic phenomena among Baptists for nearly a decade before he became pastor of San Antonio's Trinity Baptist Church.

The religious resurgence that involved Fanning and others was perhaps most uniquely dramatized in the person of a young preacher who missed the war but emerged from that time with obvious gifts for evangelism in the new age of mass communication. Billy Graham broke into the national spotlight following a large evangelistic crusade on the West Coast which was strangely hyped by the Hearst newspaper chain. Graham was later to align himself with the First Baptist Church in Dallas and call W. A. Criswell his pastor.

The history of the church that included these three men, each in himself an aspect of the unfolding Southern Baptist experience, was a prototype of the emerging urban church and one that presaged another phenomenon, the megachurch.

Begun as an outgrowth of Southern Baptists' southwestern migration in the post-Civil War period, the First Baptist Church of Dallas, according to Leon McBeth, was uniquely the product of a persistent woman, Lucinda Williams. After her move with her lawyer husband from Missouri to the Texas prairies, she determined she would have a Baptist church in which to worship.[4] Her persistent agitation paid off and the church was organized in 1868. It was in the heart of a bustling would-be city when it called the young George Truett upon his graduation from Baylor in 1897.

Whether or not other leadership would have succeeded to the degree that George W. Truett did in leading that church for forty-six years is debatable, given the dynamic experience of Dallas itself. However, Truett's successor, W. A. Criswell, so different from Truett in style and theology and focus, caught the wave of post-World War II expansion and rode it as no one else in Southern Baptist life would for two decades. At that time, the Texas church served as a model for other large urban churches that developed to meet the needs of Baptist constituencies, even as Criswell became a role model for young preachers with his flamboyance, optimism, conservative-dispensational theology, and triumphalistic views.

Southern Baptists, with a strong missionary and evangelistic commitment, were uniquely poised to capitalize on this exploding religious interest that included everything from the discovery of the Dead Sea scrolls in Wadi Qumran in 1947 to the organization of the World Council of Churches in Amsterdam in 1948, an invitation they had respectfully declined in 1940.

Indeed, religious fervor was a national epidemic. President Eisenhower was inaugurated in January of 1953, following a prayer breakfast,[5] and in 1954 the country inserted "under God" into its pledge of allegiance.

World Events and Missions

Some of the euphoria of post-war peace dissolved, however, before a new world confrontation between democracies and communism called the Cold War. Winston Churchill, in the twilight of his leadership of the disintegrating British Commonwealth, coined the term "Iron Curtain" as Stalin ruthlessly cordoned off Eastern Europe and then in 1948 blockaded Berlin. That same year Harry Truman, who had taken over the presidency following the death of Franklin D. Roosevelt near the close of the war, was elected president of the United States in his own right; Mahatma Ghandi was assassinated in India; and the new Israel emerged from a bloody partitioning of Palestine.

Throughout the world the empires of the previous era began to collapse before a tidal wave of nationalism. New countries in Africa, Asia, and the Middle East restructured world maps. These developing nations were soon termed the Third World; Baptists found their unique polity and emphases fitted this development, and mission enterprises responded.

Even the short term of peace eluded China, however, as the war continued between Communist forces under Mao Tse-tung and nationalists under Chiang Kai-shek. Once again, Southern Baptist missionaries were caught in the middle.

Bill Wallace, the young physician from Knoxville, Tennessee, who had gone to China in 1936 and led an evacuated hospital into Western China in the 1940s, once again faced long lines of refugees; this time they were not fleeing Japanese, but other Chinese. In 1951, Korea, which had been divided at the end of the World War II into a Communist-dominated north and a Western-dominated south, was plunged into war as the communist North Koreans attacked the quasi-democratic South Koreans across the thirty-eighth parallel. The United States-led United Nations' forces responded, and the world was at war again. As U.N. forces drove the North Koreans back, the Chinese Communists, victorious over Chiang Kai-shek, who had taken refuge on the island of Taiwan, swarmed across the Yalu River into the fray. The U. N. forces were driven back again by the sheer power of numbers.

Southern Baptist mission stations in South China were not only occupied by Communists but with the outbreak of the Korean War; American missionaries were considered enemies. Bill Wallace, whose personal popularity with the Chinese people impeded Communist propaganda, was arrested on trumped-up charges and placed in a Communist prison. The gentle Tennessean died there following a beating at the hands of his guards, though they tried to cover their brutality with a staged suicide.[6]

Baptists again realized the high cost of doing what they had always felt committed to do, and which had brought them together in the first place, but that did not halt the continued expansion of the missionary enterprise. In 1943, Charles Maddry, having realized his long-term goal of freeing the Foreign Mission Board from debt, stepped aside in favor of M. Theron Rankin, who had been his secretary for the Orient. Rankin, working out of war-ravaged China, appointed young Baker James Cauthen, the former Fort Worth pastor and seminary professor, to succeed him as secretary for the Orient and moved back to Richmond.

Baptist mission executives participated in the equivalent of a second London Conference in 1948, which further expanded the Southern Baptist role in Europe and in the Middle East. The Foreign Mission Board increasingly felt a mandate to go wherever doors were open, and personnel and financial resources enabled them to proceed.

In 1948, after intense prayer and planning with his fellow administrators, Rankin led the Board to call on Southern Baptists for a worldwide advance. Rankin's Advance Program was adopted by the Southern Baptist Convention in 1949, calling for goals of 1,750 missionaries and a $10 million budget.[7] Nine supportive objectives focused on methods: training centers for nationals, publications, medical efforts, and areas of works (that is among Moslems) in post-war Europe and the Near East, Africa, Latin America, Japan, and other areas in the Orient. If the program seemed broad, it simply reflected the unbounded optimism being felt among Southern Baptists.

In fact, "Advance" was the theme not only of the Foreign Mission Board but of Baptists everywhere. In 1955, various Baptist organizations, including the American Baptist Convention and the Southern Baptist Convention, joined hands to plan a Jubilee Celebration in 1964 on the Sesquicentennial Anniversary of the establishment of the Triennial Convention. Goals were set by all for that date.[8]

Yet Rankin, the soul of this vision, fell before a sudden onslaught of leukemia in 1953. At this point the "Advance" effort was still seeking momentum, with the missionary total having grown from just over seven hundred missionaries to just over nine hundred. The Foreign Mission Board with rare unanimity tapped Cauthen to take over, and the bright, slight, energetic, and compelling Texan committed himself to realizing Rankin's advance goals by the Jubilee year.

Cauthen, who had begun preaching around his east Texas home of Lufkin when only sixteen, had been strongly influenced by a missionary-minded mother active in WMU. He took a master's degree at Baylor in English after graduation from East Texas State Teachers College. At Baylor he met young W. A. Criswell, who was his age and was already attracting attention with his pulpit skills. Though Criswell and Cauthen's paths separated the next year when Criswell chose to go to Southern Seminary in Louisville, believing that it was a "more scholarly" environment, the two were friendly competitors through the years and both played pivotal roles in the Southern Baptist post-World War II experience.

But Cauthen also met Eloise Glass at Baylor. The tall, energetic woman was born in China to missionary parents and after the death of her mother was sent off to a boarding school with an older sister at age six. Now a bright and beautiful Baylor junior, she was determined to return to China. Cauthen planned to be a pastor or perhaps a professor of religion. He preceded her to Southwestern Seminary, but after her arrival they began a friendship that turned into a courtship. Though the missionary goal was some years after their marriage, her vision turned out to be the prescient one.[9]

As mentioned earlier, Cauthen, while serving as pastor of the prestigious Polytechnic Baptist Church in Fort Worth and holding the professorship of missions at Southwestern Seminary, shocked his mentors and colleagues by announcing his plans to seek missionary appointment for China. He cut his missionary teeth in North China, survived wartime displacement, and was tapped to take over Rankin's area role when the latter became head of the Foreign Mission Board. Now he had been called on a second time to follow the much-loved M. Theron Rankin.

Leadership

As Southern Baptists launched into the second century, they were blessed not only with freedom from long standing shackles of debt and with growing prosperity, but with strong, consensus-building leadership. The Convention met once in 1942 following the U. S. entrance into the war, discussed earlier with the California expansion. It met only one other time during the war, in 1944, in Atlanta, Georgia, where Pat Neff of Texas and Baylor University took over the gavel from W. W. Hamilton of Louisiana.

The Convention did not meet in 1945 and was presided over by Neff in Miami, Florida, in 1946 when it formally celebrated its Centennial. Attendance took a sharp jump at that point, going from a previous high of 5,884 in 1941 to 7,973 in 1946, 8,508 in 1947, and 9,843 in 1948 when the Convention met in Memphis, Tennessee, where Georgia Baptists' venerable Louie D. Newton presided.[10]

The epitome of old South preaching, Robert G. Lee of Bellevue Baptist Church in Memphis, Tennessee, who had served on the Statement of Principles committee, wielded the gavel in 1950 as the Convention held its first meeting outside the South in Chicago, Illinois. Northern Baptists considered that action a direct slap and a violation of the last vestige of any kind of comity and changed their name to the American Baptist Convention that same year, though a name change had been under consideration since 1948. Both Conventions now claimed a mandate to the whole country, though the numerical strength of both remained focused north and west and south.

Lee presided the next year when Southern Baptists went to California for the first time, meeting in San Francisco, as the meetings began to reflect national aspirations. The Convention jumped all the way back across the country to Miami in 1952 and registered over 10,000 messengers for the first time as J. D. Grey, pastor of the First Baptist Church of New Orleans, Louisiana, took over the presidency. He was presiding also when Southern Baptists met in Houston and nearly 13,000 messengers set still another new record in 1953.

One of Baptists' new confidence-expressing goals, a Sunday school expansion called "A Million More in Fifty-Four," was launched at the Houston meeting, and J. W. Storer of First Baptist Church, Tulsa, Oklahoma, was elected to preside over the burdgeoning fellowship. That messenger record would stand until 1960. Storer turned the gavel over to North Carolina's C. C. Warren for meetings in Kansas City and a return to Chicago in 1956 and 1957.

In Chicago, former Arkansas congressman, Brooks Hays, was elected, the first layman since 1910. Hays, whose courageous stand for Blacks during the 1958 school desegregation crisis cost him his seat in Congress, was a hero to both Blacks and young idealists. Television personality Bill Moyers was later to say Hays "was the first Baptist hero I met face-to-face."[11] Since Hays incarnated progressive views on race relations, many people thought Southern Baptists were ready to move ahead in such matters.[12]

But a strong, conservative pastor from Memphis, Tennessee, Ramsey Pollard, R. G. Lee's successor at the large Bellevue church, was elected at the record-setting convention meeting in 1960 in Miami Beach. There 13,612 messengers indicated that despite the social-justice agenda of the Statement of Principles of 1946 and an increasingly visible social justice agenda led by the Christian Life Commission, a conservative evangelism was still the top and most comfortable Southern Baptist priority.

Territorial Expansion

Southern Baptists were now expanding north from bases that stretched throughout the Old South across the Southwest to the West Coast. In part, this resulted from continued migration of Southern Baptists to the Midwest, West, and Northwest that began with the depression and continued with the Second World War. In part, the expansion was due to the collapse of the restraint that Southern Baptists had practiced, however unevenly, in Northern Baptist territories. According to H. K. Neely, Southern Baptist expansion had to overcome four barriers: (1) competition from the Home Mission Society of the northern body; (2) the sectional name of Southern Baptists; (3) limitations presented by Southern Baptists' by-Laws and constitution; and (4) fears of the size of Convention gatherings and the distances involved.[13] The California decision in 1942, the Convention meeting in Chicago in 1950, and the Northern Convention's name change to the American Baptist Convention motivated Southern Baptists to ignore all barriers.

The Northern group had been less effective than its Southern counterpart in reconciling its left and right wings. In 1946, it failed again to approve the New Hampshire Confession of Faith and from then through 1947 saw major defections to the newly organized Conservative Baptist Association of America. Few expected Southern Baptists to experience that same trauma.

American Baptist historian R. G. Torbet identified four reasons the old lines between Northern and Southern Baptists collapsed: (1) Southern Baptists migrating to northern territories were uncomfortable in Northern Baptist churches; (2) theological differences and especially Landmark-fed sensitivites about communion and immersion; (3) Southern Baptists feared losing contact with their own; and (4) the Northern Convention's name change.[14]

But whatever the reasons, the expansion's roots were already in place, and it began to flower state by state.

A Kansas Southern Baptist Fellowship was organized in 1945 and a Kansas Convention of Southern Baptist Churches in 1946. The churches involved changed the name to the Kansas Convention of Southern Baptists in 1947, and they were recognized as a cooperating constituency in 1948.[15]

Just how far this expansion would reach became evident in 1948 when the Home Mission Board was instructed by the SBC to assist a fledgling Alaska Baptist Convention. A 1951 constitutional amendment cleared the way for this and other new and small state conventions.[16]

Southern Baptist oriented churches organized a convention in Oregon in 1948 and changed its name to the Baptist General Convention of Oregon-Washington. They were accepted for affiliation with the Southern Baptist Convention in 1949. [17] In 1969 the Oregon-Washington body changed its name to the Northwest Baptist Convention and listed 22 associations and 205 churches with over 37,000 members.

Yet the SBC did draw the line. As early as 1953 the Emmanuel Baptist Church of Vancouver, British Columbia, affiliated with the Oregon-Washington body in a conscious effort to identify with Southern Baptists. Though Southern Baptists, due to their U.S.-limited polity, refused to accept it, nearly two dozen similar churches arose in the Canadian Northwest in the next dozen years. They and their supporters engaged in an ongoing debate with Southern Baptist leaders and especially those of the Foreign Mission Board, who saw the issue as a Pandora's box threatening the way they related to the national bodies that were a product of Southern Baptist missionary labors around the world.

Six years elapsed after the 1949 acceptance of the Oregon-Washington group before Southern Baptists recognized another new state convention, and this time it was again in the Midwest and in another territory, Ohio, long served by American Baptist churches. Southern Baptists in Ohio were so close to Kentucky that informal ties with Southern Baptists had been in place with many churches for quite a while, and so, in 1940, five churches organized the White Water Association of Southern Baptists. With relationships to Kentucky Baptists and the Home Mission Board, the Association hired Ray Roberts as missionary in 1952, and thereafter the Ohio work grew so rapidly that thirty-nine churches sent messengers to organize the State

Convention of Baptists in January, 1954. The Executive Committee's Porter Routh participated in the organization, giving it the tacit blessing that forecast Southern Baptist acceptance which came in 1955.[18]Ohio Baptists were equally aggressive in opening up new work in Pennsylvania and New York in Erie and Niagara Falls.

Still another state convention was added in 1955 when the Colorado Baptist General Convention was organized with messengers from ninety churches at the First Southern Baptist Church in Colorado Springs. Thirteen of the churches constituting the new convention had been related to the New Mexico Baptist Convention. They were joined by churches from Wyoming, Montana, North and South Dakota, and Nebraska, most of them the product of the Arizona Baptist Convention. In fact, Arizona Baptists' aggressive Willis J. Ray became the first executive secretary-treasurer of the new state convention. Indicative of the missionary spirit involved was a goal set in 1956 to help members in the four northern states to organize their own convention.

It seemed as if the Southern Baptist Convention was back-filling to the east when fifty-two churches constituted the Baptist State Convention of Michigan in November, 1957, and the State Convention of Baptists in Indiana was organized in October, 1958, with the help of the Kentucky and Illinois Baptist Conventions.[19]

Growth and Numbers

In 1946, as Southern Baptists commenced the second century, the Convention included 26,134 churches listing 5,865,554 members. These churches in turn were a part of 923 associations in twenty cooperating state conventions. Total gifts had reached $76,588,615, and the SBC receipts totaled $22,490,751. Southern Baptists reported 256,699 baptisms that year and Sunday School enrollment of 3,525,310. Pastors had discovered that Sunday School enrollment was the key to increased baptisms.[20]

The force of the growth that followed is evident in the corollary numbers compiled in 1964 when Southern Baptists met in Atlantic City with American Baptists to celebrate their common Jubilee. Cooperating state conventions numbered twenty-eight and recognized 1,172 associations, including 33,126 churches. The churches reported 10,395,940 members. Sunday School enrollment reached 7,610,727 and the churches reported 355,325 baptisms.

The success of Southern Baptists' stewardship emphasis, as well as their prosperity and the creeping inflation of the period was reflected in total gifts of $556,042,694 and Cooperative Program gifts of $55,695,627. The special mission offerings, which totalled $2,912,104 in 1946, reported $12,872,181 in 1964.[21]

Dissent

A few voices were raised in caution concerning the long-term effect of this rapid expansion on Southern Baptist life. One voice was that of South-eastern Seminary's founding president, Sydnor Stealey.

Stealy's father, C. P. Stealey of Oklahoma, had been the strong conservative voice that led the fight against evolution in the 1920s and the one who brought a minority report when E. Y. Mullins's Baptist Faith and Message report was adopted in 1925. C. P. Stealey joined J. Frank Norris in 1933 in organizing the Premillennial Baptist Missionary Fellowship and was elected its first president.[22]

The younger Stealey attended Southern Baptist Seminary after graduation from Oklahoma Baptist University and served as a fellow to E. Y. Mullins. After years as a pastor Stealey served as professor of Church History at Southern Seminary from 1942 until his election as president of Southern Baptists' new Southeastern Seminary in 1951.

In 1961, clearly marching to a different beat than that of his father, Sydnor Stealey warned that the Convention was "in the process of being taken over by the dominant fundamentalist elements in the southwestern and western states." From an angst made poignant by his obvious reaction to his own background, Stealey called for his "Baptist brothers to slow down the admission of new state conventions until more maturity and less divisiveness is evident." He added, ominously, "I tell you even today they are plotting to take over . . . SBC institutions and boards."[23]

Few would argue with the generally conservative nature of the work that seemed so ominous to Stealey. However, studies of the votes that brought Stealey's fears to fruition in less than two decades do not entirely support such a geographical division.

Ministry Expansion

The Executive Committee's Austin Crouch guided the Convention through a strategic era that included the Home Mission Board treasurer's defalcation, the representation change in 1931, and the California decision in 1942. He stepped down in favor of young Duke Kimbro McCall in 1946.

McCall, a polished young southerner, son of Judge John McCall of Tennessee, graduated from Furman University and earned a doctor of theology degree from Southern Baptist Seminary. After a Louisville pastorate, McCall in 1943 became the youngest president of the Baptist Bible Institute. Three years later, he was the popular choice to succeed the veteran Crouch, though he moved after four years to take the presidency of Southern Baptist Theological Seminary, where he served in that role for twenty-nine years.

McCall was succeeded at the Executive Committee by a layman, Porter Routh, the son of the Oklahoma editor who led in the 1931 representation change. Routh, who took office in 1951, brought steady and diplomatic leadership to Southern Baptists during a quarter of a century of numerical, territorial, and ministry expansion.

A Press Service

Before assuming the Executive Committee role, Porter Routh had served as director of the Sunday School Board's department of survey and statistics. In that position, the former state paper editor and son of a state paper editor began publishing weekly news releases as the Southern Baptist Press Association. Citing it as a response to needs voiced by state Baptist paper editors, Routh continued this for a year before transferring the task to the Executive Committee, where C. E. Bryant, a trained professional journalist, had been hired as director of publicity. Bryant shortened the title of the publication to Baptist Press, which was reported to the 1948 convention as a "completely new service of the Executive Committee."[24]

A year later Albert McClellan, former editor of Oklahoma's *Baptist Messenger,* succeeded Bryant and held the post for ten years before W. C. Fields took over the service which was strongly supported by the Baptist editors. Baptist Press would reach its zenith under Fields who would expand the partnership between the news service and the state papers to include SBC agencies and institutions including the establishment of bureaus.[25]

Baptist state papers had undergone a major change since the days of Landmarkism and such galvanizing events as the Whitsitt controversy. At that time, the often iconoclastic publications were privately owned and frequently challenged by rival publications for Baptist readership. This changed rapidly after World War I; in 1950, when the *Religious Herald* became the property of Virginia Baptists, all were state convention related. This tended to make the papers house organs of the sponsoring body. Individual state conventions felt the papers were of critical importance to the development of work in their state and the appearance of a state paper usually quickly followed the organization of a state Baptist convention.

Baptist Press, according to Bob Terry who would later edit Missouri's *Word and Way,* had a tremendous impact on the state Baptist papers. Baptist Press became the primary source for news of events and issues facing Southern Baptists. Since content in the state papers had largely been promotional or theological, the advent of news stories was significant. For one thing, news reporting underscored the practices of Georgia's *The Christian Index* where a professional journalist, John Jeter Hurt, was gaining a reputation as a champion of news stories. The influence of Baptist Press and Hurt would, by the 1970s, cause most Baptist editors to name "reporting the news" as their top priority.[26]

Historical Commission

A year after McCall took the Executive Committee post, the Historical Commission came into being when the Southern Baptist Historical Society was given commission status. Like most such actions, it had a long line of precedents.

An American Baptist Historical Society, chartered in 1853, included Southerners for many years and carried the historical task for Baptists in general. Then in 1916 the Sunday School Board was asked to be responsible for developing a Southern Baptist history. A writer was given the task, only to have his completed manuscript judged unsuitable for publication in 1919. Whether the manuscript was rejected for quality or controversy is not clear.[27]

In 1921, the Convention, at its meeting in Chattanooga, appointed a committee on the preservation of Baptist history. After the death in 1935 of A. J. Holt, who had chaired the committee, responsibility was assigned to the Sunday School Board, which was already the designated repository for Southern Baptist historical materials.

The next task was focused in a committee appointed in 1936 and chaired by Southern Seminary's W. O. Carver. The committee helped organize a Southern Baptist Historical Society in 1938 which began looking toward commemorative Baptist histories when the Convention reached its centennial in 1945. A curator was secured by the Society to care for a permanent collection of historical materials. That same year the committee's work was formally given to the Society which served as the Convention's history agency until the Historical Commission was chartered in 1951; however, the latter fixes its beginning in a 1947 SBC action that gave the Society commission status. The Society then became an auxiliary to the Commission.

In a near repetition of the first effort to develop a Southern Baptist history, the projected centennial volumes failed to materialize when a pre-1845 volume was never written and W. W. Barnes's Southern Baptist Convention history was delayed by the illness and death of Barnes's wife and subsequent wrangling in the committee. The Centennial history finally appeared under Barnes's name in 1954.[28]

The Commission itself fared better under its first executive, Norman W. Cox, and merged its collections with the Sunday School Board's Dargan library in what became the Dargan-Carver library. The Commission's progress was steady but low-keyed under Cox, then Davis Woolley, and finally Lynn May, until the controversies that began in 1979 dragged it into unwanted limelight in 1992.

Southern Baptist Foundation

In 1947 the Convention established a Southern Baptist Foundation to develop endowments and invest funds for any Southern Baptist entity. The idea, long a strategy of various philanthropists, was pioneered in North Carolina in the early twenties and further developed in Texas in 1931 with the establishment of what became the largest such endeavor in Southern Baptist life. Georgia followed suit ten years later, and the strategy soon became one of choice in new and old state bodies. Institutional needs in the various states highlighted in the depression undergirded the movement in the several states.

The need to seek and administer endowments for "southwide" endeavors made the Southern Baptist Foundation a natural. While not growing as fast as some of the state foundations that emerged, the Foundation was a part of the burgeoning post-war notion that Southern Baptists had a manifest destiny in the world.

Stewardship Commission

In 1960 the Executive Committee surrendered its stewardship-promotion role to a Stewardship Commission. Convention actions in 1958 and

1959 brought into being the new commission to promote the Cooperative Program and the whole concept of biblical stewardship. Its first director, Merrill D. Moore, moved smoothly into his new role, confident that everyone else would support him because he was dealing with the mother lode of advance.

The importance of stewardship grew rapidly with the creation of the denomination, even when fund raising was the primary role of agents. The Seventy-Five Million Campaign, the Cooperative Program, and the Baptist Hundred Thousand Club brought stewardship to the front of denominational aspirations, and from 1931 on, with a brief hiatus, stewardship promotion was the task of the Executive Committee and the particular responsibility of various staff members. When a Committee to Study the Total Southern Baptist Program reported in 1958 in Houston, it recommended the formation of a Stewardship Commission and the transfer of those responsibilities from the Executive Committee to the new entity. The report received second approval in 1959 at Louisville, and the Commission formally was established on January 1, 1961.

Early on, the Commission realized it would have to do its work through other program leaders and through state convention counterparts. However, since everyone had a stake, cooperation came readily.

The Baptist concept of stewardship was broad enough to include later even the environment, but focused primarily on the promotion of tithes and offerings and regularity and dependability in giving. The escalating numbers of total Baptist gifts testified both to the success of these concepts as promoted by the Commission and all involved and to the growing numbers and affluence of Southern Baptists.

Seminary Expansion

During the decade following World War II three new Southern Baptist seminaries were established in California, North Carolina, and Missouri—even as enrollments continued to expand in Southern Baptists' three older institutions in Louisville, Fort Worth, and New Orleans. By this period Southwestern Seminary had captured the "largest" title, with over two thousand students. Southern Seminary was second, and New Orleans Seminary third. The drive for new regional institutions was seen as a form of missionary effort, on one hand, and recognition of the demands of new constituents, on the other.

Golden Gate Baptist Theological Seminary

Golden Gate Baptist Theological Seminary was incorporated during the latter part of the war in July 1944 and began receiving students in Oakland, California, across the bay from San Francisco, that fall. The California Baptist Convention accepted responsibility for the new institution in 1945, but in 1950 the Southern Baptist Convention, in one of its most expansionary moods while meeting in Chicago, voted to accept ownership and support of the seminary.

After Harold Graves became president, the seminary moved to an impressive facility on Strawberry Point in Marin County.[29] The fact that the property had reportedly been considered for the headquarters of the United Nations gave the scenic location a special aura.

While the seminary began immediately to serve young church vocationists from the West Coast, a large percentage of its student body was attracted to the scene and the missionary setting from Southern Baptists' traditional bases. When later the West Coast emerged as a vital center of the developing Pacific Rim, the concept gave still more viability to the institution. The new seminary had to battle the economic success of the area which took the cost of living and working in the area out of the range of many students and especially of the faculty. This high cost-of-living would be the foundation of later financial crises for this westernmost of Southern Baptist institutions.

Southeastern Baptist Theological Seminary

In 1950, the Convention recommended the establishment of the Southeastern Baptist Theological Seminary in Wake Forest, North Carolina, envisioning an east-west anchoring of Baptists' aggressive and ambitous theological education program. It became the first seminary that the Southern Baptist Convention itself began. Southern, Southwestern, New Orleans, and Golden Gate seminaries all began under the auspices of other entities and were subsequently accepted by the Convention; Southeastern began as a Southern Baptist seminary.

The new seminary had the advantage of a ready-made campus when it took over the buildings of old Wake Forest College, which moved to Winston Salem, North Carolina, with the help of Reynolds Tobacco money. The new seminary, Southern Baptists' easternmost, began its work in September, 1951.[30]

Sydnor Stealey, previously mentioned as the son of Oklahoma's outspoken fundamentalist C. P. Stealey, was elected as Southeastern's first president. He assembled an able faculty, most of whom were Southern Baptist Seminary trained. As his warning regarding Southern Baptists' susceptibilty to fundamentalism indicated, he thought Southeastern Seminary should represent what he considered a more progressive environment, fostering scholarly enquiry in tandem with historic Baptist distinctives and responsible mission and ministry. One of its early graduates, Edwin Young, who became a megachurch pastor and president of the Southern Baptist Convention, years later would deplore what he believed was the school's dangerous liberalism. Young was a member of the forces that radically reoriented the institution in the early 1990s.

Midwestern Baptist Theological Seminary

When the Convention returned to Chicago in 1957, it voted to establish a third seminary in the middle of the country in Kansas City, Missouri, to be named Midwestern Baptist Theological Seminary. This seminary was the fruit of a special convention study on one hand and another battle with Baptists to the north on the other.

The 1949 Convention action that resulted in taking over Golden Gate Seminary and beginning Southeastern Seminary implied the principle of geographical availability to the churches that would need the seminary's product and in turn provide pastoral positions for the students. The next year the Convention reinforced this position in deciding against the sponsorship of Bible institutes, the preferred educational ministry of fundamentalists and many conservatives, in favor of more broadly based seminary curriculums.[31] It followed this with the appointment of a committee in 1953, chaired by Georgia's Louie Newton, to study the Convention's "total program of theological, religious, and missionary education, as it involves financial support."[32]

The committee in the next few years conducted a revealing study of ministerial students and those preparing for church vocations. It documented the growing western segment of Southern Baptist life, tackled relationships between Southern Baptists and Central Baptist Theological Seminary of Kansas City, and, finally, in 1956–57, selected the site for a sixth seminary.

The study revealed that Baptist college students studying for the ministry increased from 3,300 in 1946 to 5,800 in 1953. In 1955 it showed 4,379 ministerial students in seminaries and another 6,500 in Baptist colleges. It also demonstrated the continuing need for schools in the Convention's growing western section.

Central Baptist Theological Seminary was founded in Kansas City, Kansas, in 1901 and began operations in 1902 as an independent institution with a strong missionary emphasis. For years it drew support from Baptist churches in both Missouri and Kansas and, at the time of the Newton Committee study, two-thirds of Central's students and several faculty members and trustees were Southern Baptists.

The leaders of the seminary suggested joint sponsorship, but the committee pointed out that Southern Baptists' procedures require the right to nominate the trustees for institutions it finances. As a result of this position, the leadership of Central Seminary voted to align itself with the American Baptist Convention, and a number of Southern Baptist professors, trustees, and students left. After further study, the committee recommended to the Convention in 1957 a new seminary in Kansas City. After defeating efforts to locate it in Chicago and Denver, the Convention voted the operating and capital funds for what would become Midwestern Baptist Theological Seminary.

Trustees were elected, and under the leadership of Missouri's H. I. Hester, Millard J. Berquist served as the Seminary's first president. Midwestern opened to students in the fall of 1958. The first professor appointed was Ralph H. Elliott, a young Old Testament teacher who had been on the faculty at Southern Seminary. As the new institution began its work in a burst of enthusiasm, few people would have guessed that it would soon be embroiled in a convention-wide controversy foreshadowing the conflict that would dominate Southern Baptists' attention in the years leading up to the convention's sesquicentennial.[33]

The Corporate Image

World War II had developed in American industry a strong organizational awareness and a commitment to corporate efficiency. Southern Baptists, ever reflecting the cultural environment in which they found themselves, were quick to accept this model. Both the Executive Committee and the Sunday School Board employed sophisticated organizational consultants and began to redefine their tasks through program statements.

Porter Routh was uniquely prepared to lead Southern Baptists' Executive Committee. When he was a youngster his father was editor of *The Baptist Standard;* during those years the younger Routh came to know such men as

J. B. Gambrell, George W. Truett, and L. R. Scarborough. After graduating from Oklahoma Baptist University and attending the University of Missouri and Southern Baptist Seminary, Routh succeeded his father as editor of the *Oklahoma Baptist Messenger*, when the elder Routh went to the Foreign Mission Board to become editor of *The Commission*. In 1945 he joined the Sunday School Board, still being led by T. L. Holcomb, and in 1951, when Duke McCall replaced Ellis Fuller as president of Southern Seminary, Routh was tapped as the new executive secretary-treasurer of the Executive Committee.[34]

Under Routh's leadership the Executive Committee recommended a formal Advance Program to the Convention that met in Miami, Florida, in 1955. It looked to the Jubilee in 1964 and became the Baptist Jubilee Advance Program. In December of 1955, the Executive Committee appointed a sub-committee to "study the total program of Southern Baptists." At the 1956 Convention the recommendation was formalized as the Committee to Study Total Program.[35]

But this spirit was already under way at the Baptist Sunday School Board, where James L. Sullivan had taken over two years before from T. L. Holcomb. Sullivan, a native of Mississippi and the product of a devout and dedicated Baptist family, had been a star football player at Mississippi College. He graduated from Southern Baptist Theological Seminary in 1935 and served as pastor of churches in Kentucky, Tennessee, Mississippi, and finally the First Baptist Church of Abilene, Texas, where L. R. Scarborough was once pastor.

Sullivan had come to the Baptist Sunday School Board with little fanfare but with the unusual request that he might bring his educational director from Abilene, J. M. Crowe, as his assistant. In 1954 Sullivan led the Baptist Sunday School Board to hire the consultant firm of Booz, Allen, and Hamilton to study the Board and recommend reorganization. The rapid growth of Southern Baptists after the war made such a study necessary and Holcomb, admittedly a promotionally oriented man, had advised his successor that he would need to reorganize. "If I had done it," Holcomb is reported to have said, "it would have killed me."[36]

The enterprise Holcomb turned over to Sullivan provided materials for Sunday Schools enrolling over 5.7 million members, a church training program involving over 1.8 million Southern Baptists, and total receipts exceeding $12.6 million.

The Sunday School Board's corporate atmosphere grew rapidly under Sullivan's leadership with Crowe as his point man and W. L. Howse, Jr., who had been on the faculty at Southwesten Baptist Seminary, as his educational specialist. Howse's committment to modern management practices emerging in post-war corporate environments influenced all Southern Baptist agencies.

By 1956, Routh, with Howse as support, led all agencies to function together in an Inter-Agency Council to correlate their programs of work. The Committee to Study the Total Program had willing and aggressive leadership in these men and made rapid progress that had far-reaching effects. Leon McBeth says that what Howse was attempting through his educational division at the Sunday School Board and a Coordinating Committee for the Inter-Agency Council was "nothing less than the restructuring of local Baptist churches and the reshaping of the entire Southern Baptist Convention."[37] At a still later date, through a consulting relationship with the Foreign Mission Board's R. Keith Parks, he engineered what ultimately amounted to a paradigm change in that agency's program.

Gradually overcoming the traditional Baptist philosophy that if "it ain't broke, don't fix it," these corporate-model leaders updated Baptist life on almost every front for the exciting future they saw unfolding before them.

Radio and Television Commission

Riding the tide of the new technology that flooded the American scene following World War II, Southern Baptists embraced mass communications. In 1938 a convention committee headed by Samuel F. Lowe led to the formation of a Radio Committee. Later called the Radio Commission, it did not have a paid director until Lowe took the job in 1942, the year after it began what became its flagship ministry, "The Baptist Hour."

The Commission became the Radio and Television Commission in 1955 under the leadership of Paul M. Stevens, Lowe's successor. Stevens may have been the most aggressive of a whole class of aggressive leaders. Invariably gracious to one another in formal settings, they nevertheless competed fiercely for their particular vision or perceived mission.

When the Convention met in St. Louis in 1956 it approved a plan to move the Radio and Television Commission from its offices in Atlanta to Fort Worth.[38] There they planned a state-of-the-art facility, including sophisticated production equipment and sound stages, to be occupied in July, 1965. During the elaborate planning and extended construction period,

Stevens negotiated "uplinks and downlinks" with satellite companies while fighting jurisdictional and program battles with the Sunday School Board, the Home Mission Board, and even the Foreign Mission Board.

From a program involving little more than "The Baptist Hour" on radio in 1955, the Commission quickly added a television program called "This is the Answer" in 1956 and took "The Baptist Hour" into Spanish and devotional type programs into several other languages. In 1959 the Commission followed this with a magazine-style radio program called "Master Control." By January, 1961, the Commision was producing 1,100 programs per week.[39]

Brotherhood Commission

Challenged by the success of Woman's Missionary Union, men's programs expanded during this period. The Laymen's Missionary Movement formed in 1907 became the Baptist Brotherhood of the South in 1927. It moved its headquarters to Memphis in 1936 and in 1950 became the Brotherhood Commission.

Its successes had been modest to that time, featuring a Layman's Day beginning in 1933 and a Man and Boy Movement in 1949. In 1956, it defined its task as being that of seeking and discovering the talents of men and boys in Southern Baptist churches and challenging those churches to utilize them in Christ's work. George W. Schroeder took over the leadership of the Commission in 1951 from Lawson H. Cooke, who had led it since 1936. Schroeder succeeded in having the Royal Ambassador program, a long-established program of the WMU, transferred to the Brotherhood Commission in 1957. This program, however, faced sharp competition from the Boy Scouts and did not maintain the momentum under the men's guidance it had experienced under the women's aegis.[40]

Civil Rights

It was difficult for Southern Baptists to continue to develop an agenda irrespective of the demands of the environment around them. Nowhere was this more clearly evident than in the civil rights movement that was birthed during this period. The whole movement placed unusual pressures on Southern Baptists because of their identity with the culture of segregation that had been the repressive replacement of slavery.

In the early years Southern Baptists had responded to the conflict regarding the former slave population with strong home missionary efforts and educational programs. The segregation and benign neglect that developed during and after Reconstruction, however, left a painful legacy. By 1946 they realized that more was needed, and the Statement of Principles included not-so-subtle concerns about race relations.

The touchy subject was given to the Social Service Commission, which had been established in 1913 and which at this time was being led by Hugh H. Brimm. In 1953, after A. C. Miller took over from Brim, the agency's name was formally changed to the Christian Life Commission.

In 1954, the Supreme Court of the United States struck down segregation in the celebrated *Brown vs. Board of Education* case. The Southern Baptist Convention, meeting only weeks later, became the first major religious denomination to endorse the decision. The Christian Life Commission began to expand its role in helping Southern Baptists come to terms with race relations. At this point, foreign missionaries were the most avid and effective agents of change, especially missionaries stationed in Africa. They would come home to the States on furlough and point out the contradiction between what they were preaching in Africa and what was being practiced at the sending base.

In 1961 Woman's Missionary Union sponsored a study throughout its organizations of T. B. Maston's book, *The Bible and Race*. Maston, a Yale-trained lay faculty member of Southwestern Baptist Seminary, had been effectively sensitizing a long line of students to a more progressive position on race.

When Foy Valentine, one of Maston's mentees, took over from A. C. Miller in 1960, the Commission became even more aggressive, and in the program adopted at the Southern Baptist Convention in 1961, a "license to practice" was given under terms such as human relations and moral issues. While the Commission and its predecessors in early years focused on issues such as alcohol abuse, citizenship, white slavery, and child labor under the leadership of Brimm and Miller, it now moved to address more contemporary concerns, but not without persistent opposition from the culturally anchored churches of the Deep South.[41]

Possibly one of the costs of efforts to address civil rights that Southern Baptist leaders, however timidly, attempted to give was the distrust and even alienation felt by many of its more conservative constituents. When, nearly two decades later, the moderate leadership was challenged, they were shocked and dismayed by the level of distrust in place and the willingness of many conservatives to believe the charges of liberalism and heresy leveled against the leadership.

Tensions in the United States made the climate in which progressive social reformers would work hazardous. Anti-Communist emphases such as those promoted by the John Birch Society flourished. Many people feared the growing Soviet nuclear threat, which was a dark shadow over east-west struggles, and despite oft-repeated Baptist convictions on the subject some people believed restricting civil liberties was justified to temper that threat.

Advance and Crisis

The presidential election of 1960 revealed just how rapidly Southern Baptists had developed in the nearly two decades following the outbreak of World War II. At that time, saddled with debt, minimal growth, displaced missionaries in Asia and Europe, and internal questions over expansion, Southern Baptists were still regionally bound, culturally restricted, and far from realizing their inherent potential.

The changes would occur over the next twenty years. During that time they became more likely to live in the suburbs than in the country. More Southern Baptists than ever would go to college and be employed in white-collar jobs. They would expect their pastors to be educated and to educate their own children. Baptist colleges and Baptist Student Unions in state colleges would flourish. Diversity would be thrust upon them from every quarter. More non-Southerners would move in than Southerners move out—a sharp change from the depression years. As SBC leaders developed programs for suburban, better-educated, and middle-class constituents, the less educated, rural, and blue-collar Baptists felt left out.

Sociologist Nancy Ammerman has claimed "Campus ministers nurtured the young Baptist rebels who populated their campuses. Seminary teachers and scholars began to feel free to introduce their students to the wide-ranging critical perspectives that had long been part of their own thinking."[42] Those who dreamed of Southern Baptists' readiness to embrace a broader world and take on such social issues as peace and justice were heady with the times. Ammerman holds that, while such progressives leaders were in key places, they were not a majority, as subsequent events revealed.

Such progressive leadership was largely unchallenged at this time, however, as Cooperative Program gifts grew from $7.8 million in 1941 to $84.4 million twenty years later. Southern Baptists were expanding, with churches now numbering 32,600 and proliferating in cities, as compared to the 25,600 scattered in mostly rural areas in 1941. Those churches, growing most rapidly in urban areas, were a part of twenty-nine state conventions in contrast to the nineteen that were in place in 1941.[43]

Perhaps more illustrative than the numbers, however, were the implications of the campaign of the charismatic young John F. Kennedy on his way to the White House. It had been said that a Roman Catholic could not be elected President of the United States and indeed the only Catholic to try, Al Smith, had been overwhelmingly defeated by Herbert Hoover in 1928. Southern Baptists, with their history and church-state fears, had been natural enemies to a Roman Catholic candidacy. In 1919, J. B. Gambrell had written, "The inner principles and the external economy of Baptists isolate them from Rome and all ecclesiastical systems carrying the root principles of that vast, imposing heirarchy."[44]

While the South had been largely Democratic for decades, the Eisenhower administration made large inroads into that hegemony because of the more conservative social and political framework of Republicans. But Kennedy's charisma, ability to charm the media, and aggressive new kind of campaigning changed that.

In a historic meeting in Houston, Texas, which included the pastors of the Union Baptist Association, John F. Kennedy effectively defused the church-state issue in a head-on confrontation. When he was through, he was applauded and even E. S. James, Texas Baptists' strong-minded editor of the *Baptist Standard*, reluctantly commended his performance and his potential as a leader of the United States and what was now being called the "Free World."[45]

The very fact that Southern Baptists figured so strongly in the Democrats' strategy reflected how strong they had become and how influential they were, not only in their original base of the South, but throughout the Southwest, Midwest, and increasingly, the West Coast.

What turned out to be a tragically short tenure for Kennedy was almost immediately awash in crisis. Confrontations with the Soviet Premier Khrushchev brought about a call-up of reserves by the new president and the construction of the Berlin Wall in August of 1961 by Communist leadership.

Flashpoints began to appear throughout the world, and people felt very uneasy with the fact that it was now a nuclear world. In 1961 Kennedy sent military advisors to South Vietnam and in April of the same year decided not to back an effort by Cuban exiles to retake Cuba from Fidel Castro's successful insurgency that had installed a Communist government.

Castro, in the meantime, was further embraced by Russia's Khrushchev, and in October 1962 a missile crisis with Russia and Cuba brought the world to the edge of a nuclear holocaust.

However, "the Kennedy rounds" lowering tariffs with Europe, the efforts to achieve a more viable relationship with Russia, and the ambitious space program continued to reflect the spirit of advance that also characterized Southern Baptists.

But in the heartland of Southern Baptists' life, the South, civil rights agitation was escalating rapidly. The 1954 Supreme Court ruling elevated expectations, but for expectant blacks things seemed to change very little and aggressive activists began to lead blacks and white sympathizers in confrontations with established order. A sit-in in Greensboro, North Carolina, at a lunchcounter in early 1960, followed by an effort to integrate buses in Montgomery, Alabama, brought to the fore new black leaders such as the Reverend Martin Luther King, Jr., a Baptist preacher from Atlanta.

In 1962, a twenty-nine-year-old Air Force veteran, James Meredith, tried to enroll in the University of Mississippi; President Kennedy sent troops to back the effort. He confronted Alabama's George Wallace in 1963 on the same issue. In August of 1963 Martin Luther King led 200,000 demonstrators on a march on Washington. But despite media support and modifying influences among Southern Baptists, resistance was bitter and occasionally violent. Civil rights worker Medgar Evers was killed, and then in September of 1963 a black Baptist church was bombed, killing four little girls in Sunday School. Years later it would be charged that the Convention's Executive Committee, meeting a few days later on September 15, 1963, would turn aside a motion by Tennessee's Charles Trentham to specifically condemn the incident in favor of a more general statement decrying the tragedy of racial strife. Those bringing the charges termed the substitute motion a "profound failure of nerve."[46]

Women in the Wings

Another revolution was waiting in the wings. Called the Women's Liberation Movement, it was caricatured and couched in terms that seemed foreign to Southern Baptists' feminine ranks. But it did include significant moves by women into new roles in the workplace, at church, and in society at large.

Following World War II Southern Baptists noticed the change first in the number of women enrolling in their seminaries and taking assignments with the mission boards, then in the number of women holding positions in student work and in church education. Baptist leaders seemed more aware of women in the secular workplace, with divorces, and single-parent (read: women) homes on the increase. While they gave tacit support in the next few years to women's roles in ministry, a reaction nurtured by memories of traditional homes and traditional roles for women was building.

Woman's Missionary Union continued to be the most obvious vehicle for women's roles in the church. WMU's Juliette Mather, a veteran with the auxillary with the job of promoting missions education, wrote in 1958 that "Southern Baptist women do not preach and are not pastors."[47]But many of the young women responding to service soon challenged that. In the meantime, missionary service continued to be women's most available avenue, and single women, together with missionary wives, totaled over half of all missionaries for both boards.

New leadership in Woman's Missionary Union proved ready for the rapidly developing revolution among women. Alma Hunt of Roanoke, Virginia, succeeded the indomitable Kathleen Mallory as WMU leader on October 1, 1948. The energetic Hunt was a new type leader. Gymnast, volleyball player, and swimmer, Hunt became a school teacher and then a principal by age 21. Reading a biography of Henrietta Hall Shuck provided a turning point in the young woman's life, and she became an enthusiastic disciple of WMU's Young Woman's Auxiliary (YWA). Soon she was tapped for more and more tasks within the organization and spoke to the national meeting of WMU in 1940.[48]

Alma Hunt became Dean of Women at Missouri's William Jewell College in 1944. By spending summers at Columbia University, she soon earned her master's. When she was elected executive secretary of WMU in 1948, she first put her hand to organization and to purchasing a new building in 1952. But she really hit her stride in 1956 when Marie Wiley Mathis joined her as president of the WMU.

A Texas girl, Mathis was raised in Wichita Falls, where she attended Midwestern State Teachers College. After marriage to Robert L. Mathis, she plunged headlong into WMU activities wherever she and her husband lived. She was executive secretary of the Texas Union for a time. After her husband's untimely death, she worked on the staff at First Baptist Church in Dallas before becoming Baylor's Student Union Director. The SBC WMU asked her to become president in 1956, and she found a soul-mate and energetic cohort in Hunt for the exciting transition period unfolding. Together they helped reorganize the auxilliary to deal with the new roles women were taking and engineered major growth in the mission offerings.

Aware of male sensitivites, Mathis and Hunt moved circumspectly with SBC leadership in relationship to the broader women's movement, but they enjoyed increasing openness throughout the fifties and sixties. More women appeared on boards and committees, most of whom had WMU ties.

Hunt's cooperative spirit paved the way for healthy new relationships with other Southern Baptist agencies. That same spirit would allow her to preside over four major divestitures of WMU prerogatives, a feat not seen since I. T. Tichenor led the Home Mission Board to pave the way for the Sunday School Board. Under Hunt, WMU transfered the Carver School of Missions and Social Work (the old WMU Training School) to the SBC, the Royal Ambassadors to the Brotherhood Commission, and the missionaries' children's scholarship administration to the Mission Boards. They also allowed the Mission Boards to take over decisions related to the expenditures of the special offerings.[49]

Other milestones included passing the one million mark in membership in 1950, recording the first one-million-dollar Annie Armstrong Easter Offering for Home Missions in 1953, and taking the weeks of prayer and offering churchwide in 1956. By 1964 the Lottie Moon Christmas offerings had totaled over $100 million during their seventy-six-year history.

The Elliott Controversy

Meanwhile, despite such rapid growth on all fronts, Southern Baptists confronted still another crisis in their ranks that diverted energy from civil rights and women's issues. A young seminary professor, Ralph Elliott, had been one of a group of professors caught up in a controversy with President Duke McCall of Southern Baptist Seminary in 1958 over faculty contributions to a book McCall had published. Years later social historian Samuel S. Hill would label this controversy one of the last hurrahs of a progressive group of scholars attempting to respond to "modern, international currents of thought, including world class biblical scholarship."[50] While most of that group would become part of a controversial set of dismissals related to their conflict with McCall, Elliott escaped as he became the first professor to be contracted at Midwestern Baptist Theological Seminary when it began its work in Kansas City in 1958.[51]

In 1961 at the behest of the Sunday School Board's Broadman Press, Elliott completed a small book, *The Message of Genesis,* which was published by Broadman Press in 1961. An Old Testament professor, Elliott said he was seeking to clarify many of the vexing questions that blocked young intellectuals from seeing the truth of God's Word in the Book of Genesis in light of scientific advances and increasing acceptance of modern scientific theory.

As Nancy Ammerman noted, the theories advanced by Elliott were being aired with less hedging than ever in most Southern Baptist seminary classrooms. While many professors took extreme care to position such teachings beside more conservative views, the increasingly suspicious conservative constituency was uncomfortable with the thought that such views were aired at all. A flurry of questions and then reactions followed the publication of *The Message of Genesis.*

Baptist reaction to modern theories of biblical scholarship and efforts to reconcile science and religion had not changed in many ways from the days of Crawford Howell Toy's experience at Southern Baptist Seminary in 1879. W. A. Criswell, extremely successful as pastor of the First Baptist Church of Dallas after assuming the mantle of George W. Truett in 1946, had become a spokesman for a conservative reaction. He gained a reputation by supporting a biblically justified segregation of the races for a time, though in a highly publicized turnaround he later confessed that he had been wrong and embraced a more open approach to intergration and civil rights.[52]

One of Criswell's favorite stories was that of Crawford Howell Toy. He would point out John A. Broadus's pride in Toy. He would talk about Toy's "tender romance" with Lottie Moon and his mission aspirations, and then he would turn to the deadly "virus" that he contracted while studying German rationalism in Berlin. Criswell was able to evoke not only the tragedy of Toy's defection, but the danger of entertaining such ideas. In Criswell's mind, Toy's Unitarian affiliations a few years after he went to Harvard simply confirmed what that kind of thinking would do, and Criswell was able to voice the fears and convictions of many others in the process.[53]

By the time the Convention gathered in San Francisco in 1962, the Elliott issue had heated up dramatically with many Baptist papers leading the outcry. Herschel H. Hobbs, pastor of the First Baptist Church of Oklahoma City, presided, having been elected at the Convention the previous year in St. Louis, and taking over the gavel from Ramsey Pollard of Tennessee.

The conservative attack was led by K. Owen White, pastor of the First Baptist Church of Houston who in October of 1961 wrote an article based on 2 Kings 4:40 called "Death in the Pot," which he sent to all Baptist state papers, to the seminary presidents, to the Sunday School Board, and to many other leaders. In the article White decried Elliott's work as undermining the historical accuracy of the Bible.[54]

White's warning helped the cause of conservatives in Missouri and Oklahoma who began to develop organization and network to address the issue of liberalism in Southern Baptist life. The fact that *The Message of Genesis* had been written by a professor in a Southern Baptist Seminary and published by Broadman Press, the arm of The Southern Baptist Sunday School Board, was intolerable to many conservative pastors and a number of theologians.

According to Elliott in a book written years later to show this issue as the beginning of the battles that rocked Southern Baptist life in the eighties, one of the letters Midwestern's President Millard Berquist received was from Paul Pressler of Houston, Texas. Pressler said he was praying that "Dr. Elliott will be quickly dismissed for his denial of the inerrancy of Scripture."[55]

In fact, he was dismissed, but not for denying inerrancy. He was dismissed for insubordination when he refused to promise that he would not allow his book to be reprinted. This action was taken by trustees of Midwestern in the fall following the Convention of 1962, but not before the heat peaked with a bomb explosion at the door of Elliott's Kansas City home.

After Elliott's dismissal the controversy continued to dog him, and a call for him to become pastor of a church was withdrawn after pressure was applied. He later found a teaching post with Crozer Theological Seminary and subsequently was pastor of churches affiliated with the American Baptist Convention where he became a rather prominent leader. An editorial in *Christian Century* said "the issue is not heresy or the right of a professor to teach such mild biblical criticism. The issue is a much more vast one: control of the Southern Baptist Convention's academic institutions and, through this, of the training of the ministry." As it turned out later, both conservatives and moderates saw it just that way.[56]

Elliott's book, *The Message of Genesis,* was reprinted the following February by Bethany Press, publishing arm of the Christian Board of Publication of the Disciples of Christ.

The Convention in 1962, held in San Francisco, was all but consumed by the Elliott issue or as others termed it, the Genesis Crisis. State papers fueled the controversy with articles, editorials, and letters to the editor. At San Francisco the Pastor's Conference became a forum for the issue, presaging a growing role for this preconvention meeting in Southern Baptist life. In the Convention meeting itself there were efforts not only to call for Elliott's dismissal, but to recall the book and censure the Sunday School Board and its president, James Sullivan.

Also presaging later battles, trustee selection came into focus as a strategy to control Convention institutions. In his later book Elliott quotes an article by Sally Rice, a Duke graduate student, and claims four trustees were not reelected because of their stands in his behalf.[57]

Herschel Hobbs's skillful handling of motions, as well as his presidential address, were designed to control damage. It became evident that this was part of a leadership plan in place to do just that. Earlier in the spring of 1963, Porter Routh and his associate, Albert McClellan, had gone to Oklahoma City for the fiftieth anniversary of the *Baptist Messenger* which they had both edited in past years. While there, they met with Herschel Hobbs to discuss the growing Genesis Crisis. According to Hobbs, Routh said, "If the Convention was drifting to the left then the fact should be known."[58] They decided to propose to the Executive Committee the appointment of a special committee to study the Statement of Faith that had been developed from the New Hampshire Confession of Faith and adopted by the Southern Baptist Convention in 1925. The 1946 Statement on Principles did not figure into this consideration for reasons previously noted.[59]

The Routh-McClellan-Hobbs plan was a page out of the notebook of history, and these leaders felt that what worked in 1925 to resolve the controversy over evolution would work now. The initial plan envisioned a committee including the seminary presidents, but Baptist editors led by E. S. James protested. Since seminaries were "being investigated," James contended, their presidents should not be included. Hobbs and Routh conceded the point. However, at the Convention a motion was made to include them. It was soundly defeated, indicating the mood of the messengers on this issue and growing conservative suspicions about the institutions. The Convention's final recommendation called for a Committee of State Convention Presidents to be chaired by Hobbs to bring a report to the 1963 Convention.

Baptist scholars, still leery of creedalism, were only partially reassured with such language as "which shall serve as information to the churches, and which may serve as guidelines to the various agencies of the Southern Baptist Convention."[60] The whole exercise, however, was directed to conservative concerns in hopes that it would contain the spreading suspicion of liberalism in SBC seminaries and universities.

The Committee made a crucial decision from the beginning. It saw its options as a new statement, a reaffirmation of the 1925 statement, or a revised form of the 1925 statement; it opted for the third. The Committee then spent much time on a preamble which included the five key concerns of the 1925 preamble and "safeguards of the individual conscience in the interpretation of Scripture."[61]

To the article on the Scriptures they added, "The criterion by which the Bible is to be interpreted is Jesus Christ." And because of increasingly heated racial concerns, they added to the article on man, "The sacredness of human personality is evident in that God created man in His own image, and in that Christ died for man; therefore every man possesses dignity and is worthy of respect and Christian love."[62]

The 1963 document reduced the 1925s' twenty-five articles to seventeen by combining certain items. The only real controversy in committee was on the Lord's Supper when one member insisted on a Landmark treatment or "closed communion." Admitting that many Baptists believed otherwise, however, the member finally relented and supported the majority. There is no record of gender concerns being raised.

The Baptist Faith and Message Committee, as it came to be called, brought its report to almost 13,000 messengers meeting in Kansas City in May 1963. It didn't pass unanimously. Again a Landmark concern for the article on the church and specifically the committee's inclusion of the words "which includes all of the redeemed of all ages" triggered the debate. Hobbs, with Albert McClellan's coaching, called the group's attention to a J. M. Pendleton quotation acknowledging New Testament use of *church* to mean the redeemed in aggregate. Since Pendleton had been a leader of the Landmark movement, that settled matters.[63] That inclusion was arguably the first new development in ecclesiology in the Southern Baptist Convention since 1845.

After the heated debate, the Convention agreed to approve the document as presented. The Convention instructed the officers to print both the 1925 document and the 1963 version with its changes side by side in the

Annual. Again the intervening 1946 Statement of Principles was ignored. Any effort to regard the document as a creed was roundly denounced and uniformly denied by supporters, but Walter Shurden, in retrospect, would imply it was by any other name still a creed.[64]

Baptist leadership, looking toward the celebration of the post-war advance at the Baptist Jubilee Convention to be held in Atlantic City the following year in conjunction with the meeting of the American Baptist Convention and other Baptist groups, desperately wanted the celebration to stand above controversy.

As if to register a final statement on the matter, the Convention elected the leader of the Genesis reaction, K. Owen White, president. But, reflecting the growing bifurcation of focus in Southern Baptist life, it elected its first woman officer at the same convention, as WMU's Marie Mathis took her place as one of the vice-presidents.

The racial turmoil swirling around Baptists on the local level and dominating the national news took a backseat to the Genesis controversy in Southern Baptist life, even as efforts to put the Cooperative Program in place in 1925 had taken a backseat to the 1925 Statement of Faith and the evolution controversy.

Students

When John F. Kennedy was assassinated in Dallas, Texas, in November of 1963, the turmoil and continuing crises of the 1960s seemed to be dramatized in its most violent ugliness.

Young people everywhere had been politically activated by Kennedy, and despite the loss of their ideological leader, they continued to respond to social concerns. Southern Baptist youth were increasingly among them, though generally more moderate. Among Kennedy's most popular programs was the Peace Corps, which enlisted, trained, and deployed thousands of young Americans around the world in service roles. Baker James Cauthen's son, Ralph, went to the Philippines for two years in this program and helped the missions leader envision a missions role for students and young adults.[65]

Baptist Student Unions on college campuses throughout Southern Baptist life were increasingly visible and active. Seminary enrollments grew as these feeder movements delivered more and more young people who felt that the real answers to the turmoil of the period lay in the spiritual realm. Their most visible mobilization came in the next period, however.

Foreign Missions

Despite the litany of crisis in the world, Southern Baptists continued to drive ahead in their original focus, foreign missions. M. Theron Rankin's Program of Advance, developed in a prayer meeting in a hotel in Petersburg, Virginia, at the beginning of 1948, called for Baptists to strengthen the 119 centers in nineteen countries where they were at work, to open additional centers in strategic areas, and to increase personnel and finances until a missionary staff of 1,750 was in place backed by a budget of $7 million.[66]

The Board's Missionary Personnel Department had been established in the latter part of World War II and began to process larger numbers of missionaries each year during Rankin's tenure. Veterans who had seen the world in the war finished college and seminary and presented themselves for new assignments overseas, this time armed with the gospel.

As previously noted, Rankin was not permitted to see the completion of his dream. Just before the Southern Baptist Convention's meeting in Houston in 1953, a medical exam revealed he had leukemia. He died a little over a month later.

The Board next elected George W. Sadler, who had been secretary for Africa, Europe, and the Near East, as interim while they sought God's leadership. When the Board met in Richmond in October 1953, it gave command of Southern Baptists' most precious enterprise to Baker James Cauthen who since 1943 had served as Secretary to the Orient.[67]

Cauthen had received his baptism of fire in difficult times, having gone to China in 1939 during the Japanese-Chinese war. He narrowly missed Japanese capture in 1941 and 1942, as well as Communist occupation in 1951. Cauthen had already begun redeploying the missionaries being expelled from China to other countries in Asia, feeling that as tragic as the closing of that old door was, the opening of new doors was the work of God.

In his very first report, Cauthen made it clear he was committed to Rankin's Program of Advance. The Board's financial receipts had increased much faster than Rankin and his colleagues had dreamed in 1948 and had already reached $8.7 million. But Cauthen was heavily committed to entering new fields and expanding the missionary force itself. He gave strong support to the Missionary Personnel Department that had been established in Maddry's day and significantly expanded under Elmer S. West. At the close of 1963 it was obvious that the Foreign Mission Board would go to the Jubilee Advance in Atlantic City reporting more than 1,750 missionaries. In fact, a few years before this, they raised the goal to 1,800 and actually reached 1803 in time for the Jubilee year.[68]

The increasing flow of committed college and seminary graduates responding to the vision so well articulated by Cauthen allowed the Board to maintain high standards throughout this Advance. The personnel process required college and seminary degrees, robust physical and mental health, and demonstrated spiritual resolve. Experience was carefully evaluated and a high degree of resulting missionary stability allowed for the rapid growth of the force. While such standards were occasionally questioned, not until 1993 would they be seriously challenged.[69]

In 1959, the Foreign Mission Board successfully sought a ruling from the Internal Revenue Service declaring commissioned missionaries, both men and women, as ordained ministers in the eyes of the government. The move was approved by the Southern Baptist Convention without triggering the theological questions about women that emerged later. Even then the ambiguity of this action would be ignored.[70]

Besides the achievement of goals in missionary appointments, the Board reported more than $10 million in gifts. Baptists expanded beachheads throughout Asia, including Korea, Indonesia, East Pakistan, Malaysia, and even an ill-fated work in Vietnam.

African nationalism seemed to be made to order for Southern Baptists as Nigeria missionary Wimpy and Juanita Harper were sent to open up a new work in East Africa. Central African work commenced in what was then called Northern and Southern Rhodesia, while in Latin American and Middle America rapid deployment of missionaries to most of those countries proceeded with the expansion of the missionary force.

Cauthen was one of the most effective speakers in Southern Baptist life, and Foreign Mission night at the Southern Baptist Convention each year tended to be the best attended and the most emotionally charged session. Cauthen's style was part of the key to this, as well as the poignancy and the electricity of missionaries reporting from a world increasingly familiar in Southern Baptists' homes through radio and television.

Home Missions

The Home Mission Board, in the meantime, was much more in the heart of the crises wracking the American domestic scene. As late as 1959, periodic efforts to phase out its work in favor of state convention programs and those of the other agencies and conventions again came to the fore. The

Convention once again voted that year to continue the Board as a separate agency of the Convention.[71]

In 1949 the Southern Baptist Convention had given the Home Mission Board's Chaplaincy Commission full responsibility for this program and it remained a significant part of the Home Mission Board's efforts in the ebb and flow of military buildups that followed World War II. Over 1,200 Southern Baptist ministers served as chaplains in World War II, and 489 were on active duty in 1964 with 752 on reserve status.[72]

Home Mission growth developed, however, in conjunction with the new state conventions being rapidly organized, with a number of new programs emerging out of the program studies of the 1950s, and then with the leadership, first of Courts Redford and later of Arthur Rutledge.

Samuel Courts Redford was a descendant of President Zachary Taylor, but was born to a Missouri farmer in 1898 at the height of the Whitsitt controversy. The family moved to Oklahoma, where the highly motivated young man attended Oklahoma Baptist University. Pastorates, professorships, and denominational posts followed until Redford became president of Southwest Baptist College in Bolivar, Missouri. In 1943, Redford joined the staff of the Home Mission Board as assistant executive secretary. He took the top post ten years later. His tenure witnessed missionary growth from 936 to 2,353.

Arthur Bristow Rutledge, son of a painter-paperhanger, came into a changing world in 1911. In that year Sun Yat-sen was elected president of revolution-weary China, Winston Churchill became First Lord of the Admiralty, and Madam Curie won the Nobel Prize for Chemistry. Yet those who shared birth with Rutledge in this period witnessed changes that made these seem uneventful. He grew up in the relative quiet of San Antonio, Texas, and made a profession of faith in that city's Central Baptist Church, where he was also called to the ministry and ordained as a young man at the beginning of the Great Depression.

Rutledge entered Baylor University two years after Cauthen and Criswell had gone on to seminary. He married Vesta Sharden the summer he graduated and then took Criswell's path to Southern Baptist Seminary, where he received a Th.M. degree in 1939. He returned to pastorates in Texas, including his home church in San Antonio, during which time he took a Th.D. from Southwestern Baptist Seminary after months of an arduous commute. After the war, Rutledge accepted a call to the First Baptist Church of Marshall, Texas, near a small school, East Texas Baptist College.

During his twelve-year pastorate there, Texas Baptist leadership noticed his remarkable skills with people and persuaded him to become first the state's stewardship secretary and then to take its direct missions post. Courts Redford later convinced him to join the Home Mission Board staff in 1959 as Missions Division Director, where he helped initiate many of the Board's new directions. In 1965 he began his eleven-year stint as that agency's fourteenth chief executive. Rutledge's winsome personality, his work with national Baptists and the Christian Life Commission, and his progressive and conciliatory spirit helped in the passion of the Civil Rights battles.[73]

When Texan Lyndon Baines Johnson succeeded Kennedy, his liberal roots from his admiration of Franklin D. Roosevelt emerged. He quickly pushed Kennedy's stalled tax cut and civil rights bill through Congress and added proposals of his own for a billion-dollar "war on poverty." Johnson focused on Appalachia, as did the Home Mission Board, along with programs of work with Indians, Europeans, Orientals, other internationals, the deaf, Spanish-speaking persons, Cuba, and Panama.

In 1963, the Home Mission Board began training Spanish-language missionary appointees at the Mexican Baptist Bible Institute in San Antonio. The Board joined Texas Baptists in a Latin American Crusade in 1964 and then joined the Foreign Mission Board in a "Crusade of the Americas."

By 1963, and after the ill-fated Bay of Pigs, the Home Mission Board in Cuba shifted work to Miami and the growing number of refugees there. Herbert Caudill and his son-in-law David Fite, Home Mission Board missionaries, were imprisoned by the Castro regime, Fite for almost four years.

In 1963, however, the Home Mission Board began giving limited assistance to churches in Puerto Rico, which again brought conflict with the Home Mission Society of the American Baptist Convention. Despite this opposition, the Home Mission Board named a general missionary and justified its work there on the basis that the Southern Baptist Agency had not initiated it.[74]

The Home Mission Board also continued to expand its role in Christian social ministries. It expanded the number of Baptist centers and added juvenile rehabilitation and migrant ministries. Rapid Baptist expansion throughout the United States was well underway when Redford stepped aside in 1964 for Arthur Rutledge. Other Home Mission ministries included work related to nonevangelicals, which included Catholics, Mormons, and non-Christian world religions.

Thirty Thousand

When Southern Baptists met in Atlantic City in May of 1964, it culminated a long period of promotion under the leadership of North Carolina's C. C. Warren who had presided over the Convention in 1956 and 1957. Warren led the Convention to strive for thirty thousand new churches and missions before the Jubilee of the Triennial Convention. It was Southern Baptists' most ambitious promotion since the Sunday School Board led out in an effort to enlist a million more Sunday school scholars by 1954.[75] In many ways the Thirty Thousand movement was simply an exercise in reporting, because the momentum was already underway. Both the Home and Foreign Mission Boards had moved ahead, the Radio and Television Commission continued to expand its ministry, and the Sunday School Board had become a corporate giant. Also, Woman's Missionary Union was more and more aggressive in mission support and in tackling social problems at home, the Brotherhood Commission was defining its role, Baptist Student Unions were growing, Baptist colleges and universities were prospering, and the seminaries were turning out more and more young ministers and missionaries, both male and female.

It was obvious long before the Atlantic City meeting, however, that the numbers were not developing for the Thirty Thousand movement as envisioned when Warren launched the effort in 1956. In some desperation, a more inclusive count was approved which would also count mission points. Even this failed to deliver the results required, and a best-face approach was taken, pointing out how much had been achieved in the effort.[76]

SBC Presidents

For a number of years the election of a president at the Southern Baptist Convention had been a loosely structured exercise of key leaders developing a consensus among themselves about whom they would support and that person's invariably being elected. It included both conservatives and moderates, as such leaders as Lee, Warren, Criswell, Hobbs, White, and Paschall demonstrated. But conservatives, who led what they called a "conservative resurgence" two decades later and were chided about their precinct style politics, often pointed to this "old boy network" as less than a paragon of the democratic process.[77]Once in power, the conservatives would be accused of essentially the same small-group nominating process, but without including any moderates.

Midwestern Seminary historian Hugh Wamble, in a study of Southern Baptist Convention presidents, noted several key changes in this process over the years. The term of service initially had no limit, for instance. The first forty-three years saw only six presidents; three of those served thirty-four years. P. H. Mell's fifteeen years held the record.[78]

After 1900, a custom developed to limit the president to three years, though this was broken once, when J. B. Gambrell was persuaded to accept a fourth term in the euphoria of the 1920 meeting. The Convention formally imposed a two-term limit in 1951 following R. G. Lee's third term. The only exceptions to this since then have been four cases where presidents limited themselves to a single term.

Another change in 1932 made the effective hour of the president's term, which in the beginning commenced at the election, run from the end of one annual meeting to the end of the next.

Other changes were in the practice rather than the rule, such as regionalism, which since World War I "trended westwardly." Wamble noted that since that time twenty-six of thirty-two presidents were from trans-Appalachian and trans-Mississippi areas. Since his study, two were elected from Florida and Tennessee and two from Texas. In 1992, when a president was elected from Texas once again, it was only the third time in SBC history that presidents from the same state had succeeded one another.

Particularly significant over the years have been the professional identification of the presidents. Two educators served twenty-four years in the beginning, with a layman serving ten years and three pastors, nine years. Between 1900 and World War II, the results were equally diverse, with six pastors serving fifteen years; five laymen serving fourteen years; educators thirteen years; and a state-missions official, four years.

Since the beginning of Southern Baptists' second century, sixteen pastors have presided thirty-three years; two laymen four years; and a retired denominational executive one year. This clear trend toward pastor-presidents is seen more clearly in the statistics that show pastors served 21 percent of the time until the end of the century, 32 percent of the time from then until the Centennial, and 86.5 percent since.[79]

Two other trends noted were the increased incidence of pastor-presidents from large churches (over two thousand members) and until 1960 strong Cooperative Program giving churches. That changed in 1979 and declined generally until 1990.

The final trend Wamble noted was evident with the election of K. Owen White in 1963 in Kansas City. The presidency began to reflect current issues in Southern Baptist life. White's high visibility leadership against the "liberalism" which he felt was illustrated in Elliott's book on Genesis, evidently led to his election as president.

The Southern Baptist Convention in 1964 in Atlantic City provided for spirited competition between two candidates reflecting two strongly held Southern Baptist positions. Because the Jubilee Advance was a cooperative effort among Baptists throughout America and a celebration of the denominationalism that had begun with the Triennial Convention in 1814, many leaders wanted to turn to a president who would typify that inclusive spirit. None did so more, it seemed, than the genial Theodore Adams, pastor of Richmond Virginia's First Baptist Church. From 1955 to 1960 Adams served as president of the Baptist World Alliance, joining the distinguished train of Mullins and Truett. Moreover, he was reared in Northern Baptist churches, was educated in Northern Baptist institutions, and pastored Northern Baptist churches before beginning his long tenure in Richmond. Tall and statesman-like, with a pleasing speaking voice and a record of progressive views on civil rights and Baptist cooperation with other Christian groups, Adams was the favorite of many Baptists on the East Coast. In addition, his work as chairman of the Jubilee program impressed many agency leaders and certainly the more moderate wing of Southern Baptist life.[80]

K. Owen White had announced that he would not run for president of the Convention again, and the conservative forces and probably the "old boy network" backed Wayne Dehoney, pastor of the Walnut Street Baptist Church in Louisville, Kentucky. Dehoney, gregarious and at home in all areas of Baptist life, served on a variety of committees and boards and at the same time helped run a very aggressive travel agency.

Both candidates fit all but one of the trends. Both were pastors of large churches; both churches supported the Cooperative Program well; they certainly represented current issues. Neither, however, was from the West; both represented founding states in the Southern Baptist Convention. On the other hand, Dehoney was serving as president of the Pastor's Conference, a role that would later be a staging ground for Southern Baptist Convention presidents.

With conservative backing that was more in evidence following the Genesis controversy than it had been in previous years, continued Southern anxiety about rapid cultural change attendant to civil rights, a continuing fear of ecumenicalism and liberal thinking, Dehoney won, though narrowly. The Virginia Baptist paper complained that the chair had announced a runoff between Dehoney and Adams for the next morning, but in fact, held the vote that evening while many Adams supporters were in other services.[81] Some people felt that race confirmed a growing factionalism within Southern Baptist life unlike any evident since the days of Landmarkism.

The Jubilee Advance was dutifully observed, though the number of messengers, 13,136, fell short of 1960's Miami total of 13,612. An effort to include Southern Baptists in a North American Baptist Fellowship was rejected at this convention. As it turned out, however, Southern Baptists would see even greater Convention gatherings and more galvanizing issues.[82]

7

The Uneasy Consensus

1964–1979

If Southern Baptist leaders hoped that the 1963 Baptist Faith and Message statement and the 1964 Jubilee Advance celebration would provide a working consensus for the years ahead, it quickly proved to be a uneasy one. Rapidly unfolding developments made it increasingly obvious that both the nation and Southern Baptists were entering one of the most socially and politically troubled periods of their interwoven history. The November 1963 assassination of John F. Kennedy in Dallas was a traumatizing introduction to the period.

Less than a year later, the country became embroiled in the most unpopular and ambiguous of wars. In tiny Vietnam, where Southern Baptists had begun a small but promising mission effort in 1959 led by Herman and Dottie Primeaux Hayes, the United States had, under President Kennedy, commited military personnel and resources to support the anti-Communist regime. Under President Lyndon B. Johnson that process continued until more than 800,000 military personnel were involved, and the ambivalent, divided nation suffered 211,000 American casualties and mourned 57,702 dead or missing before the painful event came to an unsatisfactory end.

At home student rebellions, race riots, a developing drug culture, and escalating crime began to trouble and reshape American life.

In the spring of 1968, the nation's most visible and effective civil rights leader, black Baptist minister Martin Luther King, was shot to death in Memphis. The shock had not subsided two months later when presidential-candidate Robert F. Kennedy, like his brother before him, became an assassin's victim. Strangely, the same day, the Southern Baptist Convention, meeting in Houston, Texas, approved a document titled "Concerning Crisis in Our Nation." Decrying racism and violence and calling for healing and renewal, it was Southern Baptists' most direct reaction to moral and political turmoil in its history—yet 2,119 messengers opposed the affirming 5,687.[1]

By 1967, the war in Vietnam was also taking its toll on the nation's economy, and inflation heated up with the consumer price index going from 100 in 1967 to 229 by 1979. Yet Southern Baptists seemed to prosper. Their total gifts doubled the rate of inflation, and Baptists' investment in brick and mortar skyrocketed. Albert McClellan later observed, "If the years 1944–64 were the golden years of church membership growth, the years 1964–84 were the golden years of church building."[2]

Missions in the Midst

The charismatic Baker James Cauthen of the Foreign Mission Board and the likable Arthur Rutledge of the Home Mission Board took full advantage of the uneasy consensus in place after the 1963 Convention and its Baptist Faith and Message agreement.

Cauthen's leadership, following the untimely death of Theron Rankin in 1954, was marked by unprecedented success in pursuing the Rankin "Advance" program. The twenty-two countries where new mission work was started after Cauthen took office were augmented by forty-four new entries in the next fifteen years.[3] In the midst of national and world turmoil, Southern Baptists managed the most aggressive mission era.

Late in 1963, Cauthen gave the Foreign Mission Board's personnel secretary, Jesse Fletcher, permission to pursue a short-term program for young adults in missionary service. Cauthen had relaxed his long-term commitment to the sole use of career missionaries in missionary advance a year earlier when he approved an associate program for experienced men and women beyond the age of missionary appointment for single terms of service in English-language work.

The short-term program, however, capitalized on a major phenomena that had begun under the youth-capturing leadership of President John Kennedy. The Peace Corps had taken the country's imagination, even the world's imagination, by storm when it was introduced in 1961. Cauthen's own son served as a peace corpsman in the Philippines.

Fletcher recruited fellow Texan Louis R. Cobbs to develop what would become the Missionary Journeyman program, and those two—along with Truman S. Smith, who would later become the board's family consultant, William W. Marshall, who after a stint as a missionary and a return to the staff would become executive secretary of Kentucky Baptists, and Samuel A. Debord, former missionary to Africa and Southwestern Seminary professor—designed the program that was launched in 1965.

After a ground-breaking ten-week orientation session, something not yet required of career missionaries, the energetic and idealistic young college graduates were deployed in several dozen countries, beginning with a class of forty-six.[4] The innovation, which would reach its zenith under the direction of Cobbs's successor, Stanley A. Nelson, would send more than two thousand young people overseas for two years of service in the next twenty-five years, including such troubled areas as Vietnam. The popular program would later be downgraded under the Parks administration only to be restored to its original form after R. Keith Parks's retirement.[5]

The enthusiasm of the Journeyman group was more than matched, however, by an ever-increasing pool of older seminary-trained career candidates. The total force continued to grow, and new mission work was launched in Africa and Asia.

Cauthen enjoyed tremendous respect among virtually all Southern Baptists who, for a decade, had been mesmerized by his preaching. But he was not without his detractors.

In 1960, some of his board members decided to back the ambitious plans of one of his missionaries to Japan, W. H. Jackson, Jr., of Texas, for a great evangelistic crusade in that country. Jackson had secured the backing of one of the leading pastors in Japan, but he did not have full support of the mission nor of area leadership in Richmond. He did have the strong support of the Texas Baptist General Convention's executive secretary, T. A. Patterson. Faced with Texas pressure, Cauthen overruled his staff and decided to support what was called the New Life Crusade. Despite mission leaders' fear that Japanese culture was not ready for a western mission that included not only witnessing laymen from farms and offices and living-rooms of Texas homes, but the Hardin-Simmons University Cowboy Band, the program went well and left an indelible impression on its American volunteers.[6]

Cauthen's intuition was good. The New Life Crusade triggered a trend of involving Southern Baptist churches in short-term witnessing efforts overseas. Later, Jackson resigned as a missionary to run a parallel program called the World Evangelistic Foundation with strong support from such conservative leaders as James Draper of Euless, Texas, a former associate of W. A. Criswell. Still later the Foreign Mission Board worked out an agreement with Jackson whereby he phased out his organization in favor of a Partnership Missions endeavor at the Foreign Mission Board.[7]

T. A. Patterson had been pastor of the First Baptist Church in Beaumont, Texas, for many years before taking over the leadership of Texas Baptists, and he was one of the first to challenge openly Cauthen's intimidating leadership. Patterson believed that Southern Baptists' Foreign Mission Board too often became bogged down in institutional efforts and bureaucratic ties with national bodies, instead of aggressively pursuing evangelism.

At this point, T. A. Patterson, whose son Paige attended Hardin-Simmons University and had already evidenced a capacity to challenge the powers-that-be, reflected the same views as one of Cauthen's successors at Southwestern Baptist Theological Seminary.

R. Cal Guy, Bottoms Professor of Missions, championed the methods of the old China hand, John Nevius, in his classes at Southwestern. Nevius had influenced T. P. Crawford who fathered "gospel missionism" three-quarters of a century before. Guy considered Cauthen unresponsive to those Nevius voices that urged less commitment to institutions and more to evangelism, less financial support of national Christians and more incentives to self support.[8]

Few people questioned Cauthen's orthodoxy, conservative views, or heart for evangelism and missions. That, and the forceful personality and incisive mind he brought to his task, ensured his staying in control and on course. It was his successor who changed the paradigm under which the mission board worked and moved more toward the Patterson-Guy emphases.

Home Missions

Under the leadership of the genial and statesman-like Arthur Rutledge, who took over from Courts Redford on January 1, 1965, the Home Mission Board was more aggressive than ever.

Rutledge had proven his skills at the Home Mission Board while serving as the director of the Division of Missions under Redford. He negotiated new agreements with most of the state conventions providing for cooperative efforts in new work, the appointment of missionaries, and percentage sharing in budgets and financing.

The progress achieved in the combined efforts of the Cooperative Program and the Home Mission Board's special offering (the Annie Armstrong Easter Offering) during the Redford era gave the agency more than eight million dollars to work with in 1965 when Rutledge assumed office. By 1970 the total exceeded fourteen million dollars. That same year the missionary force related to the Home Mission Board would approach 2,250.

Rutledge quickly launched the Board into a long range planning process that first developed fourteen basic guidelines to undergird the twelve program statements for the Board adopted by the Convention in 1966. That same year the Department of Christian Social Ministries was organized, focusing on Baptist centers, youth and family services, migrant missions, and literacy missions. Reflecting the Board's more aggressive stance, disaster relief and child-care-agency liaison ministries were soon added.

Glendon McCullough, personnel secretary at the Home Mission Board, and his colleague Nathan Porter, the son of missionaries in Brazil, fashioned a program similar to the Foreign Mission Board's Journeyman program. It was called US-2, signifying two years of service in the United States. Porter would direct the effort which also had a national counterpart, a domestic Peace Corps called Vista. McCollough later headed up the Brotherhood Commission and launched it on an aggressive new course, before an untimely death in an automobile accident ended his outstanding missionary career.

Work related to nonevangelicals was also added that year, picking up the traditional Jewish and Catholic attention and adding Christian sects and non-Christian world religions. In the spring of 1967 a set of ten-year goals titled Directions '77 was approved. These goals subsequently gave way to a

Crossing Barriers emphasis, and then the more far-reaching Bold Mission Thrust, nomenclature that the Home Mission Board initially developed but which was later adopted by the whole Convention and all of its agencies.[9]

Along with the Foreign Mission Board, Rutledge and his colleagues joined the Crusade of the Americas in 1969, with three ministry-encompassing objectives: (1) deepening spiritual life within the churches, home and individual Christians; (2) evangelizing the American continent; and (3) establishing true moral and spiritual bases for the betterment of mankind's economic, social, and physical welfare. Without reference to the 1946 Statement of Principles, these objectives seemed to reflect its flavor in a remarkable way.

Also in 1969, Rutledge named Kenneth Chafin to the Home Mission Board to succeed C. E. Autry as secretary of evangelism. With stints as professor of evangelism at Southwestern Seminary and in the Billy Graham chair of evangelism at Southern Seminary, the New Mexico native brought a new perspective to the task. Earlier, Rutledge had tapped Southern Seminary's professor of missions and world religions, Hugo H. Culpepper, to head the Missions Division along with *Home Missions* editor Walker L. Knight, who later published an independent paper called *Baptists Today*; Chafin, who returned to influential pastorates; and Culpepper, who returned to teaching. Rutledge gave the often-challenged Board new stature. Interestingly, all three of Rutledge's lieutenants became strong voices for moderate dissent after the 1979 conservative resurgence was launched.

Rutledge himself retired at the end of 1976 and died in November 1977, giving his initial "Direction '77" planning a prescient personal significance.

During the twelve years of the Rutledge watch, gifts tripled and the missionary force reached 2,839. One of the Rutledge-led Board's more effective accomplishments was an accelerated effort to embrace the proliferating ethnic communities in ministry along with traditional Hispanic and Black ministries.[10]

But Rutledge's lasting legacy was not so immediately recognized as a paradigm shift in the pattern of the oft-challenged enterprise. The Home Mission Board moved from a direct mission program to a cooperative mission program. Agreements that Rutledge negotiated under Redford laid the groundwork, but the careful implementation Rutledge presided over was the key. He often referred to this new role as one of "catalyst."[11]

The paradigm change freed the Home Mission Board from doubts about its role vis-à-vis state conventions. It did not fully resolve the challenge given it by the Southern Baptist Convention in 1959 to develop "a single uniform mission program." But its new role and aggressive program innovations under Rutledge allowed it to emerge from the shadows of the questions it had faced since its early battles with the Home Mission Society and its later conflicts with developing state conventions. The agreements with the state conventions and its new program statements gave it a national strategic role that became more evident in the upcoming Bold Mission Thrust era. Thanks to a popular and well-written *Home Missions* magazine edited by Walker Knight, the Board even enjoyed popularity comparative with that of the Foreign Mission Board for the first time since the days of I. T. Tichenor. That Board's paradigm shift was yet to come.

Women's Ordination

An almost unnoticed event in August 1964 presaged growing implications for Southern Baptists. In the Watts Street Baptist Church of Durham, North Carolina, a young Virginia woman named Addie Davis, a 1963 graduate of Southern Seminary, was ordained a minister of the gospel. Not since the days of the evangelistic Separate Baptist churches in the South and the like of Martha Stearns Marshall had a Southern Baptist church recognized a woman for ministry.

Davis had already proved her mettle in service as assistant pastor of the First Baptist Church of Elkins, North Carolina, and as dean of women at a small West Virginia college. The pastor of the ordaining church, Warren Carr, explained simply that her testimony and her sense of call were taken seriously by the church.[12]

While what Leon McBeth called "a storm of protest" followed, Davis' acceptance of a church in Vermont probably kept it from becoming more intense.[13] Too, Baptists respected the autonomy of the local church and gave the Durham church the right to take such an action even when they disagreed.[14]

Addie Davis's ordination at first seemed an isolated event. In fact, it was 1971 before the next ordination of a woman in Southern Baptist life was recorded when the Kathwood Baptist Church of Columbia, South Carolina, ordained Shirley Carter. That action was rescinded the next year, however. Also in 1972, the Bainbridge Baptist Church of Richmond, Virginia, ordained Marjorie Lee Bailey, a chaplain at the Virginia State Industrial Farm. Some opposition was registered in the Richmond Baptist Association, but no action was taken.[15]

Again in 1972, the Metropolitan Baptist Association of New York, which was a Southern Baptist group, admitted the Christ Temple Baptist Church in Harlem to its membership. This church's pastor since 1963 was a widow, Druecillar Fordham, who had been ordained among National Baptists in 1942. The church's admittance made Fordham the dean of such women in Southern Baptist life.[16]

McBeth notes that the first Southern Baptist Convention employee to be ordained, Elizabeth G. Hutchens, received her credentials from the Baptist Temple Church in Alexandria, Virginia, while on sabbatical from Southern Seminary. A year later, 1974, Jeanette Zachry, a graduate of Southwestern Seminary, received ordination from Broadway Baptist Church in Fort Worth, as Hazel Grady did from the Oakhurst Baptist Church in Decatur, Georgia. Grady did not ask for hers, but she accepted the church's recommendation, even as George Truett had done so long ago.[17]

While opposition in many of these churches was present, it was minor. When Willow Meadows Baptist Church in Houston ordained Susan Sprague in late 1975, 16 percent of the church opposed as did one member of the ordaining council.[18]

One interesting turn in this still-modest development in Southern Baptist life was that numbers of couples were ordained for either joint or separate ministries. Darryl Tiller, a Southern Seminary graduate received ordination before his wife Aldrede was ordained by the First Baptist Church of Rockmart, Georgia. Her service was notable in that Hazel Grady and Pearl Duvall took part in her ceremony as ordained women.

Yet the phenomena was still a trickle. McBeth said that between 1964 and 1978 the total number of women ordained numbered around fifty. The number later increased dramatically.

During the same period even more churches began to ordain women as deacons or deaconesses. However, even as the setting aside of deacons in the New Testament preceded that of pastors, so this practice among Southern Baptists preceded women's ordination for ministry. The First Baptist Church of Waco appointed (rather than ordained) deaconesses as early as 1877 to assist deacons with the poor and in the baptism of women and girls.[19] Women deacons have served the Wake Forest Church in North Carolina since 1924 and the Danville Church in Georgia since 1931. The BSSB publication, *The Deacon*, estimated that two or three hundred Southern Baptist churches had women deacons by 1973, and Virginia Baptist churches recorded 520 women deacons in 1976.[20]

The scattered opposition to the ordination of women began to coalesce in 1976 when Arkansas's Black River Association passed a resolution that cited the practice as "unbiblical" and took the state's executive secretary, Charles Ashcraft, to task for an article perceived to be favorable to the practice. The Arkansas Convention itself passed a resolution the next year opposing the Home Mission Board's support of an ordained woman, Suzanne Coyle, who had been ordained in Kentucky after graduation from Southern Seminary and was working under Home Mission Board auspices in a Philadelphia mission.[21]

Arkansas's opposition was preceded, however, by an Oklahoma resolution decrying ordination of women as ministers or deacons. As early as 1972, an article in the *Baptist Messenger* of Oklahoma said, "The Bible teaching on the subject is so plain that it would seem unnecessary and a useless waste of time to discuss ordaining women as preachers or deacons in the churches."[22]

Defenders such as Arkansas's embattled Charles Ashcraft stood their ground, saying, "Any lack of serious assessment of these delightful handmaidens of Almighty God will not meet the smile of God."[23]

It was only an introduction to one of the key issues of the upcoming Southern Baptist battles.

Marking 125 Years

When the two mission boards celebrated their 125th anniversaries in 1970, both were in an expansive posture, increasingly confident of the churches' support. Both were well funded by the Cooperative Program and special offerings, the Lottie Moon Christmas offering for Foreign Missions and the Annie Armstrong Easter offering for Home Missions. In addition, they were registering a wealth of missionary prospects emerging from Baptist college campuses and, through Baptist Student Unions, state colleges and universities and the burgeoning seminaries.

Their progress was unrivaled in Christian denominational circles, but interdenominational missionary programs such as Wycliffe Translators and Campus Crusade, though more narrowly focused, did match them in personnel numbers. The neo-evangelicalism feeding these efforts found its way into Southern Baptist ranks in the next period and challenged Southern Baptists' missionary directions and progress.

New State Conventions

With the Home Mission Board both leading and following, Southern Baptist work continued to expand throughout the sixties and seventies into traditional American Baptist areas with the resulting state conventions being organized and then recognized by the Southern Baptist Convention.

The western mission efforts of the Arizona Baptist Convention, which had, along with the Home Mission Board, spawned much new work, saw its latest hatch come of age in the birth of the Utah-Idaho Southern Baptist Convention in October of 1964. With headquarters in the heart of Mormon country in Salt Lake City, the Convention included fifty churches and a budget 90 percent funded by the Home Mission Board.[24]

Three years later, work sponsored first by the Arizona Baptist Convention and later by churches in Colorado came to fruition for Southern Baptist churches in the states of Montana, North Dakota, South Dakota, and Wyoming with organization of the Northern Plains Baptist Convention in November 1967 in Rapid City, South Dakota.

The Baptist Convention of New York came into being in September 1969 with seventy churches. It was the thirty-first state convention to be affiliated with the Southern Baptist Convention. As in the West, new work was the constant focus of each church. The Metropolitan Baptist Association of New York, for instance, was composed of churches primarily developed by the work of the Manhattan Baptist Church.[25]

When the Northeastern Baptist Fellowship split into smaller units, the Pennsylvania-South Jersey Baptist Fellowship was established and became the Baptist Convention of Pennsylvania-South Jersey in early October 1970, with ninety churches and 10,000 members in three associations.[26]

In contrast, the West Virginia Convention of Southern Baptists had a long history of Southern Baptist churches when in October 1970, they achieved a long sought goal and organized the West Virginia Convention of Southern Baptists in Belle, West Virginia.[27]

The thirty-fourth state convention to affiliate with the Southern Baptist Convention was another product of Southern Baptists' great western initiative. Seventy-one churches sent messengers to organize the Nevada Area Baptist Convention in October 1978 in Las Vegas, though it quickly dropped the "Area" from its name.[28]

This post-war expansion throughout the United States was due to many factors. In the West, the aggressive work of the Arizona Baptist Convention and the Southern Baptist Convention's pivotal decision in 1942 admitting

California Baptists certainly facilitated it. Moreover, the ethos of western Baptists was missionary, and even the smallest and newest churches endeavored to start missions and new churches.

In the Midwest and the Northeast, new work was more intentional, and the Home Mission Board was aided by growing acceptance on the part of American Baptists to the inevitability of expansion. Growth of the so-called Sun Belt even involved a reverse flow of Baptists from the north who organized a few churches that affiliated with American Baptists.

The whole process rode the wave of demographic changes that followed first the displacements and westward migration after the Civil War, then the move to the West and Northwest that came on the heels of the depression and finally the major changes that were a part of the World War II mobilization. Southern Baptists' affinity for their own ecclesiology and doctrine and their missionary spirit undergirded their attitude of manifest destiny.

Agency and Institutional Growth

As they came to their 125th anniversary in 1970, Southern Baptists' four boards were ably leading the Convention's collective cause. Besides the Home Mission Board and the Foreign Mission Board were the giant Sunday School Board and the quiet, but well-trusted and rapidly growing Annuity Board.

The Annuity Board had enjoyed solid growth under R. Alton Reed, who had taken over its leadership from W. R. Alexander in 1955 and who in turn gave way to Darold H. Morgan in 1972. In 1959, during Reed's administration, the name of the agency was changed from the Relief and Annuity Board to the Southern Baptist Annuity Board.[29] It subsequently changed the name of its chief executive to "President," which became a model for other boards and commissions in the years that followed. The Annuity Board had one-third of a billion dollars in trusts at the turn of the decade and provided programs not only for churches and their staffs, but for colleges and universities, seminaries, children's homes, homes for the aged, hospitals, SBC agencies, and thirty-three state convention headquarters. In the troubling years that followed the breakup of the uneasy consensus, pastors were heard to say more than half seriously, "I go with the side that gets the Annuity Board."[30]

Much of the focus of Southern Baptist life during this period was shared by six seminaries. The oldest seminary, Southern, had been under the leadership of Duke McCall since 1951. McCall had previously served as president of New Orleans Baptist Theological Seminary during the time it was still known as Baptist Bible Institute. Before that he had a brief stint as executive secretary-treasurer of the Executive Committee prior to going to Southern.[31]

In 1958 McCall fought a revolt of seminary professors which cost him thirteen of his best professors. These men in turn helped staff the new seminaries, as their battles with McCall were judged to be with McCall's administrative style rather than theological differences. Southern Seminary enjoyed an outstanding reputation as the Convention reached its 125th birthday and reported over 1,300 enrolled two years later with a faculty of fifty-four, in contrast to the original four who started the seminary in 1859.[32]

Southern Seminary's rival institution, Southwestern, which had, shortly after its founding, come under the aegis of the Baptist General Convention of Texas, became a Southern Baptist Convention institution in 1925. Under Presidents Scarbrough, E. D. Head, J. Howard Williams, and Robert E. Naylor, the Fort Worth seminary had outgrown the older institution in Louisville. At the time Southern Seminary's enrollment reached 1,300, Southwestern's had passed 2,400 with a faculty of seventy-five.[33] It was then the largest institution of its kind in the world.

As mentioned earlier, the Baptist Bible Institute had become New Orleans Baptist Theological Seminary in 1946 and was led during this period by H. Leo Eddleman (1959–70) and Grady C. Cothen, who took over in 1971. It registered roughly half of the student attendance of Southern at this time, with just over seven hundred students and thirty-eight faculty members.[34]

The new institutions, Golden Gate Baptist Theological Seminary, Southeastern Baptist Theological Seminary, and Midwestern Baptist Theological Seminary were, in contrast, much smaller, but as Protestant seminaries go, still large.

Golden Gate, which was located in Mill Valley, California, had moved to a new campus on Strawberry Point in Marin County under the leadership of President Harold K. Graves. It had a fairly stable enrollment of three hundred-plus with sixteen faculty members at this same period. While Graves sought to increase the number who came from California Baptist churches and the funds that came from those churches, he found himself traveling back to the Old South both to recruit students and to raise funds.[35]

Southeastern Baptist Theological Seminary, which had been established largely in a tandem program with Golden Gate, had grown to well over six hundred students with twenty-five faculty members by this period. Its Ivy League look came from the inherited old campus of Wake Forest University at Wake Forest, North Carolina.[36]

Midwestern Baptist Theological Seminary survived the turmoil surrounding the Elliott controversy and began to experience solid growth under founding president Millard Berquist, who was succeeded in 1973 by former Southwestern Seminary philosophy professor, Milton Ferguson.[37]

Nashville was the base for the six seminaries' Seminary Extension department which represented them through correspondence work and enrolled over six hundred people. Nashville was also the home of the Southern Baptist Foundation, which by this period had $13 million in trusts, though it was eclipsed by larger state foundations. In fact, the same year (1959) that the Home Mission Board survived a challenge when the Convention reaffirmed its existence, the Foundation faced the same fire, also because of perceived overlap with state efforts. Its existence was also reaffirmed.[38]

Commissions and Committees

The Southern Baptist Convention did its work through standing committees, especially the Executive Committee and its boards, institutions, and commissions. There were eight commissions in this period, though one, a hospital commission was phased out in 1971 as the Southern Baptist Convention decided to get out of the hospital business. State conventions continued to sponsor hospitals despite ambiguities over federal funding.[39]

The American Baptist Seminary Commission in Nashville, Tennessee, provided for Southern Baptists' continuing work among black Baptists in a cooperative program with the National Baptist Convention, Inc. During this period the American Baptist Seminary enrolled approximately one hundred students.[40]

Despite the fact that WMU was an auxiliary to the Southern Baptist Convention, the Brotherhood continued to operate as a Commission. The successor of the Laymen's Missionary Movement of 1907, the Brotherhood Commission, which had taken this name in 1950, was led by George W. Schroeder until 1970 when Glendon McCullough left the Home Mission Board to head up that Commission. Despite significant progress in lay witnessing emphases and improved publications, Brotherhood, as it was called, continued to struggle in the shadow of the much larger, more aggressive Woman's Missionary Union.[41]

Though the women had transferred the Royal Ambassador program to the Brotherhood in 1954, the men had not been able to generate the kind of popularity in this program that the women had nurtured for many years.

The Education Commission worked to support the colleges and universities that were a part of the various state conventions. While sometimes a spokesman for the oft-troubled group, its job was more often a clearing house and correlation function.

In addition, the Historical Commission was in place as a successor to the Southern Baptist Historical Society which became an agency of the Convention in 1951. Its predecessor had played a strong role in the Convention's effort to secure a centennial history under the authorship of Southwestern Seminary's W. W. Barnes. Norman Cox, followed by Davis C. Woolley, led the Commission into this period, and Lynn E. May, Jr., took over in 1971.[42]

The most aggressive commissions of this period, however, were the Christian Life Commission, led by Foy D. Valentine, and the Radio and Television Commission, led by Paul M. Stevens. Valentine had succeeded A. C. Miller in 1960, and Stevens had followed S. F. Lowe in 1953.

Because of the continuing civil rights crisis in the nation, the Christian Life Commission was drawn more and more into a vortex of controversy. After Kennedy's assassination, Texas's Lyndon Baines Johnson led a remarkable legislative landslide called the Great Society, which included the Voting Rights Act of 1965. This act further galvanized militant black leadership and sympathetic white civil rights supporters. The assassination of Martin Luther King, Jr., in Memphis, Tennessee, in 1968 robbed the movement of its most charismatic leader. But by then civil rights was no longer just a black issue; it was a national issue.

The Christian Life Commission took a very aggressive approach in trying to make inroads to entrenched Southern views that had existed since the days of the Civil War. Under the broad program title Christian Morality Development, Valentine kept his staff and a small but enthusiastic cadre of followers on the leading edge of national social change.[43]

By the Convention's 125th anniversary, the Radio and Television Commission was "originating a broadcast somewhere in the world on the average of every three minutes." With programs of preaching on radio and television, audience building, inquiry and counseling, and technical assistance to agencies, churches, and individuals, Stevens kept the Commission moving ahead on a tidal wave of developing technology.[44]

Church services throughout the South were being televised, and prominent evangelists developed regular programming that was self-sustaining through audience solicitation.

The eighth commission, the Stewardship Commission, enjoyed the support of all agencies and commissions through its undergirding role. It was still in the beginning of this period by its first executive director Merrill D. Moore. Moore was succeeded in 1971 by James V. Lackey, then in 1974 by A. Rudy Fagan.

Two standing committees that served Southern Baptists during this period, the Denominational Calendar Committee and the Baptist General Committee on Public Affairs, were less front-and-center, though the latter became the focus of a firestorm two decades later.

Auxiliaries

Three auxiliary organizations were serving with Southern Baptists by this time. Woman's Missionary Union—under the leadership of Alma Hunt and Carolyn Weatherford and strong presidents, Mrs. R. L. (Marie) Mathis and Mrs. Robert Fling—expanded the influence of the women's program through their publications, their organizations, and especially their annual missions offerings. Reflecting their working camaraderie, Alma Hunt convinced Marie Mathis to resign as president to become director of the Union's Promotion Division in 1963, shortly after Mathis was elected second vice-president of the SBC.[45]

Not surprisingly, WMU enjoyed the total confidence of the Foreign Board's Baker Cauthen and the Home Board's Arthur Rutledge. The three presented a solid front in denominational affairs, a condition that fell victim to the factionalism that soon developed.

With a program of teaching missions, engaging in mission action, supporting world missions through prayer and giving, and providing interpretive information regarding the work of the church and the denomination, Alma Hunt led the WMU toward its centennial in solid fashion before giving way to Carolyn Weatherford in October of 1974.

Weatherford, who headed Florida's WMU prior to her election to the national post, early embraced the need to help women in their drive for roles in church vocations. Her actions guaranteed opposition, as many conservative women strongly resented anything that would take away from women's roles in home and family or would question their being subject to men. Conservative opposition was obvious in the 1973 convention when a resolution by Texas's Jessie Tillison Sappington called for a return to traditional women's roles and proved that the women's movement was still suspect among many Baptists.[46]

This did not deter Weatherford, however, and she requested the Christian Life Commission to conduct a seminar on Freedom for Christian Women at WMU's 1975 executive board meeting. Eight years later she helped Southern Baptist Women in Ministry organize. Hunt, in her retirement address, had expressed her own views that WMU "lifts a woman's perspective above the kitchen sink, or above the desk, or above the industry where she works, to see a world in need and to see that she herself can have a part in it."[47]

Weatherford's more immediate challenge was to reverse declining enrollments which hit WMU as more women moved into the workplace in the seventies. In 1975, Helen Fling stepped aside as president in favor of Christine Gregory of Virginia, who teamed with Weatherford for long-range planning and appropriate reorganization. In 1981, Gregory, like Mathis before her, was elected a vice-president of the Southern Baptist Convention.

WMU was especially involved with the denomination's Mission Challenge Committee and helped birth the Bold Mission Thrust program in the late seventies. By 1979, total enrollment stood at 1,086,785, led by Baptist women with 494,273 members, and including Baptist Young Women, Campus BYW, Acteens, Girls in Action, and Mission Friends. They numbered 80,195 individual organizations.[48]

Another auxillary organization was the Baptist World Alliance, which was begun in 1905 and periodically headed by Southern Baptist leaders. In fact, Southern Baptist Robert S. Denny was the general secretary of the BWA during this period, which by now included six groups of Baptists in North America as well as national groups of Baptists throughout the world—many established by the missionary efforts of American Baptists and Southern Baptists.

The third auxiliary organization was the American Bible Society which was only loosely supported by the Southern Baptist Convention at this time, but helped Southern Baptists highlight their self-identity as a people of the Book.

WMU presented a significantly different kind of auxiliary relationship to the SBC from that of the Baptist World Alliance and the American Bible Society. WMU participated in program planning and coordination with the other agencies and had representatives on the Executive Committee. This meant much more direct involvement. Yet WMU received no Cooperative Program funds in contrast to BWA and ABS.

Continuing Crisis

Despite overall progress, Southern Baptist life, like the larger environment, was anything but tranquil during this period. The focal point for much of Southern Baptists' conflict was the Baptist Sunday School Board, now a corporate giant continuing to operate out of Nashville. In some ways the turbulence that engulfed it in the 1970s was but a mirror of turmoil already engulfing the nation.

President Johnson had all but abandoned his Great Society program, commiting his resources instead to stopping Communism's advance in Vietnam. While Johnson's policy was consistent with the predominant theories of the time, reaction to the Vietnam War became more and more vehement in the late sixties. By 1968 he thought he could not win an election with that burden on him and announced that he would not run and would retire to his ranch in his beloved Texas Hill Country.

With Johnson out, former vice-president Richard Nixon moved back on the scene, defeating the Democrat's George McGovern. Nixon escalated the war in Vietnam and opened negotiations toward its end.

Overwhelmingly reelected in 1972, Nixon immediately encountered a series of disasters. First, his vice-president, Spiro Agnew, was forced to resign. Then after the break-in at Democratic headquarters at Washington's Watergate Hotel that had ties to White House staff and a botched coverup, Nixon was forced to resign in August 1974.

Gerald Ford, who had become vice-president by virtue of the U. S. Constitution's twenty-fifth amendment—which allows a president to nominate a replacement for a vice-presidential vacancy to take effect upon a majority vote by both Houses of Congress—now became president. Having been "selected rather than elected," Ford's position was weakened from the outset.

Nixon and his intrepid Secretary of State, Henry Kissinger, had managed to extricate the United States from Vietnam in 1973, but the country then had to watch helplessly as the South Vietnamese proved unable to handle the Communists by themselves and collapsed in 1975.

These overwhelming setbacks in Republican ranks enabled an unknown Democrat, Jimmy Carter from Plains, Georgia, to defeat Ford and win the presidency in 1976. Carter looked like an anti-establishment type who would at last bring the people's point of view to entrenched bureaucratic government. After his swearing in ceremonies he eschewed the traditional limousine and hand-in-hand with his wife Rosalynn led the parade down Pennsylvania Avenue.

Jimmy Carter was not the first Southern Baptist ever to be elected President of the United States. While the press and public made little of it, Harry S. Truman's church in Independence, Missouri, is affiliated with the Southern Baptist Convention. But Carter's affiliation was high-profile, as he unashamedly referred to himself as "a born-again Christian" when he embarked on what was to be a troubled four years in office. His deep Christian convictions were demonstrated in the Camp David peace accords between the Egyptians and the Israelis, who had fought two disastrous wars during this period. But he was unable to break into the bureaucratic inner circles in Washington and encountered a fervent conservative opposition.

In this sense Carter mirrored the feelings a cadre of Southern Baptists who felt that they were unable to break into the bureaucratic inner circle of Southern Baptist life. While some of these were on the left of the Baptist spectrum, more were on the right.

Controversy at the Sunday School Board

The Sunday School Board epitomized for many people a forbidding bureaucratic structure, and many Southern Baptists found themselves in a love-hate relationship with that extremely successful product of its common life.

Sunday School enrollment doubled in Southern Baptist life just about every forty years from 1880 on, but beginning in 1960 it slowed dramatically. In fact, for the twenty years from 1960 to 1980 enrollment only increased from 7.3 million to 7.4 million, almost a standstill by previous standards.[49]

In addition, the Church Training programs which had been the successor of Baptist Young People's Union (BYPU) suffered a drastic decline in the mid-sixties. Consideration must be given to the possibility that the Convention's subsequent conflicts were due at least in part to the lack of understanding of denominational history and a lack of awareness of its doctrinal development that had previously been provided through the work of Church Training and its predecessors.

The Sunday School Board endeavored to pump new life into the Sunday evening program in 1969 by changing the name of Church Training to a well-researched and tested name, Quest. But at about the same time a national company began to produce women's hygiene products under the same name. Baptists defeated the name-change by ridicule as much as by anything else.[50]

Still, through corporate restructuring and astute marketing leadership, the Sunday School Board grew dramatically in influence and financial strength. But these visible setbacks robbed it of some of its invincibility.

The Sunday School Board had barely recovered from the Elliott controversy in the early sixties when the *Broadman Bible Commentary* was published and its Genesis and Exodus sections came under heavy fire from conservative voices. Led by Ross Edwards, editor of the *Baptist Word and Way* in Missouri, and a pastor, M. O. Owens, from North Carolina, an aggressive conservative group still in touch with one another following the Elliott controversy leveled a blistering criticism at the Sunday School Board. Even such strong denominationalists as Joe Odle of the Mississippi *Baptist Record* questioned the direction of the Sunday School Board in its publishing ventures. Specifically, Odle cited tendencies to allow biblical criticism in its new materials, to move away from a doctrinal stand, to overemphasize social action, and to emphasize an intellectual rather than biblical approach.[51]

W. A. Criswell was elected president of the Convention in Houston in 1968 and presided when the Convention registered a record 16,678 messengers in New Orleans in 1969. Criswell took over the gavel from H. Franklin Paschall, who served as pastor for many of the Sunday School Board employees and had presided for two terms following Wayne Dehoney's tenure. Given the recent controversies, Sunday School Board employees could have felt less secure under the fiery Criswell, but Criswell later confessed that he did essentially what the denomination's leadership told him to do.[52]

The Sunday School Board's Broadman Press, under fire from conservatives for the *Commentary*, drew criticism from its more moderate elements when in 1968 it published W. A. Criswell's book entitled *Why I Preach That the Bible Is Literally True* at the beginning of his tenure as president of the Convention. Many Baptists of more moderate views, still wincing over treatment of the Elliott book, reacted strongly against Broadman's promotion of

Criswell's effort. Confirming the suspicions of many conservatives was a strong reaction by the Association of Baptist Professors of Religion at their meeting in 1969 that criticized Criswell's book and the Sunday School Board's promotion of it.[53]

The professors' move, based upon their belief that Criswell's book denied the historical-critical approach to the Bible, encountered an immediate backlash. A few letters to editors and one editorial called for investigations by trustees of Baptist schools into what their professors were teaching about the Bible.

Despite evidence of strong support for Criswell's book and maybe because of it, the professors and their supporters organized a short-lived entity called the E. Y. Mullins Fellowship. They even decided to run one of their own, Richmond University professor W. C. Smith, Jr., against Criswell at the convention in New Orleans. Smith garnered 450 votes to Criswell's 7,482. Thus supported, Criswell lashed back in a speech to the Executive Committee in Nashville. Urging "arch-liberals" to get out of the Convention, he confessed his growing frustration with the range of beliefs sheltered under the Southern Baptist Convention. "How far do you compromise what you believe in order to stay together?" he asked.[54]

The following year, 1970, emboldened by Criswell's presiding and with the Convention meeting in the conservative stronghold of Denver, Colorado, opponents of the Sunday School Board's perceived liberal tendencies promoted an "Affirming the Bible Conference" just preceding the Southern Baptist Convention. Led by Missouri's Ross Edwards and several previous SBC presidents, including Ramsey Pollard and K. Owen White, the conference, together with the Denver Convention, clearly demonstrated the growing power of the conservative voice and the galvanizing of the forces of the disaffectioned in Southern Baptist life.

Despite efforts by the Sunday School Board's Sullivan to promote the idea of unity amidst diversity and to point out that no SBC position was intended by Broadman publications and Clifton Allen's plea to give the next generation "a heritage of the open mind and open Bible" (Allen was general editor of the *Commentary*) a motion was passed to withdraw volume 1 from distribution and rewrite it.[55]

A year later the Convention met in St. Louis, and, though North Carolina's Carl Bates had succeeded Criswell in the presidency, the SBC majority present hardened the Denver action by instructing the Sunday School Board to rewrite the *Commentary* with another writer. The action of the Convention was unprecedented and should have clearly demonstrated the potency of the conservative bent among Southern Baptists and its growing desire to influence the agencies more directly. On the other hand, as certain agency heads would try to point out, the move demonstrated the effectiveness of existing denominational procedures to correct matters deemed amiss. No changes were needed, they would argue.

The next year, in Philadelphia, Bates lashed out at a conservative group committed to rewriting the entire twelve-volume *Broadman Bible Commentary*. He said, "If any member of this convention and its affiliated churches is determined to have theological and ecclesiastical sameness, let him know at the outset that he has one of two choices. He must either join another denomination or deny the basic democratic principles for which our people have been known across the years."[56]

The Convention defeated a motion to rewrite the whole commentary, but as the years ahead would show, many Baptists were committed to the theological "sameness" that Bates felt was incongruous with Baptist principles.

Sullivan tried to control the damage and regain convention confidence for the agency by hiring former New Orleans Baptist Theological Seminary president H. Leo Eddleman to be "doctrinal reader." It was hoped that Eddleman's well-known conservatism would placate the growing assertiveness of the Board's detractors.

The damage, however, did not reach to the Sunday School Board's bottom line as it continued to grow and pursue its programs aggressively, including its program of publications. But the ability to develop and promote its programs without fear of criticism and protest, if indeed it ever existed, was gone. Traditional agency leadership, which had all but become the dominant force in Southern Baptist life, was both sobered and puzzled by the Sunday School Board's experience. Things were less rancorous during Bates's second term. His successor was a moderate layman, Owen Cooper of Yazoo, Mississippi.

With both distance and absence of a galvanizing controversy working together, the Convention's next meeting in Portland, Oregon, registered only 6,638 messengers, the lowest number in twenty-two years. A resolution asserting that "many of our churches are disturbed and fellowship hindered because of a liberal drift in theology" died in the resolutions committee. An attack on the women's liberation movement was rewritten to be less strident. These efforts continued to demonstrate, however, the Convention's growing conservative bent, and its sessions continued to reflect a growing conservative reaction.[57] Observers would later note that this tendency mirrored directions in the nation as a whole.

Total registration nearly doubled when the Convention returned to its heartland in Dallas the following year and conservative Texas pastor Jaroy Weber was elected to succeed Cooper.

Sunday School Board chief, James Sullivan, however, continued to be harrassed by reactionary elements despite his own well-known conservatism. Having tried to handle earlier conflicts by changing his residence and securing an unlisted phone number, he now began to feel the burden was threatening his health. He let the Sunday School Board know that he would be retiring at the end of 1974, and in February of 1974 the Board turned to Grady Cothen, president of New Orleans Baptist Theological Seminary, to head up the giant enterprise.

Cothen, the first non-Southern Baptist Theological Seminary-trained person to head the publishing giant, was, like Sullivan, a Mississippian. He graduated with a Masters of Christian Training from New Orleans Baptist Theological Seminary, served as a chaplain during the war, and was a pastor in Alabama and Oklahoma before becoming executive secretary of the Southern Baptist Convention of California in 1961. His intense leadership qualities identified him as a comer and, despite his lack of an earned doctorate, he served as president of Oklahoma Baptist University for a time before being tapped for the presidency of New Orleans Seminary.[58]

Obviously, to the Board members looking to recoup Southern Baptists' confidence in the Sunday School Board, Cothen was ideal for the job. But they spared no effort to make sure of that. He was the first prospective president to be required to take psychological testing before his election. Sullivan, however, had introduced that corporate trend to the Sunday School Board some years before for his top lieutenants.

Anxious to win back the confidence of Southern Baptists, Cothen set up listening meetings designed to negate the perception that the rank and file had no influence on the Sunday School Board. He told the Board he wanted to concentrate on "in-depth Bible study, equipping the saints, supporting and enriching family life, and aiding and encouraging pastors and church staff."[59]

Cothen called Southern Baptists "a people of the Book" and introduced a new Sunday School series called "The Bible Book Series." Since 1891, the Sunday School Board had been publishing the uniform Sunday School series in connection with all denominations involved in Sunday School work, and in 1966 introduced an alternate plan called The Life and Work curriculum. "The Bible Book Series" took its genius from the highly successful January Bible Study Program which had been inaugurated in 1948. Bringing in new lieutenants such as Harry Piland in Sunday School and Roy Edgemon in Church Training, Cothen moved the church programs forward again. Sunday School growth gained momentum under this new leadership, and Church Training made some adroit moves to carve out for itself a new role in Southern Baptist life.

Other programs, however, had prospered during Sullivan's administration including the Church Music Department, which had published with great fanfare in 1975 a new *Baptist Hymnal,* replacing the time-honored hymnal of 1956 and the *Broadman Hymnal* of 1940.

Baptist Book Stores continued to be a vital part of the aggressive marketing of the Sunday School Board. The Baptist Conference Centers at Ridgecrest and Glorieta also played a central part in helping Southern Baptist leadership support the various programs that its institutions and agencies were promoting.

Conflicts with the Radio and Television Commission emerged from time to time between the aggressive Stevens and both Sullivan and Cothen, but the Baptist Telecommunications Network (BTN) put the Sunday School Board solidly in the business. Next, the Cothen-led corporation bought the Holman Bible Company. Both of these programs, however, came in the next period which Cothen's Sunday School Board bracketed.[60]But that next period was greeted by collapse of the uneasy consensus under which all Southern Baptist programs had made progress during the preceding fifteen years.

The Cracking Consensus

The success of coalescing conservatives in compelling Midwestern Baptist Seminary to dismiss Ralph Elliott and the Baptist Sunday School Board not to print a second edition of his book—and their ability to get the first volume of the *Broadman Commentary* recalled and its writers changed—did not lessen the resolve of a growing number of people to "recapture" the structures of Southern Baptist life for what they felt was a truly conservative position.

W. A. Criswell and members of the First Baptist Church of Dallas set up the Criswell Institute of Biblical Studies as an adjunct to that great church—

itself something of a corporate giant—in 1971. Former New Orleans Seminary president H. Leo Eddleman became the first president and was succeeded by T. A. Patterson's son, Paige, in 1975. Paige Patterson completed his doctorate at New Orleans and was, at this time, one of Criswell's associates. In 1972 a former missionary, Gray Allison, established the Mid-America Baptist Theological Seminary as an alternate to the liberalism he and his backers felt had invaded the existing seminaries. After a brief stay in Little Rock, the institution came under the protection of young Adrian Rogers, the strong-minded conservative pastor of Bellevue Baptist Church in Memphis, Tennessee. Rogers, Criswell, and Patterson became a vital part of what was soon called the conservative resurgence in Southern Baptist life.

In retrospect much of this was presaged by historian Robert A. Baker in a history of the Southern Baptist Convention published by the Sunday School Board's Broadman Press in 1972. Moving into the historical gap left by Barnes's centennial history, Baker wrote an elaborately documented and data-supported history of the Convention. Writing in the midst of the cracking of the consensus, however, he spoke to the issue in a way that would prove prophetic. He cited the reasons Southern Baptists had grown dramatically, with membership exceeding twelve million by 1972 and registering over four hundred thousand baptisms a year. He credited: (1) the simple biblical emphasis and democratic ecclesiology, (2) the numerous self-sustaining ministries, (3) identification with cultural patterns of its environment, (4) evangelistic zeal, (5) individual leadership, (6) the structure of the Convention with special emphasis on the genius of the Cooperative Program, (7) the absence of significant controversy, and (8) the emphasis on education.[61]

Baker held that controversies in Baptist life demonstrated that it had no monolithic doctrinal stance. He noted that historians had long celebrated the lack of such a stance as a part of the Baptist genius. Baker thought that as long as Baptists had no monarchical head to forbid dissent or enforce uniformity, diversity of belief would continue.[62]

However, Baker put his finger on the sensitivities that were cracking Southern Baptists' uneasy consensus. He noted that the annual sessions themselves proved that ordinary Baptists did not have immediate sovereignty over the agencies, but only mediately through the trustees elected. He carefully pointed out that the president of the Convention had the ability to name the committees which nominate the trustees that the Convention elects. This put tremendous power in the hands of the president and the two vice-presidents, though nothing in the by-laws required the president to be guided by the two vice-presidents.[63]

Procedures had already been set up to be sure that individual agency heads could not influence that committee on the election of trustees, despite the fact that this was a practice uniformly accepted in state convention life for its institutions. Baker spoke of the alienation that was obvious among many Southern Baptists in the Elliott controversy, the initial rejection of the North American Fellowship plan in 1964, and the Commentary controversy in 1970. Of course, it could be argued that in each of these situations Southern Baptists did exercise power without elaborate political strategies.

The Structure of Dissent

Did Baker give a road map to two men who would become the generals of a march on Southern Baptists' pinnacles of power in the years ahead? The timing of his book and their unfolding strategies raise the question.

One of these men was Judge Paul B. Pressler of Houston. Pressler, a judge of the 14th State Court of Appeals in Texas, was by his own testimony a "fifth generation Southern Baptist," with very conservative biblical views and a long-standing disaffection with Southern Baptist leadership. Educated on the East Coast, first at Philip Exeter Academy and later at Princeton University, Pressler testified he saw there first-hand the faith-eroding effects of biblical liberalism. At Princeton he shared his thoughts with a young Texas graduate student named Cecil Sherman who later furnished Pressler some of his strongest opposition. After Princeton, Pressler returned to his home state and to the University of Texas, aghast at the liberalism that he felt was invading Southern Baptist ranks. He was convinced that this was the disease that had devastated older denominations in the Northeast.

Pressler saw evidence of his concerns in two of the leading pastors in Austin, Texas, where he went to law school: Blake Smith of University Baptist Church and Carlyle Marney of First Baptist Church. This was the same Blake Smith who had joined Theodore Adams and others in dissenting the rejection of the World Council of Churches' invitation in 1940. Both Smith and Marney had embraced many modern critical views of the Bible and some aspects of evolutionary theory, but they primarily found the limelight of controversy for their progressive racial views in the early days of the civil rights movement.[64]

Pressler, first as a lawyer and later as a judge, taught Bible classes to high-school students in his church in Houston, and many of these students went on to Baylor University. He recalled that in the mid-1970s some of these students told him of "liberal views" being taught at Baylor University and invited him to come and see for himself. So Pressler read their textbook which had been coauthored by the chairman of the Religion Department and was disturbed by what he considered its liberal thought.[65]

A growing desire to head off this trend occupied Pressler's thoughts throughout the sixties. In 1967 he was attracted by the position on biblical inerrancy of theology professor Clark Pinnock at New Orleans Baptist Theological Seminary. He convinced the Seminary's administration to accept a scholarship gift for students favoring that position.

During this time Pressler met the ally that was to galvanize his thoughts into actions when he and his wife met young Paige Patterson and his wife, Dorothy, at a Bible Conference at New Orleans Seminary. The two later remembered their meeting in the French Quarter over coffee and beignets and their resolve to recover Southern Baptist life for its "conservative roots." Twenty years later, achieving the victory that they had pursued single-mindedly, they would celebrate in that same location.[66]

Pressler had grasped the key to control of Southern Baptist institutional life delineated in Baker's history and, with Patterson's intuitively shrewd and enthusiastic support, came up with the plan to storm those heights. Meanwhile, those who later attempted to defend the status quo had other problems.

Courts and Culture

Baptist churches had through the years occasionally been forced into litigation over church splits. The results had been uneven. The First Baptist Church of Philadelphia was awarded to a minority as "the rightful church" in 1784. In 1953, in Rocky Mount, North Carolina, a court again awarded the church to a minority. On appeal, the result was upheld but was based solely upon testimony from the local body without reference to denominational affiliation. Since the issue was generated by a new majority taking the church independent, there had been much denominational testimony. The court ruled the new majority was taking the church away from its "fundamental usage, customs, and doctrine."[67]

Another case in 1960, involving the First Baptist Church of Wichita, Kansas, awarded the church to a majority that wanted to withdraw from its American Baptist Convention affiliation. But the Kansas Supreme Court reversed the decision, awarded the church to the minority, and said repudiation of its affiliations constituted a departure from its original principles, rules, and practices.

This meant that not even in Baptist polity, where the majority rules, can the church change denominations by a mere majority vote. Historian Robert Baker said these rulings robbed an autonomous church of its autonomy, but Baker's successor, Leon McBeth, pointed out that such a decision protects a Baptist church from an influx of members bent on changing it into something else. McBeth also warned that it gave a Baptist convention a vested interest in every affiliated church. How these rulings might play out in Baptist battles was yet to be seen. By this time, Baptist bodies were more concerned about the potential liability that might ascend from one of its institutions in an increasingly litigious environment.[68]

If the courts struggled to define Southern Baptists, social historians and students of cultural change also took a turn. Baptists were alternately concerned and totally oblivious to how they were seen by their culture. In turn, that culture has not found it easy to define Southern Baptists. Religious and social historians have struggled between defining Southern Baptists as a church or as a sect. The simplest definition of the difference—of the many advanced by scholars—is that a church is a religious group that accepts the social environment in which it lives and a sect is a religious group that rejects it.

By this time, many social historians followed John Lee Eighmy's approach in his posthumously published book, *Churches in Cultural Captivity,* which was a history of Southern Baptist social attitudes from 1840 to 1970. Eighmy held that Southern Baptists had been so dominant in their heartland that they determined the social environment instead of just accepting it.[69]

Much later, an Episcopal writer would say of Southern Baptists, "This unusual denomination was born in the murky back waters of the Reformation; nurtured in the slums of London, Bristol, and Liverpool; experienced a very uncertain transplantation to the New World; and finally blossomed in the fresh air and sunshine of the New South. They began as radical social activists and have ended up the reactionary religious 'establishment' of the South."[70]

In contrast, other scholars held that Southern Baptists have a sect-like view of the world and have always felt like theological outsiders.[71] David

Downs holds that Southern Baptists fell into an ethnic response to the pluralism of their culture which produced a fortress mentality and an identity need that was met by being a Southern Baptist.[72]

Numerous efforts to change the name of the Southern Baptist Convention in later years have underscored that identity need. After the California decision in 1942, and as nonsouthern state conventions affiliated with the Southern Baptist Convention, pressure grew to approve a less exclusive, more expansive name. A committee appointed to study the matter had agreed on American Baptist Convention when the Northern Baptist Convention beat them to it and preempted the most desirable terminology. W. A. Criswell suggested the Continental Baptist Convention, but despite his influence, such suggestions were turned aside as it became evident that the name was not regional, but comprehensively delineated a people almost ethnic in their cohesive quality.

Names notwithstanding, by 1972 Southwestern Seminary's William Estep claimed Southern Baptists had an identity crisis.[73] Many people have agreed with Edward L. Queen II that "the Southern Baptist Convention has always been a complex and plural institution based on compromise and consensus."[74] Historian Bill Leonard later said that the compromising nature of the Convention meant it always lived on the edge of controversy and potential schism, which explains why the denomination's history has been one of continual controversy and political struggle.[75]

Anthropologist Ellen M. Rosenberg in her 1989 book, *The Southern Baptists: A Subculture in Transition*, claimed that all this was due to changes in the Southern caste system. For her, "religious groups select for emphasis those aspects of their tradition which are congruent with their class interests, express their prejudices, reinforce their identity, or at the very least support their claims to authority."[76]

Despite such less-than-supportive views of Southern Baptist dynamics and whether due to an identity crisis, a changing caste system, a pluralism-driven collapse of compromise, inherent contradictions, or something far more elemental—controversy and political struggle were pushing other concerns aside in their move toward center stage.

Baptist Faith and Message Fellowship

The initial centers of opposition to perceived liberalism in Southern Baptist ranks came primarily from Missouri, where conservatives had done battle with William Jewell College and then Midwestern Seminary, and from North Carolina where conservatives had cut their teeth in battles with Wake Forest University. That center moved to Atlanta, Georgia, in 1973.

The First Baptist Church, Atlanta, had been a bastion of Southern Baptist orthodoxy for many years and in recent years had been led by the well-known pulpiteer, Roy McClain. In that church during McClain's pastorate the Association of Baptist Professors of Religion met when denouncing Criswell's book in 1969.

McClain, on the other hand, trying to lead his church to a more inclusive racial position retired when he thought virulent opposition had undermined his leadership.[77]

Charles Stanley, a strong conservative, who had come to Southern Baptist life as a young adult even though he had attended the University of Richmond in Virginia, succeeded McClain in an unlikely way. Serving as associate pastor at the time, McClain stepped down and rejected as a successor by the pulpit committee, Stanley's supporters managed to get a voice vote on him before the congregation. To the shock of many church leaders, he was called as pastor. Involved in an altercation in a subsequent service and stung by the departure of thirty-eight deacons, Stanley nevertheless consolidated his hold on that church and began to attract a conservative constituency with a strong television ministry.[78]

Ironically, most of the thirty-eight deacons who left went to Second Ponce De Leon Church in northern Atlanta where a young Texan named Russell Dilday was pastor. Dilday, a Baylor graduate and a Southwestern Seminary graduate, was pastor of a church in Houston before going to Atlanta and while there had been elected a vice-president of the Southern Baptist Convention. In Atlanta, Dilday became a stalwart member of the Home Mission Board, ultimately serving as its chairman. When Stanley was later elected SBC president, and Dilday was president of Southwestern Seminary, Dilday played a major role in opposition to Stanley's Southern Baptist Convention leadership.

In 1973 in Stanley's First Baptist Church a group of conservatives met and incorporated an organization they called the Baptist Faith and Message Fellowship. They agreed to start publishing a paper to be called *The Southern Baptist Journal* and named former Home Mission Board employee, William A. Powell, as editor. Powell took the *Journal* on an aggressive path from the first publication, attacking "liberal" professors and through letter and print challenging leaders to affirm their conservative positions.[79]

One of Powell's early targets was the erudite William Hull, provost of Southern Baptist Theological Seminary. Hull had written an article challenging certain theories of inspiration including inerrancy. The Baptist Faith and Message Fellowship group took some credit for Hull's decision to leave the seminary in 1975 to become pastor of the First Baptist Church of Shreveport, Louisiana. Hull denied such pressure was behind his move and later reentered academic life as provost of Samford University.

A strong conservative leadership group was beginning to develop behind the scenes of Powell's efforts. Judge Pressler and Paige Patterson were the activists, strategists, and tacticians, but the backbone of the movement was a strong cadre of pastors in large, aggressive, high-growth churches in metropolitan areas, who believed that only an inerrancy approach to Scripture would ensure Southern Baptists' integrity.

No one epitomized this group more than Adrian Rogers, pastor of Bellevue Baptist Church in Memphis. The successor to Robert G. Lee and Ramsey Pollard was a tall, ruggedly handsome "all-America" type. Rogers grew up in a traditional Baptist home, starred as a high school football player, and attended Florida Baptists' Stetson University. Marrying his high-school sweetheart, he responded to a call to ministry and enrolled at New Orleans Baptist Theological Seminary. After seminary, a series of pastorates revealed him as a gifted comer and a fervent conservative, and few people were surprised when he was tapped to succeed Ramsey Pollard for the historic Bellevue pulpit in Memphis.

Rogers's friends wanted him to run for the convention presidency in 1976, and this thought began to trouble many in leadership roles even though the very conservative Jaroy Weber of Lubbock was then president of the Convention.

According to some reports, the *Kentucky Baptist* editor Chauncey R. Daley and several likeminded editors took credit for heading off a Rogers candidacy. They claimed that Daley, in a lecture he delivered at Southern Baptist Seminary some years later, said, "The kind of leader that most of us felt we needed was a fellow like Dr. Sullivan."[80]

Others questioned Daley's memory of an editor-led effort. Jesse Fletcher, pastor of the First Baptist Church, Knoxville, Tennessee, who was asked to nominate Sullivan at the 1976 annual meeting in Norfolk, Virginia, was not approached by any of Daley's group, but rather by Atlanta pastor, Russell Dilday, and a few others who knew of Fletcher's respect for Sullivan. Dilday, who had discussed the matter with a few others and had joined them in talking Sullivan into standing for election, was not aware of any editor's involvement. But such loosely connected consensus making was the hallmark of the system in place and, as soon developed, highly vulnerable to well-organized opposition.

Both were among those nominated, but Rogers came to the platform following Fletcher's nomination of Sullivan and, after graciously thanking the person who had nominated him, withdrew his name. Sullivan was elected on the first ballot, but Rogers had whetted conservative appetites. Many denominational leaders hoped this effectively headed off what they saw as a divisive trend, but it wasn't even the first round.

A less obvious event that year laid significant groundwork for what would follow. Harold Lindsell, editor of the evangelical periodical, *Christianity Today*, published a book entitled *The Battle for the Bible*. He defended the concept of biblical inerrancy and launched an attack on teachers and writers by name, including some Southern Baptists claiming certain quoted passages clearly defined them as liberals. His list and others that began to appear were touted as "the smoking gun" of the conservatives' cause.[81]

Patterson would later admit that few true liberals could be found in Southern Baptist churches. Glenna Whitley, in a Dallas magazine article, reported that "Patterson felt that 'Save the Bible from the Neo-Orthodox' would be a hard sell. So he borrowed a sure-fire red flag from his conservative brethren in politics: when in doubt, brand 'em a 'libber.'" In her admiring article on the conservative leader Whitley said, "But he went out on the stump anyway, preaching the need to flush the 'liberals' from the Southern Baptist system."[82]

The Southern Baptist experience was not an isolated phenomenon. A conservative groundswell was taking place across the United States. Ronald Reagan, former motion picture star and California governor emerged as a Republican presidential candidate from the right to challenge Jimmy Carter, who, despite his identity as a Southern Baptist, did not appeal to conservatives. In fact, the once-solid Democratic South was becoming ripe for passionately conservative Republican conquest.

Women's Roles

During the period leading up to 1979, as discussed in reference to women's ordination, women made dramatic progress in their involvement and roles in Southern Baptist life. As previously noted, in 1963, the same year the Baptist Faith and Message statement was adopted, the Convention elected the popular WMU president, Mrs. R. L. (Marie) Mathis, as second vice-president of the Convention. Having appeared often before the convention in WMU and Foreign Mission Board slots, the Texan and former First Baptist Church, Dallas staff member was adroit and appreciated in denominational life.

In addition, resolutions perceived as friendly to women were passed in 1967 (support for birth control) and 1969 (support for sex education). The most controversial issue of all, abortion, was tackled in 1971 and passed in a resolution favoring abortion in cases of rape, incest, and danger to the mother.

In such a climate, the nomination of Marie Mathis for president of the Convention in 1972 was not unexpected, nor was her failure to make a run-off. But in 1973, the same year the Baptist Faith and Message Fellowship was organized, the nucleus of a strong reaction became evident.

As previously noted, a messenger from Houston, Jessie Tillison Sappington, presented a resolution against women's liberation and in support of traditional roles for women. Despite efforts by the resolutions committee to tone it down, the original version passed, and Sappington and similarly motivated conservatives were much in evidence from then on, especially in opposition to the ill-fated Equal Rights Amendment.[83]

The ERA was a proposed amendment to the federal constitution that would grant constitutional equality to women. When it was passed, the U. S. Congress set a seven-year limit on its ratification, something it had not done with suffrage in 1919. They even extended it once for three more years before it failed, three states short ,on June 30, 1982.

A generally negative outlook on women's initiatives, however, did not keep Mrs. Carl Bates of Charlotte, N. C. from being elected vice-president in 1976.[84]

Bold Mission Thrust

In 1978 the Southern Baptist Convention concluded a long (nearly a decade) formulation of a new missions initiative by giving final approval to a program called Bold Mission Thrust. This endeavor had to fight for the attention of Southern Baptists increasingly preoccupied with internal politics. Its roots could be traced to the success of Jubilee Advance programs and efforts to mount an even greater crusade and especially one that would involve the laity who represented much untapped and yet eager potential.

The latter part of the sixties included plans by staff members of the Foreign Mission Board, the Home Mission Board, and the Sunday School

Board for a great youth conference in Atlanta between Christmas and New Year's to introduce the seventies. Mission Seventy would grapple with the problem of Vietnam-reactive young people that the Board hoped might staff the dream.

In 1970, the Executive Committee established a special Committee of Fifteen to survey the agencies; its goal was to develop new plans that would involve the total Baptist task in a bold new effort. A conference of laymen in Nashville followed the next December. Out of this came a SBC Missions Challenge Committee in 1974, which asked the Convention in 1976 to "set as its primary challenge that every person in the world shall have the opportunity to hear the Gospel of Christ in the next twenty-five years."

In 1977, the Convention approved a three-fold goal of doubling three times by A.D. 2000 the combined receipts of state conventions and the Cooperative Program, extending bold missions programs, and calling for five thousand lay persons to serve one or two years on home and foreign mission fields. The Convention assigned coordination for this to the Executive Committee and in 1978 renamed the whole effort, Bold Mission Thrust.[85]

The stewardship implications of Bold Mission Thrust called forth a support plan called Planned Growth in Giving, focused on discipleship and commitment and increasing personal giving toward a double-tithe by A.D. 2,000.

Efforts to focus Southern Baptists' energies did succeed in setting a registration record of 22,872 messengers as the Convention met in Atlanta in 1978, though registration fell off sharply to 15,947 when it returned to Houston, despite an Astrodome Extravaganza that drew 50,000 persons. Billy Graham was the speaker and 1,200 responded to an impassioned invitation.[86]

But political disagreements beginning the morning before the Graham event dogged leadership efforts to make Bold Mission Thrust succeed. A favored tactic to moderate the upcoming conflict was to appeal over and over again to the claims of Bold Missions Thrust. Both sides would echo the appeal and ignore the claims.

Inerrancy and Change

Conservative leaders focused the battle cry on a single word in the late seventies, which helped galvanize their direction and, as it turned out, helped neutralize their opposition. That word was *inerrant.* Whereas the

Bible had been called inspired and infallible by most Southern Baptist leaders and theologians, the word *inerrant* soon became a codeword for the conservative movement.

An International Council on Biblical Inerrancy was formed in 1977, running across denominational lines and headed by a conservative leader of the Lutheran Church, Missouri Synod, which had been captured earlier by conservative forces.

At the risk of oversimplification of the strongly nuanced statement, the concept of inerrancy was based on the belief that the original manuscripts (none of which were existent, all agreed) were without any error and that the Bible was true, whether read religiously, scientifically, historically, or geographically.[87] Bible scholars confronting apparent inaccuracies fell into two camps very quickly. Some held that the higher truth by which Scriptures had to be interpreted could admit these "errors" without any loss to a strong doctrine of inspiration. Inerrantists, on the other hand, said there were no contradictions except those that might have resulted from faulty translations.[88]

Some people said it was a simple contest between literal interpretations and nonliteral interpretations of the Scriptures. Efforts to attack the banner of inerrancy proved futile, however, and more and more conservative leaders used the word *inerrancy* to declare themselves to each other—whether on television, in print, at evangelistic conferences, or in the powerful Pastor's Conference that preceded each Southern Baptist Convention.

Pastor's Conference

The previously documented trend in Southern Baptist life toward the election of pastors as president seems to owe much to the creation in the early thirties of a preconvention Pastor's Conference. M. E. Dodd led it for most of its early years before giving way to a conference president selected annually. Eleven presidents of the Southern Baptist Convention elected since 1951 have previously wielded the gavel for the Pastor's Conference. Many went directly from that office to the Convention presidency and others, such as R. G. Lee and W. A. Criswell, while not serving as president, were repeatedly called on to preach at the conference.[89]

A number of reasons have been cited for the beginning of the Pastor's Conference including the men's need of a place to go while their wives attended the WMU Convention. For many it was an annual "preacher's revival." For others it was a talent show for revival prospects and platform personalities for evangelistic conferences and state convention programs. Increasingly, it was a place where megachurch leaders could demonstrate the kind of preaching that found success in the new environment that more and more pastors faced. It became a bastion for proactive conservatives and a place where an increasing number of speakers, picking up on the Patterson strategy, called attention to what they called "rampant liberalism." Attendance grew dramatically.

In 1978, the year that the record-setting Convention in Atlanta adopted its Bold Mission Thrust goals, Adrian Rogers was overwhelmingly elected president of the Pastor's Conference and it was obvious that, when the Convention met in Houston in 1979, conservatives intended to run the popular Memphis pastor as president of the Southern Baptist Convention.

Changing the Guard

Sullivan declined to be reelected after his 1976–77 term and Jimmy Allen, the highly visible pastor of the First Baptist Church of San Antonio who would later head the Radio and Television Commission, was elected after declaring himself a candidate. In a way, he became the first to step forward and declare his own candidacy. Allen was elected over Jerry Vines of Alabama and Richard Jackson of Arizona in a runoff with Vines.

Since it was assumed that Allen would be reelected to the customary second term in 1978, the rapidly coalescing conservative coalition set its sights on the 1979 convention in Houston. Yet the 1978 Southern Baptist Convention which convened in Atlanta seems to contraindicate the approaching battle. As mentioned earlier, attendance records were shattered as 22,903 messengers registered and, according to the *Baptist Standard*, "rolled through the Georgia World Congress Center like a huge convoy of Sherman tanks, overpowering almost every controversial issue they encountered with a counter-emphasis on commitment to Bold Mission Thrust."[90]

Jimmy Allen, in his presidential speech and associated news conferences, gave support for Baptists' middle-of-the-road position and faith in the Baptist process to work out any problems. The Convention even declined to vote on the controversial question of women's ordination.

At this point Judge Pressler and Paige Patterson took control, organizing rallies all over the Southern Baptist Convention as Pressler, independently wealthy, not only spoke everywhere he found opportunity but computerized an effective mailing list. Together they developed an organization of like-minded persons throughout the Convention.

By the time the Convention convened in Houston the great sky boxes in the Astrodome were under Pressler's control, and floor lieutenants had been organized to be in direct contact with the leaders high in the boxes.

The Pastor's Conference, presided over by the popular Rogers, proved to be an effective staging ground for the convention coup. Leading personalities for the unfolding conservative effort were prominent, including James Draper of Texas, who succeeded Rogers in the Pastor's Conference role; Jerry Vines, now a Florida pastor who had lost to Allen in 1977; and Georgia's Charles Stanley.[91]

On the other hand, as the Convention itself convened, Rogers was reportedly reluctant to run. Only after a late visit by retired missionary, Bertha Smith, formerly of China and Taiwan, and a still later prayer meeting with two friends, Paige Patterson and Jerry Vines, did he agree to let his name be presented. Six persons were nominated, but Rogers won on the first ballot, just as Sullivan had done three years before, though Roger's victory margin, 51.36 percent, was significantly smaller.

Denominational leaders, many of whom were increasingly called moderates, were shocked but divided in their reactions. Some felt it was a one-shot anomaly, while others began to worry about the implications. The first group assumed that the rank and file of Southern Baptists, though conservative, were not "fundamentalists" and could be rallied to their cause. On the other hand, no leadership available came close to the organizing skills of Pressler and Patterson.[92]

Conservatives continued to press their strength at the Houston Convention, when Larry Lewis, a pastor in Missouri, introduced a resolution calling for "doctrinal integrity." Lewis and friends had succeeded with a similar measure before the Missouri Baptist Convention the year before, and with it "exhorted trustees to employ only teachers who believe in the inerrancy of the original manuscripts, the existence of a personal devil and a literal hell, the actual existence of a primeval couple named Adam and Eve, the literal occurrence of the miracles as recorded in the Bible, the virgin birth and bodily resurrection, and the personal return of Jesus Christ."[93]

Jimmy Allen was presiding at this point and recognized former president Wayne Dehoney, who introduced a motion to reaffirm the Bible to be "truth without any mixture of error" in order to conform it to the Baptist Faith and Message statement adopted in 1963. Adrian Rogers came to the platform and asked Dehoney to be more specific on the subject. According to Lewis, Dehoney agreed that he meant that it was perfect and without error doctrinally, historically, scientifically, and philosophically. Herschel Hobbs, who had chaired the Baptist Faith and Message Committee, added his weight to Dehoney's substitute motion and Lewis withdrew his.

A controversy arose, however, when the *Baptist Press* failed to report the agreement and simply reported the substitute motion. It was the beginning of a running battle with both the religious and secular press. Lewis later became president of the Home Mission Board after conservatives secured a majority of its trustees.[94]

In retrospect, the Houston meetings not only introduced Southern Baptists to the personalities involved, but also to the issues. The number one issue, of course, was inerrancy. Yet motions and resolutions, whether or not acted upon positively, revealed other issues that would constitute the larger checklist for conservative convictions. Besides the previously mentioned motion for doctrinal integrity, efforts were made to block women's ordination, to disavow the role of the Baptist Joint Committee, to disavow political activity, and to take a strict and uncompromising stand against abortion.[95]

Delighted with the victory, conservative forces were warned by Pressler that the battle had only begun and that conservatives had to repeat it year after year to control the agencies and institutions which he and Patterson defined as their real goal.

Leadership on the Defensive

The heads of these institutions were, for the most part, new and not sure how to react to the developing storm clouds. Russell Dilday, who had left Atlanta's Second Ponce de Leon Church to become president of Southwestern Baptist Theological Seminary in 1978 and who was busy reorganizing an institution literally exploding with burgeoning enrollments, did begin to voice concerns regarding the Pressler-Patterson efforts as Rogers took over as SBC president.

Roy L. Honeycutt, writer of the monograph on Exodus in the withdrawn commentary, had survived that battle and succeeded Duke McCall as president of Southern Seminary in 1981. Landrum Leavell, a former Texas pastor, was elected president of New Orleans Baptist Theological Seminary in 1975, and former Southwestern Seminary professor, Milton Ferguson, had headed Midwestern Theological Seminary since 1973. Former Southwestern Professor of Ethics, Bill Pinson, headed up Golden Gate Baptist Theological Seminary, having been elected in 1977. A North Carolina pastor, Randall Lolley, had guided Southeastern Seminary since 1973. While most of the group, Dilday notwithstanding, hoped they could stay out of the battle, Lolley was already on the defensive.

Bill Powell had often pummeled Lolley in the *Southern Baptist Journal* for leading a "liberal seminary" and cited as evidence the fact that Lolley had once prayed at the opening of a brewery in North Carolina.[96]

The Sunday School Board's Grady Cothen, whose conservative credentials were impressive, was too busy trying to reestablish confidence in that agency among the Convention's rank and file to jump into the battle, though, according to a book detailing his experience and published over a decade later, he expressed his anxieties on a number of occasions.[97]

Carolyn Weatherford, Alma Hunt's successor with Woman's Missionary Union, initially continued the tried-and-true WMU strategy of avoiding convention controversy, though her support for the women's movement and the roles of women in church vocations was well-known. She later found a high profile role in opposition to the conservative regimes.

Foy Valentine, a veteran of the battle, was more outspoken, as was the new head of the Baptist Joint Committee on Public Affairs, James Dunn, who had already gone head-to-head with conservatives over the issue of prayer in schools. In turn, both felt the full heat of the new conservative coalition.

Arthur Rutledge's style at the Home Mission Board was nonconfrontational, and he was succeeded in 1977 by the Oklahoma Baptist University president, William Tanner, a skilled denominationalist. The Oklahoma native had earned degrees at Baylor and Southwestern. He left a pastorate in Gulfport, Mississippi, in 1967 to begin ten years as a college president, first at Texas's Mary Hardin-Baylor and then at Oklahoma Baptist University. He also shied from confrontation.

Veteran Porter Routh undoubtedly felt both relief and trepidation as he concluded his twenty-eight-year tenure a month later. The Convention-adopted resolution honoring him noted that during his leadership role, the Convention had grown from 28,289 churches to over 35,000, from 7,373,498 members to more than 13 million, from total mission gifts of $37.2 million to $318.3 million with SBC Cooperative Program receipts going from $21.5 million to $150 million.[98]

The epitome of Southern Baptist cooperation, the Foreign Mission Board, was also in the throes of a change of leadership. Baker James Cauthen, after leading that organization for twenty-five years, was stepping down. Cauthen's leadership had been dramatic and his hold over the Convention sure. When he began his quarter-century command, Southern Baptists had fewer than 750 missionaries serving in 23 countries with total revenues of less than $9 million. When he stepped down, Southern Baptist missionaries numbered over 3,000 deployed in 95 countries with revenues exceeding $70 million.[99]

The end of his era seemed to symbolize changes throughout Southern Baptist life. The Foreign Mission Board meeting in Miami heard a report of its Search Committee which had narrowed its consideration to Keith Parks, a former missionary in Indonesia and head of its Missions Support Division since 1975; William O'Brien, a colleague of Parks's in that division; and Jimmy Allen of San Antonio and immediate past-president of the SBC.

Allen, pastor of San Antonio's First Baptist Church, obviously had more visibility than Parks as well as more extensive denominational experience. On the other hand, given the climate, Allen's well-known efforts to head off the Pressler-Patterson onslaught were a minus, and Parks's less well-known status may have been regarded as a plus. His missionary experience certainly followed the Rankin-Cauthen trend.

So Parks was elected. Because some Board members were sensitive to Parks's lack of denominational experience, O'Brien was named as executive vice-president to help him negotiate those waters. It turned out that Parks got a crash course.

The Advance and consensus years, however uneasy, that Cauthen had exploited and somehow epitomized were over.

8

The Battle for the Gavel

1979–1990

The election of Adrian Rogers as president of the Southern Baptist Convention in June 1979 was not the end of a campaign, but the beginning of one. Those who engineered the charismatic Bellevue Baptist pastor's victory backed a battle plan that called for a patient but persistent ten-year effort. It soon became obvious this controversy would be different from anything Southern Baptists had experienced. In retrospect a dozen years later, Dan Vestal claimed "a new kind of politic was introduced into the SBC. It was a politic of purposeful control and intentional exclusion." Vestal had served on the Peace Committee and had led two ill-fated efforts to stop Rogers and his successors. He lamented "they have systematically and consistently shut out of leadership and meaningful decision-making anyone who will not participate in their movement and continued control."[1] Conservative leadership believed that was precisely what was required to achieve its goals.

A History of Conflict

Born in the immediate aftermath of the Campbell battles and the anti-mission rhetoric rampant especially in Kentucky in the 1830s, Southern Baptists had never been far from the beginning of a battle or the aftermath of one. Immediately after their organization they were engulfed in the Landmark controversies and often divided by them. The incident with Crawford Toy was more of an internal question for Southern Baptist Theological Seminary, though it introduced Southern Baptists to the modernist controversy, and the Whitsitt conflict was another chapter in the Landmark controversy. The fundamentalist wars led by J. Frank Norris left more scar tissue, but the battles that began in Houston cut much deeper into the ranks of Southern Baptists' fellowship than any that had gone before.

This conflict was a civil war with a difference. This time there was no Mason-Dixon line neatly dividing the antagonists. Only where the Civil War had divided families along its borders was there a counterpart, in that brother and sister were increasingly divided from brother and sister.

Without territorial lines and natural divisions, the inerrancy controversy, as some called it, divided churches, associations, and state conventions; but churches tended to follow pastors, associations tended to follow dominant churches, and state conventions tended to follow state leadership. Suspicion, distrust, acrimony, and poorly substantiated charges were rampant.

The commanding and articulate Rogers tried initially to alleviate anxiety. In a postelection press conference, he said, "I was not a part of this campaign. I never went to a single meeting. I don't belong to Paige Patterson or Judge Paul Pressler or even to this Convention. I belong to Jesus Christ. I am not here to represent any splinter groups. I'm here to represent the Lord Jesus Christ. I love Paige Patterson and Judge Paul Pressler, but if I can't be the president of all Southern Baptists, then I do not want to be here."[2]

On the other hand, during the debates in Houston, Rogers joined Larry Lewis in pressing Wayne Dehoney and Herschel Hobbs to clarify the meaning of the Baptist Faith and Message article on Scripture. In essence, they wanted reassurance that the article was interpreted to mean inerrant. The responses satisfied them, but subsequent *Baptist Press* releases did not include the reassurances Dehoney and Hobbs gave Rogers and Lewis, and they claimed they had been betrayed.[3]

For Rogers, the problem was not a question of the method of inspiration, but the result. Was the result inerrant? Rogers said he was happy with the Convention's decision to reaffirm support of the Scripture section of the 1963 statement on Baptist Faith and Message, though at the time he said that he was not aware that the *Baptist Press* report would not include the platform reassurances.

Rogers distanced himself from concerns about the political maneuvering and controversies related to the election itself, specifically Judge Pressler's use of sky boxes in the great Houston arena from which to view and direct the floor fights, as well as Pressler's credentials. In actuality, Pressler, a member of First Baptist Church of Houston, was also an "honorary member" of First Baptist Church of Bellaire, a Houston suburb, and was elected a messenger from that church. He apologized when it was pointed out that this was a violation of Article III of the Constitution.

Registration secretary, Lee Porter, also noted other irregularities that included some churches who had more than their ten-messenger maximum, a few who had double registered, and a number of pastors who had registered for all ten of their messengers and collected their ballots.[4]

In a pattern that would not often be repeated, those who lost the presidential vote won several subsequent votes including the rest of the officers and a resolution condemning "overt political activity." The author of that resolution feared that Baptist conventions would fall victim to politics and the pocket book.[5]

The New Mason-Dixon Line

As indicated earlier, the Mason-Dixon line in Southern Baptists' new civil war was neither territorial nor clear. In studies attempted in subsequent years and especially in one published eleven years later by sociologist Nancy Ammerman of Emory University, the complexity of those lines was documented.[6]

Ammerman divided Southern Baptists into self-identified fundamentalists, fundamentalists-conservatives, conservatives, moderate-conservatives, and self-identified moderates. Her survey showed the fundamentalists with 11 percent, the fundamentalist-conservatives with 22 percent, conservatives with 50 percent, the moderate-conservatives with 8 percent, and the moderates with 9 percent. This meant that the great host of Southern Baptists were in the middle, being fought over by forces representing smaller groups. She pointed out that the first group, self-identified fundamentalists, included so-called "super church pastors," members of the Baptist Faith and Message Fellowship, and most of the movement's leadership.

In the second group, the fundamentalists-conservatives, she included fundamentalists in theology, but people strongly identified with the denomination. In the third group of conservatives, which included a full 50 percent of Southern Baptists, Ammerman placed some of the denomination's statesmen and people who differed from fundamentalists' theological points of views, but who saw themselves as conservative in their theology.

The fourth group, the moderate-conservatives, were strongly opposed to fundamentalists' approach to the Scriptures and deeply committed to the denomination. Ammerman put most of the "denominational establishment" in this category.

The final group, self-identified moderates, were not only opposed to fundamentalist beliefs about the Bible, but strongly committed to delineating those differences.[7]

Her studies pursued the differences through these categories in such matters as biblical authority, pastoral authority, women in ministry, social and political agenda, and such traditional Baptist concerns as swearing, drinking alcoholic beverages, smoking, social dancing, movies, and card-playing. She then considered each categories' attitudes toward evangelism, cooperation, freedom, and toleration.[8]

Those who were courted and won by the new leadership following Adrian Rogers and his successors favored biblical inerrancy and authority and strong pastoral authority. They were against women taking leadership roles in religious life, supported a strong conservative social and political agenda, and supported strict moral standards. While they professed a deep commitment to evangelism and cooperation, they thought that those who did not agree with them had neither the missionary zeal nor the commitment to Scripture to make missions and evangelism succeed.

Ammerman's studies concluded that with the exception of the pastors of super churches and others who were giving leadership to the new conservative movement, the rank and file were prone to be less educated, lower on the social scale, and more apt to be disturbed and frustrated by all aspects of modernity and progress. Larry L. McSwain later claimed that while the leadership core of the new movement would build its power base in megachurches, it would find its most loyal support among small, rural churches.

According to McSwain, "The most modern beneficiaries of the New South built constituencies out of the Old South."[9]

Ammerman also maintained that there were remnants of the old Eastern establishment-Western frontier divisions that had been present in the Land-mark controversy. Social differences, region, and social status were key components, according to Ammerman, and those who were overthrown in the subsequent battles were more likely to be insiders, privileged, established, and less disturbed with change.[10]

Despite such studies, the lines remained blurred throughout the eleven-year battle and featured, as much as anything else, constant efforts on the part of the most polarized groups to preempt the categories and name the agenda.

Preempting the Categories

The question of categories has to be resolved early on in a narrative such as this, if for no other reason than to give clarification to subsequent use of language. The categories bandied about initially were fundamentalists, conservatives, moderates, combinations of these, and liberals. A second line of categories include inerrantists, traditionalists, denominationalists, and progressives.

Those leading the new movement surrounding Adrian Rogers proved to be more successful at preempting the categories. Before many years passed they were referring to themselves as "conservatives," to their movement as the "conservative resurgence," and to their theological designation as "inerrantists." In turn, they designated their opponents as "moderates" or "liberals."

In a way, the battle focused on how each group saw itself and how they would be reported in the secular and religious press. At that point, the conservative resurgence tended to be more often than not referred to as fundamentalists, while their opposition began to be referred to as moderates. Baptist state papers, trying to respond to the sensitivities of both groups, referred to one as fundamental/conservatives and the other as conservative/moderates. The pejorative for the first group meant calling their opposition liberals, while the people they opposed gave pejorative connotations to the term fundamentalist.

As indicated in the introduction to this book, in an effort to avoid such pejorative meanings, this author uses the word *conservative* for those who elected Rogers and his successors, and *moderate* for those who were on the other side, except where the terminology is that used by named sources whether descriptively or pejoratively.

The conservative group may have included fundamentalists, and the moderate group may have included liberals. Yet, as more than one observer noted, on any Christian-wide scale the overwhelming majority would appropriately be termed conservatives.

The Bold Mission Thrust Agenda

Just as Southern Baptist leadership in 1925 and in 1963 had hoped that a combination of confessions of faith and a new focus on tasks would deter Baptists from polarizing conflict, so the denominational leadership in place following Adrian Rogers's first-ballot victory at Houston tried to rally Southern Baptists to the Baptist Faith and Message and the Bold Mission Thrust agenda that was approved by the Convention in 1977.

As previously noted, that emphasis, which was the product of inter-agency meetings for several years in the mid-seventies, was the most aggressive and triumphalistic of Southern Baptists' programs. Its scope ranged from a challenge to let every person in the world hear the gospel by A.D. 2000 to radically enhanced stewardship goals to underwrite the effort that would be effected by the agencies, commissions, and institutions of the Convention.

Following the 1977 action, convention agencies went all out in preparation for the effort. Five-year planning cycles and performance goals were set by agencies, and churches were challenged to enlarge their financial base by 15 percent annually and to double their cooperative mission gifts.

Sunday School Board President Grady Cothen later said: "The people were ready. The agencies were fully supportive of Bold Mission Thrust, the laity were buying into the effort in large numbers, and financial support was increasing. Mission volunteers were coming to the mission boards in large numbers. The colleges, universities, and seminaries had more mission volunteers than ever . . . Almost all was in readiness for accelerating the cumbersome machinery of the largest non-Catholic denomination in America. It was beginning to move in new ways with new levels of cooperation in every area of denominational life."[11]

The report filed by Paul Stevens and the Radio and Television Commission at the 1979 Convention undergirded Cothen's contention: "The Radio and Television Commission's 'game plan' for all its activities this year has been Bold Mission Thrust; Bold Mission Thrust was the Radio and Television Commission's 'game plan' last year; and Bold Mission Thrust will be the Commission's 'game plan' in 1979 and 1980 and the years after, every year until the end of this century and/or until Jesus returns."[12]

Cothen and other traditional agency leadership obviously thought that "the controversy" sidelined this potentially great effort, though most conservative leaders continued to support Bold Mission Thrust. Dan Vestal, later a leader in moderate ranks though an inerrantist himself, remembered how he felt when Bold Mission Thrust was adopted: "The ambitious goal of preaching the gospel to everyone in the world by the year 2000 was set forth. I stood on the floor of the convention as a young pastor and wept with joy. I felt an enthusiasm and an exhilaration. I shared in a dream, a romance, a hope."[13]

Convinced that this grand dream was set aside for "doctrinal dispute, denominational control, and secular politics," Vestal's disappointment was keen. "I will go to my grave believing that Southern Baptists faced a crossroads in those years and made the wrong choice." It must be noted, however, that all of the presidents elected after 1979, as well as new agency heads, continued to support the Bold Mission Thrust goals.

New Leadership

Did leadership changes during this period contribute to the inability to resolve the conflict? As previously noted, in April 1979, a few weeks before Rogers was elected, Porter Routh, the veteran secretary-treasurer of the Southern Baptist Convention's Executive Committee, retired and was replaced by Harold C. Bennett.

Bennett, who had served for twelve years as executive-director-treasurer of the Florida Baptist Convention, seemed ideal for the job. Prior to his tenure in Florida he was Director of Missions for the Baptist General Convention of Texas, and before that, secretary of the Metropolitan Missions Department of the Home Mission Board. He also was Superintendent of New Work in the Sunday School department of the Baptist Sunday School Board before moving to Atlanta. When he succeeded Routh, much was made of this experience and of a stint with the FBI after World War II service as a naval aviator.

Throughout the conflict that commenced at the beginning of his administration and continued through the end of it, Bennett struggled to be even-handed with all parties. This caused some moderates to be frustrated with his lack of clear-cut allegiance and to accuse him of compromising his convictions to protect his job. Conservatives, aware of his long ties with denominationlists hostile to their agenda, responded by leaving him outside their inner decision-making procedures. Thus, while Bennett was loyal to the denominational program throughout, he was not a factor in the dynamics of the conflict itself, except when required to use his office to effect conservative majority decisions or to the degree that his active opposition might have slowed the conservative agenda.

His situation stood in sharp contrast to predecessors Routh and Crouch, who worked very closely with the establishment in power throughout their tenures and helped orchestrate the successful efforts to paper over differences during the years from 1927 to 1979. In all fairness to Bennett, however, he had to play the hand he was dealt, and his support of Bold Mission Thrust never wavered.

As discussed earlier, the Foreign Mission Board's Baker James Cauthen stepped down the following year in favor of R. Keith Parks, who had been one of his division directors, served in other functions on the Richmond staff, and was a long-time missionary in Indonesia. Parks declared his chagrin with the conflict over and over again, and he was often accused of siding with moderate forces whose commitment to the missionary task he thought ran deeper. He expressed his fear that the conservatives' efforts to dominate the Convention would slow Southern Baptist missionary momentum and the Bold Mission Thrust agenda. His outspoken style ultimately brought about acrimonious confrontation and a shortened tenure.[14]

William Tanner headed the Home Mission Board following the retirement of the widely appreciated and low-keyed Arthur Rutledge in 1977. A skilled southwestern denominationalist, Tanner tried to avoid antagonizing either side, but, possibly frustrated with the growing polarization, he left the Home Mission Board in 1986 to become executive secretary of the Oklahoma Baptist Convention.

At the seminaries, as already noted, Russell Dilday followed Robert Naylor at Southwestern in 1978 and Roy Honeycutt succeeded Duke McCall at Southern in 1981. Landrum Leavell had headed New Orleans Baptist Theological Seminary since 1975, and William Pinson guided Golden Gate Seminary from 1977 till 1981 when he accepted the executive secretaryship of Texas Baptists, and was succeeded by Franklin Pollard. Milton Ferguson, at Midwestern since 1973, thus became the dean of the group.

Leading the Commissions were Foy Valentine, who was nearing transition at the Christian Life Commission; James H. Smith at the Brotherhood

Commission since the untimely death of Glendon McCullough in 1978; Lynn May, who took over the Historical Commission in 1971; and A. R. Fagan, who had led the Stewardship Commission since 1974.

The Radio and Television Commission, which developed major visibility and program clout under the leadership of Paul Stevens, elected former SBC president Jimmy Allen, pastor of the First Baptist Church of San Antonio, to head the agency in 1980, a few months after Allen had been bypassed in favor of Parks for the Foreign Mission Board's leadership post.

Grady Cothen still led the Sunday School Board. Cothen early on had opposed the conservative coalition, but his position was increasingly undermined by personnel problems at the Sunday School Board and personal health problems. He gave way in 1984 to Lloyd Elder, who had been serving as executive vice-president to Russell Dilday at Southwestern Seminary.

Convention annuals in 1979, 1980 and 1981 reflect that while the agencies were aware of what was happening, they tried valiantly to keep Southern Baptist momentum on track. Many were convinced that if they did so, Baptists would once again set aside their differences for the common cause. It was an historically informed position, but events were unfolding in response not to a common past, but to a future envisioned more effectively by the conservatives than the one projected by the moderates.

Setting the Agenda

Moderate hopes that the Rogers victory and the Pressler-Patterson strategies were a flash in the pan disappeared at St. Louis, Missouri, when the Convention met in 1980. While Missouri had been a stronghold for conservative denominational reaction since Landmark days, St. Louis was earmarked as a potentially controversial Convention. Then, one month before the Convention, Adrian Rogers announced, even as Sullivan had done in 1976, that he would not stand for a second term. Moderates were not geared up for an election and the two thousand fewer delegates than had gathered at Houston revealed that fact. Bailey Smith, a megachurch pastor from Del City, Oklahoma, and well known for his evangelistic preaching, was the conservatives' choice for president. Even as Rogers had done, Bailey Smith won on the first ballot with 51.67 percent of the vote over five opponents including an avowed inerrantist, Richard Jackson, pastor of the North Phoenix Baptist Church in Arizona—itself a megachurch.

Some felt that Jackson might have won had not a rumor swept the Convention hotels that he had made a deal with the denominational power brokers, who were strongly supportive of Jackson because they thought he would prove that the issue was not theological but rather one of control. The impact of rumor mills was significant at a number of Conventions that followed, and each side accused the other of planting them for their own purposes.

The true impact of presidential appointments did not affect trustee appointments for another year, due to the lag-time between appointment of the Committee on Committees and the appointment of the Committee on Boards. But Rogers's Committee on Resolutions was able to assert the power of the new agenda.

A resolution for doctrinal integrity which had been passed over in Houston reappeared. Unlike previous committees who would have tried to rewrite such resolutions to a less controversial level, this committee moved it right to the floor.

Herschel Hobbs, the denominational statesman who was the architect of the 1963 Baptist Faith and Message as a way of quieting the furor related to the Genesis controversy, took the floor on the point of personal privilege. In the past this had become a way for influential personages to restore perspective. Hobbs urged the Convention to make a renewed commitment to its common denominational task of evangelism and missions, and he cautioned them against creeping creedalism. Historian Bill Leonard later wrote that if there was ever evidence that the grand compromise upon which Southern Baptists' consensus had been built had failed, it was when Herschel Hobbs was booed for his efforts.[15]

It was certainly obvious that denominational compromise was not the compelling solution it once was, and traditional leadership no longer wielded its old power. According to Leonard the "fundamentalists and the conservative resurgence" knew that the traditional viewpoint no longer commanded the same respect and that denominational loyalty had waned dramatically. They sensed what denominational loyalists refused to believe and that was that single-issue-oriented politics was carrying the day.[16]

It was now obvious that the conservative resurgence knew not only how to preempt the categories, but how to set the agenda.

Reaction

Perceiving this in the fall of 1980 following Bailey Smith's election, Cecil Sherman, pastor of the First Baptist Church, Asheville, North Carolina, called on a group of pastors to meet him in Gatlinburg to discuss ways and means of mounting organized opposition to the new movement in their midst. Conservative opponents called this group the Gatlinburg Gang.[17]

Sherman, a native of Texas and a graduate of Baylor and of Southwestern Seminary, was a Baptist traditionalist in every sense of the word, but a very outspoken preacher. Friends regarded him as a sharp-tongued prophet because he spoke what he felt was the truth whether friend or foe was in the way.

He grew up in the Polytechnic Baptist Church in Fort Worth, Texas, when Baker James Cauthen was its pastor. He was at Baylor during the heady post-war days of youth-led evangelism and even headed collegiate evangelism for the Evangelism Department of Texas Baptists for a time. He also spent a year studying at Princeton and was there at the same time as Paul Pressler.

Conservatives quickly accused Sherman's Gatlinburg Gang of overt political activity. Sherman tried to tell Baptist moderates that they were going to have to organize and work just as the Pressler-Patterson coalition had done if they hoped to preserve the traditions that had been in place in Southern Baptist life for so long and for which they had worked so hard.

Paige Patterson debated Sherman and another moderate leader, Kenneth Chafin, before the next Convention. Neither Sherman nor Chafin made much headway against the feisty Patterson who kept the focus on inerrancy and perceived liberalism in the schools and seminaries.

Chafin, professor of evangelism at Southern Baptist Theological Seminary, had previously held that post at Southwestern Seminary and served as Director of Evangelism at the Home Mission Board and as pastor of a prestigious church in Houston. Much more visible in the previous decade than Sherman had been, Chafin yet was unable to make a dent in the conservative resurgence. In a short time he and Sherman both felt left out on a limb by denominational leadership who did not come to their aid. They had especially harsh words for agency heads whom they felt were staying silent far too long.

Sherman and Chafin were able to convince moderates, however, that they must mount a challenge to Bailey Smith, and they did so in Los Angeles, California, in 1981, going against the traditional reelection of an incumbent. Richard Jackson, who had offered stiff resistance to Bailey Smith the year before, this time was tapped by Smith to nominate him. Smith defeated Baylor President Abner McCall with a 60.24 percent majority. Conservative dominance in the resolution committee was evident as they tried to further define the 1963 Baptist Faith and Message's statement on the Bible.

But the real change at Los Angeles was the obvious strength of committed conservatives who moved to fill the vacancies on the boards of Southern Baptist agencies. Moderate reaction successfully challenged several of the new nominees, but the handwriting was on the wall.

In the Trenches

Traditionalist Southern Baptists, more and more called moderates, reacted sharply in 1982 to a speech by Adrian Rogers calling the Cooperative Program a "golden calf."[18] Rogers was correctly measuring the depth of antipathy toward the old denominationalism consensus that traditional Southern Baptists thought would be a rallying point. Yet it was faith in that position that probably caused moderates to choose retiring Southern Seminary President Duke McCall as their candidate to succeed Bailey Smith, completing his two terms.

The campaign was fierce. Bailey Smith, a firebrand of a preacher, had whipsawed the moderates with charges of liberalism, support of evolution and historical criticism, and a swipe at Southeastern Seminary's Randall Lolley's invocation at the dedication of a brewery. Bill Powell's *Southern Baptist Journal* even published a rumor that Duke McCall, the moderate candidate, had a drinking problem. McCall explained that the perception, false as it turns out, had been brought on by misunderstanding of something he had said.[19]

Conservative candidate James Draper, pastor of the First Baptist Church in Euless, Texas, was elected the new president over McCall in a runoff with 56.97 percent of the vote. Another strongly conservative slate was presented by the Committee on Boards to make their presence among Southern Baptist trustees even stronger.

Kenneth Chafin led moderate opposition to the slate, again finding himself head to head with Larry Lewis of Missouri. Lewis, president of a small Baptist college in Missouri, was a floor-fighter for the conservative cause from 1979 on. He and Chafin finally agreed to allow three nominees to be replaced, but the rest took their place on the Boards.

Strong resolutions for school prayer and support for scientific creationism to be taught in the schools passed over moderate objections, though moderates did manage to get a resolution against abortion tabled.

Support for school prayer was opposed by the Baptist Joint Committee on Public Affairs in which Southern Baptists were the most prominent members and which Southern Baptist James Dunn served as executive director. Dunn was under fire by the conservatives from this point forward.

Draper called for a "summit discussion" between leaders of the conservative resurgents and agency heads in August of 1982. The conservatives told the agency leaders to give conservatives parity in employment, especially on seminary faculties. Parity turned out to be a transitional notion only, however, for conservative leaders later made inerrancy and loyalty to the conservative resurgence the litmus test for trustee nominations with implication it would filter down.[20] At this time, though, they pushed for either an inerrancy affirmation by employees and faculty members or a clear statement about what they believed about the Bible. Conservatives also advocated a restructure of the Cooperative Program so selective support could be given by churches who felt their consciences violated by certain programs. As it turned out, this concept suggested by the conservatives who, despite a string of presidential victories were still in the minority on the Boards, would be used by moderates when they became a minority.

Draper was able to give some hope to the moderates that more even-handed days would come, by calling what was going on in Southern Baptist life a "midcourse correction." He was reelected in Pittsburgh in 1983 without opposition and with forty-two hundred fewer messengers than had been in place for election at New Orleans in 1982.

A group of moderate sympathizers pulled away for a fellowship meeting in protest to the conservative dominated Pastor's Conference while in Pittsburgh and promised that they would meet again in 1984 when the Convention gathered in Kansas City.

Little note was taken of a modest beginning in Atlanta of a moderate publication called *SBC Today*. Funds for the start-up were raised by an organization led by Cecil Sherman and Ken Chafin to counter the conservative resurgence. The monthly publication was edited by Walker L. Knight who had retired from his post with the Home Mission Board where he earned repeated honors as editor of the *Home Mission* magazine.[21]

Women in Ministry

The Pittsburgh convention witnessed the beginnings of a significant new initiative on the part of the growing ranks of women called into ministry. In March, 1983, Nancy Hastings Sehested enlisted several like-minded women to plan a conference for women to help open doors for ministry. Meeting in Louisville, thirty-three women organized Southern Baptist Women In Ministry with three objectives. First, they wanted to encourage women in ministry in Southern Baptist churches and in denominational ministries. Second, they determined to provide the support system needed for encouragement and contact. Third, they sought to "explore new paradigms of leadership" in Southern Baptist churches.[22]

More than two hundred women joined them at a pre-Convention meeting in Pittsburgh. That summer Reba Cobb and Betty McGary organized a Center of Women In Ministry at Louisville's Crescent Hill Baptist Church. They also began a newsletter-type publication called the *Folio*.

While this movement in Southern Baptist life mirrored the larger American environment where women's roles and rights continued to expand, it also confronted a growing conservative resistance. Conservative leaders noted with distaste the growing number of women being ordained as deacons and ministers.

They staked out their theological ground on the issue at the 1984 Convention when former *Christianity Today* editor, Carl F. H. Henry, now a Southern Baptist, introduced a resolution regarding the roles of women in the church. The notion held that while both men and women had roles of ministry and service in the church, 1 Timothy 2:12ff. excluded women from pastoral leadership "to preserve a submission God requires because the man was first in creation and a woman was first in the Edenic fall."[23]

The motion passed with 58 percent. Support was probably due to the growing conviction that the disintegration of the modern home was partially caused by women's efforts to move outside their divinely appointed roles. Some of the most intense support for the conservative position came from women themselves.

While resolutions carried no intrinsic authority, the Home Mission Board, now dominated by the new conservative trustees, ruled that no mission money would go to churches with women ministers.

In 1987 Nancy Sehested, a third-generation Baptist minister, was called as pastor of the Prescott Memorial Baptist Church of Memphis. The Shelby Baptist Association immediately "disfellowshipped" the church from that body.[24]

Program Momentum

Almost lost in the charged atmosphere of "the controversy," as it was increasingly called, was continued Southern Baptist expansion in states previously claimed by the American Baptist Convention. Two new state conventions were organized in 1983 and another in 1984, bringing the total number to 37. While the bulk of Southern Baptist members remained concentrated in the first fourteen states, no one doubted the impact of the largely conservative new bodies.

Four families in Madison, Wisconsin, with the help of an Illinois area missionary, had founded the first Southern Baptist church in that state in September 1953. Three years later, seven churches, including one from Minnesota, organized the Wisconsin-Minnesota Baptist Association. They had come under the direct sponsorship of the Baptist General Convention of Texas which provided support along with the Home Mission Board. A Minnesota-Wisconsin Southern Baptist Fellowship organized in 1969 and in 1975 established its headquarters in Rochester. This fellowship had nearly one hundred churches when it became a state convention in 1983.

When a Southern Baptist church was established in Vermont in 1963, Southern Baptists could point to at least one church in every state. The first church in New England had been established earlier in 1960, which was the Screven Memorial Church in Portsmouth, New Hampshire. By 1962 there were two associations in New England sponsored by the Baptist Convention of Maryland and the Home Mission Board. By 1980 there were four associations and 74 churches. Making their headquarters on the property that was the birthplace of Luther Rice, the drive to organize a state convention was steady, and it bore fruit in 1983.

By 1985, Wyoming churches were strong enough and conscious enough of their state identity to pull out of the Northern Plains Baptist Convention and organize the Wyoming Baptist Convention.

While the new state bodies included people with sympathies on both sides of the controversy, many felt that the majority of the incoming leadership favored the conservative resurgence and that the additions of these new state conventions only strengthened the conservative cause.

Blacks, Hispanics, and Ethnicity

Few aspects of Southern Baptist progress during this period have been more overlooked and eclipsed by its controversy than the Convention's remarkable progress regarding Blacks, Hispanics, and other ethnic groups, particularly Asians, despite Southern Baptists' beginnings with reference to slavery, its years of support of racial segregation, and its resistance to civil rights. Its current attitude can only be explained in terms of radical changes in the larger culture, paired with the slow but sure effect of biblical principles as advocated by such Baptist pioneers in race relations as Blake Smith, Theodore Adams, Clarence Jordan, T. B. Maston, and Foy Valentine.

Most Southern Baptist churches now welcome all races and many have black members. Many predominantly black congregations are now dually aligned with their historic denominations and the Southern Baptist Convention. The Home Mission Board's Victor Glass, a white man, pioneered a program of active efforts to work with black churches, but a major step forward was taken when black theologian Emmanuel McCall was named to succeed him.

By 1993, a black member of the Home Mission Board's staff, Willie McPherson, led conferences among SBC churches on the "starting and development of black churches." The Foreign Mission Board's David Cornelius, also a black, served as that Board's Director of Black Church Relations, and he was not the first of his race in that position. Both Boards had appointed black missionaries in the seventies, a pre-Civil War practice with a long hiatus. Even more significant were the four blacks serving as members of the Home Mission Board: Cecil Rhodes of Ohio, Japhus Haley of Nevada, Willie Gaines of California, and Jo Ann Britton of the District of Columbia; the two serving on the Annuity Board: Christene Walker of Texas and James Shelton of D.C.; and two serving on the Historical Commission: Joyce Austin of D.C. and Theodore D. Wilson of Indiana.

Hispanic work, previously centered in New Mexico and Texas, proliferated beginning with the Rutledge era in Home Missions. Oscar Romo, a Hispanic pastor from Texas, was added to the Home Mission Board's administration in 1971, and state convention programs addressing the growing national Hispanic population were further undergirded under the administrations of William Tanner and Larry Lewis. By 1991, Hispanic leaders such as Omar Pachecano and Rudy A. Hernandez of Texas occupied trustee roles at the Foreign and Home Mission Boards, and New Mexico's Frank Zamaro served on the Sunday School Board.[25]

In a doctoral dissertation for Southwestern Theological Seminary, Jose A. Hernandez would claim in 1983: "Southern Baptists have been particularly successful in both evangelizing and congregationalizing Mexican Americans." He cited 2,030 Hispanic congregations with over 200,000 members by 1985.[26]

Following the Vietnam War, a trickle of Asian immigrants turned into a flood, and Southern Baptist churches everywhere began to sponsor language ministries to these groups. Commenting on this phenomenon, Oscar Romo said, "The land that received the world's tired, poor, huddled masses that yearn to be free has become the American mosaic of people whose lives reflect in excess of two hundred ethnic groups and communicate in 276 languages and 360 Amerindian dialects." [27] By 1992, the Home Mission Board would support 1,825 missionaries and pastors among 102 ethnic groups using 98 languages and dialects. They registered 515 new language congregations that year. [28]

Few can argue that this trend has stood above Southern Baptist controversy and been a source of gratitude to all positions. It has probably reflected both a belated but growing rejection of Southern Baptists' segregated heritage and further evidence of its missionary convictions. On the other hand, despite the ethnic and racial diversity of churches within the Southern Baptist Convention by that date, most churches were still largely homogeneous in their racial makeup.

Shift in Foreign Missions

R. Keith Parks, even as Arthur Rutledge had done for the Home Mission Board in the sixties, presided over a major restructuring of the Foreign Mission Board in the eighties and a refocusing that would, in retrospect, contribute to a paradigm shift in the Board's traditional way of operating.

Born in Arkansas to a farm family, Parks received his education at what is now the University of North Texas and at Southwestern Seminary, where he earned his doctor of theology degree. He married Helen Jean Bond, the daughter of a Hardin-Simmons University professor and taught there in the Bible department before he and his wife were appointed missionaries to Indonesia in 1954. Serving as treasurer and theological professor, Parks came home for a brief stint in the Board's personnel department in 1964 and returned permanently in 1968 when he was named area secretary for Southeast Asia in 1968. In 1975 he became Mission Support Division Director.

Prior to Parks's leadership, the singular role of the Foreign Mission Board was the sending and enabling of missionaries to other lands. As they were successful in winning converts and planting churches, they helped these indigenous groups organize into autonomous national bodies. Missionaries then provided leadership and financial support as these bodies matured and became self-sufficient. Strategy was field-based and field-developed. It usually involved a mosaic of ministries and supporting institutions, often mirroring home patterns. The Mission, as the organization of missionaries in a particular field was called, developed its own strategic plans and sought resources from the Foreign Mission Board to accomplish them. The Board in turn developed coordinating policies regarding these allocations and the deployment of the missionaries.

When Parks took over, the administration included the support division he had headed, a financial division, and an overseas division, with area secretaries and field representatives functioning under a presiding director reporting to Parks. The role had been so focused in the previous paradigm that Cauthen was often accused of being concerned only with "men and money" or more missionaries and more resources to send and enable them.

Parks changed that by developing a strategic approach to world evangelism. He organized a Global Strategy Group that brought the world to a Richmond planning table and began to consider personnel and resources as assets to be strategically deployed to carry out a hard-data and prayer-backed global strategy developed in the Board's "War Room."

Widely hailed by many people as a timely innovation, it nevertheless troubled some. One older missionary thought the move changed missionaries from apostles to agents. The shift moved the Board from a sending agency paradigm to a global evangelistic center paradigm. The staff in the Board's Richmond headquarters increased sharply in the next few years to effect the change. Most of the new administrators, like Parks, were veteran missionaries.

Though Parks took over from Cauthen in 1980, the restructuring was not immediate. The beginning was in all likelihood a carefully planned Global Evangelization Strategy Consultation, held at Ridgecrest Baptist Conference Center in North Carolina in June 1985, two months after Cauthen's death. The picture unfolded there among missionaries and Baptist leaders from twenty-one nations.[29]

One national leader later said that Parks began efforts here "to emancipate [missions] from their old syndrome and stereotypes with their pronounced demarcations between 'givers' and 'receivers'...one that sometimes served as a subtle disguise for paternalism."[30]

One of Parks's staff members, Louis R. Cobbs, a holdover from the Cauthen era, said later: "In a series of identifiable steps, the FMB changed from a denominational, church-related mission board which served as a channel for Baptists to express their mission as concern and commitment to a board of global evangelization, working with various organizations and people in a coordinating and motivating role toward the goal of global evangelism." Cobbs went on to say, "Dr. Parks has probably done more to change the Foreign Mission Board than any other leader in all its history."[31]

One of the earliest products of such centralized direction was a seventy-thirty directive that said the Board would, over the course of ten years, place 70 percent of its personnel and resources into evangelism resulting in the planting of new churches, with support roles and other ministries utilizing 30 percent. With the centralizing move already causing some missionaries to feel less in charge of their own destinies, the seventy-thirty directive was broadly misinterpreted and caused some wives, medical personnel, educators, business administrators, and other specialists in the missionary force to feel like "second class citizens."

Yet the Global Strategy Group continued to expand its planning role and to push that role as far into the ranks of its missionary organization as possible. It was not all smooth going. One administrator said later that the moves kept "staff and missionaries off balance and resulted in lost momentum." He added, "Overlapping and top-heavy administration has tended to create too much of a bureaucratic system, rather than streamlined decision-making. This also has had an adverse effect on morale."[32]

While Parks and his administrators held their course, they later confessed that they had neglected the process that has to take place between policy and implementation. Parks' executive vice-president, William O'Brien, admitted that interpretation to the missionaries by regional vice-presidents as they were now called was uneven.[33]

In retrospect, a number of significant developments gave a certain inevitability to this shift. One was the continuing influence of the corporate model, another was Bold Mission Thrust, and a third was Partnership Missions.

Shortly after Parks became Mission Support Director under Cauthen, he retained then-retired Sunday School executive W. L. Howse to help him learn organization skills. Howse, one of the prime developers of the corporate model at the Sunday School Board, tutored Parks in organization theory, reporting and accountability functions, and strategic planning. Howse's influence was evident when, soon after Parks succeeded Cauthen, the Board approved title changes, beginning with Parks. His title was changed from executive director to president, and the titles of the rest of the Richmond staff were similarly changed to appropriate corporate nomenclature. This was not as radical a move as it might seem, in that the

Home Mission Board under William Tanner had taken such a move in 1980.[34]

Howse was dispatched then to mission fields to help develop strategic planning skills, though it soon became obvious that the core planning was to be accomplished in Richmond. The Global Strategy Group with its centralizing focus was a natural outcome.

Bold Mission Thrust, with its aspirations to let everybody in the world hear the gospel by the year 2000, also influenced this paradigm shift. The harnessing and directing of all resources available was believed to be the only way the far-reaching goal would be accomplished. The institutional emphasis—whether medical, educational, or other—had to take a back seat to the more immediate task of evangelism. In many ways this vindicated some of the T. P. Crawford-embraced Nevius's emphases. Cal Guy, Park's missions professor at Southwestern Seminary and a continuing supporter of Parks, may also have influenced this evangelism-first focus. But the move also suited the more conservative, evangelistic, and often, dispensational views of the Foreign Mission Board's new trustees.

A third influence was the Partnership Missions program which the Board took under its own wing. Begun by W. H. Jackson, Partnership Missions was a program to move large numbers of Southern Baptist church members into short-term witnessing jaunts overseas. Missionaries would then serve as advance persons, arranging for interpreters, accommodations, and places to work. Such efforts have continued to grow and need central planning. When one of Parks's staff, Betty Law, later resigned largely in support of Parks, she said the emphasis had swung from meeting needs overseas to serving the aspirations of Southern Baptist church members.[35]

Jackson himself, who coordinated many Partnership efforts, maintained that the real benefit was the direct role given national groups and leaders. Frustrations between reported results and actual baptisms and church growth often placed the program on the defensive, but its continuing popularity kept it growing.

Parks's staff also moved to facilitate the new paradigm with a groundbreaking new network of evangelical missionary agencies. Bill O'Brien convinced Parks that the Foreign Mission Board needed to serve as a catalyst in world evangelism by interrelating with other Great Commission sending agencies. The move represented a kind of missionary ecumenicity that had been held at bay since the rejection of interchurch movements after World War I. Long standing concerns about entangling alliances were allayed by the reach of Bold Mission Thrust's "that everyone might hear" goal. To O'Brien, it was obvious that Southern Baptists could not do it by themselves. As the architect of this aspect of the new paradigm, O'Brien developed broad ties with the international missionary community, but he also incurred the ire of the incoming conservatives of the Board for his ecumenical views.

Many people credited O'Brien with bringing Anglican missionary researcher David Barrett to the Foreign Mission Board, giving it a leadership role among the international missionary community by making his extensive missionary data available to all groups. Cobbs says his influence went further than statistics and analysis. According to the former personnel secretary of the Board, Barrett held that the missionary of the future must be a global citizen, globally aware and globally informed. Barrett contended that he or she must be one who understands the great advantage of being a missionary of the Board in contrast to being an independent missionary, must be oriented to the unfinished task, must be adept at adopting a low profile, must be nonresidential, must be narrowly focused, and must be supportive.[36]

In 1986, the Foreign Mission Board hosted a conference for other missionary organizations to promote global evangelistic cooperation and to focus on "World A." The term was coined by Barrett to focus on those peoples yet to hear the gospel. A foreign mission program primarily focused on evangelism and reaching out to World A on a priority basis was popular among the Board's conservative trustees. Many premillenialists believed the very return of Christ hinged on all peoples "hearing the gospel" as implied in Matthew 24:14.

Regardless of the range of reasons applicable, the Foreign Mission Board now had its own paradigm shift. Parks, and even Board members who would later oppose him, felt the potential under the new paradigm could awaken what for many had been, despite Cauthen-era advances, a sleeping giant. Yet the change, as far-reaching as it was, continued to take a backseat to what continued to be called "the controversy."

Agency Heads React

In 1984 in Kansas City the moderates made their strongest run to that time against the new conservative coalition. Conservatives had decided to go with Charles Stanley as their standard bearer. Stanley, pastor of the First Baptist Church of Atlanta, was host to some of the earliest efforts to organize the conservative coalition that ultimately gained the upper hand, and whether he wanted the position or was convinced by coalition leadership, he agreed to stand. Conservatives knew they would have to overcome the impact of the 2.7 percent that the Atlanta church gave the Cooperative Program to elect Stanley, but by that time they felt strong enough to do so.

Actually, when Rogers attacked the Cooperative Program as a sacred cow, he knew the constituency better than the traditionalists did. Conservative leader churches included Bellevue Baptist Church, Memphis, with a 4.3 percent CP budget, First Baptist Church of Atlanta, with 2.7 percent, and First Southern Baptist Church of Del City, Oklahoma, with 1.6 percent. This was significantly less than the percentages recent moderate presidents' churches gave. The difference, as Rogers perceived, was lost on the majority of voters.

Moderates were encouraged by a new pre-Convention group called the Forum. The Forum gave moderate pastors a place to gather and hear their own kind of thinking, in contrast to the Pastor's Conference, now a well-structured rally for conservative causes. And Women in Ministry continued their still small but very focused meetings.

Moderates fielded retiring Sunday School Board president Grady Cothen as their candidate. Stanley, who was well-known throughout the United States because of the widespread television ministry of his church, was elected on the first ballot with 52.18 percent of the vote over Cothen and a third candidate.

A measure of salt was rubbed into the wounded moderates when Paul Pressler was nominated to Southern Baptist Convention's Executive Committee. A motion made by Winfred Moore, pastor of the First Baptist Church of Amarillo, to replace Pressler failed. Moore, a well-known conservative pastor, began to be more and more identified with moderate causes. His role, like that of Richard Jackson, strengthened the moderates' convictions that the controversy was more about power and conservative political issues than about theology.

The real bombshell at Kansas City, however, was not Stanley's election over one more moderate-backed candidate, but Southwestern Seminary President Russell Dilday's convention sermon. Since the time delay related to the Executive Committee's work had taken so long to ensure conservative appointees' control, Dilday was to be the last moderate to preach the Convention sermon. He made the most of it. Decrying the temptation to camp on the "misty flats of forced uniformity," he urged the Convention to return to the higher ground of "autonomous individualism." He argued for the higher ground of "spiritual persuasion" over the "muddy swamps of political coercion." He concluded with a passionate appeal for Southern Baptists to abandon the "barren grounds of egotistical self-interest" in favor of the higher ground "of Christ-like humility."[37]

It was not Dilday's first venture into the controversy; he had done that before in articles for *Southwestern News.* In an article dated January 1983, he said, "I long for the day when we can again affirm the diversity within our unity as a Bible-believing convention of Southern Baptist churches and recognizing the pettiness of it all, laugh at ourselves a little bit, and get back to the main task our Lord has given us." [38] He also tackled the issue on a scholarly level with his book, *The Doctrine of Biblical Authority,* published by Convention Press in 1982. In it, according to Southern Seminary's David Dockery, Dilday "carefully affirmed the inspiration and authority of the Bible while pointing out the weaknesses of the inerrancy position."[39] James T. Draper's *Authority: The Critical Issue for Southern Baptists,* published in 1984 by Fleming Revell, though not an effort to answer Dilday, defended the inerrancy position. Yet Dilday's Convention sermon was more the prophet's protest than the theologian's dialogue.

Conservatives immediately protested an agency head's taking such a strong political stance. But Dilday was not alone. Southern Seminary's Honeycutt, in a semester-beginning speech, referred to the moderates' cause as a "holy war."

Keith Parks put himself on the line a few months later when he opposed Charles Stanley's reelection in 1985 in Dallas. The battle was heating up, but there was no sign that the conservatives were losing their ability to deliver the votes. Moderates became convinced that they would just have to beat the conservatives at their own game.

At this point, historian Bill Leonard points out that there was a major advantage discernible in conservative ranks, despite denominational efforts to counter it in speeches like Dilday's. Conservatives were simply better at the forms of communication now dominant in American religious life, especially Southern Baptist life. Leonard says the average denominational leader had not mastered the ability to preach in this new environment, and the super-church pastors who were leading the conservative cause were experts. Most of them had cut their teeth in evangelism and knew how to make the most of populist issues, simplified doctrinal statements, and especially strong appeals to the emotions. They could decimate with ridicule the arguments of their opposition, especially "liberals," in whatever form or fashion they were perceived.[40]

Moreover, conservative leaders had mastered the use of television and the "sound bite." They knew that carefully reasoned arguments were not nearly as powerful as a forceful, carefully placed phrase. They continued to preempt the categories and set the agenda, and some thought they had moderates on the ropes.

Ironically, the strongest moderate resistance began to emerge not from Virginia or North Carolina, but Texas, the home state of Pressler and Patterson and the conservative spiritual leader, W. A. Criswell.

Watershed in Dallas

The year between Charles Stanley's election at the Southern Baptist Convention in 1984 in Kansas City and the Convention that met in Dallas in 1985 was marked by agency reinforcement for the moderate position. Buoyed by Russell Dilday's Convention sermon at Kansas City, Missouri, angered over Paul Pressler's election to the Executive Committee, and the minimal support that new Baptist leaders like Charles Stanley had given to Convention causes, moderates intensified their efforts.

Russell Dilday's Convention sermon was widely understood to have slapped the hands of conservative leaders and signaled a change of strategy on the part of a few agency leaders. Moderate leaders, who deplored the lack of agency leadership involvement in the controversy, were heartened as Dilday was joined by Southern Seminary's Roy Honeycutt when he launched his "holy war" against "unscrupulous and unethical acts."

Landrum Leavell indicated that he had no respect for pastors who utilized institutions but did not lead their churches to support the denomination. Later, both Parks of the Foreign Mission Board and the Home Mission Board's Tanner added their voices by indicating that the controversy would adversely affect missions. Randall Lolley of Southeastern Seminary and Herbert Reynolds of Baylor University also jumped into the battle, with Reynolds calling conservative leadership a "college of cardinals" out to "clone" the SBC educational system.[41]

But conservative leadership continued to gain strength and took on new allies in the national conservative scene. With strong roles in the reelection of Ronald Reagan, Stanley, Draper, and Rogers were a part of the American Coalition for Traditional Values. This coalition focused on a conservative political agenda, including constitutional amendments prohibiting abortion and supporting prayer in public schools, tuition tax credit for parochial schools, and restriction of welfare programs. The new Southern Baptist leaders often appeared alongside high-profile television personalities such as Jerry Falwell and Pat Robertson.

New efforts on the part of moderates who had not been able to put together any kind of grassroots organization were evident before the Dallas Convention in 1985. Led by a layman from Second Baptist Church in Houston, John Baugh, and another from Dallas, Dewey Presley, they enjoyed the support of a large group of the Texas Baptist Convention's leadership which was still firmly in the hold of the moderates. They decided to back Winfred Moore again and, despite tradition, challenge Charles Stanley's incumbency.

But the more experienced conservatives seemed able to match them step for step, and when all messengers were registered in Dallas the total was an all-time record of 45,531.

Moore, a very conservative pastor from the First Baptist Church of Amarillo, which had traditionally been one of the strongest supporters of the Cooperative Program, was a winsome challenger. Feeling that Moore was far more grounded in traditional Baptist life than Stanley, moderates were encouraged about the possibility.

When the count was over, however, the incumbent had garnered over 55 percent of the vote for a clear reelection. Many observers suggested that a telegram from an associate of Billy Graham indicating the evangelist was endorsing Stanley had been the decisive factor.[42]

Surprisingly, Moore was elected first vice-president over incumbent Zig Ziglar by a two-to-one margin. It was hard to tell whether it was an accident of nomination (Moore was on the floor at the time and, in an exchange with Stanley, elicited from Stanley a willingness to work with him) or whether it was strictly the personality and appreciation of Moore that prevailed.

Moderates tried to elicit from Stanley a commitment to let the vice-presidents have a say in the appointment of committees. Stanley only said he would consult them; later he pointed out that is all he was obligated to do. A moderate challenge to the Committee on Committees' report to replace the entire slate was stopped by effective presiding. Stanley first ruled that they could only be challenged one by one. However, this ruling was overturned 12,576 to 11,801. That evening Stanley announced that the parliamentarians had decided that only the Committee on Committees could nominate the Committee on Boards. The frustration that came from this parliamentary haggling produced howls of protest and charges of voting irregularities and by-law irregularities.

The year-long involvement of agency heads came to the floor as a motion was made to forbid denominational employees from taking sides in the SBC battle. There was no doubt that Russell Dilday, Roy Honeycutt, and Keith Parks were in the minds of the voices supporting that motion. Stanley defused the issue, however, by ruling it out of order.

Herschel Hobbs was roundly defeated when he made an effort to alter the Baptist Faith and Message to a more conciliatory position for inerrantists.

Peace Committee

Almost lost in all of the furor in Dallas was the appointment of a twenty-two-person Peace Committee—twenty men and two women—to look into the roots of the denomination's ongoing division and propose solutions leading to reconciliation. Stanley and Moore were named *ex-officio* members of this committee with full voting rights. The committee was given two years to do its task, though requested to make an interim report at Atlanta.[43]

Because of the Peace Committee, the *Baptist Standard* summarized the event by saying, "Southern Baptists in record-shattering numbers poured into Dallas last week poised for battle and left scarred but with a sliver of hope that peace between warring factions may yet salvage the nation's largest evangelical denomination from self destruction."[44]

Though the result of diplomatic efforts by several state presidents and Franklin Paschall of Tennessee, the Peace Committee chaired by Pastor Charles Fuller of First Baptist Church, Roanoke, Virginia, was not destined to bring peace, but rather new division. Even before Atlanta, in February of 1986 the Peace Committee announced that an investigatory subcommittee sent to six seminaries and five agencies had found "significant theological diversity."

Focusing on the historicity of Adam and Eve, miracles, and the authorship of individual biblical books, the thrust of the committee's initial findings was that conservative charges of liberal leanings in Southern Baptist institutions had substance.

However, the committee's report in preparation for the 1986 Atlanta Convention referred to both sides being guilty of political activities and using "intemperate, inflammatory, and unguarded language." The committee also took to task independent journals and denominational papers for choosing sides. The reference was to the moderate publication *SBC Today* and the conservative's *Advocate* as well as perceived biases in state paper editorials.

But the conservative resurgents plowed right ahead in 1986 as Adrian Rogers, emerging as the strongest leader of the conservative movement, was once again nominated and pulled 55 percent of the vote to defeat Winfred Moore for a second time. Reports from the Peace Committee said Rogers had been the undisputed leader of the conservative majority on the committee. His second stint with the gavel seemed to indicate he held that role for the movement as a whole.

Following the Atlanta meeting, Presnall Wood wrote, "not since William Sherman's troops sacked the city in 1864, has a battle been so one-sided. With President Charles Stanley at the helm, the fundamental-conservatives won almost every skirmish, including the election of a new leader."[45]

As the balance of conservative appointees on Southern Baptist boards and agencies reached the 40 percent point, many moderates assumed a siege mentality. Roy Honeycutt told his alumni, gathered at the Convention "we may have to do as they did in Rome, when they survived the dark ages by creating pockets of civility, intelligence, and morality."[46]

Trustee Majorities

What was ultimately at stake, however, was not electing a president of the Convention or even dominating business done in the form of motions or resolutions, but rather the control of the agencies owned and operated by the Southern Baptist Convention. The Home Mission Board and the Christian Life Commission gave the conservatives their first opportunities to place their own people in agency leadership.

Even before they had a clear-cut majority on the Home Mission Board, the conservative members were able to elect one of their own as its board chairman. The new chairman, in turn, secured the resignation of the moderate-dominated Search Committee, which had been appointed earlier when William Tanner, who had led that agency since 1977, announced that he was stepping down to take the executive secretaryship of Oklahoma Baptists.

Clearly the new search committee would be looking for a person more acceptable to conservative members of the Board. These members demonstrated their power by blocking the appointments of ordained women to Home Mission positions. A staff veteran, Robert T. Banks, Jr., took the touchy interim situation.

The Christian Life Commission was a slightly different story. Long time activist Foy Valentine announced that he would retire a bit early because of health conditions and asked the Board to begin looking for his successor. Valentine's unabashed goal was to allow the Commission to secure his replacement while a moderate majority was still in place. Again conservatives tried to elect one of their own to chair the Commission, but they lost by a vote of 15 to 13, which clearly revealed the slim majority the moderates still held. Early in 1987, the Commission elected Larry Baker, a former professor at Midwestern Seminary, to succeed Valentine by a vote of 16 to 13. Conservatives were incensed and vowed that Baker's tenure would be short.

In the meantime, conservative pressure against the seminaries continued, with charges being hurled against Southern Seminary's Glenn Hinson and Midwestern Seminary's Temp Sparkman. At their Board meetings Russell Dilday, Randall Lolley, and Roy Honeycutt received bitter complaints from their conservative board members over their own roles in the conflict.

The Glorieta Statement

The Peace Committee requested a meeting with the Seminary presidents in Glorieta in October of 1986. Responding to a plea from the committee to help them get off dead center, the presidents attempted to craft a conciliatory statement. Randall Lolley drafted that report for the presidents; it included a statement drawn from a Fuller Seminary document which used language the presidents felt was middle ground: "The sixty-six books of the Bible are not errant in any area of reality." In their statement, the presidents also pledged to balance their faculty with "the entire spectrum of scriptural interpretation represented by our constituency." They also promised to sponsor three national conferences over the next three years, beginning with biblical inerrancy in 1987, biblical interpretation in 1988, and Biblical imperatives in 1989.[47]

Included as a release from the Peace Committee, the presidents initiative was called the Glorieta Statement. The presidents evidently felt it would be hailed as a breakthrough, and in several places it was. But at Southern and Southeastern it unleashed a firestorm. Lolley and Honeycutt found troubled faculties waiting upon their return, and efforts to explain their actions only added fuel to the fire. According to Bill Leonard, "the statement meant that the fundamentalists had won and that the seminary presidents knew it."[48]

People hoping for some kind of genuinely peaceful resolve of the Southern Baptist conflict thought the Glorieta Statement was a needed concession. But many moderates felt they had been abandoned by the presidents, and Cecil Sherman, an early leader of the moderates, resigned from the Peace Committee in protest of the presidents' statement.

Leaving no doubt as to how he felt about the Glorieta Statement, Paul Pressler said, "I'm extremely grateful for the seminary presidents finally admitting the legitimacy of the concern we have been expressing these eight years."[49]

Conservative Gains

The Convention also had to cope with a lawsuit filed against the Convention and the Executive Committee, based on Stanley's rulings at Dallas. Costs approaching $300,000 were forecast, but the conservative domination of the Atlanta Convention enabled a change in by-law 16 that would cure the problem James Slatton of Virginia had so determinedly tried to exploit in the 1985 Convention.

When the Peace Committee brought its report and recommendations to the Convention in 1987 in St. Louis, it was seen by most as a clear-cut Conservative victory.

The Peace Committee's report affirmed all of the issues that the conservatives wanted. It was consistent with the concept of inerrancy and gave many agencies fears that it would be treated as a creed. When the Committee was continued at the St. Louis Convention, moderate Winfred Moore resigned in protest, saying the committee was never meant to be an oversight or policing committee, nor to monitor the work of institutions.

At the St. Louis meeting moderates were also aware of the inroads of the conservative resurgence in the agencies. The Home Mission Board elected Larry L. Lewis as its new president that spring.[50] Lewis had led many of the early conservative fights and was seen as a clear-cut partisan, though he cited a desire to represent all Southern Baptists.

A Missouri native, Lewis at the time of his election was president of Hannibal-LaGrange College of that state, where he began his own education. Besides a B.A. from the University of Missouri, Lewis had earned both the Master of Divinity and the Master of Religious Education from Southwestern Seminary. He took a Doctor of Ministry degree from the independent

Luther Rice Seminary in Jacksonville, Florida. Prior to his six-year stint at Hannibal-LaGrange, Lewis served as pastor of the Tower Grove Baptist Church in St. Louis, long a stronghold of conservative action among Baptists.

Under Lewis's direction, the Home Mission Board soon refused financial support to women pastors and moved to enforce restrictions on the appointment of divorced persons and people in the charismatic movement. But he also showed a strong administrative hand and the ability to relate to other agency heads.

The Home Mission Board, which had often played second fiddle to the Foreign Mission Board, prospered in the new convention climate while the Foreign Mission Board, still dominated by moderate leadership, increasingly came under fire.

After St. Louis there was no doubt that the conservatives had a majority in Southern Baptist agencies and institutions. Randall Lolley, president of Southeastern Seminary, resigned in the fall of 1987 in protest, even as the faculty formed a chapter of the American Association of University Professors to prepare for the battle. Lolley's dean and three other administrators followed him. Seizing the opportunity, conservative trustees elected Lewis Drummond of Southern Seminary. An inerrantist and professor of evangelism for several years, Drummond became Southeastern's third president.

Skirmishes

In the fall each year, state conventions became skirmish sites for Southern Baptist battles where the sides of the national group was mirrored in state conflicts. Not only the seminaries came under fire, but the Baptist colleges owned by the state conventions such as Mercer in Georgia and Baylor in Texas, were drawn into the acrimonious debates, though they were not new to charges of liberalism.

The only encouragement for moderates during this period was a public-broadcasting television special hosted by Bill Moyers. Moyers, a product of an East Texas Baptist church and an alumnus of Southwestern Seminary, achieved national stature first in posts with President Lyndon Johnson and then as a broadcast journalist. Conservatives thought his piece reflected them in unfair light. Moyers especially targeted the conservative strategist, Paul Pressler.

A continuing frustration for conservatives during this period was the perceived support of the national press for the moderate cause. A story on the front page of *The Wall Street Journal* featured the heading "Fundamentalists Fight to Capture the Soul of Southern Baptists. Purges and censorship grow as conservatives try to finish takeover from liberals."[51]

WMU Centennial

Desperately hoping for an oasis experience in the midst of the rancor and bitterness of Southern Baptist infighting, Woman's Missionary Union gathered in Richmond, Virginia, May 13–14, 1988, to celebrate its centennial. The *Religious Herald* reported over eleven thousand participants in the drama-and-pagentry-dominated event. "Taking part in the parades were representatives of the 37 state WMU organizations, 670 district associations, and 24 countries; hundreds of Southern Baptist foreign and home missionaries; and executives of denominational agencies and institutions." [52]

The Foreign Mission Board's Keith Parks told the gathering that it was the most prosperous time "since Adam and Eve," and the resources to evangelize the world were available. Parks said the only thing lacking was "the sacrificial commitment" of God's people. The Home Mission Board's Larry Lewis shared his dream of "a heaven-sent Holy Ghost revival" among Southern Baptists and hopes of reaching the Bold Mission Thrust goals of fifty thousand Southern Baptist congregations and ten thousand home and foreign missionaries by the year 2000.

The auxilary's four living presidents, Helen Fling (1963–69), Christine Gregory (1975–81), Dorothy Sample (1981–86), and Marjorie McCullough, first elected in 1986, addressed the meeting, along with former WMU executive Alma Hunt and its current executive, Carolyn Weatherford.

Weatherford said of the organization, whose Lottie Moon and Annie Armstrong offerings had become key to foreign and home mission endeavors, "We are a missions organization composed of women, not a women's organization that happens to support missions." Julian Pentecost, editor of Virginia's historic Baptist paper said, "Both she and Marjorie McCullough, WMU president, are fully committed to the organization's auxilary status which, although a historical necessity, is a present blessing. We share their hope and prayer it will continue to be so."[53]

It would be four more years before the substance of the anxiety behind Pentecost's words would be fully evident.

The Moderates' Alamo

As Convention time neared in 1988, moderate hopes began to rise once more, despite the nine straight losses they had suffered. Especially encouraging were the increased efforts on the part of organized Baptist moderates led by Houston layman, John Baugh. Jerry Vines, co-pastor of the First Baptist Church in Jacksonville, became the conservative candidate for president at San Antonio, after years of playing a prominent role in articulating the conservative position.

Moderates planned to back Richard Jackson and initially pushed Randall Lolley to be his running mate. They backed off when they perceived Lolley's identity with Southeastern Seminary and that the more liberal wing of theological life would hurt Jackson's chances.

Others were more concerned about the impact of the WMU's centennial meeting in Richmond the previous month, which they feared would reduce their attendance at the San Antonio meeting. That their role was considered so critical is more understandable in light of subsequent WMU problems with the conservative leadership. While some claimed it may have been the crucial difference, no substantial evidence exists to support that conclusion. WMU had not registered the attendees of its annual meeting for over three decades when they gathered in San Antonio, and its officials felt its sessions were as well attended as usual. It would be 1991 and the annual meeting in Atlanta before the auxilary would once again register its participants.

The popularity of Richard Jackson, the efforts of the moderate organization, Baptists Committed, and the less well-known candidacy of Jerry Vines brought the closest election in the ten-year history of the controversy. A strong effort was made at the pre-convention Pastor's Conference to build support for Vines. W. A. Criswell fired the passions of conservative followers with a blistering sermon grouping liberals and moderates in the same category and saying, "Liberals today call themselves moderate." He added, "A skunk by any other name still stinks."[54]

Vines was elected by a margin of 692 votes out of 32,436 cast. But the most controversial event at San Antonio was a resolution supporting the authority of the pastor at the expense of more traditional views concerning the doctrine of the priesthood of the believer. While it passed by a margin of nearly 11,000 to 9,000 it incensed moderates as much as the election discouraged them.[55] Some of the deeply disappointed moderates followed

Randall Lolley to the historic Texas shrine, the Alamo, where they burned their ballots in protest.

The Alamo, where Mexican General Santa Anna and five thousand troops overwhelmed, killed, and burned the bodies of 187 defenders may have been too strong a metaphor. However, a San Antonio newspaper columnist, writing in the shadow of the Alamo several years later, probably voiced the feelings of the dispirited moderates when he said, "Without a twinge of conscience or hint of remorse, conservative laymen and preachers smeared the names of Baptist brothers and sisters and conducted witch hunts that battered the reputations of holy men and women. In their wake, they left damaged institutions, wounded spirits, and broken hearts. All in the name of God." [56] The rhetoric on both sides now reflected the intensity of the conflict.

The victorious majority also supported the conservative leadership in the Executive Committee when it proposed that a smaller percentage of messengers be considered a quorum for business, to offset the now predictable exodus of messengers after the election of the president.

Texas Baptist Pastor Joel Gregory preached a Convention sermon that urged the Convention not to "tear down the castle" while "building the wall." Despite the conciliatory sound of Gregory's position, many conservatives thought he was already in their camp secretly. While his superb preaching talents lifted him above the fray on this occasion, a more combative role for Gregory in the controversy would soon come. [57]

Moderate Organizations

In 1986 a group of moderates formed an organization they hoped could move beyond politics on the Southern Baptist scene. Meeting in Charlotte, North Carolina, in November, they formed the Southern Baptist Alliance and elected North Carolina pastor Henry Crouch as chairman. According to Crouch, "The SBA would be a voice of conscience in the Convention." The SBA was a societal type of organization open to both individuals and congregations and advocating seven principles which reflected reaction to much of the conservative agenda.

The seven principles developed in a "covenant" cited the individual's freedom to read and interpret Scriptures; the freedom of a local church to shape its own life and mission, including the ordaining of males or females for ministry; cooperation with believers everywhere; the servant role of leadership; theological education characterized by reverence for biblical authority, inquiry, and responsible scholarship; a gospel that calls people to repentance and faith as well as to social and economical justice; and the principle of a free church and a free state.[58]

Moderates did not flock to the ranks of the Southern Baptist Alliance, however. Some explained that they did not want to do anything that would undermine their efforts to assert themselves as the real Southern Baptists or to regain their role in Southern Baptist life.

Women's Ordination Opposition

As has been noted numerous times in this narrative, women's roles have been significant, though often ignored and controversial throughout Southern Baptist history. Despite pivotal contributions by Baltimore's Ann Baker Graves, Virginia's Lottie Moon, Alabama's Martha Crawford, along with Annie Armstrong, Kathleen Mallory, Alma Hunt, Marie Mathis, and many others, women's roles remained constrained by the theology and practice of Southern Baptists. Apart from the seating question and the reversing of that ban following the successful progress of women's suffrage, the ultimate question of women's ordination did not come to the floor for Convention deliberation.

That began to change noticeably in the mid-sixties in conjunction with major social turmoil in the nation as a whole. After the 1964 ordination of Addie Davis by the Watts Street Baptist Church in Durham, North Carolina, the issue was ripe for debate. Historian Leon McBeth, in a singular study on women's roles, called it a first. While granting that women had enjoyed ministry-related roles in early Separate Baptist life, he cited reaction to suffragettes, the WMU outlet, and the church committee structure outlet, and the change of the diaconate from ministry to management roles as the reasons that Southern Baptists had taken an opposite tack.

Davis's ordination did not trigger an avalanche of such events, though more and more churches did ordain women as deacons and deaconesses. Most women who were ordained as ministers served in staff roles, and the increasing numbers graduating from the seminaries began to put pressure on the more moderate churches for this kind of recognition.

In 1980, Anne Rosser, who copastored a church in Richmond, Virginia, with her husband, Aubrey, baptized three new Christians, also a suspected first in Southern Baptist circles. A few women deacons chaired deacon groups in more moderate churches stretching all the way from Richmond's First Baptist to Austin's First Baptist.[59]

Heightened reaction to this trend became a part of the platform for the conservative resurgence, despite moderate assertions that the question of ordination was the prerogative of the local church. Thus, women ministers were refused subsidy by the conservative-led Home Mission Board, and later an ordained couple was rejected by the Foreign Mission Board.[60] In the Convention meeting in 1984 in Kansas City where Charles Stanley was elected president, a resolution opposing women's ordination was passed despite strong protests that it violated local church autonomy.[61]

As late as 1978, Southern Baptist agencies jointly sponsored a national consultation on the subject of women in church-related vocations, and one state convention, the District of Columbia, had even taken a stand in favor of women's ordination three years before that. But the resistance that found majority support in conservative ranks was also evident.

In 1985, a Sunday School Board editor, Howard Bramlette, was forced to resign after protests over an issue on women's roles in Southern Baptist life printed in *The Baptist Student*, followed a few months later by one critical of right-wing politics and religion. The latter forced the issue more nearly than the former, however.[62] Sunday School Board president Lloyd Elder's handling of Bramlette's case incensed many moderates and probably cost Elder some support when the same sword was turned against him.

Women in Ministry also constituted a moderate organization by definition. Though organized with the help of WMU's Carolyn Weatherford, WIM was independent. It continued to meet in connection with the Southern Baptist Convention and to publish its highly respected periodical *The Folio.* One of its leaders, Martha Marshall, a Southern Baptist Theological Seminary professor, survived a challenge by conservatives to her receiving of tenure at Southern because of an adroit move by Roy Honeycutt, in which he paired her tenure recommendation with the hiring of an inerrancy professor, David Dockery.

Another strong woman's leader, Nancy Sehested, the first woman pastor of a Southern Baptist church, was nominated by a supporter of Woman In Ministry to bring the Convention sermon during the naming of that preacher at the San Antonio Convention. The nominator was ruled out of order.[63]

Baptists Committed

The Forum continued to be a pre-Convention protest to the conservative-dominated Pastor's Conference; it served for nearly ten years as a staging ground and rally for moderate positions at the Convention itself. Though the Forum met a fellowship need for messengers who felt disenfranchised, its gatherings were always dwarfed in numbers by the traditionally well-attended Pastor's Conference. Control of the Pastor's Conference was undoubtedly one of the keys to conservative success.

The Southern Baptist Alliance, while including a significant group on the East Coast and giving vital support to Women In Ministry, was still not a comfortable choice for many Southern Baptists. In December 1988, a group of moderate laymen meeting in Dallas formed "Baptists Committed to the SBC." Their goal was singular: to make a concerted effort to defeat candidates of the fundamentalists.

Winfred Moore was named chairman of this group, which hired a former Christian Life Commission staff member, David Currie, as a salaried coordinator. The group, citing declines in baptisms and contributions and shattered unity, said they wanted to "lead us out of this despair" and proceeded to organize chapters in a number of states.[64] In 1990, Moore was succeeded by Jimmy Allen, following Allen's retirement from the Radio and Television Commission.

Turning Up the Heat

When the Convention made its controversial trip to Las Vegas in 1989 (many opposed going to the "city of sin and gambling"), Morris Chapman, in his Convention sermon, questioned the doctrinal integrity of many state convention-related colleges and universities. His speech met with strong conservative approval and moved the Texas pastor into the front ranks of the conservative resurgence.

Conservative leaders continued to take issue with Southern Baptists' participation in the Baptist Joint Committee on Public Affairs directed by the combative James Dunn. Pressler and Patterson, committed to a national conservative political agenda often opposed by the Dunn-led organization, felt that the B.J.C.P.A. had outlived its usefulness to Southern Baptists. They wanted their own public affairs committee, and the SBC Executive Committee supported the idea. The matter should have been voted on at Las Vegas, but SBC president Jerry Vines thought it would be too controversial an issue and that opposition was growing while support was not yet focused. Even the conservatives' own Larry Lewis was opposed to anything that would take dollars away from missions.

Moderates made a reasonably strong effort to elect a president at Las Vegas in the person of Dan Vestal, the conservative and well-liked pastor of the First Baptist Church, Midland, Texas. Vestal himself had confessed that he had been galvanized to action after listening to a tape of a radio interview of Judge Paul Pressler.

A measure of the growing discouragement of moderate factions was the partnership of the Southern Baptist Alliance and *SBC Today* to produce an alternate Sunday School commentary to the Sunday School Board's Life and Work series. It later gave way to a full set of lesson materials published by a new moderate-focused firm called Smyth and Helwys.

The SBA employed Stan Hastey as executive director, changed its name to the Alliance of Baptists, and dropped any reference to Southern Baptists in its purpose statement. Since the larger part of its membership was from the East Coast, the events at Southeastern Seminary were especially galling. At its meeting in Greenville, S.C., in March of 1989, the SBA committed itself to beginning a new seminary in Richmond, Virginia.[65]

The Smell of Victory

It was obvious that the dominant majorities of conservatives on the Boards were having their way, and the only question was just how quickly their agenda would unfold.

The Christian Life Commission majority was the first to act. Larry Baker was forced out in favor of Richard Land, a former administrator at the Criswell Bible Institute and colleague of Paige Patterson. Land, well-educated and articulate, was committed to a conservative social and political agenda.

For many conservatives and their supporters from outside the Southern Baptist Convention, all this had the sweet smell of victory. In the *Fundamentalist Journal*, published by Independent Baptist Jerry Falwell, the editorial asserted, "It has been done." With Vines and his wife on the cover, the July-August 1989 issue focused on the SBC conservative leadership, identifying with them as fundamentalists.[66]

The feature article said, "After the 1988 and 1989 elections of Jerry Vines as president of the Convention, Conservative leaders breathed a sigh of relief. Over the last ten years a succession of Bible-believing presidents has appointed Fundamentalists to leadership positions. The Convention, for all practical purposes, is back on track."[67]

Paige Patterson, predicting that the next few years would be peaceful, said, "The energy we've spent on the issues of the last ten years will be channeled into more productive areas." W. A. Criswell was quoted as saying, "It will finally turn our Southern seminaries into great fundamental, Bible-believing, and Bible-teaching institutions." Judge Paul Pressler announced, "As Conservatives lead in our institutions, the fears generated by others will dissipate. Southern Baptists will see the tremendous benefit in missions and evangelism that comes from biblical theology, and will recognize the purity of the motives of those who have sought a return to this basis."[68]

The magazine also focused on what might happen to Southern Baptist moderates. The Christian Life Commission's new director, Richard Land, said, "Some will be forced to come to a decision about their present beliefs versus historic Southern Baptist beliefs on issues and will have to decide whether they can function comfortably with the tension between the two."[69]

Criswell was more direct, "Like sin and the Devil, we shall have the so-called Moderates among us. I am praying that as time goes on, our fundamental, Bible-believing people will become so numerous and so dedicated until the voice of the Moderates subsides into an indistinguishable whisper."[70]

A California pastor, Bill Hann, claimed that some Moderates would join the American Baptists or the Episcopalians. He also added, presciently, "There are probably some churches that will stay in the SBC and form a fellowship within it. Others may stay in their local churches and not get involved in Convention work or denominational affairs."[71] Vines simply said, "Time will tell."

Despite such sentiments, the battle for the gavel was not quite over. The candid remarks of Pressler about efforts to control Southern Baptist life had incensed the mild-mannered Vestal. Despite his defeat in Las Vegas and his having accepted a new pastorate in Dunwoody, Georgia, a few weeks after that meeting, he committed himself to make an all-out try to capture the presidency at New Orleans in 1990.

The Baptist Committed group out of Texas geared to back him and make one last effort to turn the conservative juggernaut aside and win the battle for the gavel.

Agency Leadership under Fire

Events of the Convention quickly paled, however, beside efforts at the August 1989 meeting of the Baptist Sunday School Board to fire Lloyd

Elder as president. Despite the fact that conservative trustees had already elicited a commitment from Elder for an inerrantist commentary and the inclusion of anti-abortion programs and materials, he continued to encounter conservative opposition. His involvement with the Baptist Joint Committee on Public Affairs became the catalyst when it spilled over into a controversial Elder-led gift of $400,000 to the Executive Committee to help retire a building mortgage. Elder was accused of linking support to the BJC with the gift.

The opposition was led by trustee Larry Holly, a physician from Beaumont, Texas. Before the Board's meeting at Glorieta, Holly circulated a list of concerns about Elder's leadership, based on the $400,000 gift and other questions. A number of trustees moved to censor Elder. One of the Board members even urged that Elder be fired. When it was obvious that this motion did not have sufficient backing, it was withdrawn and a number of instructions to Elder were adopted instead.[72]

Upon his return to Nashville, Elder spoke to nearly one thousand employees of the Board and said, "After the motion was withdrawn—which I consider the depth of cowardice on the part of the trustee who withdrew it—I felt as if I had been laid out on a table for surgery and cut wide open, and left there to see if I would live. I've not felt so abandoned since our daughter died in an automobile accident."[73] A standing ovation by his employees was some comfort to Elder, but the question to whether he would live or die as president of the Board was the open wound of his metaphor.

Rumor and rancor dominated the fall of 1989 and the spring of 1990 as Southern Baptists moved toward what many thought would be the final confrontation between its polarized ranks.

At the Radio and Television Commission, conservatives gained a long-awaited opportunity when Jimmy Allen stepped down after a financially troubled ten years. Despite his own clearly stated moderate views, most of Allen's opposition developed from growing financial problems and failed efforts to negotiate a super network. He would be succeeded by Arizona's state executive secretary, Jack Johnson, who was clearly conservative in his views. Allen, in turn, would use his new status to give major leadership to moderate initiatives yet to come.

Southeastern Seminary continued in turmoil during this year and came under fire from its accrediting agencies. Reports claimed that faculty members were looking for other posts and that students planned to transfer. Drummond was also criticized by his trustees for moving too slowly.

Southwestern Seminary's new conservative-dominated board took Russell Dilday to task over his outspoken opposition to the new leadership's tactics. Stung by what he felt was an orchestrated political process of appointing new trustees, Dilday had been very critical of some of the new Board members' inability to "read a balance sheet" or to do anything other than carry the "party line." He had spoken at a meeting of Baptists Committed and continued to refer to the conservative efforts as a "takeover effort."

Dilday's impeccable character, orthodoxy, and administrative ability made him a tough target. After an effort to fire him failed to garner necessary support, he was bumped dramatically by his trustees before an accommodation was reached in which both Dilday and his board agreed to avoid overt political activity, though each reserved the right speak their convictions. The accommodation would become the grounds for a new round of acrimony.

The Last Battle

It was clear to Southern Baptist Convention strategists on both sides even before they left the 1989 convention site in Las Vegas that the 1990 convocation in New Orleans might constitute the last battle between conservatives and moderates.

Dan Vestal came away from his run at the presidency at Las Vegas even more committed to tell Southern Baptists his side of the story. While Vestal's own well-known inerrant position on the Bible left him above conservative reproach at that point, he was convinced that the real issue was not the authority of Scripture, but rather that of power and control of denominational agencies and institutions. The organization formed a few months earlier under the leadership of John Baugh stepped up its activities to back Vestal. Conservatives charged that Baugh had 27,000 locked-up reservations in New Orleans. Since conservatives had traditionally been accused of working the reservation opportunity, observers were not sure whether this was a turning of the tables or a new tactic.

Vestal secured the support of the church at Dunwoody for an all-out effort. A friend from his former church at Midland offered his airplane and his pilot to facilitate Vestal's ability to attend meetings to rally moderates and still honor his commitment to his new church.

At the fall meeting of the Executive Committee in Nashville, Jerry Vines turned the Committee loose on the question of the Baptist Joint Committee on Public Affairs and the proposed Religious Liberty Committee. Vines had asked the Executive Committee in February not to vote on that issue so that the focus could be on personal evangelism in Las Vegas. He trumpeted the results of the grassroots effort among Las Vegas neighborhoods, thanked the committee for their patience, and said he was now willing for the Executive Committee to move ahead to resolve the issues before it.

After a good deal of parliamentary maneuvering by people opposed to the defunding of the Baptist Joint Committee, votes that all but did just that prevailed, and it was obvious that the conservative majority was going to pursue its agenda on all fronts.

That next spring of 1990, Russell Dilday came under fire again from trustees at Southwestern Baptist Theological Seminary over a conversation reported between him and Convention President Vines in Nashville on the occasion of the February 1990 Executive Committee meeting. Dilday, who had undergone a triple heart bypass two weeks before, was confronted in late March by his trustees. He assured the Board that he was in full health again and gave his side of the conversation, reported by a number of people and even recorded by some who accompanied Vines that day.[74]

Several Southwestern Seminary trustees thought Dilday had broken an agreement reached with them in the spring not to engage in political activities. Dilday indicated that he was trying to resolve a matter with Vines, and apologized if he had offended. Again, after some additional warnings, the Board backed off.

Roy Honeycutt of Southern Seminary also came under fire from a trustee who mailed out a voluminous report to fellow trustees charging Honeycutt with theological impropriety. Honeycutt's trustees refused to censor him after he answered the charges, but moderate supporters at Southern Seminary were aghast at what was happening to their institution under the pressures coming from the conservative-dominated trustees.

Two of their professors incurred the wrath of conservatives during the course of the year preceding the final battle. Glenn Hinson, speaking in Chattanooga in a hard-hitting statement that was well-reported, impugned the preparation and motives of the trustees appointed to Southern Seminary. Fellow faculty member Paul D. Simmons, professor of Christian ethics, spoke to a Planned Parenthood meeting and incurred the wrath of the pro-life forces in the conservative movement.

But conservatives were heartened by the increasingly strong role that Richard Land's new Christian Life Commission was playing in the Right to Life Movement as well as his actions on other conservative agendas. Land and W. A. Criswell were on opposite sides of this issue, which many thought was the most potentially explosive in all the conservative majority's new agenda, the right-to-life or anti-abortion issue. Land identified that as his major difference with his predecessors. He said, "I'm executive director of the Southern Baptist Christian Life Commission and I'm very pro-life . . . that's a change."[75]

On the other hand, David Beale, a fundamentalist historian, said in 1985, "Following the 1973 pro-abortion ruling by the U. S. Supreme Court, Dr. Criswell publicly expressed satisfaction. A Religious News Service in Dallas quoted his remarks: 'I have always felt that it was only after a child was born and had life separate from its mother, that it became an individual person, and it has always, therefore, seemed to me that what is best for the mother and for the future should be allowed.'" Beale said, "Criswell has not changed his views on the matter since he made this statement, a fact which this writer verified by calling his office."[76]

Keith Parks received the support of Jerry Vines and other conservatives in calling for a strong Lottie Moon Christmas offering. Parks had felt that the offering was going to suffer severely under the cloud of the conflict. Giving to the offering which had grown dramatically for a dozen years had begun to flatten. The Foreign Mission Board's operations depended on the offering for roughly 50 percent of its annual budget.

While Baptists continued to buy Sunday School Board literature, support the Lottie Moon Christmas and Annie Armstrong Easter offerings, send their young men and women to Southern Baptist seminaries, support the Radio and Television Commission's broadcasting efforts, and witness and study as before, it was obvious that a great deal of energy was being spent getting ready for New Orleans.

Conservative leadership came together shortly after Christmas on a Caribbean cruise under the leadership of Adrian Rogers, the unofficial but unchallenged head of the movement. Their task was to agree on a candidate to field opposite Vestal in New Orleans. Some conservatives had said in other elections that it did not matter whom they put forward; if he was their candidate, he would be elected. But conservative leadership felt that this was a critical time when it was imperative they select the right man.

According to conservative reports, Rogers, Vines, and others thought that Fred Wolfe, pastor of the Cottage Hills Baptist Church in Mobile, Alabama, was the man. His church was close to New Orleans and he had received a lot of national exposure. Other strong candidates included Morris Chapman and moderate leader John Baugh's pastor, Ed Young, who despite Baugh's activities, remained a conservative insider. The cruise meeting settled on Wolfe, and Wolfe tentatively agreed.[77]

A few years later writer Helen Lee Turner would attach eschatological meaning to such cruises. "Led by pastors of SBC's megachurches, the apocalyptic conquest is symbolically enacted at sea. Worldly evils are literally pushed aside." She quoted conservative accounts to highlight the triumphal feelings as bars and casinos were closed and Christian entertainers replaced the usual fair.[78]

Meanwhile, moderates continued to rally their forces with Baptists Committed leading the way. Under the chairmanship of Jimmy Allen, former president of the Radio and Television Commission, as well as of the Southern Baptist Convention, moderates thought there was reason for genuine optimism. He was joined by the Southern Baptist Alliance's Stan Hasty and *SBC Today* principals, publisher Walker Knight and editor Jack Harwell. When Harwell had been forced from his position as editor of Georgia's *Christian Index* in 1988, he had been quickly enlisted by Knight.

Moderate leaders were joined by a new face in the person of Carolyn Weatherford Crumpler, who had served for a number of years as executive director of Woman's Missionary Union, but had recently resigned to marry a widowed Illinois pastor named Crumpler. She made an announcement in Dan Vestal's church that she would be willing to run as first vice-president and support Vestal in his efforts to unseat the conservatives. Yet any headlines that moderates grabbed were soon eclipsed by stories of new additions to the conservative bandwagon.

The first convert was the highly respected John Bisagno, pastor of the First Baptist Church of Houston, who had been widely understood to be neutral in the battle, though his own biblical position, like Vestal's, included inerrancy. Just before the Convention had met in San Antonio, Bisagno had issued a strong statement urging both parties to come together around the Scriptures and a new commitment to missions and evangelism. Now he decided to support the conservative cause—coming out of the closet, as some conservatives put it.

Before moderates could get over the announcement by Bisagno, new endorsements came from Joel Gregory, pastor of Travis Avenue Baptist Church in Fort Worth and rumored to be in line as W. A. Criswell's successor at First Baptist Church, Dallas, and from Kenneth Hemphill, pastor of the First Baptist Church in Norfolk, Virginia, a traditionally moderate state. For Gregory, it meant abandoning the neutrality he had claimed in San Antonio in 1988. Many moderates accused him of opportunism.

Chapman Chosen

The triggering event for these endorsements was a decision by Fred Wolfe, who had become increasingly uncomfortable with his agreement to run in New Orleans, to step aside in favor of Morris Chapman. Rogers and the other conservative leaders evidently agreed and noted the strong history of Cooperative Program support by Chapman's church, the First Baptist Church in Wichita Falls. In comparison with any of the previous conservative resurgence-backed presidents, Chapman had far and away the best record in Convention support.[79]

Chapman had served the First Baptist Church during some stormy years when several members of the traditionally centrist church, formerly pastored by New Orleans Baptist Seminary's Landrum Leavell and the Texas Baptist Convention's William Pinson, mounted strong opposition to his conservative involvement. Before going to Wichita Falls he had served the First Baptist Church in Albuquerque and had twice served as president of the state convention there.

Conservatives were delighted with the endorsements and their timing, but they took issue with several state papers, including the *Baptist Standard* over the perceived lack of attention given to the story. Conservative writer James Hefley, after carefully measuring the words given to all of the participants, claimed bias by the *Baptist Standard's* editor Presnall Wood and associate Toby Druin in favor of moderates. According to Druin, Joel Gregory felt especially slighted by the lack of notice given his endorsement of Chapman.[80]

Meanwhile, moderates were buoyed by a member of the Committee on Nominations' announcement that he would give a minority report championing more broad-based nominations for the New Orleans Convention. Dan Montoya, one of the area lieutenants in Arkansas for the conservative movement, had defected rather spectacularly with a secretly taped transcription of one of the conservative strategy meetings in that state.[81]

In February 1990 in Atlanta, conservatives had their most public planning meeting yet, led by Adrian Rogers. Rogers set forth the game plan for conservatives in that meeting. He urged his followers to keep the focus on the Peace Committee report showing the "duplicity of moderates" and to keep the issue on biblical inerrancy. Above all, Rogers urged the veteran group to once again get their messengers to the meeting and support their candidates.[82]

New Orleans

As the Convention gathered, moderate political activity was evident. Baptists Committed had managed its most aggressive program yet of printing, distribution, and organization.

The pre-Convention meetings went according to the now-established pattern of moderates attending the Forum and the Women In Ministry meetings as well as the WMU meeting, and of conservatives packing the Pastor's Conference where Chapman was showcased and championed.

As the convention convened with Vines presiding, Bisagno made a strong nominating speech for Chapman. While the messenger count did not reach the startling Dallas number, it did total 38,456. Chapman won nearly 58 percent of the votes for president, and conservatives dominated all proceedings until defections from both sides left the Convention without a quorum to act on most of the resolutions developed by the Committee on Resolutions. This embarrassing situation developed, despite the fact that the percentage required for a quorum had been lowered at the preceding meeting to 25 percent. With less than 15 percent of the registered messengers present, Vines was left with no alternative but to adjourn after a series of reports.[83]

A final flap allowed diehard moderates to vent their feelings when a motion to remove from the Southern Seminary Board the trustee who had mounted the attack on Roy Honeycutt was loudly approved by those still there. The motion was ruled out of order, however, and the matter was referred to the Southern Seminary trustees, where the person being challenged would have an appropriate opportunity to answer.[84]

The battle of New Orleans was over, but more importantly, the battle over the SBC leadership was over. In a post-Convention press conference, Chapman said the question of whether the issue was really settled was up to future actions of the 42 percent who had voted against him. He held, as Rogers had held before him, however, that the vast majority of Baptists supported the conservative position despite the decade-long 55 percent-45 percent split. Chapman tried to reassure nervous Baptist agency and institution employees, but he also reiterated his commitment to the conservative program.

Second Guessing

While the victorious conservatives savored their triumph, moderate scholars reviewed the futile twelve-year battle. What had gone wrong? Where and how was the battle lost?

Southern Seminary's Larry McSwain claimed that moderates lacked the "motivation to fight a political conflict with ideological values at its heart." He noted the irony of moderates becoming the conservatives in the new resistance, by their efforts to defend the old denominational consensus that had served the body prior to the social changes of the 1960s and 1970s. His assessment was unsparing. "Lacking highly visible leadership and depending on the structures of the denomination itself, they preached too ineffectively with too little visibility, spent too little money and failed to organize the intensity needed to defeat the fundamentalist juggernaut."[85]

Samford University's Bill Leonard cited five reasons for the moderate's overwhelming defeat: First, the so-called moderate coalition was virtually no coalition at all, with members lacking consensus and direction, especially in the early years. Second, moderates misread the times and stayed with the old methods for coping with controversy. Third, moderates failed to perceive the nature of the controversy by refusing to admit it was theological. Fourth, moderates' promotion of the old program and corporate identity of the past reinforced "the bureaucratic image that the fundamentalists exploited." Fifth, too many moderate sympathizers failed to get involved.[86]

Some scholars thought the determinative factor was the larger environment. George Marsden, writing in the *Reformed Journal* in 1988, noted that the inerrancy movement had been strategically allied with the New Christian Right and its national political agenda.[87] Even more global causes would be cited in later years, including the effects of "post-denominationalism," "post-modernity," and changes in "organizational theory."[88]

And Celebration

Such analysis, however, was far from the minds of victorious conservative leadership, who thought the victory could at last be celebrated. A large number of them gathered at the Cafe du Monde in New Orleans' French Quarter the evening after the election. It was there in the early 1970s that Judge Paul Pressler and Paige Patterson had begun to plan what they would subsequently call the conservative resurgence and what defeated moderates would decry as a ruthless takeover.

The SBC parliamentarian, Barry McCarty, a Church of Christ minister retained by the Executive Committee, presided over the victory party. Plaques commemorating the event and their roles were presented to Paige Patterson and Paul Pressler. Those assembled then sang "Victory in Jesus."[89]

9

New Initiatives

1990–1993

As the final decade of the twentieth century unfolded and the Southern Baptist Convention approached its sesquicentennial, it was obvious that its more conservative elements were in full control and anxious to consolidate their position. It was less obvious what the defeated moderates were going to do. Few from either side felt they would simply take a back seat and watch the conservative agenda play out. New initiatives were in the air, but they had to await a round of consolidation and reaction.

Conservative Aspirations

For conservatives, the program was simple. Conservative writer James Hefley outlined that course as one in which the emphasis would move from attaining trustee majorities to restaffing the agency leadership positions, to changing literature, educational emphases and programs, and to state convention and association control.[1]

The beliefs and convictions the conservatives hoped to institutionalize by these actions had been deducible through a variety of statements throughout the controversy, but in an article in Southern Seminary's *Review and Expositor* in the winter of 1991, conservative strategist Paige Patterson systematized the convictions the dominant conservatives hoped to inculcate in the denomination they now controlled.[2]

All of the decade-long controversy's high particulars of inerrancy, women's biblical roles, pro-life stands, pastoral authority, the priesthood of the believer, and church-state balance were contained in the broad approach Patterson sketched in his article. Historians will subsequently have to judge whether those high particulars were dictated by the emphasis of conservatives, the reaction of moderates, or a combination of action and reaction.

Moderate Reaction

Reaction began in July of 1990, when Dan Vestal and other leaders of Baptists Committed called for a national consultation in Atlanta to discuss alternate ways of dealing with their sense of disenfranchisement. While admitting that they were not able to unseat the conservatives in Convention meetings, most moderates still refused to believe they were in the minority. But a larger and larger group felt that conservative domination made it a moot point.

Surprising even the most optimistic moderates, more than three thousand registered for a meeting expecting five hundred. Leadership from Baptists Committed, the Forum, *SBC Today*, and Women in Ministry all took part. When the meeting was over they had approved a newly chartered Baptist Cooperative Missions Program, Inc. as an alternate funding program to bypass the SBC Executive Committee. The charter for the tax-exempt channel was taken out by Duke McCall, Grady Cothen, Hettie Johnson, and others. Since the charter predated the call for the meeting, it was obviously a part of a developing strategy.[3]

Conservative leaders were even more determined to pursue their program, despite the new turn in moderate opposition. James Draper, reflecting his reputation as the most conciliatory of that leadership, called a meeting of moderates and conservatives, but when it yielded little, he deferred to Morris Chapman, who made another attempt two months later. Draper put the matter of the new alternate funding program bluntly, "We are struggling with whether or not to let someone blackmail us into a sort of detente." After Chapman's meeting, conservatives decided they could weather the storm, and they resolved to maintain their course.[4]

Conservative Consolidation

Despite these conciliatory efforts the victorious conservatives quickly revealed a relentless resolve to realize all they had so persistently pursued. Rapidly developing events showed that resolve would be acted out by the trustee majorities in the Executive Committee and on each of the Boards of the agencies and institutions.

That resolve was felt that fall when the Executive Committee decided to oust two Baptist Press staff members, Al Shackleford and Dan Martin. Martin and Shackleford refused ultimatums to resign and declined to attend the closed meeting.[5] While their ouster was widely thought to have been engineered by Paul Pressler, the Texas jurist was in Europe at the time of the meeting.

Associated Baptist Press

The firings precipitated a new uproar in Baptist state papers still largely supportive of moderate causes and dominated by state conventions where, arguably, moderates often still prevailed. After the advent of advocacy journalism among Southern Baptists through conservative ventures like *The Southern Baptist Journal* in 1973 and *The Southern Baptist Advocate* in 1980 and the moderate's *SBC Today* in 1983, state Baptist papers were seen as defenders of the status quo. While only gradually becoming more aggressive, these papers' influence continued to be significant.

In the first forty-five years of the twentieth century, eight new state papers had joined the twelve surviving publications from the previous century. As already noted, this formerly private enterprise by 1950 had become totally owned by state conventions. By 1990, eighteen more state Baptist papers had been established during Southern Baptists' nationwide expansion. Circulation rose from 547,254 in 1945 to 1,462,474 by 1992. All of the eighteen had developed since the advent of *Baptist Press,* and most had a loyalty, however occasionally critical, to the service.[6]

It was therefore not surprising when many Baptist editors moved to establish an alternative Baptist press service to supply them with "unbiased" material. Chartered and based in Jacksonville, Florida, Associated Baptist Press was organized with a self-perpetuating board, designed to be free from the control of any denominational agency or faction. Its goal was to provide news about Baptists and of interest to Baptists to secular newspapers, Baptist newspapers, and other Christian publications.[7] Presnall Wood, editor of the *Baptist Standard* of Texas, said he and other editors had often considered such a move, feeling that Baptist Press was too beholden to the Convention program to provide unbiased reporting. He said that only their confidence in *Baptist Press* staff members over the years had deterred them. The deterrent disappeared with the firing of Shackleford and Martin.[8]

In 1993 Associated Baptist Press would begin accepting support from the moderate's Cooperative Baptist Fellowship.

Sunday School Board

In January of 1991, the Sunday School Board met and forced Lloyd Elder into early retirement in a not-unexpected turn of events following his Glorieta trials. The final blow descended from a new controversy over a centennial history of the Sunday School Board written by Baptist historian Leon McBeth of Southwestern Baptist Theological Seminary.

McBeth's commission was to write an interpretive history of the Board's first one hundred years. Elder made available whatever material the writer requested, and McBeth used a combination of interviews and records in completing his manuscript. Not surprisingly, given the climate between trustees and Elder following Glorieta, questions were raised about the project as it went into the editing stages.

Texas trustee Larry Holly demanded all internal documents related to the book as well as the manuscript. Trustee chairman Bill Anderson said the book was biased against the conservative resurgence, and he questioned its account of the Glorieta meeting and treatment of an embarrassing slander trial initiated by a former employee of the Board over incidents that took place during Grady Cothen's administration. Calling the manuscript unbalanced, the Board voted in August 1990 not to publish McBeth's manuscript entitled *Celebrating Heritage and Hope.*[9]

Faculties at Southern and then Southwestern, knowing McBeth's superior credentials as a scholar, protested the decision, but to no avail. Since the Sunday School Board claimed that McBeth's contract gave them ownership of the manuscript, it was decided that all but one copy was to be destroyed. It soon became obvious, however, that even before that decision had been made, copies of portions and even complete manuscripts had made their way to numerous people.

Elder caught the blame for the whole uproar, and Anderson told him he could not save his job. The Board cited him for financial mismanagement, taping of phone calls without second-party consent, and editorial bias in the centennial history. But Anderson was reported to have said, "It was the book that got him."[10]

Pressures mounted to secure Elder's resignation, and a special meeting of the Board was called for January 17, 1991. Elder, fully aware that he lacked the support to stay on, retained the services of a lawyer and negotiated a generous separation fee that also covered his legal expenses. In return, he agreed to take no action nor make any statement not in the best interest of the Board. Despite outcries from the right that the Board had given Elder a "golden parachute" and outrage from the left that he had been forced out on trumped up charges, the decision stood.[11]

Southern Seminary

The trustees at Southern Seminary turned up the heat on that administration by pressing for a new test for the hiring of faculty based on the Peace Committee report rather than the historic Abstract of Principles signed by all previous faculty hired at that Seminary.

After the accrediting agencies raised questions about the trustees' actions, the trustees accepted negotiations initiated by the Seminary president, Roy Honeycutt, in the form of a "covenant," which included faculty input and which the trustees agreed to as a compromise with the outside accrediting pressures as well as with the Southern faculty, staff, and alumni.[12]

Moderate Dreams

Any doubt that moderate support had collapsed at New Orleans with Morris Chapman's victory over Dan Vestal was settled after the 1990 Fellowship meeting held in August following the New Orleans Convention.[13]

It was clear that a new form of dissent was in place when the leadership that had coalesced at that meeting, including Baptists Committed and Southern Baptist Alliance members and other moderate leadership, called for a meeting in Atlanta two weeks prior to the meeting of the Southern Baptist Convention there in 1991. In concepts drafted by Baptists Committed's Jimmy Allen, John Baugh, and Daniel Vestal, the idea that would become the Cooperative Baptist Fellowship was conceived. Less than a year later, before six thousand Baptists meeting in Atlanta's Omni Coliseum, it was delivered [14]

Initially designed not to be an alternate Southern Baptist Convention, but an alternative within the Southern Baptist Convention, the Cooperative Baptist Fellowship was a call for churches to use state conventions to bypass traditional Cooperative Program lines and still support Southern Baptist mission work and institutions, especially those such as the Baptist Joint Committee, which had been kicked out of the trough by the conservative-dominated Executive Committee.

One participant, Bill Bruster, pastor of First Baptist Church of Abilene, reported in his church bulletin, "It had the kind of enthusiasm and the kind of fellowship we haven't seen since the fundamentalist takeover began." To many people, it was still a hodgepodge of initiatives, with the CBF as an umbrella of sorts. They included *Baptists Today* (formerly *SBC Today*), Women in Ministry, the Alliance, the Baptist Theological Seminary in Richmond (which had opened its doors that fall with thirty-two students), Associated Baptist Press, and the new publishing effort in Greenville, South Carolina, called Smyth and Helwys Publishing.

Pressing the Conservative Agenda

The new Southern Baptist leaders, on the other hand, pointed out that Baptists could do whatever they chose to, but they went ahead with their plan for the Convention in Atlanta. With Morris Chapman presiding, his reelection was not contested, and final defunding of the Baptist Joint Committee proceeded as predicted. While moderates were present and made themselves known in a number of business items, it was obvious that most of the leaders, as well as others of the groups who had opposed conservative candidates for eleven years, were either not present or very quiet.

Conservative leaders now openly talked about taking the battle to the state conventions where in fact it had already been joined.

Baylor and Furman

Initially, transference to the state level of the conflict taking place on the Southern Baptist Convention level was most evident in Georgia, where controversy over the editorial policy of the Georgia *Index's* Jack Harwell and perceived liberalism and management problems at Mercer University provided the focus. Harwell had to step down, but Mercer held its ground. The Georgia Baptist Convention swung to clearly identified conservatives, and then back to moderates, and then back to a conservative. A nearly equally divided constituency emerged.

Just as heated, however, were state convention battles in Texas and South Carolina, where their leading institutions, Baylor University and Furman University, respectively, moved to make the election of trustees independent of their respective conventions.

Baylor University shocked even moderate leadership with a quick charter change in the fall of 1990, just before the Texas Baptist Convention met that year in Houston. Trustees sympathetic to the plan to protect Baptists' largest university from a hostile takeover were briefed prior to a trustee meeting, but known opponents were not. A majority approved, and an amendment to Baylor's charter and constitution was filed with the State of Texas before the information was given to all parties, including the state convention headquarters and the *Baptist Standard*.[15]

The outcry was immediate. Joel Gregory, then a pastor in Fort Worth, was especially incensed with the Baylor action, and vowed to fight it, although he was in the process of accepting a widely anticipated call to succeed W. A. Criswell at First Baptist Church in Dallas. It would be an unusual succession. Criswell was to remain as senior pastor and preach the 11:00 A.M. service, while Gregory would be pastor and handle the other services. Many predicted it would not be easy for the old patriarch to let go, but Gregory's sponsors were counting on his acknowledged oratorical skills to carry the burden of the transition. The result was that Criswell continued as an outspoken champion for conservative themes, and Gregory stepped forward as a major leader in the conservative movement.[16]

Less than a month after Baylor's initiative, Furman made the same move in South Carolina but, due to the different charters of the schools, faced less question about the legal right to do so than Baylor had encountered.[17]

Conservatives pointed out that both schools would move quickly into "secular humanist" ranks if the safeguarding right of the state conventions to elect trustees was not restored. However, W. A. Criswell, the "grand old man" of the conservative forces, said, "I've washed my hands of them. You are not going to get Baylor back . . . It's gone."[18] But his successor-designate, Gregory, was not ready to give it up, and he began a frantic recovery effort.

Both universities reiterated their commitment to Baptist life and to their historic principles, but both asserted their need to be free from what they claimed would be the oppressive control of the conservative forces. Throughout 1991, supporters and opponents of the institutions' actions jockeyed for position in their respective states.

Leadership Changes and Challenges

Conservatives had waited impatiently for a changing of the guard at Southern Baptist Convention agencies and institutions. Despite significant battles, only the Christian Life Commission, the Radio and Television Commission, the Home Mission Board, Southeastern Theological Seminary, and, some believed, Golden Gate Baptist Theological Seminary, had been turned over to conservative-sponsored presidents by mid-1991. But what many people believed was the most strategic prize of all formally came into their hands when conservative leader and former Southern Baptist Convention president, James Draper, was elected president of the Sunday School Board in the fall of 1991 to succeed the deposed Lloyd Elder.[19]

Elder took a teaching position with Belmont College, now Belmont University, in Nashville, in a carefully structured relationship that would not impinge upon conditions of the package he and his attorney had negotiated with the Sunday School Board in his agreement to step down.[20]

Draper had been seen as one of the more conciliatory leaders of the conservative resurgency in moderate eyes, but his taking over at the Sunday School Board was viewed as the beginning of a new round of changes in which loyal conservative leaders would be given leadership of Southern Baptist agencies and institutions. Moreover, expectations for changes in programs and literature controlled by the Sunday School Board were considered crucial to conservatives' long-range plans.

Many people were surprised when Russell Dilday was not challenged at his fall board meeting in 1991, despite a new chairman of Southwestern's trustees known to be a hard-liner. What really surprised Baptists was the question of Foreign Mission Board leadership coming back to the front.

Fighting at the Fountainhead

In October 1991, conservative leaders at the Foreign Mission Board overrode recommendations from its administration and voted to reverse a funding agreement previously negotiated with the Baptist Theological Seminary in Ruschlikon, Switzerland. That seminary, established in 1948 as a part of the Foreign Mission Board's post-war European strategy, had grown increasingly expensive to operate. In the 1980s the Board endeavored to negotiate a decreasing financial commitment, believing that European Baptists should carry a larger share of the responsibility. A compromise was worked out in which the Board would, at the close of 1992, begin a fifteen-year annual reduction.

The commitment collapsed, however, when Glenn Hinson began teaching as an adjunct at Ruschlikon while on sabbatical from Southern Seminary. Hinson had often been a thorn in the flesh of conservative leaders for his outspoken viewpoints. Consequently, the Board voted 35-28 to cease funding at the end of 1991; the $365,000 that would not be paid in 1992 amounted to 40 percent of the seminary's budget.

Foreign Mission Board president R. Keith Parks defended the seminary's autonomy under a European Baptist Board to utilize Hinson, and thought it imperative for the Board to fulfill agreements negotiated in good faith. With a storm of protests emerging from all over the South as well as from Europe, the chairman of the Foreign Mission Board, William L. Hancock, agreed to review the matter in December. Many Board members thought the matter would be reversed, but with Texas members Joel Gregory, now co-pastor of the First Baptist Church in Dallas, and Paige Patterson in the lead, the conservatives stiffened. They claimed that the agreement with the seminary had included a promise on the part of seminary administration to take a more conservative approach, and that had not happened. A motion to reverse failed 54-27.[21]

The Board's vice-president for Europe and the Middle East, Isam Ballinger, and its area director for Europe, Keith Parker, took early retirement in protest, and in a news conference held at the Foreign Mission Board in Richmond, blasted conservative leaders and policies, which they claimed would wreck 140 years of missionary effort.[22]

Parks came under fire from trustees for allowing the press conference in which the two staff members of his made their announcement. Since he would reach sixty-five, or retirement age, in October 1992, some Board members began talking of the need to set up a search committee in February of 1992. Others feared that forcing Parks to take retirement would antagonize still more Baptist churches and therefore stifle the flow of gifts and volunteers.

At the Foreign Mission Board's February 1992 meeting Parks asked the Board for a clear-cut affirmation of his request to stay on until 1995. He did not get it. Instead, the Board's leadership called for a spiritual retreat, which was held in March at a motel near the Dallas-Fort Worth airport.

To everyone's surprise, Parks, on the second day of the retreat, announced that he would step down in October 1992, in connection with his sixty-fifth birthday. News releases claimed Board members tried to dissuade him and wanted him to stay. A motion asking him to stay until 1995, or whenever he wanted to step down, was ruled out of order, however, and despite affirming language, it was obvious that the decision was a relief to many members who feared the downside of further confrontations with Parks.

A subsequent news release made it clear that Parks's decision was based on the differences he had with the majority. Consistent with his new role as a key conservative leader, Texas's Joel Gregory was named chairman of a search committee to seek a replacement for the veteran missionary administrator.[23]

Conservative In-fighting

All was not totally settled within the ranks of conservatives. In the fall of 1991, the trustees of Criswell College, as the former institute was now called, announced that Paige Patterson was being dismissed. This was done amid rumors that Patterson was being considered for the executive secretary's position at the Executive Committee or president at Southeastern Seminary, despite Lewis Drummond's presence there, or successor to Keith Parks if the Board forced his retirement.

Conservative leaders, including Adrian Rogers and Charles Stanley, asked for a meeting with Criswell College trustees, and out of that meeting came an announcement that Patterson would be retained at Criswell College. Insiders reported that this was simply a matter of buying time. This was confirmed in a newspaper interview a few weeks later, when Criswell himself said, "Paige . . . was gone all the time. They thought they needed someone there to build the school. . . . they have given him five months."[24] Yet, observers were amazed at this demonstration of the power of the informal conservative group presumably presided over by Rogers.[25]

Meanwhile, at Southeastern Seminary, Lewis Drummond was reported to be under pressure to retire. Drummond, who had suffered a bout with cancer early in his tenure, had seemingly recovered, but the institution continued to struggle with sharp student declines and faculty defections. He was offered a position at Samford's Beeson School of Theology and also at Houston Baptist University's Department of Religion. Taking a leaf from Lloyd Elder's notebook, Drummond negotiated a generous settlement before agreeing to step down.

Chapman Succeeds Bennett

At the same time, the Executive Committee was considering a replacement for Harold Bennett, who had served as its president-treasurer since the retirement of Porter Routh and had been the chief executive throughout the conservative ascendancy. Now it was Bennett's turn to retire. He had played a completely neutral role throughout the battle, but conservatives knew that position needed to be in their hands also. To the surprise of many people, Paige Patterson again came in second, as Convention president Morris Chapman was tapped for the position.[26]

Mixed University Battles

When the South Carolina Convention met in the fall of 1991, it narrowly supported a motion to deny Furman University support for its decision to elect its own trustees. The narrow majority instructed the Convention officers to take the matter to court if necessary.

In sharp contrast, the Baptist General Convention of Texas meeting in Waco, the site of Baylor University, overwhelmingly supported Baylor's right to elect its trustees in terms of a compromise agreement reached with the state convention. Under the agreement, convention funds would continue to go to Baylor for certain clearly defined programs. The defeated conservatives, led by Joel Gregory, vowed to rejoin the issue.

In South Carolina, after the vote failed to support Furman's move, a possible legal challenge was set aside while members of both Furman and the state convention tried to find a solution. In April, both sides reported they were unable to find grounds for compromise, and a legal confrontation seemed inevitable. In a final effort to avoid such an unprecedented action, a group of thirty-four South Carolina Baptist pastors proposed that the Convention sever all ties with Furman, much as B. H. Carroll had suggested for Southern Seminary during the Whitsitt controversy. Claiming to be bipartisan, the group's suggestion was seconded by Furman officials.[27] A special meeting of the South Carolina Convention was called to accomplish this in June 1992 and the issue was settled by cutting loose the prospering institution where much Southern Baptist history had begun.

Cooperative Baptist Fellowship Leadership

A few weeks earlier, the Cooperative Baptist Fellowship Executive Committee, led by John Hewett, pastor of the First Baptist Church in Asheville, North Carolina, met at a hotel in the Dallas-Fort Worth Airport area to consider electing an executive secretary for the Cooperative Baptist Fellowship.

Reporting that over a million dollars had been channeled through the Cooperative Baptist Fellowship since its inception in the summer of 1991 and that funds were going to the defunded Baptist Joint Committee and would now be sent to the Baptist Theological Seminary in Ruschlikon, Switzerland, the Board moved to elect an executive secretary. Cecil Sherman, who had been pastor of the First Baptist Church in Asheville at the time he first emerged as a moderate spokesman, and who for several years had been pastor of the Broadway Baptist Church in Fort Worth, was approached.

Sherman, following his resignation from the Peace Committee, had backed off from moderate leadership roles. He became very active again in the battle over Baylor University, leading the Baylor alumni fight to sustain Baylor's actions and approve the Baptist General Convention of Texas Executive Committee compromise which had been crafted to do so. Sherman, now sixty-four years of age, agreed to take the leadership of the alternate funding and program entity as moderate opposition continued to take a different tack.[28]

Southern Baptist Progress

Despite the turmoil, the continued delineation of moderate alternatives and conservative consolidation, Southern Baptist programs pressed ahead. Convention reports in 1991 showed significant progress, despite widely publicized setbacks.

During the ten years of battle for the gavel, the number of churches affiliated with Southern Baptists increased from 35,404 to 37,974. Membership grew from 13,196,979 to 15,044,413. The percentage gain in the decade was 7.26 percent in membership and 14.3 percent in baptisms.

Even more encouraging to the new leadership were Southern Baptist program numbers, as the Foreign Mission Board reported 3863 missionaries in 1991, compared to 2,897 when the battle began. Missionaries were at work in 121 countries, compared to 94 in 1979 and reported total receipts of $189,457,000, compared to $69,422,463 at the beginning of the decade long struggle.[29]

The Home Mission Board, clearly under conservative leadership for a large part of the period and using a different way of counting, reported 4,573 missionaries compared to 2,805 in 1979. The receipts were $88,438,938, compared to $30,455,926 when the battle began.

The Sunday School Board, despite being in the eye of the storm for three decades, reported sales income of $180,296,364 in 1991, in contrast to $73,846,796 at the beginning of the conservative resurgence. Inflated dollars accounted for much of this growth, however, and the Sunday School Board's new leadership faced serious financial difficulties.

The Annuity Board, never the focus of controversy and despite the election of moderate leader Paul Powell, reported assets of $3,001,065,000 in 1991, compared to $539,734,000 at the beginning of the period. Powell, a former president of the Baptist General Convention of Texas, pastor of the Green Acres Baptist Church of Tyler, Texas, and a prolific writer, came under fire when he headed Baylor's trustees at the time they withdrew from Texas Baptist control. It was a measure of how much all sides wanted the Annuity Board above the fray that no action was taken against him.

Seminary enrollments were the most obvious casualty if judged on numbers alone, with full-time equivalent enrollment in 1992 being 7,499, compared to 1979's 8,684. During the course of the controversy this figure rose to an all-time record of 9,746 in 1985, before a precipitous decline to the 1992 figure. Some said this proved that Southern Baptist momentum did not need what the conservatives termed "the correction" and that it had clearly impacted enrollments negatively when it took hold. However, many people thought the enrollment changes more nearly reflected certain age-group demographics, the cooling of the economy, and other ministry training options than the strife in Southern Baptist ranks. An upturn in 1993 partially alleviated concerns at this point.

Accommodation and Change

In the spring of 1992, seminary leaders were more worried about major changes shaping up in the locus of ministerial training. Leon McBeth noted that the stand-alone seminary phenomenon, historically speaking, was relatively recent and that this type of specialized education had emerged out of university settings in Southern Baptist life. He cited signs that it might be returning to university settings, pointing out major moves at Wake Forest University in North Carolina, Samford University in Alabama, Hardin-Simmons University in Texas, and Baylor, among others, to develop strong theological graduate schools.

The Beeson Divinity School at Samford, for example, began offering the classic Master of Divinity degree and scheduled a Doctor of Ministry program. In an effort to bridge the theological controversy, they hired well-known theologians from both sides of the spectrum, though their dean was a leading conservative, Timothy George, who was rapidly establishing himself as a popular writer of theological texts.

Equally ominous to seminary leadership was Baylor University's move to establish the George W. Truett Seminary in connection with its campus in direct competition with Southwestern. That all these moves were to some degree motivated by the long strife was obvious. The Truett seminary project, along with the Alliance-begun Seminary in Richmond, operated outside Southern Baptist control, and the university programs were under state convention control, through Baylor was now essentially independent.

On the side of the existing institutions with boards controlled by the conservative majorities, however, were the traditions, buildings, libraries, and substantial endowments which would allow them a strong position in the competitive years that lay ahead. In addition, Cooperative Program funding allowed them to offer their programs for significantly reduced costs.

Indeed, as the 1992 Convention drew near, longer-term strategies began to become clear. At Southern Seminary, Honeycutt, seemingly with the backing of his trustees and the majority of his faculty, was seeking accommodation along lines of the new Covenant agreement and the Glorieta Statement. Glenn Hinson had resigned in April 1992 to join the faculty of the Richmond Seminary, removing one of the sticking points.

At Southwestern, Russell Dilday, feeling some degree of support from his Board for the first time in six years, began to position the seminary to serve the American evangelical community as well as Southern Baptists.

Southeastern, in search of a replacement for Lewis Drummond who spent his final semester in a cloud of controversy over his settlement package, finally announced in April that Paige Patterson would be chosen. Drummond accepted a position at Samford's Beeson Divinity School. To the chagrin of many of its alumni and former supporters, it was clear that Southeastern was settling in as a clearly delineated bastion for inerrancy.

A faculty spokesman at Southeastern, Robert Culpepper, told Associated Baptist Press that the nomination of Patterson—probably the most prominent political figure in Southern Baptist life—demonstrated that positions in the SBC were being filled according to a political spoils system. "To the victor go the spoils, and Southeastern is one of those spoils," the theology professor said.[30]

Such attitudes, in addition to the fact that Southeastern's student body had dropped from roughly one thousand to around five hundred during the period following conservative control and that only seven of thirty-five faculty members in place in 1987 were still there in 1991, guaranteed Patterson a true challenge. Following Patterson's election, the president of the national alumni organization, Leon Smith of Gastonia, North Carolina, resigned in protest, claiming that alumni input had been rejected.

Indicating the hostility and difficulty that Patterson faced was a Raleigh, North Carolina, *News and Observer* editorial cartoon, picturing Patterson as Southeastern's president addressing two staff members with the words, "O.K. First thing we have to do is get enrollment up. Find me some bright young minds to close."[31]

Though Patterson achieved some early success in stabilizing enrollment in the fall of 1992 and negotiating some leeway from accrediting agencies, he and his wife felt the ire of the moderate community when their application for either membership or watchcare at the nearby Wake Forest Baptist Church was turned aside.[32] While such action was not unprecedented in Baptist church life, it certainly represented a new turn in the ongoing Southern Baptist bifurcation. Despite such difficulties, the resolute Patterson was able to register enrollment gains in 1993 and resolve most of the accreditation problems.

Golden Gate and New Orleans Seminaries were content to wait in the shadows, rather than feel the heat of the controversy anew, but tremors were felt at Midwestern when the trustees adopted an anti-abortion position and asked faculty members to affirm it. This non-theological position requirement was an unexpected turn in the consolidation strategies of the new majority. Those same trustees later put new pressures on the Midwestern faculty by approving the rights of students to tape lectures and report questionable positions.

In the spring of 1992, New Orleans Baptist Theological Seminary stepped forward with a plan to offer limited baccalaureate programs. In doing so, they were perceived as invading the traditional territories occupied by Baptist colleges and universities. When the latter protested through a meeting of their presidents, the matter was referred to the Southern Baptist Convention's Executive Committee. In its September 1992 meeting, the Executive Committee dismissed the presidents' objections and in doing so, freed New Orleans (and the other seminaries if they wished) to augment its declining student body with the lure of inexpensive baccalaureate programs. It was as much a slap at Baptist colleges and universities as it was support for the seminaries. The Education Commission's director, Arthur Walker, angrily refuted charges of liberalism in the state Baptist institutions.

Homosexuality and Church Autonomy

In the spring of 1992 conservatives took the offensive on a key issue that left moderates with little stomach for opposition. As it turned out, however, more was at stake than what was on the surface.

Two North Carolina churches, both associated with the Southern Baptist Alliance, took controversial stands on homosexual issues. The Olin Binkley Baptist Church began considering a widely publicized move to license an avowed homosexual member of its congregation to the gospel ministry, and the Pullen Memorial Baptist Church began consideration of the recognition of a homosexual marriage. A woman was pastor of the Binkley Memorial Church. The actions prompted Southern Baptist conservatives on its Executive Committee to press for a constitutional change to deny such churches seating in the Convention and to reject their gifts.

While biblically based opposition to homosexual lifestyles was one of the many areas where conservatives and moderates were generally in agreement, conservative strategists endeavored to tar moderates with the brush, while moderate strategists tried to keep their distance from the issue.[33] In 1993, Cooperative Baptist Fellowship coordinator, Cecil Sherman, released a statement through Associated Baptist Press saying, "The Bible teaches homosexuality is a sin."[34]

Alternative or Schism

The question whether the Cooperative Baptist Fellowship would remain as an alternative method for cooperating Southern Baptist churches or become a full-blown schism was the unspoken agenda when the Fellowship gathered in Fort Worth, Texas, in April of 1992. In a pre-meeting issue, *Bap-*

tists Today, the official publication for the Alliance and increasingly representative of the Fellowship, featured several positioning articles.

Sociologist Nancy Ammerman, whose social history, *Baptist Battles*, gave provocative data on Southern Baptist history, confessed that in the birthing of the Cooperative Baptist Fellowship, she was a "passionate participant." In an effort to "share her dreams" for the body, she denied that it was a protest movement, since it was no longer trying to change the status quo within an organization, but was proactively carving out a new opportunity for Baptists to do what "they had been called to do."[35]

The incoming executive for the Fellowship, Cecil Sherman, claimed in an adjacent article in the same issue of *Baptists Today* that the recovery of autonomy was the real goal of the Fellowship. Beware conformity, he urged. The Fellowship was a matter of choices, he said.

On the other hand, an editorial in the same issue claiming that eight thousand would attend the Fort Worth meeting said the Fellowship was on the way to becoming a new convention. The writer urged disaffectioned Southern Baptists "to get on board." He suggested there was a line in the sand and excoriated "fence straddlers, lukewarmists, neutrals, and cowards," in the process labeling and to some degree offending a great many people sympathetic to moderate positions.[36]

While only four thousand registered for the Fort Worth meeting, a number attributed by John Hewett to meeting west of the Mississippi where moderate support was still lukewarm, the Fellowship continued to define itself more to the new convention side than to the simple alternative side. This was most clearly seen not so much in rhetoric and resolution as in the three financial plans adopted.

The regular plan, to which most of the initial churches attracted to the Fellowship alternative subscribed, directed its money to Southern Baptist agencies in roughly the same proportions as those adopted by the Convention. It included a modest 1.65 percent for Cooperative Baptist Fellowship (CBF) operations and small amounts to the Associated Baptist Press and Baptist Joint Committee. At the Fellowship meeting in Fort Worth, however, the regular plan was amended to channel 17.5 percent of monies received into Fellowship programs.

But a Ventures Plan included 30 percent to a CBF missions program and 1–2 percent each to literature and ethics programs and the Alliance-begun Richmond Theological Seminary and Baylor's George W. Truett Seminary.

Still more in the direction of a separate convention was a Vision 2,000 Plan, which eliminated all SBC programs and projected 72 percent to CBF Global Missions.

A highlight of the meeting was a prolonged standing ovation for the Foreign Mission Board president, Keith Parks, attending as "a private citizen" as his own leadership role wound down. It was no secret that Parks had been offered a number of positions, including direction of the CBF Global Mission project.

Conservative Containment

Initially, agency heads, including James Draper at the Sunday School Board, planned to place exhibits and booths at the Fellowship meeting. But conservative leadership, including the yet-to-assume-command Morris Chapman, moved to reverse that. By the time the Fort Worth meeting convened most agencies had backed out, though a few seminary alumni meetings were held, including one by Southwestern Seminary, which also had a display booth. Russell Dilday raised some eyebrows by addressing his alumni group.

Even before the meeting, the Alliances' Stan Hastey complained of "the sting of rejection." He said too many denominational people were unable to deal with the ambiguity of the present moment and resorted to what Hastey called "blackmail." In a play on a mid-eighties "flap" when Adrian Rogers called the Cooperative Program a "sacred cow," and a denominationalist replied it was a "sacred how," Hastey said it was now a conservative sacrament. He reserved his harshest judgment for state executive secretaries and Baptist paper editors who, he predicted, would not be in attendance. There was no doubt that a conservative containment had not only begun but was enjoying early success.

The Anatomy of Conservative Decision Making

How the core of conservative leadership effected decisions had long been clouded in informality, though the Caribbean cruise mentioned earlier that dealt with the 1990 conservative candidate for president of the SBC was often cited as delineating the real decision makers. Its power and method had become a bit more evident at the meeting with Criswell trustees that bought Patterson additional time to relocate. However, an Associated Baptist Press story in May of 1992 may have been the most revealing yet.

The story datelined Richmond, Virginia, reported a conference call "between the most powerful leaders in the Southern Baptist fundamental-conservative movement" designed to talk Pressler out of allowing himself to be elected to the Foreign Mission Board. The story's source said the group thought it smacked of the "cronyism" they had so often assigned to the moderates.

More important than the mission of the call were the members and the light shed on conservative decision-making. Adrian Rogers, Jerry Vines, Jimmy Draper, Fred Wolfe (the only one quoted), and Ed Young, who was an announced SBC presidential candidate for the 1992 meeting, all called Pressler, urging him to decline the nomination. A seventh participant was not identified by Wolfe. Evidently, Pressler did not accede but did promise to pray about their request. The Baptist Press story also pointed out that Pressler was not the only resurgence leader being cycled from one trustee-ship to another. Moderates claimed that the fact weakened Chapman's promise as president to "broaden the tent" of participation.[37]

On the other hand, pre-Convention positioning for the presidential election in 1992 indicated both the return to a semblance of pre-conflict conditions and the question of conservative decision-making in the future. Nelson Price, pastor of the First Baptist Church of Marietta, Georgia, announced that he would allow himself to be nominated. Joel Gregory announced shortly afterward that he would nominate Houston's Ed Young. Prior to either of these announcements, California's Jess Moody announced that he would seek the presidency as a reconciliation candidate. Both Price and Young were identified with the controlling conservatives.

Price said, "If it is I, it will be a new precedent in that the president will not be chosen before the Convention this year but at the Convention." Price had been elected first vice-president in 1991. He explained, "Reputedly, for some years a very small group proud of the Southern Baptist Convention chose an individual who would be their candidate for the presidency and . . . inevitably that person emerged as president." He added, "Those who did that had for some time said there's got to be a day when we get away from that and it becomes an open convention and persons can be nominated without that individual being chosen in advance of the Convention."[38]

On the other hand, Price had not been in on the Dallas meetings or the conference calls, and Young had. A variety of endorsements soon made it clear that it was Young who enjoyed conservative leadership backing.

A New Consensus?

The question being asked as the Southern Baptist Convention convened in Indianapolis in 1992 was clear: Is there a new consensus developing that could continue the conservative program and yet resume business in a more traditional manner? Bill Leonard, speaking at Samford University in April of 1992 during a celebration of William Carey's two hundredth anniversary, denied a new consensus was possible.

In fact, there is no center in the SBC now," Leonard said. "The result will be the continuation of the SBC, but within it will be multiple constituencies related to local, regional, theological, and economic concerns for mission and ministry." Leonard claimed that "the old divisions between moderate and conservative are becoming passe. Those subgroups are now factionalizing. In a sense, there are not two groups, there are too many."

Leonard, a Baptist historian who had recently transferred from Southern Seminary to Samford, continued, "We are essentially returning to the old society method for funding and for carrying out missions and ministry."[40]

Indianapolis itself, however, indicated that the conservative consolidation was gaining steam. A rousing family-values speech by U.S. Vice-President Dan Quayle and a clean sweep of all conservative-backed issues left no doubt. Young was elected with a 62 percent first ballot victory and Moody garnered 22 percent, followed by Price with 16 percent. Editors speculated that Moody's count probably measured the moderates continuing to attend and that Young's margin indicated the continuing influence of the core-leadership group.

The most far-reaching action, however, was the overwhelming support given a constitutional change recommended by the Executive Committee, requiring the Convention to deny messenger status to representatives of churches supporting homosexuality. Despite warnings that tampering with the constitution over a single issue would infringe upon local-church autonomy, it was obvious that the conservative majority present was more than willing to run that risk. Aimed at the two North Carolina churches that had supported homosexual marriage in one case and the ordination of a professed homosexual in the other, the matter required the support of two Conventions.

One conservative leader, James "Larry" Holly of Beaumont, Texas, who as a Sunday School Board trustee had led the fight to remove Lloyd Elder from the presidency of that agency, was again successful in an effort to order an inquiry into Masonic rituals, claiming they were contrary to the Bible. The Convention gave the task to a reluctant Home Mission Board and an even more reluctant Interfaith Witness Department of that Board. It was this action that received the most negative reaction in both secular and religious newspapers. It also highlighted the power of any single messenger who understood how to work the system.

Further illuminating the conservative agenda driving the controlling majority were resolutions supporting the Boy Scouts' stand against homosexuality, condemning euthanasia and abortion, and passing out condoms in schools as an effort to combat AIDS, a deadly developing sexually and drug-activity transmitted disease. The resolution urged school officials to advocate sexual abstinence outside of marriage instead. The Convention deplored television programming that, they said, "bombarded with themes, plots, images, and advertisements which promote and glorify sexual promiscuity, violence, and other forms of immorality." They also reiterated the conservative cry that Supreme Court decisions against official prayer and Bible reading had restricted religious freedom.

The one question as to conservative leadership effectiveness came when a challenge to Paul Pressler's election to the Foreign Mission Board was soundly turned back by the body. Most conservative leaders were of no mind to oppose Pressler after they failed to talk him into withdrawing. Following the vote on the challenge to his nomination to the Foreign Mission Board, which was overwhelmingly defeated, Pressler visited the press room to question their release on the action. He claimed that it showed him in a negative light and failed to emphasize the strong support he received.

According to a reporter from a secular newspaper, Judge Pressler "threatened to fire Herb Hollinger—whom Pressler had helped pick to replace Shackleford." Afterwards, a revised story was released. The writer called Pressler "the most powerful figure in the SBC fundamentalist resurgence."[40] As previously noted, there were other candidates for that role.

Two weeks later, however, it was announced that Al Shackleford, fired from directorship of *Baptist Press* in 1990, had been hired to edit the Baptist Sunday School Board's *Mature Living*. Board President Draper wanted the Shackleford hiring to be "seen as a gesture that we are trying to bring some healing to the denomination."[41]

An embarrassment for Convention leadership was failure to achieve a quorum the first evening on Home Mission night. An estimated two thousand attended the session, after an attendance of seventeen thousand in the morning session. In sharp contrast to previous conventions, less than seven thousand people heard Parks's final report the next night and an estimated two hundred walked out during his speech when he asked a series of rhetorical questions: "Has the controversy accelerated fulfilling our purpose of sharing the gospel with all the world? Do we have more commitment to pray? Are there more of us giving generously? Is our witness more effective in the world?" Parks then answered his own questions. "To these questions, from an up close viewpoint I'd have to answer no."[42]

Morris Chapman laid down the convention gavel to step into the president-treasurer's role with the Executive Committee, succeeding the retiring Harold Bennett. For Bennett, who took office in 1979, it had been a wild ride. In his last column in the *Baptist Program* he said, "These have been great years but I must add that some of the days and experiences within these years have been less than great: some have not been good. There were times of unhappiness."[43]

Southern Baptists and Politics

As the 1992 national presidential election drew near, many observers thought Southern Baptists reflected a collision between radically different concepts of moral authority. Despite Democrats' efforts to focus on the economy, hot issues for conservatives were abortion, child care, funding for the arts, affirmative action and quotas, homosexuality, prayer, and values in public education. Sociologist James Davison Hunter of the University of Virginia said, "The cleavages at the heart of the contemporary culture war are created by what I would call the impulse toward orthodoxy and the impulse toward progressivism."[44]

That Southern Baptists' conservative leadership was solidly on the side of orthodoxy and made them a formidable ally to those political forces which successfully courted them. And it was obvious in 1992 that Republicans had successfully done so.

The appearance of Vice-President Quayle at the Southern Baptist Convention in Indianapolis signaled more to many observers than the Convention's due respect to an Indiana native son. Earlier in the year Quayle had included the Morris Chapmans on a jet flight to a political event. The conservative leader of the Convention left no doubt that his sympathies lay with the Religious Right and that body's support was going to the Republican ticket of George Bush and Dan Quayle. Even when the Democratic Party nominated two Southern Baptists, Bill Clinton of Arkansas and Al Gore of Tennessee, to be their standard bearers, it changed nothing.

The September-October issue of the Christian Life Commission's publication *Light* indicated a very pro-active political position for that agency and for conservative leadership. The Family Values theme of the 1992 Republican Convention was strongly seconded by Commission Director Richard Land. A favorable article in the same publication on the Religious Right's Ed McAteer and the National Affairs briefing held in Dallas following the Convention meeting and strongly supported by key SBC leadership further endorsed the Bush-Quayle ticket.

During the briefing in Dallas, Adrian Rogers introduced President Bush with a ringing endorsement and shared the rostrum with Jerry Falwell, co-chairman of the evangelical coalition for Bush-Quayle, Richard Land, Joel Gregory, and W. A. Criswell. Falwell, referring to Clinton and Gore, was quoted as saying, "The fact that those two old boys are Southern Baptists will have absolutely no impact on the evangelical vote."[45]

The next morning President Bush and his wife attended services at First Baptist Church of Dallas.

In the Christian Life Commission publication, Land questioned the church-state separation concept so often cited by Baptist moderates. He reflected the conservative conviction that the "establishment" clause was overshadowing "free exercise." Strong support for prayers in public schools was the focus.

The Commission's director of media wrote in the same issue, "At times biblical principles will coincide with certain aspects of any particular party's platform or actions, as many Christians believe is happening today with the Republican Party's platform on abortion."[46] He also noted precedent for his actions in support given the Democrat's Jimmy Carter, a Southern Baptist, by moderate leaders in earlier elections.

Letters to editors of state papers reflected both concern and support for the actions of conservative leaders. A pastor from Fort Worth wrote, "The fact that Clinton and Gore are Baptists does not automatically qualify them to be president and vice-president. Nor does the fact that they are pro-choice automatically disqualify them. I fear Southern Baptists will make this a single issue campaign."[47]

Recognizing that there were other issues, one Clinton supporter cited his stands against homosexual marriages and that family decisions should be made by parents and not politicians. But these were positions already pre-empted by Republicans.

Texan Ross Perot entered the race between the incumbent Bush and the challenger Clinton, dropped out, and then reentered in October. Perot claimed that the threat of Republican dirty tricks had caused him to exit. He reentered in time to participate in several lively debates with Bush and Clinton and appeared to be capable of eroding support from both.

The Clinton-Gore ticket won the race in November, though the sizable Perot vote prevented the winner from securing a popular majority. The moderate paper, *Baptists Today*, featured the results under the headline "Baptists elected with little help from brethren."[48] Conservative Baptists and a majority of clearly identified evangelicals who supported the losing cause were unimpressed by the fact that both Clinton and Gore were active members of Southern Baptist churches. Despite the emotion attached to such questions as pro-choice or abortion, gay rights, and prayers in schools, the economy which had lagged so long seemed to be the deciding factor.

A Religious News Service article by Albert J. Menendez said Clinton "won among Catholics, Jews, black Protestants, religious liberals and made sharp inroads among mainline Protestants, usually a GOP stronghold." Menedez observed that the "only place where he lost was among his co-religionists: white Southern evangelical and fundamentalist Protestants, including Southern Baptists." In all probability, a large percentage of moderates also voted for Bush.

Morris Chapman, president of the Executive Committee of the Southern Baptist Convention, said he was praying that president-elect Clinton would "rethink his positions on abortion and homosexuals." In an open letter to Clinton, the Christian Life Commission's Richard Land promised to pray for the new team as the Scriptures admonish in 1 Timothy 2:1–2. He applauded Clinton's support of the Religious Restoration Act designed to protect religious freedoms, support of health warnings on alcohol advertising, and anti-pornography efforts. He supported the president's concern for human rights around the world. But Land reminded the president that "most Southern Baptists" were opposed to abortion and special civil rights for sexual preference. He said they would resist public funding of obscene and sacrilegious art. He admonished the new leader that "America needs moral conviction, not moral neutrality."[49]

On the other hand, Ed McAteer, a well-known conservative voice and a member of Adrian Rogers' Bellevue Church, said Clinton's election would hasten the decline of America. Beverley LaHaye, a Southern Baptist lay-woman said, "It's going to be devastating for the American family."[50] Most members of what the national press called the Religious Right, with whom most of the conservative Southern Baptist leaders identified, denied that the election turned on religious values.

In early 1993, a group of Independent Baptist protesters began appearing before Immanuel Baptist Church in Little Rock, Arkansas, where President Clinton maintained his membership and where he had sung in the choir while governor of the state. They demanded that Pastor Rex Horne, Jr., and the church discipline Clinton for his positions on abortion and homosexuality. [51]

WMU under Pressure

Woman's Missionary Union, under the leadership of Dellanna West O'Brien, was increasingly under pressure throughout 1992. O'Brien took the reins of the Auxiliary in September 1989, bringing impressive credentials. A graduate of Hardin-Simmons University with a B.S. degree, Texas Christian University with an M.Ed., and Virginia Polytechnic Institute and State University with an Ed.D., O'Brien's pilgrimage included experience as a missionary to Indonesia where she served with her husband from 1963 to 1971, and as mother to three children, pastor's wife, elementary school teacher, private school administrator, and president of an international family and children's educational service organization.

Her husband William had served as executive vice-president of the Foreign Mission Board, where as an expert in ecumenical dialogues, he had drawn criticism from the conservative leadership before Keith Parks reassigned him to Birmingham. While the move coincided with Dellanna O'Brien's assumption of the WMU task, Parks defended it as an experiment in "distance management via high-tech connections." Given O'Brien's skills and changing job description it was probably a reasonable assignment, but it drew strong criticism from an increasingly challenging board. Before it could come to a head, O'Brien joined Samford University as director of a global mission center.

A 1992 request by moderate leaders for Woman's Missionary Union support of Cooperative Baptist Fellowship mission projects aroused strong resistance from conservative leaders and the implied threat of a competitive program to be led by the Sunday School Board. O'Brien led the WMU into a series of dialogues with leaders from both groups as the pressure mounted and achieved a modicum of breathing room when she asked the conservatives to initiate talks with moderate leadership.

Conservative opposition to the WMU was read into a motion in Indianapolis that the Executive Committee charge Woman's Missionary Union for its meeting-hall expenses. When at the fall meeting of the Executive Committee it was reported that $169,945 had been provided for the Pastor's Conference during the years 1988–92 compared to $20,000 for WMU, the matter was referred to a policy study.[52]

In September, Sunday School Board's President Draper tried to squelch such fears in a statement to a gathering of Baptist editors. He said the Sunday School Board was not competing with WMU and that the two organizations were codeveloping a national conference for women the next year (1993). He did carve out some territory by saying work with abused wives and single parents had been assigned to the Sunday School Board's discipleship and family development division.[53]

New Initiatives

While the U.S. presidential election was still in full swing, the post-1990 rounds of consolidation and reaction were giving way to new initiatives by the fall of 1992. The newly elected SBC president, Edwin Young of Texas, led out with a call for a far-reaching series of studies looking at SBC foreign and home evangelistic outreach, theology, structure, and funding as the Convention approached its sesquicentennial in 1995. He named eighteen co-chairmen to head up nine special study groups and then serve as a special task force to make recommendations to the Convention. He asked Sunday School Board President Draper to serve as overall chairman.

In launching the new initiatives, Young said he was not a "status-quo kind of guy" and wanted to examine where we have been, where we are, and where we need to be.[54] To maintain focus, the Executive Committee turned aside suggestions to study the Cooperative Baptist Fellowship. One member said, "It is time to go on, to do our business, attack the job at hand and let others do what they want."[55]

Conciliatory to these new initiatives was Russell Dilday, still presiding over Southwestern Baptist Theological Seminary. "Some of us who once truly believed that the SBC was the best, maybe the ultimate expression of the New Testament pattern of cooperating church life, find it difficult to concede that out of the turmoil of these past dozen years an even better denomination could arise. But the intriguing possibility is there, and it offers hope and challenge in the midst of the vacuum."[56]

Yet *Baptists Today*, the moderate publication out of Atlanta, saw ominous dimensions to Young's initiatives, particularly in the study group called Cords and Stakes, where the assignment called for a review of the degree to which the Peace Committee recommendations had been carried out, with reference to the theological positions of seminary administrators and faculty members. The same issue of the moderate periodical also wondered if the Women's Ministries task force was a part of efforts to keep Woman's Missionary Union in line.

However, Roy Honeycutt of Southern Baptist Theological Seminary seemed to be going along with the new initiatives, as he accepted co-chairmanship of the theological group with conservative theologian Timothy George of Samford University. Shortly afterwards, Honeycutt made his own news by announcing that he would retire as president of the seminary at the end of 1993.

A less attention-grabbing initiative was launched by moderates at a meeting held at Georgia's Mercer University. Moderate historians organized the William H. Whitsitt Baptist Heritage Society on October 9, 1992. *Baptists Today* publisher Walker Knight was elected president of the organization, which committed itself to an historical approach to "finding answers for future structures of moderate Baptist life."[57] A subsequent advertisement seeking charter members said the Society was for "Baptists affiliated with the Cooperative Baptist Fellowship, seeking to honor, preserve, and emphasize a treasured heritage." A few weeks later, however, the Society projected for the theme of its next meeting, "Future Structures of Moderate Baptist Life: Are We Stumbling into Order or Disorder? [58]

Transitions

At the installation of Morris Chapman as president-treasurer of the executive committee, conservative leader Adrian Rogers of Memphis reflected unbounded optimism for the conservative-dominated convention. "This is going to sound like megalomania, but I believe that the hope of the world lies in the West. I believe that the hope of the West lies in America. I believe that the hope of America is in Judeo-Christian ethics. I believe that the backbone of that Judeo-Christian ethic is evangelical Christianity. I believe that the bellwether of evangelical Christianity is the Southern Baptist Convention. So I believe, in a sense, that as the Southern Baptist Convention goes, so goes the world." The *Christian Century*, an acknowledged liberal publication, reported Rogers' remarks in its No Comment Department.[59]

Within days following Chapman's installation, Joel Gregory's role as chairman of the Foreign Mission Board's search committee took a back seat to a sudden decision to resign his relatively new post at First Baptist Church. Citing the failure of Criswell to give way to his leadership as originally planned, the younger man said his decision was "irrevocable." He was gone within a week in the midst of a flurry of questions about his severance package and the future of several highly paid staff members he had brought to the church during his tenure.

Criswell remained silent for some months before offering some reflections on Gregory's move following an appearance at an Illinois evangelism conference in January of 1993. The eighty-three-year-old father-figure of the conservative resurgence said he had not talked to Gregory since the sudden termination, but confided, "It's beyond my imagination. . . . It broke my heart." He said worship attendance had dropped from about five thousand to twenty-five hundred in Gregory's tenure and that people were discouraged.[60]

Gregory later told the same Baptist paper that he did not understand "why he [Criswell] told me it would be a brief transition." Gregory said, "I did not come for a four-year transition."[61]

Criswell also offered thoughts on the continuing Southern Baptist controversy, saying, "About 99 percent of the time I cannot understand what is happening. Now that may be a strange thing to say, but it is all so different than when I was growing up."[62] Though he thought that most Southern Baptists would stay in the Convention, Criswell said, "The breach that has been created between so-called moderates and conservatives is largely in the attitudes of the people involved. Many, many of them basically believe the same thing and love the same programming. It carries with it an overtone of sadness that is almost inexplicable."[63]

Such events and feelings made it obvious that Chapman's tenure was not going to be easy. No sooner had he taken office than the Foreign Mission Board's Keith Parks generated new controversy as he accepted the position of missions coordinator for the Cooperative Baptist Fellowship.

Foreign Missions at the Crossroads

As Southern Baptists' 147th year wound down, part of its initial reason for being was at a crossroads. The Foreign Mission Board seemed to shudder with uncertainty as it passed through the boundary zones of leadership change.

In October, just prior to Parks's exit from the post he had held for thirteen years, the Board announced a ten-point agreement with European Baptists, worked out between European leaders and a group of FMB staff and trustees. The Hamburg Agreement, as it was called, allowed the European Baptist Federation to work with other Baptist groups, including Southern Baptist dissidents at work in the Cooperative Baptist Fellowship. An October 1, 1992, Associated Baptist Press release said the Europeans understood it as an apology for the Ruschlikon defunding decision. New FMB member Paul Pressler immediately denied that the agreement was an apology, though he said all concerned regretted the misunderstandings on both sides.

Don Kammerdiener, executive vice-president of the FMB and the newly appointed interim chief executive officer, pointed out that the agreement which he had helped negotiate allowed the Board to work anywhere in the world and with any group. The fifty-six-year-old graduate of Midwestern Baptist Theological Seminary celebrated his thirtieth anniversary with the Mission Board as he took over his new assignment.

The agreement and Pressler's assertions were eclipsed by a furor generated by departing FMB president Parks, when he wrote a final letter to the missionaries with copies to state Baptist editors and state Baptist executive directors. Stating his differences with the Board, Parks noted that "in Board meetings in August, October, December, February, and April, as well as the Retreat in March, every effort to vote on affirming my leadership until 1995 was delayed or ruled out of order."[64]

Parks enumerated the changes he thought had altered the way missions was done at the FMB, beginning with the assertion that large numbers of Southern Baptists were no longer represented on the Board. He went on to deplore the decisions he claimed were replacing adopted mission principles. Citing a perceived loss of trust, freedom to disagree, and pressures on the news staff, Parks hit hardest on the declining career appointment picture in favor of the growing volunteer presence.

Requirements of loyalty to the conservative movement, substitution of the Peace Committee report for the Baptist Faith and Message, and the loss of missionary volunteers to the new atmosphere where they perceived they would not be welcome were also cited by Parks, along with a declaration that he would stay in missions.

Foreign Mission Board trustee John Jackson expressed strong disagreement with Parks's assertions. While graciously thanking the Parkses for their dedication, Jackson said most of the items in the letter "were never discussed with the trustees."[65]

Overshadowed by Parks's announcement and the reaction to it was the early retirement of Betty Law, vice-president for the Americas for the Foreign Mission Board and its highest-ranking female. Also implying a growing imbalance between volunteer and career missionaries, she said, "Now this focus is shifting to meet the needs of our own constituency rather than the needs as indicated from the field." Some months later, Law joined the CBF's mission administration.

Interim chief Don Kammerdiener moved immediately to reassure missionaries and board staff. Meeting with the latter, and in a letter to the former, he said, it's time "to move forward," and he denied there was any substantive change in the appointment process. He said studies would continue on the use of volunteers and he would insist on a credible news policy. He reassured both groups that they could speak out, but he urged them to do so through channels.

Kammerdiener, who was reported to be one of those under consideration to succeed Parks, denied he had ever been asked to identify with the conservative resurgence. When asked about working with moderate Baptists, Kammerdiener said the Board would work with all "Great Commission or evangelistic Christians."

In the initial hours of the change-over, both Chairman Jackson and Interim Executive Kammerdiener had to field questions about trustees' perceived confusion between policy-making and administration. Jackson defended their role and questioned press roles in reporting trustee actions. Jackson said trustees thought Parks's letter had been harmful.[66]

The controversy over Parks's letter and Kammerdiener's damage control were in turn overshadowed by Parks's decision to become missions coordinator for the Cooperative Baptist Fellowship. He explained that he was trying to give Southern Baptists two channels for doing global missions. In his announcement and subsequent elaborations, a number of significant factors emerged regarding the futures of the Southern Baptist Convention and the dissident Fellowship.

First was Parks's revelation that the Fellowship leadership had met his three conditions for taking the job: (1) assurance that they would remain within the Southern Baptist Convention; (2) a commitment to finding new recruits for missions; and (3) a focus on unevangelized areas. The implication was that he did not want to be a part of a new denomination or convention, that he did not want to bleed off missionaries currently serving with the Foreign Mission Board (though a number had already resigned and been accepted by the Fellowship before Parks's decision), and that he did not want to compete in the same fields.

Questioned about these implications, Parks admitted that it was a return to the "society" way of doing missions, but he held that was the alternative to leaving and forming a new convention.

Challenged about the society method, Parks and others claimed the conservatives had used the same alternative before they became dominant, citing their alternative institutions and their support of non-Southern Baptist mission groups. Parks's interpretation of the Fellowship's role meant they were trying to stay in the Convention and yet develop their own avenues of missions and ministry.

In fact, Parks was joining a movement that, while technically an alternative within Southern Baptist life, was still defining itself. Increasingly, that definition evoked memories of the SBC's own separation from the Northern Convention. Its coordinator, Cecil Sherman, spoke to the movement's future in early 1993 from the Cooperative Baptist Fellowship's office in Atlanta. He asked five questions: Is CBF going to be a cutdown version of the SBC? Is CBF under the control of some special interest group? Is CBF another political organization? Is CBF going to be a regional body or a national body? And then, What is the CBF?[67]

Sherman's answers to his rhetorical queries, that it would not be near the size and would be structured differently, that it would be more societal yet would not own the entities it would support, that it was not a "front" for such issues as the woman's issue, that it was composed of people once politically active in SBC life and still active in state Baptist politics but not itself into politics, that it was definitely a national body based upon the origin of contributions, and that above all it was a mission-support system, seemed to continue to define an "other than" rather than a "internal alternative" kind of organization.

Not surprisingly, Morris Chapman, in a widely reported interview in Oklahoma City, reacted to Parks's move, the CBF's promotion of a Global Missions Offering in competition with the Lottie Moon Offering for Foreign Missions, and such definitions as Sherman's by urging the Fellowship to leave the Convention. He said, "Every indication points to the fact that they are a denomination in the making." The Executive Committee's new president said, "While Southern Baptists have always been approached with alternative funding requests such as those from Campus Crusade, the new distinctive with the CBF is the antagonism against the Cooperative Program." He asked, "How can a person be loyal both to the SBC and the CBF at the same time?"[68]

Chapman's call shocked some members in both groups, but it could be argued that if a moderate exit could be forced early on, it would involve fewer losses than if time were given to expand the new alternatives.

Analyzing the Parks Era

In his final speech to the Southern Baptist Convention, Keith Parks aligned his tenure as president of the FMB with Bold Mission Thrust, which was formulated before he took over from Cauthen but while he was leading the Mission Support Division. He reminded the gathering that the Board had accepted ten goals in the plan and that two had already been reached: the goal to have ten thousand volunteers annually by the year 2000 had been passed in 1989 (though as mentioned earlier the very success of this program had presented a problem of balance and emphasis to Parks's administration); the goal of a presence in 125 countries was reached in 1990, a full ten years ahead of the target.

But Parks warned that despite progress, it was unlikely the other goals would be met. In his speech delivered on Wednesday night of the meeting in Indianapolis, Parks noted that the Board's income had increased by 212 percent from 1979 and its missionary force grew by 47 percent. Despite the seeming increase in funds relative to personnel, he pointed out that direct missionary support grew from 46 percent of the budget in 1979 to 65 percent in 1992. Further contradicting the seeming advance in resources was the fact that the capital expenditure portion of the Board's budget decreased from 13 percent in 1979 to 3 percent in 1992. While it might be suggested the latter was a corollary of the Parks-led paradigm change and the seventy-thirty emphasis rather than an erosion of support levels, it probably indicated pressures on overall resources and the priority of personnel.

Parks expressed his fear that "the history of Southern Baptists of this period" would not "detail a golden age of mission outreach" but would focus "on the controversy." There is no doubt that controversy "hung heavy" over his tenure, but neither is there any doubt that significant progress was made on his watch.

R. Keith Parks served twelve years and nine months as the Board's chief executive. Five of his predecessors served longer terms and three served shorter ones.[69] The average term of service of the Board's nine leaders is 16.2 years, a figure Parks would have come close to, had his initial request to serve longer been supported.

Only the legendary Baker James Cauthen led the Board to enter more countries than did Parks, sixty-seven compared to Parks's forty, but Cauthen led the Board for a record twenty-six years and three months. When Cauthen took over, the Board had 910 missionaries in 32 countries. He registered a 200 percent increase in countries occupied and a 300 percent increase in missionaries under appointment. Parks, in just under half the time, saw a 40 percent increase in occupations and a 47 percent jump in personnel deployed.

Noteworthy since for most of the period between 1979 and 1992 the Home Mission Board was under the leadership of a conservative resurgence-identified leader, its force grew from 2,839 to 4,922, outstripping its foreign counterpart when it had so often before labored in its shadows. Some of the luster of these numbers faded with the information that much of the increase issued from a new way of counting personnel.

More significant therefore than numbers in an analysis of the Parks's era is the strategical paradigm change begun in 1985. The paradigm change rapidly transformed the Board from a sending agency to a global evangelistic center. Staff member Jimmy Maroney said this focused the Board's resources on "evangelism that results in churches." Area Director Jerry Rankin, who reportedly was under consideration for Parks's position along with Kammerdiener, said this focus moved the Board "away from parallelism of everything being of equal value, which characterized previous strategies."[70] Winston Crawley, an administrator who served under both Cauthen and Parks said of Parks, "The most valuable of Parks's contributions in its long-range potential is his part in developing the networking of Great Commission Christians." [71]

The Parks-led Board developed the concept of the itinerant missionary and the nonresident missionary, both designed to cope with resident restrictions and costs and to facilitate national contacts in evangelism. Parks also led the Board to recognize partnership missions, which became the point for the explosive volunteer movement, though it also presented the balance problem that Betty Law cited in her retirement statement. It was this openness to innovation that Jamaican Baptist leader Azariah McKenzie lauded by saying Parks "had visions, ideas, and approaches which are well beyond his time." McKenzie voiced the judgment of many of the retiring chief's friends when he concluded that Parks was "the victim of an inflexible orthodoxy and visionless bureaucracy that exalts conformity to the past [rather] than to change and progress for the future."[72]

In contrast, Avery Willis, former missionary who was then an administrator at the Baptist Sunday School Board and among those under consideration for Parks's position, said of Parks, "For whatever reason, he was not able to affect as much change on the Baptist constituency in the United States as he was on the missionary force and the rest of the world." Staff member Jimmy Maroney added that Parks "failed to articulate a vision," referring not to the missionary but to the average Southern Baptist and denominational leaders.[73]

A survey released by the Executive Committee in the spring of 1993 seemed to confirm Maroney's assertion when it showed concern about missions at the bottom of a series of concerns occupying Southern Baptist's attentions.[74]

Regarding Parks's battle with trustees, former chairman C. Mark Corts explained that Parks "did not take a great deal of time to build bridges. To him that seemed to take time away from nurturing his larger vision of global evangelization. That sometimes left him an adversarial role with the trustees more often than was healthy for his vision."[75]

Yet even Parks's adversaries gave him high marks, and by the time he turned to the Cooperative Baptist Fellowship role, his friends were lauding his achievements and predicting that many people would transfer their support for missions to his new endeavor. His detractors felt that any encouragement of this would be a contradiction of his professed commitment to the Southern Baptist missionary endeavor.

In the years ahead, examination of influences on the Parks era will focus on the role of William O'Brien, who was paired with Parks by the FMB Search Committee when he was elected. O'Brien, idea man and voracious reader, networked with Christian and missionary leaders of every stripe and was widely regarded as a visionary. When O'Brien moved to Birmingham as his wife took over leadership of Woman's Missionary Union, he was the focus of significant trustee opposition. Without O'Brien as a lightning rod, Parks's difficulties with his trustees escalated. O'Brien's evaluation of Parks's tenure concluded that Parks "embraced the best of our heritage while innovating for the future." O'Brien, using terms he employed while at the Board, added, "He has done so while remaining inclusive of all Southern Baptists, seeing the FMB as a servant agency of all churches and people who call themselves Southern Baptists."[76]

Conflicts between Parks and Foreign Mission Board members were on the back burner when the veteran stepped aside in October of 1992. A Resolution of Appreciation noted eleven areas of contribution headed by his emphasis on "evangelism that results in churches," prayer as a key component to missions, and the introduction of nontraditional missionaries to evangelize countries unable to be reached by traditional methods.[77]

In his response, Parks highlighted the "intensification of intercessory prayer as a strategy" and "the global approach to our mission effort." Parks began the first effort early in his tenure by inviting his former colleague from Indonesia, Catherine Walker, to undertake the promotion of a prayer strategy. In time Walker was succeeded by Minette Drumwright whose late husband, Huber, had been Executive Director of Arkansas Baptists. Well known as a writer and speaker, Minette Drumwright in 1993 led a group of Baptists on a World A on-site intercessory prayer effort, the first such effort officially noted by Southern Baptists as a conscious missions strategy.

The global approach, which refocused on neglected peoples, also included the development of a pioneering itinerant program. *Networking* and *synergistic* were key words and concepts in the Parks era. Parks own dedicated lifestyle was often cited along with his wife and family, all committed to missions and ministry.

State Convention Confrontations

State Baptist convention meetings were widely watched in 1992 in light of conservative resurgence leadership assertions that they were the next battle ground. In preparation for the effort, Adrian Rogers hosted an August strategy meeting in Memphis for fifty leaders from fifteen states. The meeting, billed as a strategy session for extending SBC hegemony to the state conventions, experienced mixed results in the October-November state Baptist conventions.[78]

Counterparts to the dominant SBC conservatives lost by large margins in leadership votes in Virginia and Texas, though their positions on homosexual rights and abortion found significant support in more than a dozen state meetings, including Texas.

Backers of the conservatives absorbed a tough loss in Tennessee when an Adrian Rogers-nominated candidate, Jerry Sutton, pastor of Nashville's megachurch, Two Rivers, lost to a moderate-backed pastor, Leonard Markham of Hendersonville.

In North Carolina a moderate-supported plan passed that allowed state institutions to have out-of-state Baptist trustees and to nominate up to 50 percent of their trustees with a corresponding decrease in state-convention support. North Carolina Baptists obviously hoped they could avoid a Baylor- or Furman-type confrontation.

Again, proving that no clear-cut Mason-Dixon line existed in the Southern Baptist conflict, a moderate-backed pastor won the presidency in Oklahoma in a close contest. In addition, former Oklahoma Baptist state executive director, Joe Ingram, came out in favor of the Cooperative Baptist Fellowship avenues in connection with the organization of the CBF of Oklahoma. Ingram's surprising announcement was balanced, in part, by a frustrated Herschel Hobbs who urged moderate Baptists to get in or get out.

On the other hand, a resurgence-backed pastor in Kentucky won the presidency, and the same majority headed off a moderate-supported constitutional amendment. Two pastors who attended Adrian Rogers' Memphis meeting in August led the successful effort, to the shock of moderates in Kentucky still grieving over the changes at Southern Baptist Theological Seminary.

Conservatives were also encouraged by a presidential victory in Georgia, along with four of the five contests where the lines were clearly drawn. They won more narrowly in South Carolina, where Furman's defection continued to rankle many people.

Of definite encouragement to the new SBC leaders was the fact that twenty-three state conventions maintained their Cooperative Program allocations, and nine even increased theirs. On the other hand, four states decreased their allocations to the SBC.

This tended to support Morris Chapman's claim "that there is a difference between being a moderate and being a member of the CBF. Not all moderates in the SBC are members of the CBF. In fact, many moderates are loyal to the Southern Baptist Convention and are strong supporters of the Cooperative Program."[79]

WMU Initiatives

Woman's Missionary Union came out of its year-long study effort with its own far-reaching initiatives in the early days of 1993. Its executive board, in a 16-1 vote, decided to expand its horizons of support to include all Southern Baptists involved in missions, to forge new relations with evangelical mission organizations, to become more involved in direct missions, and active in social issues. National WMU president Carolyn Miller of Alabama called it a giant step in WMU's historic missionary involvement. The 105-year-old auxiliary's executive director, Dellanna O'Brien, called it a freeing move that "puts us in sync with today's woman." While the plan would allow WMU to work with the Cooperative Baptist Fellowship, its six recommendations were prefaced with a new commitment to the Cooperative Program. The plan also said it would stay with the traditional special offerings for Foreign and Home missions.

The report included a core-values statement, affirming the priesthood of the believer, God's call to missions, prayer for missions, the giftedness of all women, the biblical mandate to respond to social and moral issues, the need to develop leaders, partnership with Christians around the world, and the need for diverse organizational models for missions.

A vision statement proclaimed that "WMU exists to enable churches to participate in introducing all persons in the world to Christ."

O'Brien said the women's group was not afraid of reprisal: "We fear no one but God. We cannot be fearful. We have to be faithful and God will protect us."[80]

Reactions to WMU

Many Southern Baptist leaders reacted negatively to the announcement. Morris Chapman, SBC Executive Committee president, said he needed clarifications but was "saddened" by the decision. He felt that WMU had abandoned its auxiliary role. Home Mission Board president, Larry Lewis, said, "I question the wisdom of any SBC agency or auxiliary identifying in a supportive way with any schismatic group which has set itself against SBC leaders and agencies."[81]

The most widely circulated response came later from the Foreign Mission Board's trustee chairman, John Jackson, who told Associated Baptist Press that the Foreign Mission Board would see WMU's action as a form of adultery. His remark was a reiteration of a pre-report statement to a Chattanooga newspaper, saying that such an action would be saying, "We don't see anything wrong with us going to bed with CBF as well as SBC."[82] WMU's executive director, Dellanna O'Brien, called his analogy "unfortunate."

The next week the Waccamaw Association in Conway, South Carolina scratched O'Brien's name from a 1995 speaking commitment. A spokesman claimed "WMU is linking up with the Cooperative Baptist Fellowship and seems to be abandoning its historical heritage."[83] The Association later moved to reverse this decision.

On the other hand, a Baptist pastor from Abilene, Texas, wrote his state paper saying, "As always, the WMU is seeking to lead the way for us in missions. Let us thank the Lord for any group of Baptists, whatever its label, who seek to fulfill the Great Commission. I suggest we get behind the WMU and follow their lead. They know the way."[84]

Dellanna O'Brien, explaining the auxiliary's action said, "What we have done here this week is not for ourselves alone. Our decisions first and foremost have been for the sake of lost souls around the world—souls who can't wait until we resolve our denominational controversy."[85]

In the spring of 1993, the WMU controversy escalated. WMU officials appeared before the Foreign Mission Board and Home Mission Board and the SBC Executive Committee to defend their actions. The meeting in Richmond generated considerable heat when the *Richmond Times Dispatch* story said WMU leaders had been "summoned" and that the meeting was "angry." The Board leaders responded by sending a video tape of the meeting to all missions to let them "see for themselves" and requesting the newspaper involved to send a more "competent" reporter.

The whole issue racheted to a new level when the newspaper refused and backed its reporter, Ed Briggs, a twenty-year veteran of the Foreign Mission Board beat. And WMU leaders made and sent their own video to the missionaries, feeling that the Board's tape showed them on the defensive. They said they wanted to reassure the missionaries with a more definitive statement.

In the WMU tape, Dellanna O'Brien pointed out that nothing had changed regarding their prayer support, promotion of both the Cooperative Program and Lottie Moon Christmas offering, missionary education programs, and fundamental commitment to all aspects of missionary support.

Further explaining the WMU's tent-broadening moves, O'Brien said, "There has always been a great deal of diversity within the Southern Baptist Convention. But today it is playing itself out in an unusual and different way. We're finding different coalitions and fellowships joining together, based around some common concern or sense of alienation." Noting the predictions of further splintering, O'Brien added, "Within our denomination, we're seeing a return to the societal approaches of the past." The

WMU chief said such fragmentation is "pulling the SBC apart as a denomination." O'Brien expressed WMU goals in light of this: "WMU would like to be the umbrella that will pull all Southern Baptists together again in the missions cause and effort." [86]

But the fact that there was a tacit embrace of the SBC dissidents continued to rankle SBC leadership. Each of the Mission Boards and the Executive Committee issued calls for WMU's return to its exclusive SBC position. When the Home Board voted, however, there were seven dissenting votes— all women.[87]

An editorial in the conservative-oriented *Indiana Baptist* spelled out conservative reaction. Editor Gary Ledbetter wrote, "There are some who are troubled, even offended when anyone who had influence in our denomination encourages, even tacitly, the Fellowship in their shady work." Ledbetter claimed that taking the Cooperative Program seriously meant taking the CBF personally. He concluded that the WMU statement was too mixed and hesitant. "It should be understandable that our leaders hoped for something more."[88]

A hardening resolve to confront WMU independence, despite protestations by that body's leadership that nothing had really changed, was clearly evident in statements attributed to Adrian Rogers by a group of Foreign Mission Board staff and missionaries visiting his church. Rogers, to many people still the most dominant personality in the conservative leadership core, was reported to have said the "women's auxiliary should be hardwired into the denomination's structure." According to the Religious News Service release, Rogers proposed that WMU's governing body be elected by messengers at the denomination's annual meeting rather than by state organizations of the women's auxiliary. Calling for an end to the "feminization of missions," the story said Rogers indicated missions promotion should be led by pastors and the leaders of the Brotherhood.[89]

Nine days later Rogers claimed that the article was based on "voodoo quotations." He said he affirmed WMU, but he thought that if it wanted to broaden its support, it should no longer be an auxiliary but should operate like a parachurch organization. "If it does," he said, "it should no longer have a position on the SBC Executive Committee." He further stated that his reference to the "feminization of missions" was to point out that men have not supported missions as they should. Denying he wanted to control WMU, he nonetheless claimed Southern Baptists should have complete control over its mission programs.[90]

The Eye of the Beholder

The rapid developments in Southern Baptist life were obviously being filtered through the eye of the beholder in 1993 with contradictory interpretations. Following the January meeting of the trustees of the Sunday School Board, news reports differed widely over the agency's prospects as shared by Board president, James Draper. *Baptist Press*, in a report by Sunday School Board staff member Charles Willis, began, "A short-term future 'ripe with opportunities and challenge' will lead the Baptist Sunday School Board to a long-term future of greater business and ministry effectiveness than ever before." [91] In contrast, an Associated Baptist Press report of the same meeting filed by Timothy Cornell of the *Nashville Tennessean* lead with a quite negative statement: "The Sunday School Board is 'in the process of dying' and will fade away unless drastic steps are taken to revive it."[92]

Both articles cited an 8 percent decline in literature sales, and the information that the Baptist Book Store lost $5.5 million in sales during 1992.

Conservative leaders received what they considered better news when Southern Seminary's embattled Christian ethics professor Paul Simmons took early retirement. Simmons's pro-choice stands on abortion and his stands on homosexuality had been cited in the Peace Committee's report in 1987. New questions arose in December 1992 over the approach taken in a course on the church and sexuality. A personnel committee report suggesting that the seminary buy up his contract for $362,000 had been rejected, and "heresy hearings" were expected to be called. Simmons's move saved the trustees both the money and the unwanted attention that such hearings would have brought.

Simmons later explained, "My leaving was a matter of protesting a process which has lost its bearings and is willing to sacrifice faculty for the sake of institutional stability." He thought Seminary directions were making "theological education captive to the politically correct."[93] Moderates were as distressed by Simmons's move as conservatives were pleased.

Good news for conservative leadership also came with year-end reporting of Southern Baptist gains in eight of ten key denominational ministries including numbers of churches, membership, Sunday School enrollment, mission expenditures, and total tithes, offerings, and special gifts. Only a 7.3 percent decline in baptisms and a slight drop in WMU enrollment dampened the picture of a denomination still moving ahead despite persistent internal conflict.

Perhaps nowhere was the divergent way of looking at the situation in Southern Baptist life more obvious than in remarks by Beeson School's Timothy George in contrast to the results of a survey taken by the Executive Committee. George, one of the conservative movement's theological defenders, along with Southern's David Dockery, Georgia's Albert Mohler, and Southeastern Seminary's Paige Patterson, was speaking to a pro-life conference. He said, "I, for one, regard the reversal of the denominational trends of the 1960s and 1970s as a providential moving of God in our midst." George explained that the SBC "undoubtedly would have been just another mainline denomination, bereft of missionary and evangelistic zeal and tossed and turned by every new-wave ideology which comes down the pike."[94]

At almost the same time, a survey of Southern Baptists' priorities reported by the Executive Committee, said, "Home and foreign missions was clearly ranked as least important among the seven ministry areas." The report said that the low ranking of missions "was remarkably consistent among all staff and layperson groups."[95]

The survey seemed to contradict George's assertion that the conservative turnaround had saved the day for missionary zeal, though it reinforced his feelings about evangelism. Since Keith Parks's tenure had coincided with the 1979–90 conservative drive, he had every reason to question his "golden age" assessment of missions during the period in light of the collapse of missionary priorities.

Changing the Guard

In the midst of the charges and countercharges over WMU's initiatives and the ongoing Foreign Mission Board search for Keith Parks' replacement, Southern Seminary survived press leaks, the resulting exit of one of its candidates for president, and charges of violating due process. It also announced its choice of Georgia's R. Albert Mohler, as the 134-year-old institution's ninth president in a special meeting held for the purpose.

The young theologian, already cited as one of the conservative movement's more articulate thinkers, had an advantage over the other candidates; he was a Southern graduate. Mohler, who had served as editor of Georgia's *Christian Index* since 1989, had remained fairly aloof from other Baptist state paper editors and maintained the confidence of conservative leadership. He had taken both his master of divinity and Ph.D. degree at Southern and had also served as a special assistant to retiring Roy Honeycutt. In news releases announcing his nomination, Honeycutt predicted that Mohler would have an outstanding career.

Search committee chairman Wayne Allen pointed out that Mohler would not be the institution's youngest president, since founder James Boyce had been only thirty-two. He also noted both E. Y. Mullins and Duke McCall had taken office in their thirties.

The choice, while definitely involving an individual clearly aligned with the dominant conservatives, appeared in the beginning to elicit cautious support from a variety of the Seminary's constituents. It certainly represented a determined step by the new SBC leadership to consolidate its position in key positions.

A month later, however, anti-female ordination statements by Mohler and trustee actions overturning a series of faculty appointments to endowed chairs recommended by the outgoing administration, eroded some of Mohler's early support. In the aftermath, Southern's provost Larry McSwain left to become president of Georgia Baptists' Shorter College and three moderate trustees resigned from Southern's board in protest of the directions taken.

In the midst of this, Mohler hired Marsha Ellis Smith of Broadman & Holman to be associate vice-president for Academic Planning, defusing some of the criticism of his ordination statements.

The editor of Virginia's *Religious Herald*, Michael J. Clingenpeel, said, "Southern Baptist Theological Seminary is in chaos. Total chaos." While excoriating Mohler's early actions and "immaturity and ineptness," Clingenpeel landed on the trustees. "Their agenda is to sail the ship to starboard as fast as possible, even at the expense of tossing the crew overboard and overturning every piece of furniture beneath the deck."[96]

Mohler explained his own position in a baccalaureate address at Southeastern Seminary in May of 1993. Quoting E. Y. Mullins's gratitude that the seminary was anchored to "the great and eternal certainties of our doctrine," Mohler cautioned the graduates against the temptation towards "relativism and moral revisionism."[97]

Smarting from the wave of criticism that came, Mohler gave an interview in May to answer his detractors, even though he was not scheduled to take office until August 1, 1993. "If there is a fundamentalism here," Mohler opined, "it is a fundamentalism of the left which will not allow for a diversity of opinion." He argued that conservative domination meant Southern Baptists wanted a course correction, "and the seminary is only returning to its roots."[98]

The Education Commission's Arthur Walker also announced his retirement plans, but most Convention watchers were more interested in where the Foreign Mission Board would turn.

When the Foreign Mission Board's search committee absorbed its second turndown from Oklahoma pastor and former missionary, Tom Elliff, it seemed to be in disarray. Another former missionary, Miles Seaborn, a longtime Fort Worth pastor and conservative stalwart, reportedly was approached, but he also declined. In the meanwhile, interim president Don Kammerdiener moved aggressively ahead with his responsibilities, including a necessary downsizing of the 464 employee home office in Richmond, Virginia. Citing downward trends in the Cooperative Program, a shortfall in the Lottie Moon Christmas offering and rising costs, Kammerdiener seemed determined to do whatever was necessary to keep the giant missionary force viable. While losses and some sympathies toward moderate initiatives were in evidence, the keystone enterprise of Southern Baptists seemed to be trying hard to stay its course.

The Dimensions of Dissent

As convention leaders began planning for the 1993 annual meeting to convene in Houston, Texas, at the site of the initial conservative resurgence victory in 1979, the dimensions of the Southern Baptist Convention's new dissent became clearer. The initial institutionalizing of moderate causes as they continued to lose key votes came with the organization of the Southern Baptist Alliance in 1987. The group, subsequently calling themselves The Alliance of Baptists, held its seventh annual meeting in Daytona Beach, Florida, in February 1993.

The Alliance's executive director, Stan Hastey, reported a one-third drop in membership from twenty-nine hundred to two thousand with 120 churches represented. These churches were reported to have sixty thousand members. The Alliance adopted a reduced budget, renewed its covenant to affirm inclusiveness and ecumenicity, and cited relationships with American Baptist Churches USA and the Progressive National Baptist Convention. The former is the successor of the body from which Southern Baptists separated in 1845, and the latter is made up of predominately black churches.

A key vote ensured that the group would not merge with the Cooperative Baptist Fellowship, though both groups claimed they would be complementing and not competing with each other. Both bodies claimed some of the same support.[99]

After the meeting, Hastey, quoting John Galsworthy's 1933 book *Over the River,* said beginnings and endings are untidy and ragged around the edges. In an apology for the variety of moderate initiatives, Hastey urged the disaffected to "welcome the wilderness of our own chastisement and cleansing instead of demanding some new promised land on a platter." [100]

Since the Alliance had from its beginning given support to Southern Baptist Women in Ministry, the tenth anniversary of that group was also noted. At least one speaker reminded those gathered of the 1984 SBC resolution blaming women for the presence of sin in the world.[101] Because conservative dominance clearly opposed women's ordination, it remained a measure of dissent.

Sarah Francis Anders of Louisiana College, a researcher of women's issues in Southern Baptist life for two decades, reported that the numbers of Southern Baptist women ordained to ministry had tripled in the six years from 1986 to 1992. Noting that the number reported, nine hundred, still amounted to less than 1 percent of Southern Baptists' more than ninety thousand ministers reported in its 1992 Annual, Anders said the dramatic jump moved Southern Baptists from seventh to fifth among the ten largest denominations in terms of women ministers. Her report said Southern Baptist women's biggest gains were in Kentucky, North Carolina, and Virginia, followed by Georgia and South Carolina.

Amanda Hiley, the Executive Director of Women in Ministry with offices in Louisville and herself a pastor, compared Southern Baptists' experience with moves taken to bring women into the priesthood among Episcopalians and Roman Catholics. She said, "Since Baptist churches are autonomous, the decision must be made on a case-by-case basis. By the nature of Baptist polity, we will never know when we have won the battle."[102]

Anders's report said the chaplaincy continued to absorb most women ministers with over two hundred, while the pastorate still had the smallest number, eighteen.

Both women admitted continued resistance from conservative leadership, including a failed move among Southern Seminary trustees to block the election of six faculty nominees who, though professed inerrantists, were open to women's ordination. But Southwestern Seminary historian

Leon McBeth was quoted as saying, "I would say that as we go into the twenty-first century, I expect more acceptance of women in ministry."[103]

One of the most visible voices of SBC dissent, *Baptists Today,* also celebrated its tenth anniversary with plans for a special issue and a national fund-raising campaign. Editor Jack Harwell and founding publisher, Walker Knight, called it "the nation's only autonomous publication."

Dissent continued to be measured in financial terms also. The Lottie Moon Christmas offering lagged significantly behind its 1992 total of $81.3 million, though overall designated giving was up. Cooperative Program gifts, on the other hand, were running neck and neck with the previous year at the end of April. This encouraged SBC leaders, since the Cooperative Baptist Fellowship was also reporting large percentage gains as it continued to define its programs. Yet, only nine hundred of Southern Baptists' 38,458 churches were reported as having contributed. Since that number was up from four hundred in 1992, it could be interpreted either as rapid progress or limited participation.

The alternate-funding group gathered for its third annual meeting in May of 1993 in Birmingham where Patricia Ayres surrendered the gavel to Hardy Clemons, pastor of Greenville, South Carolina's First Baptist Church, and where another woman, Carolyn Crumpler, former WMU executive director, was named moderator-elect. As the moderates gathered they noted recent resignations of Foreign Mission Board vice-president Harlan Spurgeon and Home Mission Board trustee, Orrick Bullock. Bullock, a Washington, D.C., pastor, claimed the HMB "had not knowingly appointed a missionary of the 'moderate' persuasion for at least six years."[104] Spurgeon decried the political agenda pursued at the expense of missions. They also bemoaned continued defections at Southern Seminary, as Al Mohler took over, but cheered an announcement by Baylor University that it would welcome the George W. Truett Seminary's first class in the fall of 1994 in facilities made available by Waco's First Baptist Church.[105]

Approximately five thousand persons registered for the CBF meeting, though over six thousand gathered to hear former United States president, Jimmy Carter, lend his support while cautioning the Fellowship against becoming a new denomination.

A sunset clause in the organization's original constitution brought a new one into being. Membership "will be limited to Baptist individuals and Baptist churches who contribute annually to the ministries and operations of the fellowship." The document, in an obvious reaction to conservative tactics in recent years, prohibits resolutions and similar motions from the floor of its meetings. It provides for a coordinating council of sixty-nine on a representative formula.[106]

New CBF missions coordinator, Keith Parks, was featured in a service to "bless" twenty-two missionaries supported by the Fellowship. It came at a time when he was drawing fire for a video on the Fellowship's focus on World A that failed to mention Foreign Mission Board programs he had helped initiate. "World A," or the unevangelized 21.5 percent of the world's population, stretches from North Africa through Central Asia and encompasses 1.2 billion people. Efforts to reach it were a centerpiece of Parks's FMB strategy.[107] Perhaps in response to the Parks video, the Foreign Mission Board released information that twenty new churches had been started in World A the previous year.

Hardy Clemons, incoming moderator of the CBF, said in a post-meeting publication, "We are maturing as Cooperative Baptists who honor unity-in-diversity and cooperate across chasms of disagreement about many things. We agree that God has come to us in Christ. We agree that to be a Christian means to be on mission." Unity-in-diversity and mission continued to be the themes of moderate dissent.

Cooperative Baptist Fellowship Coordinator Cecil Sherman, while claiming that while the SBC "got the property: we got the principles," nevertheless softened enough to add, "We humbly pray that God will use the Fellowship for good, not ill, and that God will use the SBC in the same way."[108]

Another Rankin

A final piece of the conservative resurgence seemed ready to fall into place as the 1993 Southern Baptist Convention drew near. In a meeting on May 25, near the Dallas-Fort Worth airport, the Foreign Mission Board's search committee again announced a choice for its president. This time the committee turned within the organization to tap veteran missionary and area director for southern Asia and the Pacific, Jerry A. Rankin, to lead the keystone enterprise. He was presented to a called meeting of the Board on June 14, 1993, in connection with the convention in Houston.

Rankin, distant kin to an earlier FMB leader, M. Theron Rankin, had been with the mission organization since he and his wife, the former Bobbie Simmons, were appointed as missionaries to Indonesia in June of 1970. Their area director at that time was R. Keith Parks and colleagues included

Bill and Dellanna O'Brien. Rankin and his wife, both natives of Mississippi and graduates of Mississippi College, had two grown children and had been living in Singapore.

Having come up through the missionary ranks with a number of field administrative positions under his belt, Rankin had been in the upper echelon of prospects from the beginning, but only rose to the top in the final days before being tapped by the search committee headed by Joel Gregory. Surprised at having been chosen over such candidates as interim director Kammerdiener, Rankin immediately said he hoped Kammerdiener would continue in his role. Board chairman, John Jackson, described Rankin as a "dark horse."

A graduate of Southwestern Seminary with a master of divinity degree, Rankin also received an honorary doctor of divinity from Mississippi College. Gregory said Rankin expressed a commitment to inerrancy and "will embrace pluralistic mission efforts of all Southern Baptists." Jackson and Gregory both expected Rankin to receive the necessary 75 percent vote of the trustees at the Houston meeting.[109]

In subsequent news releases, it was obvious that the missionaries themselves were generally pleased that the committee had turned to a seasoned missionary. Even Keith Parks gave guarded support for the choice. Parks and others praised Rankin's intelligence and commitment though noting an autocratic management style.[110]

From an historical perspective, the FMB action recalled Southern Seminary's choice of E. Y. Mullins in the aftermath of the Whitsitt controversy. Mullins, who had been far from the controversy while in a pastorate in Massachusetts, had been praised for being free of any taint of the heated affair. Some of Rankin's supporters noted he had been in Singapore and had not been identified with Southern Baptists' most recent travails.

Rankin encountered some criticism for views related to spiritual gifts that caused detractors to call him a "charismatic." Rankin replied that the committee had explored this area thoroughly with him and found "no doctrinal problem."

From a strategy aspect, Rankin was seen as primarily committed to evangelism and less committed to institutionalized missions. On the other hand, a Richmond newspaper report suggested he might turn away from a Richmond-concentrated global strategy center to a more field-based or missionary-based strategy. Rankin felt the Parks-led expansion of the Richmond office has become "too large during the past six years." He wanted to balance the World A emphasis with the "harvest fields," referring to responsive areas of missionary activity. Rankin told the same reporter that he felt the thirty-nine hundred missionary agency deployed in 129 countries should be able to meet its goal of five thousand missionaries by the turn of the century.[111]

Houston Revisited

As Southern Baptists absorbed the prospects of new presidents at Southern Seminary and the Foreign Mission Board, they completed plans for a return of the annual meeting to Houston, Texas, where the conservative strategy had been successfully launched fourteen years before. In many ways, things were radically different for Southern Baptists and, in other ways, they were reassuringly the same.

Many of those leading the Convention in 1979 were now either on the sidelines or aligned with a dissident faction. They were different in that the conservative outsiders in 1979 depending upon Mid-America Seminary, Luther Rice Seminary, and Criswell Bible Institute now controlled all Southern Baptist seminaries at the trustee level and several at the administrative level. Things were different in that a missions alternative called The Genesis Commission had been replaced with solid control of Southern Baptists' Home and Foreign Boards. Things were different in that internal opposition now included two new seminaries, a publishing house, a missions enterprise, and a gift-channeling program maintained by sizable dissident fellowships. Things were different in that the social and cultural agenda of Southern Baptists was clearly a conservative one, and its lead enterprise for confronting such issues, the Christian Life Commission, was establishing itself on the national scene through a leading role in pushing the Religious Freedom Restoration Act, as designed to restore the free exercise of religion clause to a pre-1990 Supreme Court decision status.

Things were reassuringly the same in that most of Southern Baptists' constituent churches were still aligned, though some that were close in 1979 were now on the edges and some that were on the edges were now more involved. Things were reassuringly the same in that the numbers had changed only marginally and that the core beliefs were essentially the same from both an historical and a biblical basis.

The fourth and least controversial of Convention boards, the Annuity Board celebrated its seventy-fifth anniversary in the spring of 1993. Its chief executive, former Texas pastor Paul Powell, clearly identified as a moderate in his home state, seemed solidly entrenched. The huge numbers of the agency certainly helped his cause. Powell reported that Annuity Board assets climbed by $1 million a day in 1992 and totaled $3.9 billion as the year ended.[112] Conservative activism in that agency was primarily evident in a call for shareholder action against a large American retailer in support of anti-pornography initiatives. Despite a small effort among some moderates to offer an alternative annuity arrangement, the agency reported 68,600 individual accounts and record totals in contributions and benefits.

The Radio and Television Commission began to emerge from its financial problems with aggressive new program alliances with other evangelical entities, and the Brotherhood Commission found new opportunities with a program of voluntarism. Highlighting new ways of reporting, that Commission said volunteers gave time worth $67 million in 1992. They cited the work of 75,341 volunteers in 8,905 projects.[113]

A lingering nostalgia for Southern Baptists' past was poignantly reflected in a self-published "research report" mailed to SBC leaders of all stripes one month before the Convention by deposed Baptist Sunday School Board president Lloyd Elder.

Elder called on the Baptist family to "reaffirm our historic missionary nature and purpose." His action plans to reverse decline and realize this vision included affirming the SBC Constitution's Article IV on the authority of each body. As an example, he deplored what he felt were efforts by the Mission Boards and the Executive Committee to "exercise authority" over WMU. Elder also proposed expanding representation in convention governance through a series of constitutional amendments and by-law changes. Using the analogy of owner-stockholder, Elder made an impassioned and reasoned plea for rapprochement. He called his effort a Call the Family Back Together movement.[114]

While commending its spirit and content, little enthusiasm for Elder's plan was evident from either the dominant leadership or the organized dissent in the days leading up to the 1993 Convention.

Morris Chapman, president of the SBC Executive Committee said, "If the Southern Baptist Convention were to adopt the policies suggested by Elder, it would drive the controversy deeper into the state conventions." Chapman also felt Elder's document did not correctly represent SBC progress. "You will search in vain for word that giving to SBC causes is up this year, as are foreign mission applications. You will not read that Annie Armstrong was a record, that while most other denominations are declining, Southern Baptists add twenty-four hundred new members and four new churches each week."[115]

Monday of Convention week was dominated by intrigue at the Foreign Mission Board's called meeting to consider Jerry A. Rankin as its next president. Significant opposition to Rankin's nomination implicated Paige Patterson and included Paul Pressler.[116] Efforts to secure the needed 75 percent of trustees voting to elect Rankin seemed in trouble, yet search-committee chairman Joel Gregory and trustee chairman John Jackson stood firm. Gregory said the committee would resign if Rankin were not elected. While most of the questions were raised about Rankin's beliefs and practices regarding spiritual gifts, Rankin's lack of involvement in the conservative resurgence was also a problem. Impassioned presentations to the trustees by Gregory and the committee, along with Rankin's own explanations, carried the day, however, and Rankin's nomination was approved 59-14, a five-vote margin. Pressler immediately moved to make the decision unanimous.

Rankin's election seemed to meet with wide approval, as did his announced intentions to move from "a common global agenda, to restore mission-generated strategies that will give those on the field more ownership of mission methods."[117] Rankin appeared to be positioning himself to modify the Parks-led paradigm change of 1985 that, though generating a number of key innovations, had caused many career missionaries to feel less involved in strategic decisions. One of his first decisions was to phase out the Global Strategy Group in favor of more field-based direction.

At the Convention, SBC leadership, no longer preoccupied with getting out the vote, was able to spend significant energies on a witnessing program to the city of Houston and on extravaganzas focusing on biblical preparation and missions. The theme, "Such a Time as This," was interpreted from Esther 4:14 by Adrian Rogers in a symbolic return to the site of his stunning, course-changing victory in 1979.

Both leadership and observers seemed surprised by the 1993 registration figure of 17,886. It was not only far short of the projections, but less than the membership of Convention president Ed Young's Second Baptist Church of Houston.

With few moderate activities evident other than a SBC Women In Ministry meeting and a hospitality room maintained by Cooperative Baptist Fellowship leaders Cecil Sherman and Hardy Clemons, the dominant conservatives felt secure. Pastor's Conference and Woman's Missionary

Union meetings went smoothly, though WMU ignored the resolutions directed to them earlier in the year by the mission boards and the Executive Committee. It was obvious that Convention leadership wanted no fight with its historic auxiliary and that group's poised and articulate executive, Dellanna O'Brien.

Convention leadership also had their way with regard to the much discussed Masonic report by the Home Mission Board. After half-hearted efforts to both toughen and weaken the report failed and, with the study's original sponsor, Larry Holly, silent, it passed by a "clear majority."

Despite such successes and Ed Young's urging Southern Baptists to get off the "side streets" of homiletics, politics, and inattention to evangelism and missions, the return to Houston had an agenda of its own that often focused on the very things Young felt detracted from the main mission.

The second reading passage of the constitutional amendment to bar churches that "affirm, approve, or endorse homosexual behaviour" triggered the news focus of the 1993 annual meeting. First, a Florida pastor challenged the seating of messengers from President Bill Clinton's home church, Little Rock's Immanuel Baptist Church, saying "due to their lack of action, they are by their silence supporting Bill Clinton's endorsement of the homosexual lifestyle." While other motions to end relationships with Bill Clinton and Vice-President Al Gore were ruled out of order for polity reasons, this one was referred to the credentials committee. Immanuel pastor Rex Horne and ten members of the church were seated, but Horne called it "nothing but a witch hunt" and warned that the "interrogation raised serious questions for the fifteen million-member denomination, which has prided itself on local church autonomy." [118]

Resolutions denouncing Clinton and Gore and their support of abortion rights, homosexuals in the military and in the administration, and calling for a return to biblical morality proliferated. The resolution process demonstrated not only the religious conservatism of Southern Baptists represented at the meeting but also highlighted their conservative political bent. To both the delight and embarrassment of their leadership, the whole issue-dominated process demonstrated the convention's tolerance for even its more strident voices. After Ed Young was reelected president of the body without opposition, he expressed some fears that they were crossing the line between religion and politics.

The more familiar issues of the controversy—such as inerrancy, liberalism in SBC agencies, and women's issues—took a back seat, though a resolution to ban churches that ordain women and the circulation of a Paige Patterson-authored document naming certain Southern Baptist institutions and leaders as "neo-orthodox" or "liberal" attracted some attention. The first was referred to the Executive Committee, and Patterson apologized for the latter.

Because of the lack of such fireworks, Ed Young said, "We're in the kingdom business again. There's unity and excitement." One participant echoed the sentiments of many when he said, "This has been the calmest Convention in fourteen years."

Attracting surprisingly little attention was the release of a preliminary report by the Young-appointed Theological Study Committee. The group, co-chaired by Timothy George and Roy Honeycutt, invited "critique and additional counsel" and promised a final report at the 1994 meeting in Orlando, Florida, where Southern Baptists would begin a year of sesquicentennial celebration. The report reaffirmed the Baptist Faith and Message as "the guiding confessional statement of Southern Baptists," but because of "unprecedented challenges from universalism, radical feminism, deconstruction, process theology, the New Age movement, and other ideologies" the report addressed "Holy Scripture," "The Doctrine of God," "The Person and Work of Christ," "The Church," and "Last Things" in a series of "emphases" intended "to illuminate articles of The Baptist Faith and Message."[119]

The section on Scripture gave an inerrant interpretation to the Baptist Faith and Message, citing the seminary president's Glorieta Statement of 1986, the Peace Committee report of 1987, and commending the Chicago statements on Biblical Inerrancy (1987) and Biblical Hermeneutics (1988) as guidelines for interpreting Article I of the 1963 document.

For those observing the fourteen-year-old revolution in Southern Baptist life, expectations that a maturing conservative movement would mellow received little encouragement. Efforts of Lloyd Elders and Herschel Hobbs to sell rapprochement attracted scant attention, though they managed to organize a work group composed of a few state leaders to try to keep it alive.

Despite the fact that accommodation and inclusiveness are traditionally part of the politics of progress, the conservative movement's leaders knew its success had been characterized by hard positions and doctrinaire exclusiveness. Few were willing to abandon their winning strategy despite questions as to its long-term viability. One of the conservatives' chief lieutenants,

Arkansas's Joe Atchison, headed the Committee on Nominations that was approved in Houston. He was frank to say that only inerrantists and those who did not support the Cooperative Baptist Fellowship were nominated.[120]

On the other hand, the CBF represented a significant minority of dissidents who were uneasily enclaved on the edges of the Southern Baptist Convention as the Convention's sesquicentennial celebration neared. Whether this group would split off, itself split, be pushed off, or gradually be reabsorbed took its place among the questions raised by the larger prospects of the still-expanding Southern Baptist Convention.

10

Foundations for the Future

1993–Forward

More than one historian claims that the most Baptist tradition of all is dissent. If so, midway through their fourth century as a historically recognized people and halfway through their second century as a denominational entity, Southern Baptists remained true to their tradition.

The Convention, solidly in the hands of its more conservative elements, was internally divided into at least three factions: the Convention itself, the Cooperative Baptist Fellowship, and the Alliance of Baptists; the last two dissenting groups involved less than twelve hundred of the Convention's thirty-eight thousand churches and partially overlapped. The vast majority of churches cooperating with the Convention were doing so with the Convention alone. Most of the dissenting churches were dually aligned with the Convention and the Fellowship and a smaller number with all three.

Furthermore, no one of the factions was satisfied with the situation. Many controlling conservatives wanted to make dual alignment impossible. In late 1992, the Executive Committee's Morris Chapman said integrity called for those contributing to the CBF to leave the convention.[1] In turn, many in the Fellowship and Alliance groups wanted clear-cut separation, but they faced the opposition of those who wanted to maintain the uneasy duality in hopes that a workable rapprochement would eventually be possible. The longer history of the parent body provided its cohesive force, while more recent events fueled the tangential forces. Many people were asking what aspects of the longer history were still in place. How cohesive was that force?

Conservative theologian Timothy George in 1992 said, "The SBC stands today on the brink of schism." He predicted that the next few years would see the formation of "a splinter denomination," which he said would be the work of disillusioned moderates who had given up reforming the Convention in the direction of other mainline Protestant bodies. Comparing them to earlier Landmark and Independent defections, he said they would try to exist "side by side with Southern Baptists." He cited Presbyterian bifurcation in the South as a parallel.

George cautioned the conservative ranks to seek a genuine spiritual and theological renewal and somehow negotiate a reconciliation with "cooperating, Bible-believing moderates." It was imperative, he said, that "the new consensus" lay hold of the scholarship of forty years of "evangelical renaissance."[2]

Competing Visions

In the midst of Southern Baptists' efforts to move ahead and while its factions and institutions, both old and new, continued to define their directions, a number of visions vied for credibility. One could be seen in the view and longings of conservative pastor W. A. Criswell in the twilight of his remarkable and controversial career. A second could be seen in the new excitement of Randall Lolley, former president of Southeastern Seminary before its conservative takeover, in terms of the moderate initiatives. A third, and obviously meant to be synthesizing, vision was articulated by Southwestern Seminary's enduring president, Russell Dilday.

Criswell's vision included the nostalgia of a simpler day when Southern Baptists applauded and supported their mission boards and agencies, bragged on their seminaries, and touted the Cooperative Program. Perhaps

Randall Lolley was voicing Criswell's fading dream when he said, "Once upon a time being a Southern Baptist was a fairly simple matter. Missionaries were heroes. Seminaries were centers for learning and piety. . . . Conventions were reunions of likeminded people, festivals for hope and renewal of missionary thrusts."[3] Perhaps Criswell would have agreed with Lolley's assessment that the system was held together by trust and that the trust was gone. Conservatives point out that the lack of trust dictated the need for the resurgence." Criswell himself described it as "the breach that is created between some of our dearest, sweetest pastors and people, that to me is a tragedy."[4]

Lolley's vision included recognition that because of loss of trust the system is drastically changing, that "our Baptist landscape is marked by many new institutions and programs." He claimed that has "been the way of God's people through all these centuries." Pointing out that many Baptists are excluded from the old system, Lolley said they have done "what Christians have always done. They struck out on new journeys. They have changed the ways we accomplish our Lord's mission." He then cited the emergence of The Alliance of Baptists, the Cooperative Baptist Fellowship, the Baptist Peace Fellowship of North America, Associated Baptist Press, The Baptist Center for Ethics, Smyth & Helwys Publishing Company, Baptist Theological Seminary at Richmond, Southern Baptist Women in Ministry, and *Baptists Today*. Not only was Lolley naming an approved list of moderate-backed alternatives, he was naming a counter slate to Southern Baptist Cooperative Program ventures.[5]

In contrast to these visions of the way it was and the order conservatives were now trying to stabilize and the societal alternatives rapidly coalescing into a new denominational framework was Russell Dilday's vision of what he called the "New Southern Baptist Convention." Writing in early 1993 in a series of presidential columns in the *Southwestern News*, Dilday outlined what he believed could "emerge from the dust of the controversy." His New Southern Baptist Convention would rest on five concepts: it would preserve the solidarity of the past, but not be afraid of trans-denominational networks and coalitions; it would shun "politics, power, and pressure tactics for such "spiritual weapons as persuasion and proclamation" and it would welcome believing intellectualism and reverent scholarship; it would be noncreedal and yet be willing to define doctrine and think out convictions; it would seek a balance between the personal and social aspects of the gospel, i.e., evangelism and social ministry; and it would rely on the "glue" of cooperancy to hold the Convention to its primary task.[6] The Lloyd Elder efforts reported in the previous chapter could be seen as a plan to facilitate Dilday's vision, though both proposals arose independently.

It was obvious that the traditional but conservative-dominated nostalgia of Criswell still reflected the feelings of a majority of Southern Baptists, but that Lolley's argument that the moderate initiatives were really vintage Baptist, i.e., "to be church and to change," was the focal point for a small group of displaced Baptist leaders and churches. It was equally obvious that veteran denominationalists like Dilday and Elder were scratching for a place broad enough to include both groups.

The Foundation

But as provocative and possibly prescient as such observations may be, the burden of this final chapter is neither the indulgence of nostalgia nor an exercise in futurizing, neither an effort at prophecy nor a run at synthesis. It is rather to examine the narrative for foundations in place upon which any future of the people called Southern Baptists will be built.

The foundation is defined by all that has gone before. Indeed the first nine chapters delineate the historical development of this foundation. One theologian has stated that "we are able to understand the present and illuminate the future only to the extent that we do not forsake the warranted wisdom of the past."[7] But for Southern Baptists, gathering that "warranted wisdom" into a succinct summary and evaluation is desperately needed. To serve that need, consider three nonnumerical dimensions that define Southern Baptists' foundation confessionally, connectionally, and cooperationally.

Confessionally

Much of Southern Baptists' understanding of themselves has come around their efforts to articulate their faith and to define that confession in various statements of principles, beliefs, or faith.[8]

William Lumpkin, acknowledged Baptist authority on such documents, claims they have included four distinctives from other Protestant groups who were doing the same thing during Baptist beginnings: (1) Their ecclesiology focused on local communities of believers; (2) they defined their distinctive ordinances as baptism by immersion and the supper or communion as symbolic obedience and commemorative; (3) they emphasized evangelism and missions; and (4) they stressed freedom of conscience and separation of church and state.[9]

Because Baptists were initially persecuted on the strength of violated creeds inherent in established religions, they have historically denied that their statements were creedal. But since they have thought it necessary over and over again to define their position, they have called the result confessional, a simple readiness to give reasons and definition to the faith within them. For early Baptists the difference was crucial: A confession states what a group believes at any given time, while a creed prescribes what members must believe.

Southern Baptists' founders understood this distinction and cherished it. Their 1845 "Address to the Public" recognized "a Baptist aversion for all creeds but the Bible."[10] McBeth points out that more recent "usage makes less difference between confessions and creeds," and Timothy George, a leading conservative resurgence theologian, has suggested that anti-creedalism is a legacy from Alexander Campbell.[11] He has support for this from James Boyce who described Campbell as "playing upon the prejudices of the weak and ignorant among our people, decrying creeds as an infringement upon the rights of conscience."[12]

In contrast, Slayden Yarbrough holds that creedalism "is a threat to the traditions of Southern Baptist history, theology, and mission." While admitting that theology is a legitimate concern of all Southern Baptists, Yarbrough claims "the Baptist approach to theology is confessionalism, not creedalism."[13]

Nevertheless, Southern Baptists, either as a body or through one of their agencies, have on numerous occasions attempted to define their beliefs through various statements. At the time of their founding the Baptist best-known confession was the Philadelphia Confession of 1742 which had ties to their English roots in the Second London Confession; it had also been used at Charleston. The Philadelphia Confession included a Calvinistic tenet on election and both a local and universal view of the church.

Though the 1833 New Hampshire Confession of Faith, adopted by Baptists in that state to recognize a more modified approach to Calvinism in light of the "free Baptists" emerging from the Second Great Awakening, was gaining support in the South, it was not yet as widely circulated nor as influential as the older Philadelphia document and variations. As noted earlier, its subsequent gains in popularity was due first to the appeal of its less stringent Calvinism among evangelistically inclined Baptist churches in the

South and its local view of the church, which mollified Landmark positions, and later to its identification with fundamentalist positions.

The Convention itself has adopted only four such documents: 1914, 1925, 1946, 1963. A document tentatively released in 1993 might yet have the force of a fifth such document. In addition, the Convention associated itself through committees with confessional documents in 1919 and 1987. Agency-developed documents include Southern Seminary, 1859; Baptist Sunday School Board, 1900; Southwestern Seminary, 1908; Baptist Bible Institute (New Orleans Seminary), 1918; the Foreign Mission Board, 1920; and Midwestern Seminary in 1963.

As the foregoing chapters spell out, each of these efforts speaks to some issue in place at the time with the possible exception of the 1946 Statement of Principles, which was birthed by a centennial. The fact that the latter did not speak to controversy or some dominant issue may explain its near invisibility among Southern Baptists. Even as the Abstract of Principles adopted by Southern Seminary at its founding was meant to guide this pioneer institution while reassuring the constituents it was to serve, so subsequent institutional or agency-originated confessions were meant to both guide and reassure.[14]

Committee-generated documents, such as the Pronouncement of 1914, the Fraternal Address of 1919, and even the Peace Committee Report of 1987, were carefully worded to avoid the appearance of a confession. Only in 1925, 1946, and 1963 did the Convention purposefully approve a confessional statement, albeit with creed-denying disclaimers attached to each.

And both writers and supporters in each effort were hoping for an enabling consensus to result. Only the 1946 statement had the effect and that may have been more a result of invisibility than genuine consensus. It is certain that SBC leaders in 1925 and 1963 were seeking to defuse controversy and lay the groundwork for consensus.

The evolution controversy led to Southern Baptists' first formal statement of faith in 1925. Since Mullins was the prime mover in this document also, a number of questions emerge. Why did he not use either the Philadelphia Confession or the Abstract of Principles (since he was president of Southern Seminary at the time)? Why did he turn to the New Hampshire Confession? The answer seems to be threefold. First, it fit his own theological emphasis with its more evangelistically and Christian experience-oriented language. Both Mullins and later Southwestern's W. T. Conner placed strong value on Christian experience and free grace. Second, because of its simplicity and emphasis on the local church, the New Hampshire Confession had achieved a strong following. Third, Southwestern Seminary had adopted the New Hampshire Confession at its founding. Mullins, realizing that the main agenda was to foster and maintain a consensus among Southern Baptists, went with that pre-acceptance assurance and with the generally more permissive spirit of the New Hampshire Confession to keep what historian Bill Leonard would later call the "Grand Compromise" in place.

The strange case of the 1946 Statement of Principles presents a problem of perception. The fact that this document was approved without debate could either weaken or strengthen its meaning. As for its influence on subsequent doctrinal debate, it undoubtedly weakened it. But when one looks at Southern Baptists' post-war history, the Statement could be interpreted as a blueprint. Its blue-ribbon writers may have ensured its acceptance, but an equally likely explanation is the end-of-the-war preoccupation with getting on with a totally new agenda and going with the flow of the surprising consensus that had emerged during the war.

That this consensus was a compromise and not a merging of old differences was obvious by the time of the Genesis controversy of 1962 and the 1970 Commentary controversies. That Convention leadership turned to a page out of its own history in 1962–63 with a reworking of the 1925 Baptist Faith and Message was natural. Yet given Southern Baptists' history and its persistent fault lines to be discussed shortly, the fact that it did not resolve the basic problems is not surprising. The 1963 Baptist Faith and Message continues to guide Southern Baptist agencies, but pressures exist to further define its Bible statement.

Some people think that the Peace Committee report assumed the force of a new doctrinal statement in 1987 with its assertion of "what most Baptists believe." Its centrality challenged a large segment of Southern Baptist scholarship since World War II. This assumption gained credence when Convention president Edwin Young set a theological study group in motion in the fall of 1992 and charged it to begin with the 1963 Baptist Faith and Message and the report of the Peace Committee, along with the 1978 and 1982 Chicago Statements on Biblical Inerrancy and Biblical Hermeneutics.[15] As mentioned earlier, its preliminary report reaffirmed the Baptist Faith and Message though reinforcing conservative interpretations through a series of emphases.

Connectionally

Of course, Southern Baptists' unique connectionalism, clearly stated at the beginning but both realized and modified with their experience, also defines them and constitutes a second dimension. Connectionalism refers to formal relationships between local churches whether in associational, societal, or conventional forms.

Associations are connections of churches along limited geographical lines based on a common confessionalism for fellowship and certain collective ministries. Societies are connections of individuals, churches, associations, or other entities based upon the support of a single ministry. Conventions are connections of churches united through messengers confessionally and voluntarily for the support of any number of ministries that might commend themselves to the body.

Associations are Baptists' oldest form of connectionalism and continue to exert a strong influence on Southern Baptists as evident by the Convention's recent actions exercising more associational-type prerogatives as to which churches it will seat in its annual meetings. The convention-type of connectionalism has always had more affinity with associationalism than with society models.

Societal connectionalism, on the other hand, was the vehicle which Baptists initially used to respond to the missionary mandate and to become a denomination. Societal connectionalism preserves a local congregation's prerogatives at the expense of the larger endeavors facilitated by the convention strategy. Even when Southern Baptists formed their Convention with its distinctive connectional goals, there were society-type holdovers in their use of agents in fund-raising for Southern Baptists' different entities and the autonomy given the initial Boards. The advent of the Cooperative Program in 1925, the Executive Committee in 1917 and 1927, and the representation change in 1931 greatly diminished those vestiges.

Society-type connections reappeared from time to time, however, first with fundamentalism in the 1920s, and then with the pre-cursors of the conservative resurgence, who as early as 1973 began to adopt societal strategies to support periodicals, a seminary, and even a short-lived mission organization called the Genesis Commission. Their leading churches helped in numerous para-church enterprises which were in themselves societal-type entities.

When moderates lost control of the Southern Baptist Convention to the conservatives, they followed the same resort to society type alternatives with the Alliance, Women in Ministry, the Richmond Seminary, the Truett Seminary, and finally the Cooperative Baptist Fellowship, which has been confirmed by its key leaders as a societal strategy.[16] Historically then, the society method, responsible for Baptists' initial denominationalism, has become a vehicle for dissent from those controlling its Convention apparatus at any given time.

However, as early as 1934, SBC historian, W. W. Barnes, analyzed Southern Baptist connectionalism along three lines—voluntary, federal, and ecclesiastical. He felt the voluntary model was Southern Baptists' original intent. He said, "The Convention is not an ecclesiastical body composed of churches, nor a federal body composed of state conventions." He held that "in all cooperative endeavors, the principle of autonomy or self-determination should be carefully conserved."[17]

For some, however, any form of connectionalism smacks of an intrusion into local church autonomy. Paige Patterson claimed that Baptists have strongly "resisted connectionalism while emphasizing cooperation." He urged churches "autonomously" to decide how the percentages of their mission moneys would be directed, a strategy at the heart of the churches that felt displaced by the Patterson-led conservative resurgence.[18]

Cooperationally

Patterson's admonition introduces the third dimension of the Southern Baptist foundation in place as it approached its sesquicentennial. That dimension is the level of cooperation undergirding it. Nancy Ammerman links cooperation to what she calls the "substantive rationality" of a group, "what groups think they want to do together."[19] Historically, this part of the foundation has expanded and contracted under a variety of pressures. That it was inherent in the Baptist vision in the South was confirmed in 1925 with the inauguration of the Cooperative Program. It reached its high tide in 1976 when viewed from a consensus-perspective, though its numbers continued to climb. Ammerman points out that "although the central authorities of the Convention had no coercive power over local congregations, they achieved high levels of cooperation by linking the means they employed to the common values and goals present among Southern Baptists."[20]

Cooperation is the result of formal agreement, working consensus, or either residual or incipient commitments. It is reflected in denominational loyalties and especially enthusiasm for denominational projects. It can't be measured accurately in those categories, however, and more crass instruments have to be called on, such as the number of churches giving in any certain year, the percentage of that giving relative to earlier years, along with state convention percentages going to Southern Baptist Convention causes relative to other years. Gross amounts can also be revealing of cooperation, but these are hard to separate from basic growth and economic tides.

This kind of measurement, of course, reflects the post-1925 or post-Cooperative Program situation. Prior to that, during the agent-promotion period, cooperative factors depended upon the numbers of cooperating churches, the fortunes of the individual agencies, and the success of their agents in articulating a unifying vision.

Even less measurable, but potentially very revealing, would be an analysis of extra-Convention program giving. Parachurch groups since World War II such as Campus Crusade, Young Life, Intervarsity, and a host of small mission programs have found Southern Baptists a lucrative source of funds. The more conservative churches were usually the more active para-church program supporters. Megachurches, defined as the three thousand-plus membership churches, tended to fall in this category, and most of their Cooperative Program budgets fell below 5 percent annually with few exceptions.

With conservative and megachurch pastors and leaders manning the ranks of the successful conservative resurgence, new attention was accorded the Cooperative Program in the early 1990s. In turn, the moderate churches which, again generally speaking, had been the most committed to the Cooperative Program with giving commitments in the 15-percent range and up, began to consider the society-type alternatives offered by the Alliance and the Cooperative Baptist Fellowship.

For some, the most cooperation-measuring factor available is the number of churches buying and using the literature of the Sunday School Board and to a lesser extent that of the Brotherhood and Woman's Missionary Union. Churches on the theological right of the Southern Baptist Convention, feeling keenly the need for clearly "orthodox" materials, had been notoriously prone to order from independent or evangelical publishing houses instead of Convention-sponsored sources.

Not surprisingly, after the successful conservative resurgence, the displaced moderates began to consider alternatives. A moderate-supported publishing house, Smyth & Helwys of Greenville, South Carolina, began to offer Sunday School resources and publish Baptist-oriented books. Ironically, Greenville was the location of Southern Baptists' own first publishing efforts.

Recollection that both the first Baptist Faith and Message and the Cooperative Program emerged from the same Convention in 1925 has new significance as Southern Baptists reach their 150th year. Cooperation depends upon the consensus that such doctrinal statements are meant to cement, but in turn such doctrinal statements can be used to define the arena of cooperation. In a *Baptist History and Heritage* issue on patterns of Baptist cooperation in 1989, New Orleans Seminary historian Claude Howe wrote, "The future effectiveness of the SBC may depend heavily upon reaching workable solutions regarding the Cooperative Program and the Baptist Faith and Message as parameters for cooperation for Southern Baptists."[21]

Despite its internal conflicts and disaffected members, the Southern Baptist Convention's foundation, measured confessionally, connectionally, and cooperatively, was still in place and still strong by any historical standard as it approached its sesquicentennial. While such measurements as its 38,458 churches, 15,365,486 members, 8,262,521 enrolled in Sunday School, and 367,847 baptisms offered impressive evidence, it does not tell who Southern Baptists really are as accurately as an historically informed understanding of the three conceptual dimensions.

Fault Lines in the Foundation

Crisscrossing that foundation like matrices in a piece of turquoise are fault lines that define both the Convention's history and its weaknesses, as surely as California's San Andreas fault and Missouri's New Madrid fault define the continent's. No future will be devoid of their influence, either large or small.

By fault lines, this narrative means those persistent historical differences that are present in Southern Baptist life and that have been either tolerated or papered-over in the past, but which by their presence mean tension, potential division, and constant realignment among its constituents in any conceivable future. It is vital for any rational perspective of an unfolding future to understand these fault lines and how they are currently evident and/or influential.

Calvinism and Arminianism

The oldest Baptist fault line runs along the theological question of God's sovereignty and human free will. Early Baptist life reflects the differences that emerged in the Reformation between the teachings of John Calvin and those of James Arminius.

Calvin's Augustine-type theology dominated much of the Protestant Reformation by 1600 with predestination and rigid election. It was a part of the Anglican reformation and its own puritan wing and separate splinters.

Arminius was, simply put, a moderate in the Calvinist camp. But his moderate, tempered spirit emphasized the importance of human decision in the process of conversion and salvation and attracted followers who encouraged him to distance himself from Calvinistic rigidity and move more and more toward a concept of free will in matters of grace.

Baptist beginnings reflect this raging controversy in that the Smyth-Helwys group moved to temper its reform theology to the point that they became known as General Baptists. Some scholars suggest that this embracing of a general atonement view indicated Anabaptist or Mennonite influence.

Those who took root from other separatist movements in England two decades later continued to embrace Calvin's election and were called Particular Baptists. It was this group's Second London Confession that was to lead to the Philadelphia Confession.

American Baptists reflected both groups early on, though Southern Baptists' initial confessions were more nearly particular. Arminian arguments, however, were not nearly as moderating as the experience issuing from the Great Awakenings and frontier evangelism. The simple call to embrace Christ as the key to an act of grace effectively tempered Baptists' Calvinistic tendencies. This environment provided fertile soil for the emergence of the missionary movement in America in 1814 and was, indeed, as essential to it as was Carey's challenging inquiries among England's Particular Baptists two decades earlier. It also caused a split among New England Baptists and the birth of Free Will Baptists.

A sharp reaction based upon strict Calvinism emerged in Kentucky in the early 1800s, however. Objecting to mission boards and any other effort to "use means" in the conversion of unbelievers, the movement was also a suspicion of organizations and centralization of any kind, a kind of religious counterpart to Jeffersonian democracy. The movement drew its biblical strength from strict Calvinism and, in a twist given by Daniel Parker of Illinois, birthed the Two-Seed-in-the-Spirit Predestinarian Baptists.

Such extremes further moderated main stream Baptists and paved the way for the Philadelphia Confession with its classic Calvinism to give way to the New Hampshire Confession with its modified view of election as Southern Baptists defined themselves theologically in 1925.

David Dockery gives this moderation a more personalized path, claiming that Southern Baptists started with the classical Calvinism of James Boyce and Basil Manly, Jr. According to Dockery, Southern's E. Y. Mullins and Southwestern's W. T. Conner modified the Boyce-Manly position through a move from "a hermeneutic of divine sovereignty with Boyce to one of personal revelation and experience with Mullins and to a lesser degree with Conner."[22] But it was a trio of latter-day theologians—Dale Moody, Frank Stagg, and Herschel Hobbs—that Dockery feels moved Southern Baptists to an Arminian view of atonement, election, and predestination. Moody, according to Dockery, pictured Calvinism as envisioning a tyrant God watching people go by and saying, "Number six, you're in a fix; number seven, you go to heaven. Why? God has decreed that all sixes go to hell and all number sevens go to heaven." In contrast to the formulations of such theologians, Southern Baptists, Dockery maintains, embraced a grass roots theology of deeper life emphases and dispensationalism as typified by W. A. Criswell and evangelist Billy Graham.

Dockery thinks this latter day Arminianism is common ground for Baptist factions at this point but cites "indicators of Calvinistic rebirth in some circles." He says, "It is possible we will see a return to the Calvinistic vitality of Baptists of previous generations."[23]

Few will argue that a group of scholars emerged in the 1980s affirming anew strong Calvinistic views. A. H. Newman once said, "The teachings of Calvin were so self-consistent and were systematized with such logical rigor that there was little opportunity for his followers to be in doubt as to his meaning or to base upon his teachings diverse doctrinal conceptions."[24] In the doctrinally conscious atmosphere that accompanied the conservative resurgence, such consistency found new advocates. The fact that the resurgency was an amalgamation of evangelism people who practiced their calling in free-grace terms foreign to strict Calvinism, along with theologically focused neo-Calvinists, suggested an internal fault line to the movement as well as to the larger body. Moreover, reform movements such as the resurgency, no matter its move to the right, tend to simplify rather than elaborate, whereas elaboration is a condition essential to Calvinism.

Would the neo-Calvinists reactivate the fault line that tore Baptists asunder in the 1820s and following? Since neo-Calvinism was predominately a movement of a conservative theological elite in the early 1990s, many people thought its role would more likely be played out in a studied and scholarly arena rather than in the popular and divisive arena it found in the 1820–30 period.

Society and Convention

Continuing to view fault lines in the Southern Baptist foundation along a chronological continuum introduces the clear difference in polity inherent in the Furman-Johnson tradition called the convention method in contrast to the society method present in Baptists' initial denominational effort. That this is an obvious fault line in the Southern Baptist foundation has been amply documented in earlier chapters. It is most obvious in that Baptists readily return to a societal option when cooperation breaks down or as a form of dissent.

Will this persisting fault line prove to be the simple outlet that it has been in recent years for both sides of the theological spectrum, or will it facilitate a clear and significant split among the people historically gathered as the Southern Baptist Convention?

The societal method has always had the advantage of organizational agility over its convention alternative. Individual people and churches can vote to align themselves in some cause very quickly. Convention methodology with its multilayered decision-making process is ponderous in comparison. But the society-method is vulnerable in that it can break apart just as quickly, while the convention system has so many checks and balances that it has more resistance to rapid change. It is noteworthy that it took the conservatives fourteen years to capture the machinery of the Southern Baptist Convention, while it took moderates just a few years to set up dissenting alternatives. The strength inherent in the former contrasts sharply to the tenuousness of the latter.

This fault line intersects the connectional and cooperative dimensions of the Southern Baptist foundation rather than the confessional dimension. For that reason it has strong pragmatic forces at work in it. The undeniable success of the Cooperative Program is a compelling reason to keep some kind of "grand compromise" in place, and pragmatism may temper the tangential forces in hopes of rebuilding or at least reducing the losses of the controversy involving in the conservative resurgence and its disaffected.

The real issue running along this fault line for the immediate future may, like America's secular history, be representation or lack of it. The conservative resurgence attributed much of its success to its disciplined appointment of like-minded persons to committees and boards. Moderates were strictly excluded. Their lack of participation heightened their disagreement with the actions of these conservative-dominated groups and fueled their tendency to turn to societal outlets in order to participate again. Of course, feelings of the same kind of exclusion fueled initial conservative efforts.

Early in 1993, veteran denominationalist Herschel Hobbs, who chaired the committee that produced the 1963 Baptist Faith and Message and also participated in the 1987 Peace Committee report, addressed the representation question. He called upon the SBC's new leadership to "fulfill their constitutional obligation to share power with their moderate-conservative brethren."[25] Responding to those who claimed to have been excluded by the dominant leadership, Hobbs said Convention leaders should abide by the 1987 Peace Committee's call for balanced committees and boards. Calling for a summit of leaders from all sides, Hobbs' suggestions met little enthusiasm from either SBC Executive Committee president Morris Chapman or Cooperative Baptist Fellowship coordinator Cecil Sherman. Lloyd Elder's efforts in May 1993 met the same response.

Thus, the fault line here is not so much one of differing convictions vis-à-vis connectionalism as it is one of differing options available to Baptist factions. The rapid development of societal type programs represented by the Cooperative Baptist Fellowship and its missions initiative, the Richmond and Truett seminaries, the Alliance, *Baptists Today,* the Baptist Center for Ethics, the Whitsitt Heritage Society, and the Smyth & Helwys publishing venture may at some point represent irreversible momentum and an almost insurmountable hurdle to rapprochement of any kind. At the same time, conservative leaders busy consolidating their advantage saw no reason to reach out to the dissidents.

Local Church and Larger Body

The early Southern Baptist conflict known as the Landmark controversy left indelible marks in the Southern Baptist psyche and continues as a clearly delineated fault line in their foundation. It runs through all three dimensions of confessional, connectional, and cooperative aspects of Southern Baptist life.

In the confessional sense, the definition of church as a strictly local body, rather than both local and universal, has powerful implications for the future of Southern Baptist connectionalism and cooperation. On the other hand, Baptist successionism, one of the initial and most emotional tenets of Landmarkism, is all but dead in the wake of the controversy. Moderates had, along with Whitsitt and the majority of latter-day scholars, abandoned any trace of it years ago. But the conservative thrust has been based upon evangelical ties that looked to common views of Scripture as the true basis for Christian cooperation. This may have dealt the real death blow to that aspect of Landmarkism. While moderates complained that the Landmark tenets of strict biblicism, dispensational pre-millenialism, and its tendency to divisiveness were incarnate in the conservative resurgence, its theological alliances in such matters as the Chicago Statement on Inerrancy is antithetical to classical Landmarkism.

On the other side, centralization tendencies of the Convention under conservative control seem to cut across the basic Landmark tenet of the primacy of the local church. Actions of local churches related to such moral issues as abortion and homosexuality and the broader issue of women's ordination became Convention prerogatives under the conservatives. As previously noted, President Clinton's pastor, Rex Horne, claimed the challenge to the messengers from his church threatened local church's autonomy.

The fault line related to the local church and the larger church has always tempered any form of Baptist connectionalism and cooperation. It has constrained alike Landmarkers, fundamentalists, liberals, conservatives, and moderates throughout Southern Baptist history.

By the 1990s, moderate and conservative churches were switching places in their emphasis on local church autonomy. The tendency for this fault line to appear church by church, however, operates against the forces that would fashion major splits.

Scholarly and Populist

While Southern Baptist leadership was traditionally in the hands of the educated "gentry" of the South, it has been continually challenged by a populist tradition that has often seemed anti-intellectual and anti-institutional. Historians, led by Walter Shurden, have recently looked at Southern Baptist history in terms of a series of traditions. One of these, the Sandy

Creek tradition, stands in contrast to another, called the Charleston tradition, in a way that illustrates the fault line analyzed here.

The Sandy Creek tradition represented awakening-fired growth led by self-taught and largely uneducated ministers. The Charleston tradition represented reformation-projected and tradition-tempered growth that valued and featured intellect and education. Emotional experience more nearly characterized the first, while rational understanding dominated the latter, though both constituted Christian experience.

When the Southern Baptist Convention was formed in 1845, leadership went largely to the Charleston tradition, but it was those larger numbers in the Sandy Creek tradition who led the explosive growth to the West and Southwest.

The Landmark controversy functioned along this fault line, as did the fundamentalist-modernist controversies of the 1920s. Of note is the fact that though the less educated tradition often held the educated tradition in contempt, they paid great deference to those individuals within their ranks who were educated and tended to give them an enthusiastic and noncritical following. This has certainly been true to the degree that the most recent controversies in Southern Baptist life have reflected this old fault line in the Southern Baptist foundation.

Another irony inherent in this fault line is the tendency for both sides to develop or promote educational institutions. In Southern Baptists' most recent struggles, conservatives initially grouped around Luther Rice Seminary in Florida, Criswell Bible Institute in Dallas, and Mid-America Seminary in Memphis. When moderates were displaced from leadership in the Convention, some supporting the Alliance immediately organized the Richmond Seminary and more recently Baylor University began the George W. Truett Seminary.

However, indicative of the prevalence of this fault line in SBC affairs, consider how often state Baptist convention fights have occurred around one of its colleges. Early leaders in the conservative resurgence cut their teeth on controversy in battles in Missouri over William Jewell College and in North Carolina over Wake Forest University. Recent battles between conservatives and moderates in Texas and South Carolina were fought over Baylor University and Furman University.

Considering these last two aspects of this fault line in the Southern Baptist foundation, it must be recognized that both sides of the line now value education. But one side wants education to be anchored and doctrinally focused while the other favors an educational process that is liberal (in the traditional liberal arts sense, not in a doctrinal sense) and inquiring.

History says this line is emotionally divisive, but history also says that time tends to level the differences.

Gender Roles and Gender Equality

While tensions between the sexes might also be termed a fault line in humanity, Southern Baptists were reflecting such age-old tensions in a number of areas as they neared their century-and-a-half mark.

As the foregoing chapters have shown, the expected roles of males and females in Baptist life have undergone steady change and continuing resistance since the Convention was organized by its churches' white male members in 1845. The denial of missionary appointment to unmarried women in its initial years, the change of its constitution to deny women messenger status in 1885, the prohibition of women on its Convention platform for many years, opposition to women's ordination, and especially to national feminist initiatives have clearly marked this age-old fault line among Southern Baptists.

Women's embrace of the missionary task and the success of Woman's Missionary Union began major changes in the last half of the nineteenth century and especially during the mid-twentieth century. Riding the tides of woman's suffrage and economic viability, Baptist women took on new roles in addition to the traditional domestic ones. The appointment of women to missionary and chaplaincy roles, the admission of women and the increase of their numbers in seminaries, the increasing number of women ordained either as deacons or as ministers, the growth of the number of women in church staff positions as well as Convention board and committee positions indicate that much has changed and continues to change.

The fault line found its way early on into the conservative-moderate controversy that broke in 1979 in both rhetoric and resolution. It became more pronounced in early Home Mission Board actions to defund ordained women and later Foreign Mission Board actions denying appointment to an ordained couple. Southern Baptists' Women in Ministry found early support among moderate leaders in the Alliance and later in the Cooperative Baptist Fellowship, whose second moderator was Texas homemaker, Patricia Ayres. Ayres, whose husband was an Episcopal educator, was baptized into First Baptist Church, San Antonio, and became a Christian Life Commission activist before it came under conservative control.

The fault line took a new direction in tensions that developed between the conservative leadership that emerged victorious in 1990 in the SBC and its 105-year-old auxiliary, Woman's Missionary Union, when the latter asserted its independence with an expansive new vision in early 1993 that included "all" Southern Baptists. Pressures from the new SBC leadership to force the organization to declare its singular devotion to Convention programs were strong in the spring of 1993.

Exploiting this tension for all its worth was clearly a strategy of dispossessed moderates. The election of Ayres as its second moderator was followed by the election of Carolyn Crumpler, former WMU head, to be its fourth. The proportional appointment of women in all areas delineated what moderate leadership not only held was right, but what they sensed was a weakness over the long run in the conservative position.

On the other hand, prevailing methods of interpreting Scripture among conservatives continued to press the issue back toward pre-modern positions. The convictions of an Oklahoma pastor landed in the middle of the issue in late 1992 and early 1993. When Wayne Keely, pastor of Faith Baptist Church in Claremore, Oklahoma, threatened, on the grounds of 1 Timothy 2:11–13, to challenge a scheduled woman speaker before an Oklahoma evangelism conference; the conference leader canceled her engagement. The fact that the woman, Ann Lotz, was the daughter of famed evangelist Billy Graham added to its newsworthiness. Keely thought that the biblical order precluded women ever speaking in church functions to men except under the authority of their husbands. He pointed out, "A generation ago, any denominational employee who would dare to have a woman on the program to preach to men would have been dismissed from that position."[26]

Not all of the new conservative leaders felt as strongly committed to such a literal view of such passages, but no voice emerged from their ranks to champion a less literal one. Moderates claimed that the same hermeneutical approach had led early Southern Baptists to defend slavery. Yet conservative leaders did continue to place women on boards and committees, and indeed, received some of their strongest support from women. Despite this, the differences among Southern Baptists between male and female and conservative and moderate models of womanhood were significant and constituted a clearcut fault line in 1994.

Southern and Southwestern

Ever since the post-Civil War expansion of Southern Baptists to the Southwest and especially since B. H. Carroll's development of Southwestern Seminary to challenge Southern's monopoly, there has been a fault line along the two traditions that emerged.

Some old-line Southern Baptists were convinced that B. H. Carroll's goal was a new convention built around Southwestern Seminary, as the original had gathered around Southern Seminary.[27] In part, this reflected two of the previously discussed fault lines, the local church/larger church line that took its origins from Landmarkism and the scholar/populist fault line. In Southern eyes, the Southwestern image was often relegated to the Landmark-influenced, populist side.

That a Southwestern Convention did not happen might be attributed to the statesmanship of leaders like M. E. Dodd and George W. Truett. Or it might be seen as a by-product of J. Frank Norris's brand of fundamentalism, which galvanized both sides to ward off this demanding iconoclast. Its divisive potential was certainly weakened by Southern Seminary president John Sampey's generosity during the Great Depression when he offered part of its Cooperative Program allocation to a critically strapped Southwestern.

It is doubtful that this fault line is a strong factor in the immediately unfolding future, however, as an analysis of recent Convention messengers and recent Cooperative Fellowship participants shows no geographical center, despite former Fellowship chairman John Hewett's assertion that "we still have trouble with that river."

Further weakening the fault line is the fact that the Alliance of Baptists, which definitely draws its strength from the Southern side of these traditions, is supporting the rival Richmond Seminary, while Baylor University is challenging Southwestern with the George Truett Seminary. That the Richmond Seminary supporters propose to be the heir to the Southern Seminary tradition was evident in an advertisement in behalf of the Richmond seminary in *Baptists Today* in the fall of 1992. The Truett Seminary backers, on the other hand, deny competition with Southwestern, but they are bound to be aware of the irony of once again establishing a seminary at Baylor and First Baptist Church, Waco, in light of the circumstances of B. H. Carroll's founding of Southwestern.

Orthodoxy and Progressivism

The previous fault lines do not adequately explain the conflict Southern Baptists have experienced over cultural and moral agendas. In the book *Culture Wars: The Struggle to Define America,* the University of Virginia's James Davison Hunter identifies radically different concepts of moral authority: "By moral authority I mean the basis by which people determine whether something is good or bad, right or wrong, acceptable or unacceptable." He says, "The cleavages at the heart of the contemporary culture war are created by what I would call the impulse toward orthodoxy and the impulse toward progressivism."[28] While nearly any group gathered for whatever reason will feature such a fault line, it is clearly discernible in Southern Baptists' foundation.

Orthodox Southern Baptists (in the sense of this discussion) tend to want traditional interpretations of morality to prevail, as well as traditional mores. Orthodox Baptists tend to oppose abortion rights, homosexual rights, pluralism, and leadership roles for women. They also support law and order, legislatively enforced morality, and Judeo-Christian traditions.

Progressives tend to support a woman's choice on abortion, the rights of those who follow alternate lifestyles even when they are judged to be wrong, strict church-state separation, and women's roles in the market place and in church leadership. They focus on the rights of minorities and want an accountable and tempered force of law. This is a clear fault line in Southern Baptist life.

For years the Christian Life Commission ministered to the more progressive elements and kept them within the fold of Southern Baptist ranks. Since the conservative victory, the Christian Life Commission has recentered its activities in orthodox expectation. Not surprisingly, the progressive element has felt censured and unwanted and has sought solace in the ranks of the Alliance and other moderate initiatives.

This fault line has the potential to further divide the Convention under whoever might be in control.

Fundamentalist and Evangelical

Once a fault line that some people might see as the essence of Southern Baptist friction might also be seen as a threat to the remarkably tight coalition that began to dominate the Convention after 1979. This line runs between those who perpetuated the theological and ecclesiastical spirit of

1920s-style fundamentalism and those who more comfortably identify with the evangelical movement that emerged after World War II. While the earlier reaction to modernity flourished after the war in countless centers, such as Bob Jones University and Jerry Falwell's Thomas Road Baptist Church empire, an aggressive and highly literate conservative theology was championed by leaders like Carl F. H. Henry, former editor of *Christianity Today*. Finding strong support from such educational centers as Wheaton College and Fuller Theological Seminary, evangelical thought has strongly influenced Campus Crusade, the Navigators, and Intervarsity Christian Fellowship.

One of its spokesmen, Donald G. Bloesch, author of *Theology of Word and Spirit*, defines evangelical as focusing on the gospel. He says that because of this, evangelicalism entails a respect and reverence for Scripture. But Bloesch takes issue with those fundamentalists who tie the "credibility of the gospel to strict biblical literalism, which can end in scientific creationism, dispensationalism, and other 'isms' that he feels can actually distort the message of the Gospel."[29]

Bloesch says a parallel tendency is to tie the evangelical faith to cultural ideologies, producing a cultural captivity. When dominated by this approach, Bloesch says the evangelical movement finds itself "in political bondage to Americanism, social or economic bondage to free enterprise capitalism, and epistemological bondage to rationalism."[30]

Given the fact that many of Southern Baptists' newly dominant conservatives believe in scientific creationism, dispensationalism, Americanism, capitalism, and rationalism, evangelicals who oppose such ties with old fundamentalism may find themselves on the outside. Yet, it is clear that the intellectual leaders of the conservative resurgence like to identify with postwar evangelicalism and distance themselves from 1920–30s-style fundamentalism. If the expectations of the rank and file force these conservative scholars to further define themselves along some of the more controversial issues, it could cause conservative leadership internal tension of a kind they have not yet had to confront.

Pastor-led and Democratic Church Polity

A clear-cut fault line in Southern Baptist churches throughout the long controversy has been the conflict between those who uphold a democratic style of church governance and those who feel pastors and elders are given authority by God and the congregation is to follow loyally. This fault line was clearly behind the resolution in the 1988 SBC meeting in San Antonio that questioned traditional applications of the concept of the priesthood of the believer in favor of strong pastoral leadership.[31]

Conservative pastors more and more claim that pastoral authority is biblically mandated and that God will bless those churches that recognize it. They point to the successes of the megachurches where strong leaders exercising firm authority are the rule with few, if any, exceptions.

On the other hand, seminary teachers and moderate theorists of pastoral leadership have stressed servant models of leadership based upon the example of Jesus whom they say rejected king, chief, and warrior roles for the suffering servant concept of the prophet Isaiah. Such teachers have stressed the historic Baptist principle of congregational authority. They confess, however, that such leadership styles often fail to generate large followings and that many Christians prefer strong leadership.

Despite such teaching, many young pastors seeking models to emulate find the pragmatic fact of success hard to ignore. Church members, longing for successful and prosperous fellowships, also find it hard to ignore. Hardest of all to ignore may be the fact that in 1992 the average Southern Baptist church had only 168 resident members, and with only five baptisms and six other kinds of additions, was losing ground.[32]

The fault line clearly exists, but its role in Southern Baptists' future seem embedded in cultural turns and psychological needs as the Convention nears its sesquicentennial. The reality that leadership is given and not taken, which means that the people in any given fellowship still hold the ultimate vote, may be a larger factor than the fault line itself.

Fault-line Influence

While the foregoing list does not exhaust tension points and lines of difference in Southern Baptist life, it does include the most prominent historically and the most obvious in the period leading up to the sesquicentennial. Others could arise on the heels of internal or external forces yet to appear even as cultural changes and scientific theory surfaced some of the fault lines delineated above.

The more immediate question is how these fault-lines might effect Southern Baptists' short-and long-term future. Certain speculation about the future of individual fault lines has already been mentioned, but their collective futures may be even more relevant.

One possibility is that they will not exert a collective influence but will expand and contract along individual tracks as they have in the past.

Another, more potent possibility, however, is that the present polarities in Southern Baptist life will find themselves on opposite sides of enough of these fault lines for the aggregate to constitute a basis for a bill of divorcement. Collectively, they might force the separation currently resisted by significant groups within each polarity.

A third possibility is that events will emerge that reduce the individual and collective tensions of most of these lines and Baptists, conservative and moderate, will find anew more cohesiveness in their common history than they find diviseness in their current differences. For instance, leadership might emerge in the ranks of the dominant convinced that a more inclusive policy is all that can sustain the progress of recent decades and that non-compromising grounds can be found to accomplish that. Needless to say, it would have to be matched by similar leadership among the dissenting groups.

This third possibility could also be triggered by some overriding common threat that by its very nature would mitigate the issues that divide at any given time. One such threat could be an overly controlling state that threatened cherished Baptist freedoms. While conservatives may include a few theocracy advocates within their ranks, they would not offset Baptist reaction to threats to religious freedom and a fundamental separation of church and state. Another such overriding threat might come from an increasingly aggressive secularism hostile to all religion, but particulary so to free-church traditions. Communism constituted such a threat in the old Soviet hegemony, though it was wedded to state power.

Forecasting the progress of fault lines in Southern Baptists' future is not the task at hand, however. Understanding the range of their possible influence on Southern Baptists' unique confessionalism, connectionalism, and cooperation is.

The Freedom Factor

At this point, Southern Baptists' future will more likely rest on what could be called the freedom factor. The title of a book by R. Scott Walker, formerly pastor of the First Baptist Church in Charleston, who in 1993 traded that historic charge for one at the First Baptist Church of Waco where B. H. Carroll once led, looks to the personal freedoms Baptist fought hard to enjoy.[33]

Their passion for freedom is more Baptist than even dissent—even when they are tempted to deny it for others. In 1993, moderate historian Walter B. Shurden would define the essence of being Baptist in term of four freedoms: Bible freedom, soul freedom, church freedom, and religious freedom.[34] Whether one embraces or rejects Calvinistic determinism, the assertion of freedom endemic to the Christian experience will be a factor in any conceivable future.

The freedom factor leaves opportunity for developments and directions not envisioned. The lesson inherent in the sudden collapse of the Soviet Union and the previously viewed monolithic world of Communism is still being pondered, but one principle is certainly that in human affairs sudden turns and unanticipated novelty cannot be ruled out.

For people of faith, the question of predestined events versus freedom and choice, even when that introduces danger and chaos, has a knee-jerk bias for freedom. Of course, there is a negative side to freedom, and that is that it includes the freedom to do genuine harm to one's best self, one's most cherished distinctives.

In the fall of 1991, Southwestern Seminary's distinguished professor of theology, James Leo Garrett, suggested that some of Baptists' key distinctives were in danger of "serious attrition, if not total extinction." In a chapel message that was later published in abbreviated form in the *Baptist Standard*, Garrett, playing on the biological term endangered species, pointed to believer's baptism by immersion, religious freedom for all humans, and cooperative missions as the distinctives at risk.[35]

Garrett felt the first was threatened by the tendency to baptize extremely young children and the tendency for some churches to accept nonimmersion baptisms, the second by "majoritarian" Baptists tendency to disparage the principle of universal religious freedom, and the third by tendencies to "disenfranchise and exclude."

This particular battle in Baptist life began, however, with the feeling on the part of conservatives that a high view of the Bible was being undermined in moderate-dominated Baptist institutions, and that was the distinctive they were fighting to preserve.

Moderates have felt that those leading the conservative cause were sacrificing the priesthood of the believer, the right of individual believers to interpret Scriptures for themselves, and a confessional fellowship in favor of a creedal one. Former Midwestern Seminary professor, Ralph Elliott, one part of the rancorous Genesis controversy of the early 1960s, suggests that freedom itself is gone. "There is still talk of freedom and religious liberty, but it has been a long time since those were allowed to be actualized in practice in Southern Baptist Life."[36] In other words, each side thought Baptist distinctives were in danger and, indeed, the case could be made that each side was in some degree culpable.

From the outside looking in, this internal conflict over previously perceived distinctives caused an editor of *The Christian Century* to ask whether Southern Baptists were Bible believers or inerrancy dogmatists, whether diligent missionaries or arrogant proselyters, whether rigid moralists or defender of values, whether defenders of church-state separation or anti-Roman Catholic.[37]

But the freedom factor for Baptists throughout history, while involving danger and potential chaos, has far more often worked to bring forth their best and their unique contribution to the larger Christian body. It has been a cherished principle inherent in all of their confessions, connections, and cooperation.

Clearly, the Baptist bias for freedom will exert pressures on all fault lines crisscrossing the foundation in place at the time of the Southern Baptist Convention's sesquicentennial. It will undoubtedly interact with the heritage of the foundational dimensions and the tensions of the historic fault lines to shape their future.

In light of the genuine piety of most Southern Baptists, it must be noted that all factions believe that God was in their founding and that He permissively or purposefully holds their future in His hands and that they have been raised up and sustained for a significant role.

Evolving Agenda

It was obvious that as they approached their sesquicentennial, Southern Baptists were preoccupied with a different agenda from previous years and, indeed, previous conflicts.

First was the tendency to assume associational traditions of doctrinal judgment for the Convention itself and, in the process, challenge the autonomous role of local churches that had been a Baptist hallmark and had been greatly reinforced by the Landmark legacy. This tendency surfaced over the role of women in ministry and the response of churches to homosexuality.

Second was an obvious challenge to the convention method itself, which, while it helped the conservative resurgence by elevating issues over cooperation, made it difficult to reinforce once control was gained. That the disenfranchised turned to society-style reactions raised further questions as to whether the "rope of sand," as the Cooperative Program was sometimes called, could be maintained in the new environment where issues, sometimes single issues, dominate. That the convention method predated the Cooperative Program was often noted, but did little to assuage the notion that the latter was the essence of the convention method.

Third, a new form of ecumenism was emerging in Baptist ranks aided and abetted by both sides of the controversy. The "only true church" fiction of the Landmark movement died in the process, but its local church autonomy also took a back seat to a "like-belief fellowship," focused on confessional factors on one side and on the larger Christian body on the other. The Foreign Mission Board's Great Commission networking constituted an unprecedented inter-church cooperation involving Southern Baptists. A larger non-Baptist coalition of inerrantists who were a part of the evangelical movement and conservative political causes had been a major ally to the Conservative Resurgence. An old-line Protestant expression of the body of Christ was often the refuge of disenfranchised moderates. Some scholars felt it was all a part of a larger phenomena called post-denominationalism.

Faith and Hope

Despite the drama and questions raised by its multifaceted history, the Southern Baptist Convention stands as the impressive result of 150 years of missions, evangelism, ministry, and church building. Its thirty-eight thousand-plus churches and its 15 million-plus members are significant enough, but when combined with its publishing empire, its nation-spanning educational institutions, its globe-circling missionary enterprise, its growing communications capabilities, its national clout, its growing ethnic embrace, and its viability despite tension and turmoil, the picture is impressive. That its problems and the possibility they could induce a major decline at best or a momentum-and-institution-destroying split at worst were still to be resolved was obvious from all that had gone before.

But a remarkable center that was more spiritual than numerical was still intact at its sesquicentennial. Most of its constituents still felt that the most important thing was the work of God in Christ reconciling the world unto Himself, rather than any human organization or theology or philosophy. Few of either the dominant or the disaffected were willing to deny God's purposes in history and the potential of their common heritage to evolve into a still unknown but yet to be trusted future.

The Southern Baptist Convention, flaws and trials notwithstanding, remains an evolving historical entity. A strong cohesiveness emerging from its history is still in place. Its future rests on the reality that it is composed, both historically and contemporarily, of a people who, for all their biases and weaknesses, are a people of faith and hope.

Appendix 1

Charter

An ACT to incorporate the Southern Baptist Convention.

Be it enacted by the Senate and House of Representatives of the State of Georgia, in General Assembly met, and it is hereby enacted by the authority of the same. That from and after the passing of this act, That William B. Johnson, Wilson Lumpkin, James B. Taylor, A. Docrey, R. B. C. Howell and others, their associates and successors, be and they are hereby incorporated and made a body politic by the name and style of the Southern Baptist Convention, with authority to receive, hold, possess, retain, and dispose of property, either real or personal, to sue and to be sued, and to make all bylaws, rules and regulations necessary to the transaction of their business, not inconsistent with the laws of this State or of the United States—said corporation being created for the purpose of eliciting, combining, and directing the energies of the Baptist denomination of Christians, for the propagation of the gospel, any law, usage, or custom to the contrary notwithstanding.

Approved, December 27th, 1845
(1845 Georgia Laws, Page 130, Paragraph 3)

Constitution

The messengers from missionary societies, churches, and other religious bodies of the Baptist denomination in various parts of the United States met in Augusta, Georgia, May 8, 1845, for the purpose of carrying into effect the benevolent intention of our constituents by organizing a plan for eliciting, combining, and directing the energies of the denomination for the propagation of the gospel and adopted rules and fundamental principles which, as amended from time to time, are as follows:

Article I. The Name: The name of this body is the "Southern Baptist Convention."

Article II. Purpose: It is the purpose of the Convention to provide a general organization for Baptists in the United States and its territories for the promotion of Christian missions at home and abroad and any other objects such as Christian education, benevolent enterprises, and social services which it may deem proper and advisable for the furtherance of the Kingdom of God.

Article III. Membership: The Convention shall consist of messengers who are members of missionary Baptist churches cooperating with the Convention as follows:

1. One (1) messenger from each church which is in friendly cooperation with this Convention and sympathetic with its purposes and work. Among churches not in cooperation with the Convention are churches which act to affirm, approve, or condone homosexual behavior. And, (2) has during the fiscal year preceding been a bona fide contributor to the Convention's work.

2. One (1) additional messenger from each such church for every two hundred and fifty (250) members; or for each $250.00 paid to the work of the Convention during the fiscal year preceding the annual meeting.

3. The messengers shall be appointed and certified by the churches to the Convention, but no church may appoint more than ten (10).

4. Each messenger shall be a member of the church by which he is appointed.

Article IV. Authority: While independent and sovereign in its own sphere, the Convention does not claim and will never attempt to exercise any authority over any other Baptist body, whether church, auxiliary organizations, associations, or convention.

Article V. Officers:

1. The officers of the Convention shall be a president, a first and a second vice-president, a recording secretary, a registration secretary, and treasurer.

2. The officers shall be elected annually and shall hold office until their successors are elected and qualified. The term of office for the president is limited to two (2) years, and a president shall not be eligible for reelection until as much as one (1) year has elapsed from the time a successor is named. The first vice-president shall be voted upon and elected after the election of the president has taken place;

and the second vice-president shall be voted upon and elected after the election of the first vice-president has taken place.

3. The president shall be a member of the several boards and of the Executive Committee.

4. The treasurer of the Executive Committee shall be the treasurer of the Convention.

5. In case of death or disability of the president, the vice-presidents shall automatically succeed to the office of president in the order of their election.

Article VI. The Boards, Institutions, and Commissions—Their Constitution and Powers:

1. The general boards of the Convention shall be composed as follows, unless otherwise provided in their charters.

    (1) Twelve (12) members chosen from the city or vicinity of the state in which the board is located, but not more than three (3) local members elected from the same church.

    (2) One (1) member chosen from each cooperating state; and one (1) additional member from each state having two hundred and fifty thousand (250,000) members, and another additional member for each additional two hundred and fifty thousand (250,000) members in such state.

    (3) The members shall be divided into four (4) groups as nearly equal as possible, and one (1) group shall be elected each year to serve four (4) years. Board members having served two (2) full terms of four (4) years shall not be eligible for reelection until as much as one (1) year has elapsed. This shall also apply to the Executive Committee.

2. The trustees of institutions and commissioners shall be composed as follows:

    (1) The trustees or commissioners shall be elected in keeping with the requirements of the charter of the agency as printed in the 1948 Book of Reports or subsequently amended with the prior approval of the Convention.

(2) If the composition of the trustees or commissioners is not determined by charter requirements, the body of trustees or commissioners shall be composed of one (1) member chosen from each cooperating state and eight (8) local members from the city or vicinity in which the agency is located, but not more than two (2) local members shall be chosen from the same church.

(3) Unless it is contrary to the charter requirements of the agency, the trustees or commissioners shall be divided into four (4) groups as nearly equal as possible and one (1) group shall be elected each year to serve four (4) years. Members having served two (2) full terms of four (4) years shall not be eligible for reelection until as much as one (1) year has elapsed after one has served two (2) full terms.

(4) Regardless of charter provisions, no trustee or commissioner shall be eligible for reelection until as much as one (1) year has elapsed after the trustee or commissioner has served two (2) full terms.

3. Terms of Service: No trustee of a board, institution, or commission, or a member of the Executive Committee shall be eligible to serve for more than two consecutive terms. A trustee or member of the Executive Committee who has served more than half a term shall be considered to have served a full term.

4. The governing groups of the agencies may elect executive, administrative, finance, investment, and other committees if desired.

5. Each agency shall elect a president, a recording secretary, a treasurer, and such other officers as may be required. The president may be named as treasurer.

6. The compensation of its officers and employees shall be fixed by each agency, but no salaried employee or officer shall be a member of the directors of the agency.

7. Each agency is authorized to adopt its own bylaws.

8. Fifty percent of the members of the governing group shall constitute a quorum of the agency directors for transaction of any business.

Article VII. Duties of Officers of Boards, Institutions, and Commissions:
All officers shall be subject to the control and direction of their directors in matters pertaining to the work and obligations of the board, institution, or commission. They shall perform such duties as commonly appertain to such officers.

1. The executive head of each board, institution, and commission shall be responsible to the directors for all the work of the agency and shall carry on the work as the directors may direct.

2. The recording secretary of each agency shall keep a record of all meetings of directors, if not otherwise provided for, and shall keep the records in fireproof safes, vaults, or files.

3. The treasurer of each agency shall follow approved methods of accounting, keep the books, receipt for all monies and securities, deposit all funds with a depository or depositories approved by the directors, and render full statements as required to the directors or to the Convention. The treasurer shall not pay out money except as the directors may order and direct.

Article VIII. Church Membership: Officers of the Convention, all officers and members of all boards, trustees of institutions, commissioners, and all missionaries of the Convention appointed by its boards shall be members of Baptist churches cooperating with this Convention.

Article IX. Missionaries' Qualifications: All missionaries appointed by the Convention's boards must, previous to their appointment, furnish evidence of piety, zeal for the Master's kingdom, conviction of truth as held by Baptists, and talents for missionary service.

Article X. Distribution of Funds: The Convention shall have the right to designate only undesignated funds, the right of contributors to the work of the Convention to designate the objects to which their contributions shall be applied being fully recognized.

Article XI. Meetings:

1. The Convention shall hold its meetings annually at such time and place as it may choose.

2. The president may call special meetings with the concurrence of the other officers of the Convention and of the Executive Committee.

3. The Executive Committee may change the time and place of meeting if the entertaining city withdraws its invitation or is unable to fulfill its commitments.

4. The Convention officers, the Executive Committee, and the executive heads of the Convention's boards and institutions acting in a body may, in case of grave emergency, cancel a regular meeting or change the place of the meeting.

Article XII. As to Conflict with State Laws: All incorporated agencies of the Convention shall be required to comply with the letter and spirit of this Constitution, the Bylaws, and the Business and Financial Plan insofar as they are not in conflict with the statute law of the state in which an agency is incorporated, and nothing herein contained shall be construed to require any such incorporated agency to act and carry on its affairs in conflict with the law of the state of its incorporation. In case any action of any agency of the Convention is found to be a violation of the law of the state of its incorporation, said action shall be reported by that agency to the Convention for appropriate action.

Article XIII. Definition of a State: The District of Columbia shall be regarded as a state for the purpose of this Constitution, the Bylaws, and all actions of the Convention.

Article XIV. Amendments: Any alterations may be made in these Articles by a vote of two-thirds of the members present when the vote is taken without regard to total enrollment at any annual meeting of the Convention, provided (1) that no amendment may be considered after the second day of the Convention and (2) that an amendment shall be so approved by two (2) successive annual sessions of the Convention.

Appendix 2

Annual Meetings

Date	Meeting Place	Reg.	President
1845	Augusta, Georgia	236	W. B. Johnson, S.C.
1846	Richmond, Virginia	162	W. B. Johnson, S.C.
1849	Charleston, South Carolina	103	W. B. Johnson, S.C.
1851	Nashville, Tennessee	124	R. B. C. Howell, Va.
1853	Baltimore, Maryland	154	R. B. C. Howell, Va.
1855	Montgomery, Alabama	235	R. B. C. Howell, Va.
1857	Louisville, Kentucky	184	R. B. C. Howell, Va.
1859	Richmond, Virginia	580	Richard Fuller, Md.
1861	Savannah, Georgia	177	Richard Fuller, Md.
1863	Augusta, Georgia	181	P. H. Mell, Ga.
1866	Russellville, Kentucky	244	P. H. Mell, Ga.
1867	Memphis, Tennessee	250	P. H. Mell, Ga.
1868	Baltimore, Maryland	327	P. H. Mell, Ga.
1869	Macon, Georgia	266	P. H. Mell, Ga.
1870	Louisville, Kentucky	399	P. H. Mell, Ga.
1871	St. Louis, Missouri	360	P. H. Mell, Ga.
1872	Raleigh, North Carolina	304	James P. Boyce, S.C.
1873	Mobile, Alabama	259	James P. Boyce, S.C.
1874	Jefferson, Texas	222	James P. Boyce, Ky.
1875	Charleston, South Carolina	302	James P. Boyce, Ky.
1876	Richmond, Virginia	289	James P. Boyce, Ky.
1877	New Orleans, Louisiana	164	James P. Boyce, Ky.
1878	Nashville, Tennessee	253	James P. Boyce, Ky.
1879	Atlanta, Georgia	313	James P. Boyce, Ky.
1880	Lexington, Kentucky	360	P. H. Mell, Ga.

1881	Columbus, Mississippi	270	P. H. Mell, Ga.
1882	Greenville, South Carolina	335	P. H. Mell, Ga.
1883	Waco, Texas	612	P. H. Mell, Ga.
1884	Baltimore, Maryland	637	P. H. Mell, Ga.
1885	Augusta, Georgia	528	P. H. Mell, Ga.
1886	Montgomery, Alabama	488	P. H. Mell, Ga.
1887	Louisville, Kentucky	689	P. H. Mell, Ga.
1888	Richmond, Virginia	835	James P. Boyce, Ky.
1889	Memphis, Tennessee	706	Jonathan Haralson, Ala.
1890	Fort Worth, Texas	801	Jonathan Haralson, Ala.
1891	Birmingham, Alabama	915	Jonathan Haralson, Ala.
1892	Atlanta, Georgia	978	Jonathan Haralson, Ala.
1893	Nashville, Tennessee	818	Jonathan Haralson, Ala.
1894	Dallas, Texas	772	Jonathan Haralson, Ala.
1895	Washington, D.C.	870	Jonathan Haralson, Ala.
1896	Chattanooga, Tennessee	819	Jonathan Haralson, Ala.
1897	Wilmington, North Carolina	724	Jonathan Haralson, Ala.
1898	Norfolk, Virginia	857	Jonathan Haralson, Ala.
1899	Louisville, Kentucky	869	W. J. Northen, Ga.
1900	Hot Springs, Arkansas	646	W. J. Northen, Ga.
1901	New Orleans, Louisiana	787	W. J. Northen, Ga.
1902	Asheville, North Carolina	1093	James P. Eagle, Ark.
1903	Savannah, Georgia	1136	James P. Eagle, Ark.
1904	Nashville, Tennessee	1095	James P. Eagle, Ark.
1905	Kansas City, Missouri	816	E. W. Stephens, Mo.
1906	Chattanooga, Tennessee	1451	E. W. Stephens, Mo.
1907	Richmond, Virginia	1411	E. W. Stephens, Mo.
1908	Hot Springs, Arkansas	1258	Joshua Levering, Md.
1909	Louisville, Kentucky	1547	Joshua Levering, Md.
1910	Baltimore, Maryland	1641	Joshua Levering, Md.
1911	Jacksonville, Florida	1558	Edwin C. Dargan, Ga.

1912	Oklahoma City, Oklahoma	1228	Edwin C. Dargan, Ga.
1913	Saint Louis, Missouri	1403	Edwin C. Dargan, Ga.
1914	Nashville, Tennessee	1930	Lansing Burrows, Ga.
1915	Houston, Texas	1408	Lansing Burrows, Ga.
1916	Asheville, North Carolina	2125	Lansing Burrows, Ga.
1917	New Orleans, Louisiana	1683	J. B. Gambrell, Tex.
1918	Hot Springs, Arkansas	2043	J. B. Gambrell, Tex.
1919	Atlanta, Georgia	4224	J. B. Gambrell, Tex.
1920	Washington, D.C.	8359	J. B. Gambrell, Tex.
1921	Chattanooga, Tennessee	5313	E. Y. Mullins, Ky.
1922	Jacksonville, Florida	4272	E. Y. Mullins, Ky.
1923	Kansas City, Missouri	4193	E. Y. Mullins, Ky.
1924	Atlanta, Georgia	5622	George W. McDaniel, Va.
1925	Memphis, Tennessee	5600	George W. McDaniel, Va.
1926	Houston, Texas	4268	George W. McDaniel, Va.
1927	Louisville, Kentucky	4424	George W. Truett, Tex.
1928	Chattanooga, Tennessee	3810	George W. Truett, Tex.
1929	Memphis, Tennessee	3999	George W. Truett, Tex.
1930	New Orleans, Louisiana	3342	W. J. McGlothlin, S.C.
1931	Birmingham, Alabama	3195	W. J. McGlothlin, S.C.
1932	St. Petersburg, Florida	2178	W. J. McGlothlin, S.C.
1933	Washington, D.C.	2765	F. F. Brown, Tenn.
1934	Fort Worth, Texas	4435	M. E. Dodd, La.
1935	Memphis, Tennessee	4268	M. E. Dodd, La.
1936	Saint Louis, Missouri	3702	John R. Sampey, Ky.
1937	New Orleans, Louisiana	4507	John R. Sampey, Ky.
1938	Richmond, Virginia	5785	John R. Sampey, Ky.
1939	Oklahoma City, Oklahoma	4598	L. R. Scarborough, Tex.
1940	Baltimore, Maryland	3776	L. R. Scarborough, Tex.
1941	Birmingham, Alabama	5884	W. W. Hamilton, La.
1942	San Antonio, Texas	4774	W. W. Hamilton, La.

1943			
1944	Atlanta, Georgia	4301	Pat M. Neff, Tex.
1945			
1946	Miami, Florida	7973	Pat M. Neff, Tex.
1947	St. Louis, Missouri	8508	Louie D. Newton, Ga.
1948	Memphis, Tennessee	9843	Louie D. Newton, Ga.
1949	Oklahoma City, Oklahoma	9393	Robert G. Lee, Tenn.
1950	Chicago, Illinois	8151	Robert G. Lee, Tenn.
1951	San Francisco, California	6493	Robert G. Lee, Tenn.
1952	Miami, Florida	10960	J. D. Grey, La.
1953	Houston, Texas	12976	J. D. Grey, La.
1954	St. Louis, Missouri	10962	J. W. Storer, Okla.
1955	Miami, Florida	10837	J. W. Storer, Okla.
1956	Kansas City, Missouri	12254	C. C. Warren, N.C.
1957	Chicago, Illinois	9109	C. C. Warren, N.C.
1958	Houston, Texas	11966	Brooks Hays, Ark.
1959	Louisville, Kentucky	12326	Brooks Hays, Ark.
1960	Miami Beach, Florida	13612	Ramsey Pollard, Tenn.
1961	St. Louis, Missouri	11140	Ramsey Pollard, Tenn.
1962	San Francisco, California	9396	Herschel H. Hobbs, Okla.
1963	Kansas City, Missouri	12971	Herschel H. Hobbs, Okla.
1964	Atlantic City, New Jersey	13136	K. Owen White, Tex.
1965	Dallas, Texas	16053	W. Wayne Dehoney, Tenn.
1966	Detroit, Michigan	10414	W. Wayne Dehoney, Tenn.
1967	Miami Beach, Florida	14794	H. Franklin Paschall, Tenn.
1968	Houston, Texas	13071	H. Franklin Paschall, Tenn.
1969	New Orleans, Louisiana	16678	W. A. Criswell, Tex.
1970	Denver, Colorado	13692	W. A. Criswell, Tex.
1971	St. Louis, Missouri	13716	Carl E. Bates, N.C.
1972	Philadelphia, Pennsylvania	13153	Carl E. Bates, N.C.
1973	Portland, Oregon	6638	Owen Cooper, Miss.

1974	Dallas, Texas	12927	Owen Cooper, Miss.
1975	Miami Beach, Florida	12485	Jaroy Weber, Tex.
1976	Norfolk, Virginia	14107	Jaroy Weber, Tex.
1977	Kansas City, Missouri	12189	James L. Sullivan, Tenn.
1978	Atlanta, Georgia	17833	Jimmy R. Allen, Tex.
1979	Houston, Tex.	12514	Jimmy R. Allen, Tex.
1980	St. Louis, Missouri	10537	Adrian P. Rogers, Tenn.
1981	Los Angeles, California	13529	Bailey E. Smith, Okla.
1982	New Orleans, Louisiana	20456	Bailey E. Smith, Okla.
1983	Pittsburgh, Pennsylvania	10603	James T. Draper, Tex.
1984	Kansas City, Missouri	13013	James T. Draper, Tex.
1985	Dallas, Texas	45519	Charles F. Stanley, Ga.
1986	Atlanta, Georgia	37603	Charles F. Stanley, Ga.
1987	St. Louis, Missouri	22438	Adrian P. Rogers, Tenn.
1988	San Antonio, Texas	29987	Adrian P. Rogers, Tenn.
1989	Las Vegas, Nevada	18085	Jerry Vines, Fl.
1990	New Orleans, Louisiana	31856	Jerry Vines, Fl.
1991	Atlanta, Georgia	23465	Morris H. Chapman, Tex.
1992	Indianapolis, Indiana	17956	Morris H. Chapman, Tex.
1993	Houston, Texas	17886	Edwin Young, Tex.
1994	Orlando, Florida	Approx. 21000	Edwin Young, Tex.
1995	Atlanta, Georgia		
1996	New Orleans, Louisiana		
1997	Dallas, Texas		
1999	Atlanta, Georgia		
2001	New Orleans, Louisiana		

Appendix 3

Agencies, Institutions, Commissions, and Auxiliaries

ENTITY	YEAR EST.
Foreign Mission Board	1845
Home Mission Board	1845
Southern Baptist Theological Seminary	1859
Woman's Missionary Union	1888
Baptist Sunday School Board	1891
Baptist World Alliance	1905
Southwestern Baptist Theological Seminary (started at Baylor University)	1908
American Baptist Seminary Commission	1913
Christian Life Commission	1913
Education Commission	1915
Executive Committee	1917
New Orleans Baptist Theological Seminary	1917
Southern Baptist Convention Executive Committee	1917
Annuity Board	1918
Brotherhood Commission (preceded by Layman's Missionary Movement)	1918
Baptist Hospital Commission (later discontinued)	1919
Commission on the American Baptist Theological Seminary	1924
Public Affairs Committee (later part of Baptist Joint Committee)	1936
Golden Gate Baptist Theological Seminary	1944
Radio and Television Commission	1946
Southern Baptist Foundation	1947
Historical Commission	1951
Seminary Extension	1951
Southeastern Baptist Theological Seminary	1951
Midwestern Baptist Theological Seminary	1957
Stewardship Commission	1960

Appendix 4

Cooperating State Conventions*

	State Convention	Est.	Churches	Assoc.	Membership
1.	South Carolina	1821	1,789	43	563,057
2.	Georgia	1822	3,076	93	959,720
3.	Alabama	1823	3,070	75	779,819
4.	Virginia	1823	1,529	43	463,963
5.	North Carolina	1830	3,557	79	935,423
6.	Missouri	1834	1,848	73	421,888
7.	Mississippi	1836	1,990	73	488,795
8.	Maryland-Delaware	1836	300	12	78,255
9.	Kentucky	1837	2,292	78	560,890
10.	Arkansas	1848	1,305	42	335,393
11.	Louisiana	1848	1,359	48	401,229
12.	Texas	1848	4,381	112	1,672,591
13.	Florida	1854	1,777	50	708,583
14.	Tennessee	1875	2,828	68	819,109
15.	District of Columbia	1877	66	1	21,194
16.	Oklahoma	1906	1,488	41	472,838
17.	Illinois	1907	938	35	167,102
18.	New Mexico	1912	269	15	67,976
19.	Arizona	1928	280	14	83,782
20.	California	1940	1,122	33	289,900
21.	Hawaii	1943	58	5	11,399
22.	Kansas-Nebraska	1945	262	12	57,232
22.	Alaska	1946	61	6	12,543
24.	Northwest	1948	332	18	51,311
25.	Ohio	1954	500	19	120,915

* Figures are from 1992.

State Convention	Est.	Churches	Assoc.	Membership
26. Colorado	1956	205	11	44,614
27. Michigan	1957	240	14	35,314
28. Indiana	1964	312	14	74,459
29. Utah-Idaho	1964	93	11	12,644
30. North Plains	1967			
31. New York	1969	211	10	20,370
32. West Virginia	1970	129	10	24,250
33. Pennsylvania/S. Jersey	1971	154	8	21,777
34. Nevada	1978	82	4	17,580
35. Minnesota-Wisconsin	1983	90	7	13,415
36. New England	1983	141	6	16,198
37. Wyoming	1984	66	8	8,627

Notes

Introduction

1. Lance Morrow, "A Cosmic Moment," in *Time* (Fall 1992), 9.
2. Jimmy Carter, as quoted in an Associated Press release in *Nashville Banner* (May 1992), 1.
3. Bill Moyers, "On Being a Baptist," in *Religion & Values in Public Life* (Spring 1993), 1.
4. Timothy George, "Conflict and Identity in the SBC," *Beyond the Impasse,* ed. by Robison B. James and David S. Dockery (Nashville: Broadman Press, 1992), 202.
5. Susan Harding, "Observing the Observers," in *Southern Baptists Observed* (Knoxville: University of Tennessee Press, 1993), 332.

Chapter 1

1. *Southern Baptist Convention Annual, 1845,* 7–11. An analysis can be found in William W. Barnes, *The Southern Baptist Convention 1845–1953* (Nashville: Broadman Press, 1954), 310–12.

2. H. Leon McBeth, *Women in Baptist Life* (Nashville: Broadman Press, 1979), 37ff.

3. William Henry Brackney, *The Baptists* (New York: Greenwood Press, 1988), 200. This author notes that when J. B. Jeter took the pastorate of First Baptist Church, Richmond, Va., there were 1,384 black members and 333 whites.

4. Richard Fuller and Francis Wayland, *Domestic Slavery Considered as a Scriptural Institution* (New York: Lewis Colby, 1845), 101–4. As cited in Robert A. Baker's *The Southern Baptist Convention and Its People 1607–1972* (Nashville: Broadman Press, 1974), 158.

5. Jeremiah Bell Jeter, *The Recollections of a Long Life* (New York: Arno Press, 1880), 234–35.

6. Joe M. King, *A History of South Carolina Baptists* (Columbia: the General Board of the South Carolina Convention, 1964), 13.

7. Baker, *The Southern Baptist Convention*, 33–34.

8. Ibid., 33.

9. Robert A. Baker and Paul J. Craven, Jr., *Adventure in Faith: The First 300 Years of First Baptist Church, Charleston, South Carolina* (Nashville: Broadman Press, 1982), 80, quoting from Basil Manly's "Mercy and Judgment," a discourse containing some fragments of the history of the Baptist church in Charleston.

10. H. Leon McBeth, *The Baptist Heritage: Four Centuries of Baptist Witness* (Nashville: Broadman Press, 1987), 206.

11. Walter H. Burgess, *John Smyth the Se-Baptist, Thomas Helwys, and the First Baptist Church in England* (London: James Clarke & Company, 1911), 350.

12. Leon McBeth, *A Sourcebook for Baptist Heritage* (Nashville: Broadman Press, 1990), 83, quoting from *Winthrop's Journal* (March 16, 1639).

13. McBeth, *Heritage*, 131.

14. Ibid., 132.

15. Robert G. Torbet, *A History of the Baptists* (Philadelphia: Judson Press, 1950), 220.

16. Ola Elizabeth Winslow, *Master Roger Williams* (New York: The Macmillan Company, 1957), 152.

17. McBeth, *Heritage*, 131, n. 19. Leon McBeth has come to believe immersion may have been practiced from the beginning by the new Baptist churches in America. How else would you explain the absence of transitional evidence? he argues. He also points to a document by Richard Coddington referring to Williams and the Providence church as having "dipped, head and heels."

18. Albert Henry Newman, *A History of the Baptist Churches in the United States* (Philadelphia: American Baptist Publication, 1915), 147–57.

19. Lynn E. May, Jr., "Clarke, John," in *Encyclopedia of Southern Baptists*, vol. 1, ed. by Norman Wade Cox (Nashville: Broadman Press, 1958), 293, quoting the *Rhode Island Charter*.

20. Isaac Backus, *A History of New England with Particular Reference to the Denomination of Christians Called Baptists* (Newton: Backus Historical Society, 1871), 400.

21. Ibid., 30.

22. William Bradford, *Of Plymouth Plantation 1620–1647* (New York: Alfred A. Knopf, 1959), 9.

23. James Robert Coggins, *John Smyth's Congregation* (Waterloo, Ontario: Herald Press, 1991), 34.

24. Burgess, *Smyth, Helwys, and FBC in England,* 208, quoting the Declaration of Faith issued by Helwys, Murton, and group after the split.

25. Ibid., 96.

26. Ibid., 127, quoting Smyth's *Differences,* ch. 6.

27. Ibid., 307, citing Murton's *Supplication.*

28. A.C. Underwood, *A History of English Baptists* (London: The Carey Kingsgate Press, 1956), 45.

29. Brackney, *The Baptists,* 4.

30. Torbet, *A History of the Baptists,* 64.

31. Lonnie D. Kliever, "General Baptist Origins: The Question of Anabaptist Influence," in *Mennonite Quarterly Review 36* (1962), 291–321. Kliever argues persuasively against significant influence.

32. Henry M. Dexter, *The True Story of John Smyth* (Boston: Lee and Shepard, 1818), 36.

33. Kenneth Ross Manley, "Origin of the Baptists: The Case for Development from Puritanism–Separatism," in *Baptist History and Heritage* (October 1987), 41.

34. McBeth, *Heritage,* 38.

35. Ibid., 47.

36. William R. Estep, "Biblical Authority in Baptist Confessions of Faith," in *Baptist History and Heritage* (October 1987), 9–10.

37. Don A. Sanford, *A Choosing People: The History of the Seventh Day Baptists* (Nashville: Broadman Press, 1992), 41.

38. Brackney, *The Baptists,* 7.

39. McBeth, *The Baptist Heritage,* 52–53.

40. David A. Benedict, *A General History of the Baptist Denomination in America and in Other Parts of the World,* vol. 1 (Boston: Lincoln & Edwards, 1813), 264. Also see *Baptist History and Heritage* (October 1977), 200.

41. Lynn E. May, "Hubmaier, Balthasar," in *Encyclopedia of Southern Baptists,* vol. 1, ed. by Norman Wade Cox (Nashville: Broadman Press, 1958), 658.

42. William R. Estep, "Anabaptists and the Rise of English Baptists," in *The Quarterly Review* (October-December 1968, January-March 1969).

43. Paige Patterson, "My Vision of the Twenty-First Century SBC," in *Review and Expositor,* 88 (1991), 43.

44. James Leo Garrett, "Restitution and Dissent Among Early English Baptists," in *Baptist History and Heritage* (April 1978), 200.

45. E. Butler Abington, *Perpetuity of Baptist Churches* (Eureka Springs, Ark.: Times-Echo Press), 1962, 7.

46. Brackney, *The Baptists,* 9.

47. "An Orthodox Creed, or A Protestant Confession of Faith, Being an Essay to Unite and Confirm All True Protestants in the Fundamental Articles of the Christian Religion, Against the Errors and Heresies of Rome" (London, 1679) as cited in William L. Lumpkin, *Baptist Confessions of Faith* (Valley Forge: Judson Press, 1969), 327.

48. Slayden A. Yarbrough, "The Origins of Baptist Associations Among the English Particular Baptists," in *Baptist History and Heritage* (April 1988), 15.

49. W. T. Whitely, *A History of British Baptists* (London: Charles Griffin & Company, 1923), 59.

50. Ibid., 129.

51. *On Forms of Baptist Connectionalism,* see 573–75.

52. Thomas Armitage, "Pennsylvania's Great Law," in *A History of the Baptists* (New York: Bryan, Taylor, & Company, 1887), 706.

53. Ibid., 707–08.

54. Anne Thomas Neil and Virginia Garrett Neely, *The New Has Come* (Washington, D.C.: Southern Baptist Alliance, 1989), 12.

55. Leah Townsend, *South Carolina Baptists 1670–1805* (Baltimore: Geneological Publishing Company, 1978), 18.

56. Torbet, *A History of the Baptists,* 258–61.

57. Albert H. Newman, *A Manual of Church History,* vol. 2 (Philadelphia: The American Baptist Publication Society, 1902), 539.

58. William H. Brackney, *Baptist Life and Thought: 1600–1980, A Source Book* (Valley Forge: Judson Press, 1983), 86.

59. Brackney, *Source Book,* 88.

60. Brackney, *Baptists,* xx.

61. McBeth, 186.

62. Brackney, *The Baptists,* 141.

63. King, *South Carolina Baptists,* 158.

64. Brackney, *Baptists,* 14, 279.

65. James D. Knowles, *Memoir of Mrs. Ann H. Judson* (Boston: Lincoln and Edmands, 1829), 63.

66. Hortense Woodson, "Johnson, William Bullein," in the *Encyclopedia of Southern Baptists,* vol. 1, ed. by Norman Wade Cox (Nashville: Broadman Press, 1958), 709.

67. W.W. Barnes, *The Southern Baptist Convention 1845–1953* (Nashville: Broadman Press, 1954), 2–3.

68. King, *South Carolina Baptists,* 157.

69. Rueben Edward Alley, *A History of Baptists in Virginia* (Richmond: Virginia Baptist General Board, 1974), 171.

70. A.H. Reid, *Baptists in Alabama* (Montgomery: Alabama State Convention, 1967), 27.

71. McBeth, *The Baptist Heritage,* 222.

72. Paul Weber, "Missouri Baptist General Association" in *Encyclopedia of Southern Baptists,* vol. 2, 910.

73. J. L. Boyd, "Mississippi Baptist Convention," in *Encyclopedia of Southern Baptists,* vol. 2, 885.

74. William D. Nowlin, *Kentucky Baptist History 1770–1922* (n.p.:Baptist Book Concern, 1922), 66ff.

75. Baker, *The Southern Baptist Convention,* 153.

76. McBeth, 384.

77. Torbet, *A History of the Baptists,* 302.

78. Robert A. Baker, *A Baptist Source Book* (Nashville: Broadman Press, 1966), 100.

Chapter 2

1. James A. Rogers, *Richard Furman: Life and Legacy* (Macon, Ga.: Mercer University Press, 1985), 3.

2. Ibid., 37.

3. Ibid., 179.

4. Hortense Woodson, *Giant in the Land* (Nashville: Broadman Press, 1950), 4.

5. *The Christian Index* (Georgia: January 27, 1835) as cited in Baker, *Southern Baptist Convention and Its People*, 109.

6. Baker, *Baptist Source Book*, 62, 116.

7. Joe W. Burton, *Road to Augusta* (Nashville: Broadman Press, 1976), 107.

8. *Southern Baptist Convention Annual, 1845*, 12–13.

9. Timothy George, "Conflict and Identity in the SBC: The Quest for a New Consensus, in *Beyond the Impasse*, ed. by Robison B. James and David S. Dockery (Nashville: Broadman Press, 1992), 204.

10. Francis Wayland, *Daily Chronicle and Sentinel* (Augusta, Ga.: May 10, 1845), as cited in Baker, *Baptist Source Book*, 116.

11. Jeter, *Recollections*, 236.

12. *Southern Baptist Convention Annual, 1845*, 3–5.

13. Robert A. Baker, "The Magnificent Years (1917–1931)," in *Baptist History and Heritage* (July 1973), 145.

14. Ibid., 146.

15. Burton, *Road to Augusta*, 164.

16. *Southern Baptist Convention Annual, 1845*, 14–15.

17. Jesse C. Fletcher, "Letters from Burma: The Personal Side," *Quarterly Review* (April-May-June, 1964), 40–48.

18. Jesse C. Fletcher, "Foreign Mission Board Strategy," in *Baptist History and Heritage* (October 1974), 212.

19. *Encyclopedia of Southern Baptists*, vol. 1, 105.

20. Baker James Cauthen, *Advance: A History of Southern Baptist Foreign Missions* (Nashville: Broadman Press, 1970), 80.

21. *Southern Baptist Convention Annual, 1847*, 15; and *Southern Baptist Convention Annual, 1848*, 10.

22. E.C. Routh, "Bowen, Thomas Jefferson," in *The Encyclopedia of Southern Baptists*, vol. 1., ed. by Norman Wade Cox (Nashville: Broadman Press, 1958), 183.

23. *Southern Baptist Convention Annual, 1860*, 364–78.

24. Arthur B. Rutledge, *Mission to America: A Century and a Quarter of Southern Baptist Home Missions* (Nashville: Broadman Press, 1969), 21–25.

25. *Southern Baptist Convention Annual, 1861*, Domestic Mission report.

26. Ibid., 45.

27. Robert A. Baker, *The Blossoming Desert* (Waco: Word Publishers, 1970), 25.

28. J.M. Dawson, "Texas Baptist General Convention," in *Encyclopedia of Southern Baptists*, vol. 2., ed. by Norman Wade Cox (Nashville: Broadman Press, 1958), 1375.

29. Baker, *The Southern Baptist Convention*, 180.

30. Gordon C. Reeves, "Florida Baptist State Convention," in *Encyclopedia of Southern Baptists*, vol. 1., ed. by Norman Wade Cox (Nashville: Broadman Press, 1958), 451.

31. Baker, *The Southern Baptist Convention*, 201.

32. McBeth, *The Baptist Heritage*, 447.

33. Harold S. Smith, "The Life and Work of J. R. Graves," in *Baptist History and Heritage* (January 1975), 19–27.

34. This letter is found in McBeth, *Sourcebook for Baptist Heritage,* 317–18.

35. Ibid.

36. James E. Tull, "The Landmark Movement: An Historical and Theological Appraisal," in *Baptist History and Heritage* (January 1975), 9–12.

37. Robert A. Baker, "Factors Encouraging the Rise of Landmarkism," in *Baptist History and Heritage* (January 1975), 18.

38. Bob Compton, "J. M. Pendleton: A Nineteenth-Century Statesman," in *Baptist History and Heritage* (January 1975), 28–35.

39. G.H. Orchard, *A Concise History of Foreign Baptists* (Nashville: Graves and Marks & Co., 1838).

40. Barnes, *The Southern Baptist Convention,* 103.

41. Smith, "J.R. Graves," 27.

42. Tull, *Shapers of Baptist Thought,* 129.

43. Weatherford, Kenneth Vaughn, "The Graves–Howell Controversy" (Ph.D. diss., Baylor University, 1991), 254.

44. Baker, *The Southern Baptist Convention,* 217.

45. Ibid.

46. *Southern Baptist Convention Annual, 1858,* 13.

47. Keith E. Eitel and James Madison Pendleton, *Baptist Theologians,* ed. Timothy George and David S. Dockery (Nashville: Broadman Press, 1990), 191.

48. Barnes, *The Southern Baptist Convention,* 84–85.

49. Ronald H. Noricks, "Misguided Missionaries: New Englanders View Frontier Baptists, 1804–1831," in *Baptist History and Heritage* (January 1993), 46.

50. Jonathon A. Lindsey, "Basil Manly: Protean Man," in *Baptist History and Heritage* (July 1973), 134.

51. William A. Mueller, *A History of Southern Baptist Theological Seminary* (Nashville: Broadman Press, 1959), 22.

52. Ibid., 6ff.

53. *Southern Baptist Convention Annual, 1861,* 62–64.

54. Ibid., 62.

55. E. B. Pollard, "Life and Work of Whitsitt," in *Review and Expositor* (April 1912), 161–62.

56. Billy Grey Hunt, "Crawford Howell Toy: Interpreter of the Old Testament," (Th.D. diss., The Southern Baptist Theological Seminary, 1965), 35.

57. Ibid.

58. Baker, *The Southern Baptist Convention,* 229–30.

59. Ibid., 229. (See also J. William Jones, *Christ in the Camp* [Richmond: B.F. Johnson & Co., 1887] for a detailed story of that work.)

60. Ibid., 230.

61. Ibid., 229.

62. Rutledge, *Mission to America,* 30–31.

63. Barnes, "The Southern Baptist Convention" and "Japan, Mission In," in *Encyclopedia of Southern Baptists,* vol. 1, 39, and 697.

64. *Southern Baptist Convention Annual, 1862,* 26–27.

65. Barnes, *Southern Baptist Convention,* 114.

66. *Southern Baptist Convention Annual, 1863,* 11.

67. George B. Taylor, *Life and Times of James B. Taylor* (Philadelphia: The Bible and Publication Society, 1872), 269.

68. *Southern Baptist Convention Annual, 1863*, 55.

Chapter 3

1. *Encyclopedia Britannica,* 1970 ed., vol. 1, 730.

2. Paul H. Buck, *The Road to Reunion* (New York: Vintage Books, 1937), viii–x.

3. Ibid., 62.

4. John A. Broadus, *Memoir of James Petigru Boyce* (Nashville: Sunday School Board of the Southern Baptist Convention, 1927), 239.

5. Ibid., 66–69.

6. Broadus, 243–44.

7. Mueller, *A History of Southern Baptist Theological Seminary,* 32. See also *Abstract of Principles,* 238–41.

8. Broadus, *Memoir,* 267–69.

9. Archibald T. Robertson, *Life and Letters of John Albert Broadus,* 8.22 (Philadelphia: American Baptist Publication Society, 1910), 165.

10. Baker, *The Southern Baptist Convention,* 232–33.

11. Robert A. Baker, *Relations Between Northern and Southern Baptists* (Ft. Worth: Marvin D. Evans Printing Company, 1954), 95–96.

12. Baker, *The Southern Baptist Convention,* 234–36.

13. Torbet, *A History of the Baptists,* 370.

14. Ibid., 362.

15. Rutledge, *Mission to America,* 34–35.

16. Ibid., 35.

17. Cecil Ray and Susan Ray, "Roots and Change in Southern Baptist Life," Unpublished Manuscript, 1989, 91.

18. Graves, *Old Landmarkism: What Is It?* (Arkansas-Texas: Baptist Sunday School Committee), 1880, xvol.

19. Tull, vii.

20. Cauthen, *Advance,* 81, 4.

21. Catherine Allen, *The New Lottie Moon Story* (Nashville: Broadman Press, 1980), 58.

22. Ibid., 58.

23. "Questions Answered," *Western Recorder* (May 5, 1904), 2.

24. G.B. Taylor, *The Life and Times of James B. Taylor* (Philadelphia: Bible and Publication Society, 1872), 305.

25. Gregory Vickers, "Models of Womanhood and the Early Woman's Missionary Union," in *Baptist History and Heritage* (January 1989), 41.

26. Ibid., 45.

27. Cauthen, *Advance,* 272.

28. Merrill D. Moore, "Foreign Mission Board," in *Encyclopedia of Southern Baptists,* vol. 1, 462.

29. Alma Hunt, *History of Woman's Missionary Union* (Nashville: Convention Press, 1964), 12ff.

30. Allen, *The New Lottie Moon Story,* 119.
31. Ibid., 120.
32. Irwin T. Hyatt, Jr., *Our Ordered Lives Confess* (Cambridge: Harvard University Press, 1976), 97.
33. J. B. Jeter, "Southern Baptist Convention," in *Religious Herald* (May 20, 1869), 2.
34. C. H. Toy, *The Claims of Biblical Interpretation on Baptists* (New York: Lange & Hillman, 1869), 13.
35. Glen E. Hinson, "Between Two Worlds...," in *Baptist History and Heritage* (April 1985), 31.
36. Patterson, "The Twenty-First Century SBC," 40.
37. Mueller, *A History of Southern Baptist Theological Seminary,* 139.
38. Robertson, *John Albert Broadus,* 313.
39. Allen, *The New Lottie Moon Story,* 138.
40. Ibid.
41. James Powhatan Cox, "A Study in the Life and Works of Basil Manly, Jr." (Doctoral diss., Southern Baptist Theological Seminary, 1954), 291.
42. Baker, *Relations,* 158–61.
43. *Southern Baptist Convention Annual, 1879,* 26.
44. Rutledge, *Mission to America,* 36.
45. *Southern Baptist Convention Annual, 1882,* 29.
46. Kimball Johnson, "Isaac Taylor Tichenor," in *Encyclopedia of Southern Baptists,* vol. 2 (Nashville: Broadman Press, 1958), 1416.
47. Victor I. Masters, *A Historical Sketch* (Atlanta: Home Mission Board, 1912), 32.
48. B. Gray Allison, "Notable Achievements in Missions and Evangelism since 1845," in *Baptist History and Heritage* (July 1989), 35.
49. Joe W. Burton, *Epochs of Home Missions* (Atlanta: Home Mission Board, 1945), 98.
50. McBeth, *Women in Baptist Life,* 77–79.
51. Hunt, *History of WMU,* 34–35.
52. Juliette Mather, "Woman's Missionary Union," in *Encyclopedia of Southern Baptists,* vol. 2, 1513.
53. Allen, *Century to Celebrate,* 48.
54. Ibid., 132.
55. Ibid., 148.
56. Baker, *The Southern Baptist Convention,* 298.
57. Barnes, *The Southern Baptist Convention,* 92–93.
58. E. C. Routh, "James Bruton Gambrell," in *Encyclopedia of Southern Baptists,* vol. 1, (Nashville: Broadman Press, 1958), 524.
59. McBeth, *Sourcebook for Baptist Heritage,* 301–02.
60. Ibid., 302.
61. File 8, Carroll Collection, Southwestern Baptist Theological Seminary.
62. Baker, *The Southern Baptist Convention,* 261–62. See also Baker's *A Baptist Source Book,* 159–60.
63. Hyatt, *Ordered Lives,* 6.
64. Ibid., 8.
65. L. S. Foster, *Fifty Years in China* (Nashville: Bayless–Pullen Company, 1909), 145.
66. Baker, *The Southern Baptist Convention,* 279.

67. Hyatt, *Ordered Lives*, 58.
68. Cauthen, 30.
69. Allen, *Century to Celebrate*, 349.
70. Ibid.
71. W. O. Carver, "William Whitsitt: The Seminary Martyr," in *Review and Expositor* (October 1954), 453–56.
72. Rosalie Beck, "The Whitsitt Controversy: A Denomination in Crisis (Ph.D. diss. Baylor University, 1985), 67.
73. Charles B. Bugg, "The Whitsitt Controversy: A Study in Denominational Conflict" (Th. D. diss. The Southern Baptist Theological Seminary, 1972), 112 and 134.
74. Beck, "The Whitsitt Controversy," 119ff.
75. Mueller, *A History of Southern Baptist Theological Seminary* 160.
76. Alan J. Lefever, "The Life and Work of Benajah Harvey Carroll" (Ph.D. diss., Southwestern Baptist Theological Seminary, 1992), 145.
77. Albert H. McClellan, "The Leadership Heritage of Southern Baptists," in *Baptist History and Heritage* (January 1985), 12.

Chapter 4

1. Baker, *The Southern Baptist Convention*, 249–50.
2. *Southern Baptist Convention Annual, 1902,* 10 and 63.
3. W. James Powhatan, *George W. Truett: A Biography* (New York: Macmillan Company, 1939), 81–82.
4. Robert A. Baker, *Tell the Generations Following* (Nashville: Broadman Press, 1983), 178.
5. H. E. Dana, *Lee Rutland Scarborough: A Life of Service* (Nashville: Broadman Press, 1942), 17.
6. Ibid., 54–57.
7. Lefever, "B. H. Carroll," 22.
8. Ibid., 26ff.
9. Ibid., 62.
10. Baker, *Tell the Generations Following,* 120–39.
11. J. M. Gaskin, "Oklahoma, Baptist General Convention of," in *Encyclopedia of Southern Baptists*, 1029.
12. Ibid.
13. Ibid., 1032.
14. Calowa William Stumph, "New Mexico, Baptist Convention of," in *Encyclopedia of Southern Baptists,* vol. 2, 960.
15. Ibid.
16. Baker, *The Southern Baptist Convention,* 339.
17. L. H. Moore, "Illinois Baptist State Association," in *Encyclopedia of Southern Baptists,* vol. 1, 672.
18. Baker, *The Southern Baptist Convention,* 321–22.
19. J. B. Gambrell, "A Long Look for Baptists," in *Baptist Standard* (May 8, 1919), 7.
20. James E. Tull, *A Study of Southern Baptist Landmarkism in the Light of Historical Baptist Ecclesiology* (New York: Arno Press, 1980), 566–67.

21. Don Kammerdiener, "Mission and the Church," in *The Commission* (September 1991), 70.

22. John Franklin Loftis, "Factors in Southern Baptist Identity as Reflected by Ministerial Role Models, 1750–1925" (Ph.D. diss., Southern Baptist Theological Seminary), 260.

23. S.P. Brooks, "Southwestern Baptist Theological Seminary," in *Encyclopedia of Southern Baptists*, vol. 2, 1277.

24. Baker, *Tell the Generations Following*, 118.

25. Ibid., 121 and 127.

26. James Carl Hefley, *The Conservative Resurgence in the Southern Baptist Convention* (Hannibal, Mo.: Hannibal Books, 1991), 322.

27. Baker, 136.

28. Ibid., 236, 239.

29. James F. Loftis, "Factors," 264. Loftis cited letters to Mullins from Fred W. Freeman, William E. Hatcher, T. B. Ray, and P. C. Schilling in this general period.

30. B. H. Carroll, letter to Mullins, 3/16/1919, (Mullins Collection: Boyce Library, Southern Baptist Theological Seminary).

31. J. Frank Norris, "Fort Worth Gives $200,000 for Seminary," in *Baptist Standard* (November 11, 1909), 1.

32. Roberta Turner Patterson, *Candle by Night* (Dallas, Tex.: Woman's Missionary Union of Texas, 1955), 65

33. Ibid., 73.

34. Barnes, *SBC*, 206.

35. Baker, *Tell the Generations Following*, 177f.

36. Ibid., 178 (quoting a Frank Norris written history.)

37. Baker, *Tell the Generations Following*, 179.

38. Ibid., 220–21.

39. McBeth, *Heritage*, 565.

40. *Southern Baptist Convention Annual, 1914*, 73–78.

41. James E. Carter, "The Fraternal Address of Southern Baptists," in *Baptist History and Heritage* (October 1977), 211.

42. Ibid.

43. *Southern Baptist Convention Annual, 1919*, 29.

44. *Baptist Standard* (May 13, 1920), 5.

45. Baker, *Relations*, 191–96.

46. Hyatt, *Ordered Lives*, 93.

47. Ibid., 94.

48. Ibid.

49. *Foreign Mission Journal* (February 1913).

50. Hunt, *History of Woman's Missionary Union*, 56.

51. Ibid., 84.

52. *Southern Baptist Convention Annual, 1929*, 102.

53. Hunt, *History of WMU*, 102–03.

54. *Minutes Woman's Missionary Union, 1921*, 29.

55. Roland Q. Leavell, "New Orleans Baptist Theological Seminary," in *Encyclopedia of Southern Baptists*, vol. 2, 969.

56. C. Anne Davis, "Women in Southern Baptist History," in *Baptist History and Heritage* (July 1987), 2.
57. Ibid., 15. See also H. Leon McBeth's comments, 4.
58. McBeth, "Perspectives," in *Baptist History and Heritage* (July 1987), 9.
59. Ibid.
60. J. B. Cranfill, "The Greatest Convention of All," in *Baptist Standard* (November 1901), 1.
61. Margaret Lackey, *Decade of WMU Service, 1913–1923* (Nashville: Sunday School Board, 1924), 105.
62. David M. Reimers, *White Protestantism and the Negro* (New York: Oxford University Press, 1965), 54.
63. John Lee Eighmy, *Churches in Cultural Captivity* (Knoxville: University of Tennessee Press, 1972), 19.
64. H. E. Dana, *Lee Rutland Scarborough*, 99.
65. *Southern Baptist Convention Annual, 1919*, 17–23.
66. James E. Carter, 211.
67. *Baptist Standard* (May 22, 1919), 12.
68. Ibid., 8.
69. *Southern Baptist Convention Annual, 1920*, 157.
70. *Southern Baptist Convention Annual, 1888*, 34.
71. Bill Sumners, "Southern Baptists and the Liquor Question 1910–20," in *Baptist History and Heritage* (April 1983), 75ff.
72. Lefever, "B. H. Carroll," 81.
73. James O. Combs, *Roots and Origins of Baptist Fundamentalism* (Baptist Press, 1984), 3–5.
74. Ibid., 8–9.
75. Hefley, *The Conservative Resurgence*, 15ff.
76. Glenn Thomas Carson, "Lee Rutland Scarborough," (Ph.D. diss., Southwestern Baptist Theological Seminary, 1992).
77. Brackney, *Baptists*, xix.
78. Ibid., xxi.
79. *Southern Baptist Convention Annual, 1920*, 197–98. (*Baptist Standard* report printed it with no comment.
80. *Southern Baptist Convention Annual, 1919*, 43 and 197.
81. E. Y. Mullins to J. P. Love, June 18, 1919, Mullins Collection, #753.
82. James E. Carter, "A Review of Confessions of Faith Adopted by Major Baptist Bodies in the United States," in *Baptist History and Heritage* (April 1977), 83.
83. Herschel H. Hobbs, "Southern Baptists and Confessionalism: A Comparison of the Origin and Contents of the 1925 and 1963 Confessions," in *Review and Expositor* (Winter 1979), 56.
84. Herschel H. Hobbs, "The Baptist Faith and Message—Anchored but Free," in *Baptist History and Heritage* (July 1978), 34.
85. *Southern Baptist Convention Annual, 1925*, 76.
86. Ibid., 71. (See also Hobbs's article in *Baptist History and Heritage* [July 1978, 34.])
87. Hobbs, 34.
88. *Baptist Standard*, (May 21, 1925), 1ff.
89. Ibid.

90. *Southern Baptist Convention Annual, 1917,* 33–35.

91. *Southern Baptist Convention Annual, 1927,* 66–68.

92. Nancy T. Ammerman, *Baptist Battles: Social Change and Religious Conflict in the Southern Baptist Convention,* (New Bruinswick: Rutgers University Press, 1990), 47.

93. *Southern Baptist Convention Annual, 1919,* 77–79.

94. See ch. 9, 333.

Chapter 5

1. Baker, *The Southern Baptist Convention and Its People,* 394.

2. Ibid., 393–94.

3. *Southern Baptist Convention Annual, 1928,* 51.

4. Rutledge, *Mission to America,* 56–58.

5. Ibid., 57.

6. Albert McClellan, *The Executive Committee of the Southern Baptist Convention—1917–1984* (Nashville: Broadman Press, 1985), 83–86.

7. *Southern Baptist Convention Annual, 1929,* 274.

8. Rutledge, *Mission to America,* 61.

9. William W. Barnes, *The Southern Baptist Convention; A Study in the Development of Ecclesiology* (Fort Worth: Southwestern Seminary Press, 1934), 32.

10. Ibid., 38.

11. *Southern Baptist Convention Annual, 1931,* 43–46.

12. Ibid., 44.

13. *Southern Baptist Convention Annual, 1946,* 66–73. See also *Southern Baptist Convention Annual, 1947,* 19–23.

14. Ibid.

15. Robert A. Baker, "The Magnificent Years (1917–1931)," in *Baptist History and Heritage* (July 1973), 145.

16. Baker, *The Southern Baptist Convention,* 405.

17. G. Hugh Wamble, "History of Messengers to Baptist Denominatinal Bodies," in *Baptist History and Heritage* (April 1987), 13.

18. Pageant, 740.

19. John A. Garraty and Peter Gay, eds., *The Columbia History of the World* (New York: Harper and Row, 1972), 1008.

20. Thomas A. Bailey and David M. Kennedy, *The American Pageant* (Lexington: D.C. Heath and Company, 1983), 708.

21. Garraty and Gay, *Columbia History,* 1011.

22. Ibid.

23. Baker, *Southern Baptist Convention,* 394.

24. *Southern Baptist Convention Annual, 1934,* 106, 111–12.

25. Gaines S. Dobbins, *Great Teachers Make a Difference* (Nashville: Broadman Press, 1965), 44. Robert A. Baker quoted from this book in his history of Southwestern, *Tell the Generations Following,* and demonstrated that this episode probably took place on September 11, 1930, rather than 1933 as Dobbins remembered years later.

26. Baker James Cauthen and Frank K. Means, *Advance to Bold Mission Thrust, 1845–1980* (Nashville: Foreign Mission Board of the Southern Baptist Convention, 1981), 37.
27. Ibid., 38.
28. Ibid., 40.
29. Ibid., 41.
30. *Southern Baptist Convention Annual, 1936*, 150.
31. Arthur B. Rutledge, *Mission to America*, 63.
32. Ibid., 63–67. See also *Southern Baptist Convention Annual, 1928*, 55.
33. *Southern Baptist Convention Annual, 1933*, 65.
34. Merrill D. Moore, "Hundred Thousand Club," in *Encyclopedia of Southern Bapitsts*, vol. 1, 660.
35. Ibid.
36. Ibid.
37. Yvonne Stackhouse, *Hardin-Simmons University—A Centennial History* (Abilene, Tex.: Hardin-Simmons University, 1991), 126.
38. Baker, 357. See also Robert G. Torbet, "Historical Background of the Southern Baptist 'Invasion,' " in *Foundations* (October 1959), 317–18.
39. *Southern Baptist Convention Annual, 1909*, 33.
40. H.K. Neely, *The Territorial Expansion of the Southern Baptist Convention 1894–1959* (Ft. Worth, Southwestern Baptist Theological Seminary, 1963), 65.
41. *Southern Baptist Convention Annual, 1929*, 303.
42. C. L. Pair, *A History of the Arizona Baptist Convention 1928–1984* (Arizona Baptist Convention, 1989) 42.
43. Mrs. G. D. Crow, "Arizona, Baptist General Convention of: History of General Convention," in *Encyclopedia of Southern Baptists*, vol. 1, 60–62.
44. See respective *Southern Convention Annuals—1925, 1930, 1935*.
45. Garraty and Gay, *Columbia History*, 1016.
46. Ibid.
47. H. Leon McBeth, "Celebrating History and Hope" (unpublished manuscript in the Fletcher/H.S.U. file of Southern Baptist History, 1990), 155.
48. Ibid., 396–97.
49. Ibid., 170.
50. Bobbie Sorrill, "Southern Baptist Laywomen in Missions," in *Baptist History and Heritage* (July 1987), 22.
51. Ibid., 24.
52. *Southern Baptist Convention Annual, 1934*, 154.
53. Beck, "The Whitsitt Controversy," 245.
54. James C. Hefley, *Truth in Crisis*, vol. 4 (Hannibal: Hannibal Books, 1989), 43.
55. Ibid.
56. Jesse C. Fletcher, *Bill Wallace of China* (Nashville: Broadman Press, 1963).
57. Jesse C. Fletcher, *Living Sacrifices: A Missionary Odyssey* (Nashville: Broadman Press, 1974), 48ff.
58. Cauthen, *Advance*, 94.
59. Jesse C. Fletcher, *Baker James Cauthen—A Man for All Nations* (Nashville: Broadman Press, 1977), 94–101.
60. Ibid., 98.

61. Cauthen, *Advance*, 96.
62. "Home Mission Report" in *Southern Baptist Convention Annual—1925 and 1935.*
63. *Encyclopedia of Southern Baptists*, vol. 1., 18.
64. *Southern Baptist Convention Annual, 1942,* 50.
65. *Western Recorder* (May 27, 1943), 8.
66. Harold E. Dye, "Matchless California," in *The Quarterly Review* (April-June 1961), 19.
67. *Southern Baptist Convention Annual, 1940,* 99.
68. Ibid.
69. Gambrell, *Baptist Standard* (May 20, 1920), 8.
70. Baker, *The Southern Baptist Convention*, 428.
71. Cauthen, *Advance*, 94.
72. Lois Whaley, *Edwin Dozier of Japan: Man of the Way* (Birmingham, Ala.: Woman's Missionary Union, 1983), 168.
73. Allen, *Century to Celebrate*, 351–52.
74. *Southern Baptist Convention Annual, 1942,* 104.
75. *Southern Baptist Convention Annual, 1946,* 141 and 224.
76. *Southern Baptist Convention Annuals, 1939,* 16; *1942,* 49; *1946,* 76.
77. *Southern Baptist Convention Annual, 1946,* 38–39.
78. James E. Carter, "The Southern Baptist Convention and Confessions of Faith, 1845–1945," (Ph.D. diss., Fort Worth: Southwestern Baptist Theological Seminary, 1964), 194.
79. Ibid., 195. (See also *Southern Baptist Convention Annual, 1946,* 59–60.)
80. Baker, *Tell the Generations Following*, 263.
81. *Southern Baptist Convention Annual, 1946,* 154.

Chapter 6

1. Bailey and Kennedy, *American Pageant,* 820.
2. Buckner Fanning, "Remember," Sermon on file Trinity Baptist Church, San Antonio, Tex., December 8, 1981.
3. H. Leon McBeth, *The First Baptist Church of Dallas* (Grand Rapids: Zondervan Publishing, 1968), 225–26.
4. McBeth, *Women in Baptist Life,* 101.
5. *Encyclopedia Britannica,* 1970, vol. 18, 42.
6. Fletcher, *Wallace,* 155–56.
7. *Southern Baptist Convention Annual, 1949,* 87.
8. Baker, *A Baptist Source Book,* 195–96.
9. Fletcher, *Cauthen,* 44–45.
10. *Southern Baptist Convention Annual, 1941, 1946, 1947, 1948.*
11. Moyers, "On Being a Baptist," 1.
12. James T. Baker, *Brook Hays* (Macon: Mercer University Press, 1989), 113.
13. H.K. Neely, Jr., *The Territorial Expansion of the Southern Baptist Convention 1894–1959* (Fort Worth: Southwestern Baptist Theological Seminary,, 1963), 6.
14. Torbet, *A History of the Baptists,* 450.

15. Hoyt S. Gibson, "Kansas Convention of the Southern Baptist: History of Convention," in *Encyclopedia of Southern Baptists,* vol. 1, 719.
16. *Southern Baptist Convention Annual 1951,* 50.
17. R.E. Milam, "Oregon-Washington, Baptist Convention of," in *Encyclopedia of the Southern Baptists,* vol. 2, 1060–61.
18. Nobel Thomas Cottrell, "Ohio, State Convention of Baptists in," in *Encyclopedia of Southern Baptists,* vol. 2, 1027.
19. A. Ronald Tonks, "Indiana, State Convention of Baptists in," in *Encyclopedia of Southern Baptists,* vol. 3, 1777–78.
20. *Southern Baptist Convention Annual, 1946,* 494.
21. *Southern Baptist Convention Annual, 1964,* 116.
22. Combs, ed., *Roots and Origins of Baptist Fundamentalism.*
23. James Hefley, *The Conservative Resurgence in the Southern Baptist Convention* (Hannibal, Mo.: Hannibal Books, 1991), 41, quoting from "Voice from the Past," in *The Enquiry* (October 1987), 3.
24. McClellan, *Executive Committee,* 172.
25. Bobby S. Terry, "Southern Baptist News Media 1945: Purpose, History and Influence," in *Baptist History and Heritage* (July 1993), 39.
26. Ibid., 40.
27. Judson Boyce Allan, "Historical Commission of the Southern Baptist Convention, " *Encyclopedia of Southern Baptists,* vol. 1, 623.
28. Barnes, *The Southern Baptist Convention,* ix. See also H. I. Hester's *Writing Southern Baptist History.*
29. William A. Carleton, "Golden Gate Baptist Theological Seminary," in *Encyclopedia of Southern Baptists,* vol. 1, 568–69.
30. Pope A. Duncan, "Southeastern Baptist Theological Seminary," in *Encyclopedia of Southern Baptists,* vol. 2, 1239.
31. *Southern Baptist Convention Annual, 1950,* 38.
32. *Southern Baptist Convention Annual, 1953,* 38.
33. G. Hugh Wamble, "Midwestern Baptist Theological Seminary," in *Encyclopedia of Southern Baptists,* vol. 3, 1839–41.
34. McClellan, *Executive Committee,* 177.
35. *Southern Baptist Convention Annual, 1956,* 44.
36. H. Leon McBeth, *Baptist Sunday School Board,* 209.
37. Ibid., 216.
38. Clarence Duncan, "Radio and Television Commission, The," in *Encyclopedia of Southern Baptists,* vol. 3, 1932.
39. Ibid., 1932.
40. McBeth, *The Baptist Heritage,* 655.
41. Robert A. Baker, *Southern Baptist Convention,* 441. See also Leonard E. Hill, "Southern Baptist Convention, The," in *Encyclopedia of Southern Baptists,* vol. 3, 1968.
42. Nancy Ammerman, "The SBC: Retrospect and Prospect," in *Review and Expositor* 88 (1991), 12.
43. *Southern Baptist Convention Annual, 1941, 1961.*
44. Gambrell, *Baptist Standard* (May 8, 1919), 7.
45. *U.S. News and World Report* (September 26, 1960), 74–78.

46. Paula Womack, "Baptist group confesses racism to historic church," in *Baptists Today,* (August 26, 1993), 3. SBC Executive Committee minutes of September 15, 1963, note Trentham's specific recommendation, which was referred to the Administrative Committee that reported out the more general resolution. See also "The Birmingham Confession" in the *Baptist Peacemaker* (Summer 1993), 1.

47. Juliette Mather, "Women, Convention Privileges of," in *Encyclopedia of Southern Baptists,* 1958, vol. 2, 544.

48. Catherine B. Allen, *Laborers Together with God* (Birmingham, Ala.: Woman's Missionary Union, 1987), 194ff.

49. Ibid., 47.

50. Samuel S. Hill, "The Story before the Story: Southern Baptists Since World War II," in *Southern Baptists Observed,* Nancy Ammerman, ed., 36.

51. Ralph H. Elliot, *The "Genesis Controversy" and Continuity in Southern Baptist Chaos—A Eulogy for a Great Tradition* (Macon, Ga.: Mercer University Press, 1992), 3–5.

52. Al Fasol, *With a Bible in Their Hands: Baptist Preaching in the South, 1679-1979* (Nashville: Broadman and Holman, 1994), 145–46.

53. Ammerman, *Battles,* 81.

54. K. Owen White, "Death in the Pot," in *Baptist Standard* (January 10, 1962).

55. Elliot, *Genesis Controversy,* 3–5.

56. *The Christian Century* (November 14, 1962), 1376.

57. Elliot, 99, quoting Sally Rice.

58. Hobbs, 34.

59. McClellan, 209.

60. Ibid., 36.

61. Ibid., 36.

62. Ibid., 273.

63. Hobbs, 38.

64. Leonard, *God's Last,* 80. See also McBeth, *Baptist Heritage,* 687.

65. Fletcher, *Cauthen,* 257.

66. Cauthen, *Advance,* 52.

67. Ibid., 59.

68. *Southern Baptist Convention Annual, 1964.*

69. One of Jerry Rankin's appointments, Thurmon Bryant, in a report to the Foreign Mission Board in the fall of 1993 suggested reviewing requirements as a way to expand the pool of applicants. Presented to Foreign Mission Board trustees by Rankin and Bryant, August 18, 1993.

70. *Southern Baptist Convention Annual, 1959,* FMB report.

71. *Southern Baptist Convention Annual, 1959,* 61.

72. *Southern Baptist Convention Annual, 1964,* 151.

73. Edmund William Hunke, Jr., "Arthur Bristow Rutledge," in *Encyclopedia of Southern Baptists,* vol. 4, 2444.

74. Rutledge, *Mission to America,* 164.

75. *Annual of the Southern Baptist Convention, 1964,* 261.

76. Ibid., 262–63.

77. Hefley, *Truth in Crisis,* 147, quoting Emory Univeristy sociologist, Nancy Ammerman.

78. G. Hugh Wamble, "The Leadership of Southern Baptist Convention Presidents," in *Baptist History and Heritage* (January 1985), 17.
79. Ibid., 18.
80. *Southern Baptist Convention Annual, 1964,* 260.
81. "Southern Baptist Convention," in *Religious Herald* (June 4, 1964), 10.
82. *Southern Baptist Convention Annual, 1964,* 58.

Chapter 7

1. Lynn E. May, Jr., "Statement Concerning Crisis in Our Nation," in *Encyclopedia of Southern Baptists,* vol. 3., ed. by Davis C. Wooley (Nashville: Broadman Press, 1971), 1668–69. The article is followed by the full text of the document.
2. Albert McClellan, "The Southern Baptist Convention, 1965–1985," in *Baptist History and Heritage* (October 1985), 13.
3. *Southern Baptist Convention Annual, 1979,* 86.
4. Cauthen, *Advance,* 72.
5. Mary E. Speidel, "Journeyman Program Will Be Restored," in *Baptist Standard* (February 24, 1993), 19.
6. *Baptist Standard* (June 1963). The author witnessed these events as a staff member of the Foreign Mission Board and was in Japan in 1963.
7. FMB Minutes, Overseas Committee (December 8, 1980), #1.
8. Fletcher, *Cauthen,* 242.
9. "Hunke," in *Encyclopedia of Southern Baptists,* vol. 4, 2444.
10. *Southern Baptist Convention Annual, 1977,* 112–13. Home Mission Board report showing Rutledge contributions.
11. Walker L. Knight, "Home Mission Board, SBC," in *Encyclopedia of Southern Baptists,* vol. 4, 2271.
12. *Biblical Recorder* (August 15, 1964), 5.
13. H. Leon McBeth, *Women in Baptist Life* (Nashville: Broadman Press, 1979), 42–43.
14. Ibid., 153.
15. Ibid., 156.
16. Ibid.
17. Ibid.
18. *Baptist Press* (January 2, 1976).
19. Lefever, 44.
20. *The Deacon* (April-June 1973), 14.
21. *Southern Baptist Convention Annual, 1977,* Arkansas Baptist Convention, 44.
22. *Baptist Messenger* (May 4, 1972), 2.
23. *Arkansas Baptist* (December 4, 1975), 2.
24. Anita Lemke, "Utah–Idaho Southern Baptist Convention," in *Encyclopedia of Southern Baptists,* vol. 3, 2031.
25. Paul S. James, "Baptist Convention of New York," in *Encyclopedia of Southern Baptist Convention,* vol. 3, 1866.
26. George W. Bullard, "Baptist Convention of Pennsylvania-South Jersey," in *Encyclopedia of Southern Baptists,* vol. 4, 2412.

27. Jackson C. Walls, "West Virginia Convention of Southern Baptists," in *Encyclopedia of Southern Baptist Convention*, vol. 4, 2542.

28. Donald H. Ledbetter, et al., "Nevada Baptist Convention," in *Encyclopedia of Southern Baptist Convention*, 2365.

29. *Southern Baptist Convention Annual, 1959*, 75.

30. Baker, *The Southern Baptist Convention*, 433.

31. Mueller, *Southern*, 226.

32. McBeth, *Heritage*, 668.

33. Baker, *Tell the Generations Following*, 417ff.

34. Claude L. Howe Jr., "New Orleans Baptist Theological Seminary," in *Encyclopedia of Southern Baptists*, vol. 4, 2371ff.

35. W. Morgan Patterson and Harold K. Graves, "Golden Gate Baptist Theological Seminary," in *Encyclopedia of Southern Baptist Convention*, vol. 4, 2251ff.

36. James H. Blackmore, "Southeastern Baptist Theological Seminary," in *Encyclopedia of Southern Baptist Convention*, vol. 4, 2459ff.

37. G. Hugh Wamble, "Midwestern Baptist Theological Seminary," in *Encyclopedia of Southern Baptist Convention*, vol. 4, 2341ff.

38. *Southern Baptist Convention Annual, 1959*, 75.

39. Baker, *The SBC and Its People*, 439.

40. Ibid.

41. Ibid., 440.

42. Ibid., 442.

43. Ammerman, *Battles*, 99.

44. McBeth, *Heritage*, 660.

45. Allen, *Laborers Together*, 109.

46. Allen, *A Century to Celebrate*, 340.

47. Ibid., 341.

48. Ibid., 474ff.

49. McBeth, *Celebrating*, 306.

50. McBeth, *BSSB*, 221–22.

51. Hefley, *Truth in Crisis*, vol. 1, 56–57.

52. Ibid., 65.

53. Ibid., 53.

54. Billy Phagan Keith, *W. A. Criswell: The Authorized Biography* (Old Tappan, N.J.: Revell, 1973), 199ff.

55. *Southern Baptist Convention Annual, 1970*, 77–78.

56. *Southern Baptist Convention Annual, 1972*, 93.

57. *Southern Baptist Convention Annual, 1973*, 87.

58. McBeth, *BSSB*, 291ff.

59. Ibid., 296.

60. Ibid., 317ff.

61. Baker, *The Southern Baptist Convention*, 447.

62. Ibid.

63. Ibid., 449.

64. John J. Carey, *Carlyle Marney: A Pilgrim's Progress* (Macon, Ga.: Mercer University Press, 1980).

65. Hefley, *Truth in Crisis*, 63. See also "An Interview with Paul Pressler," in *The Theological Educator*, 1985, 15–24.

66. Glenna Whitley, "Baptist Holy War," in *D Magazine* (January, 1991), 65.

67. Baker, *SBC*, 422.

68. McBeth, *Heritage*, 696.

69. John Lee Eighmy, *Churches in Cultural Captivity*, xviii.

70. Tony B. Whittington, "Christ's Wider Kingdom," in *The Adventure* (November-December 1992), 12.

71. Loftis, *Queen*, 115.

72. David William Downs, "The Use of the 'Baptist Faith and Message,' 1963–1983: A Response to Pluralism in the Southern Baptist Convention" (Ph.D diss. The Southern Baptist Theological Seminary), 106.

73. William R .Estep, "Southern Baptists in Search of an Identity," in *The Lord's Free People in a Free Land*, (Fort Worth, Tex.: Evans Press, 1976), 164.

74. Edward L. Queen, *In the South the Baptists Are the Center of Gravity* (New York: Carlson Publishing, 1991), 117.

75. Leonard, *God's Last*, 34.

76. Ellen M. Rosenberg, *The Southern Baptists: A Subculture in Transition* (Knoxville: University of Tennessee Press, 1989), ix.

77. Hefley, *Truth in Crisis*, 58

78. Ibid., 58.

79. Ibid., 59.

80. Ibid., 62.

81. Harold Lindsell, *The Battle for the Bible* (Grand Rapids: Zondervan Publishing House, 1976).

82. Whitley, *A History of British Baptists,* 65.

83 *Southern Baptist Convention Annual, 1973,* 87

84. *Southern Baptist Convention Annual, 1976,* 52.

85. *Southern Baptist Convention Annual, 1977,* 37.

86. *Southern Baptist Convention Annual, 1979,* 52.

87. See "The Chicago Statement on Biblical Inerrancy," in Carl F. Henry, *God, Revelation and Authority* (Waco: Word Books, 1976–1983), 4:211–19.

88. James T. Draper, Jr., *Authority: The Critical Issue for Southern Baptists* (Old Tappan, N. J.: Fleming H. Revell Company, 1984), 82.

89. Wamble, *Baptist History and Heritage* (January 1985), 18.

90. "Convention Wrap-Up," in *Baptist Standard* (June 1978).

91. *BP,* June 12, 1979.

92. Rob James, *The Takeover in the Southern Baptist Convention* (Decatur, Ga.: SBC Today, 1989), 37–38.

93. Hefley, *Truth in Crisis,* 69ff.

94. Ibid.

95. *Southern Baptist Convention Annual, 1979,* 50.

96. Hefley, *Truth in Crisis*, vol. 2, 8.

97. Grady Cothen, *What Happened to the Southern Baptist Convention?* (Macon, Ga.: Smith & Helwys, 1993).

98. *Southern Baptist Convention Annual, 1979,* 54.

99. *Southern Baptist Convention Annual, 1980,* 80ff.

Chapter 8

1. Dan Vestal, "Quest for Renewal," in *Review and Expositor,* vol. 88, no. 1 (Winter 1991), 57.
2. "Rogers Press Conference," in *Baptist Press* (June 12, 1979).
3. Hefley, *Truth in Crisis,* 69ff.
4. "Irregularities," in *Baptist Press* (June 14, 1979).
5. *Southern Baptist Convention Annual, 1979,* (for resolution on political practices).
6. Ammerman, *Baptist Battles: Social Change and Religious Conflict in the Southern Baptist Convention.*
7. Ammerman, *Battles,* 78–79.
8. Ibid., 72ff.
9. Larry L. McSwain, "Anatomy of the SBC Institutional Crisis," in *Review and Expositor* 88 (1991), 29.
10. Ibid.
11. Cothen, *What Happened?,* 4.
12. *Southern Baptist Convention Annual, 1979,* 182.
13. Vestal, "Quest for Renewal," 60.
14. Parks retired at age 65, but had expressed publicly that he hoped to continue three more years. His predecessor retired at age 70.
15. Leonard, *God's Last,* 52–53.
16. Ibid., 176.
17. Hefley, *Truth in Crisis,* 81.
18. Dan Martin, "Rogers: Program Has Become 'Golden Calf,'" *Baptist Standard* (May 19, 1982), 10. On the other hand, Hefley reported it as a "sacred cow," *Truth in Crisis,* 87.
19. Hefley, *Truth in Crisis,* 2:8.
20. See page 354.
21. Walker L. Knight, "Moderate Organizations Fill Vacuums in SBC," in *Baptists Today* (December 15, 1992), 7.
22. Ibid., 8.
23. *Southern Baptist Convention Annual, 1984,* 65.
24. "Baptist Congregation Ousted for Hiring a Woman," in *Ft. Worth Star Telegram* (October 20, 1987), 4.
25. *Southern Baptist Convention Annual, 1991,* 415–20.
26. Jose A. Hernadez, *Training Hispanic Leaders in the United States* (Ph.D. diss., Southwestern Baptist Theological Seminary, 1985), 3.
27. Oscar I. Romo, "Ethnic Southern Baptists: Contexts, Trends, Contributions," in *Baptist History and Heritage* (July 1983), 3.
28. "Home Mission Board Supplement" in *Missions USA* (March 1993).
29. *The Commission,* (October-November 1992), 25.
30. Ibid., 26.

31. Louis R. Cobbs, "The Student Worker as 21st Century Missionary," in Lectures to Korean Baptist Student Workers, 1989. Papers contained in Southern Baptist History Collection, Hardin-Simmons University.
32. Ibid.
33. Leland Webb, "The Parks Era," in *The Commission* (October-November 1992), 34.
34. Walker L. Knight, "Home Mission Board, SBC," in *Encyclopedia of Southern Baptists*, vol. IV, 2272.
35. Robert Dilday, "Top Female FMB executive resigns, cites 'growing conformity' demands," in *Baptists Today* (November 12, 1992), 3.
36. Cobbs, "The Student Worker."
37. Russell H. Dilday, Jr., "On Higher Ground," Convention Sermon (June 13, 1984), in *Southern Baptist Convention Annual, 1984.*
38. Russell Dilday, "A Denominational Word," in *Southwestern News* (January 1983).
39. David Dockery, "Southern Baptists and Recent Theological Developements, Audio Tape from Louisville Institute's 'Case Study: Southern Baptists,'" 1993.
40. Leonard, *God's Last,* 121.
41. "Reynolds Hits 'Cardinals,' " in *Baptist Standard* (October 17, 1984), 5.
42. Toby Druin, "Graham Wanted No Word on Stanley Support," in *Baptist Standard* (June 26, 1985), 3.
43. *Southern Baptist Convention Annual, 1985,* 64.
44. Stan Hastey, "Peace Committee Emerges from Scarred SBC," in *Baptist Standard* (June 19, 1985), 3.
45. Toby Druin, "SBC: A Fundamental-Conservative Sweep," in *Baptist Standard,* (June 18, 1986), 3.
46. Hefley, vol. 5, 35.
47. *Southern Baptist Convention Annual, 1987,* 235.
48. Leonard, *God's Last,* 145.
49. Steve Maynard and Julia Duin, "SBC Fundamentalists Win Victory on Bible's Inerrancy," *Houston Chronicle* (October 24, 1986), 13.
50. *Southern Baptist Convention Annual, 1988,* 156.
51. *Wall Street Journal* (March 7, 1988), 1.
52. "WMU Returns to Richmond for Centennial," in *The Religious Herald* (May 19, 1988), 3.
53. Julian Pentecost, "A Century to Celebrate, A Future to Fulfill," in *The Religious Herald* (May 19, 1988), 6.
54. Hefley, "Resurgence," 68.
55. *Southern Baptist Convention Annual, 1988,* 68–69.
56. Roddy Stinson, "And there was unity at the Alamo after the battle, too", in *San Antonio Express–News* (June 18, 1993.),
57. *Southern Baptist Convention Annual, 1988,* 70.
58. Ammerman, *Battles,* 272.
59. McBeth, *Heritage,* 691.
60. Art Toalston and Eric Miller, "Ordained Couple Turned Down by FMB Trustees," in *Baptist and Reflector* (July 5, 1989), 1.
61. *Southern Baptist Convention Annual, 1984,* 65.
62. *The Baptist Student* (February 1985 and August 1985). See also McBeth, *Celebrating,* 342.
63. *Southern Baptist Convention Annual, 1988,* 70.

64. "Coalition Chooses Coordinator, Plans to Recapture Convention," in *SBC Today* (January 1989), 1.

65. Marv Knox, "New Seminary Approved at Alliance Annual Meeting," in *Biblical Recorder* (March 18, 1989), 1 and 8.

66. Jerry Falwell, "The SBC: Revived and Rebuilding," in *Fundamentalist Journal* (July–Aug 1989), 10.

67. Angela Elwell Hunt, "SBC Looks to the Past for Future Success," in *Fundamentalist Journal*, 12ff.

68. Ibid.

69. Ibid.

70. Ibid.

71. Ibid.

72. Toby Druin, "Motion to Fire Elder Discussed, Withdrawn," in *Baptist Standard* (August 16, 1989), 3, 4.

73. *Baptist Press* (August 16, 1989).

74. Hefley, *Truth in Crisis*, vol. 5, 167.

75. *Fundamentalist* (1989), 60.

76. David Beale, *Southern Baptist Convention: House of Sand?* (Greenville, S.C.: Unusual Publications, 1985), 33. Criswell's authorized biography by Bill Keith confirmed the Dallas pastor's position on abortion. See Billy Phegan Keith, *W. A. Criswell: The Authorized Biography* (Old Tappan, N.J.: Fleming Revell, 1973), 123.

77. Hefley, *Truth in Crisis*, vol. 5, 144.

78. Helen Lee Turner, "Myths: Stories of this World and the World to Come," in *Southern Baptists Observed*, Nancy Ammerman ed., (Knoxville: The University of Tennessee Press, 1993), 118.

79. Dan Martin, "Bisagno to Nominate Chapman in New Orleans," in *Baptist Standard* (February 14, 1990), 5.

80. Hefley, vol. 5, 164.

81. Ibid., 128.

82. "Fundamental–Conservatives Map Strategy," in *Baptist Standard* (March 7, 1990), 5.

83. *Southern Baptist Convention Annual, 1990,* 66.

84. *Southern Baptist Convention Annual, 1990,* 63.

85. McSwain, *Anatomy,* 29.

86. Leonard, *Last and Only,* 180–81.

87. George Marsden, "The New Paganism," in *Reformed Journal* (January 1988), 3.

88. Tape Recordings by Russell Ritchey, Nancy Ammerman, and Bill Leonard from Conference titled "The American Denominational Future: The Southern Baptist Case," Louisville Institute for the Study of Protestantism and American Culture (March 12–13, 1993).

89. "Pressler, Patterson Honored," in *Baptist Standard* (June 20, 1990), 11.

Chapter 9

1. Hefley, *Resurgence,* 311.

2. Patterson, "My Vision of the Twenty-First Century SBC," in *Review and Expositor* 88 (1991), 37ff.

3. Greg Warner, "3,000 in Atlanta Approve Alternate Funding Plan," in *Baptist Standard* (August 29, 1990), 5. See also David T. Morgan, "Upheaval in the Southern Baptist Convention, 1979–1990," Perspectives in Religious Studies, *Journal of NABPR*, 69–70; Knight, "Organizations Fill Vacuum," in *Baptists Today*, 7.

4. Ibid., Walker, 70.

5. Tami Ledbetter, "Shackleford, Martin Fired By Executive Committee," in *Indiana Baptist* (July 31, 1990), 1, 9.

6. *Southern Baptist Handbook*, (1991), 129ff.

7. "Associated Baptist Press to begin coverage this fall" in *The Baptist Record* (September 20, 1990), 3.

8. "Associated Baptist Press Will Begin Reporting News This Fall" in *Baptist Standard* (September 19, 1990), 10.

9. Marv Knox, "Trustees Cancel Book on Sunday School Board," in *Baptist Standard* (August 22, 1990), 4.

10. Cothen, *What Happened*, 322.

11. Dan Martin, "Elder, Sunday School Board Trustees Agree to 'Retirement,'" *Associated Baptist Press Release* (January 17, 1993).

12. "Covenant Renewal Between Trustees, Faculty and Administration of the Southern Baptist Theological Seminary," (March 25, 1991). See also Marv Knox, *Western Recorder*, as reported in *Baptist Standard* (April 17, 1991), 9.

13. Jim Newton and William Fletcher Allen, "Moderate fellowship moves to alternate funding" in *Baptist and Reflector* (August 29, 1990), 1.

14. "Cooperative Baptist Fellowship formed in Atlanta," in *Word and Way* (May 16, 1991), 2.

15. Toby Druin, "Baylor Changes Charter: 'Regents' Will Govern," in *Baptist Standard* (September 26, 1990), B 3.

16. Helen Parmley, *Dallas Morning News* (November, 21, 1990).

17. Hefley, *Resurgence*, 304.

18. Mark Wingfield, *Western Recorder*, "Criswell comments on divorce, America, SBC" in *Baptist Standard* (March 25, 1992), 7.

19. Linda Lawson, *Sunday School Board News Service* (July 18, 1991).

20. Hefley, *Resurgence*, 276.

21. Robert O'Brien, *Foreign Mission Board News Service* (October 16, 1991).

22. Robert O'Brien, "FMB Leaders of Europe Will Retire Early," in *Baptist Standard* (January 15, 1992), 3.

23. Robert O'Brien, "Parks shares his heart with FMB staff," in *Florida Baptist Witness* (April 2, 1992) 6.

24. Bill Finch, *Alabama Sta.* (February 4, 1992).

25. "Criswell Leadership Unclear," in *Baptist Standard* (November 13, 1991), 5.

26. Greg Warner, *Associated Baptist Press Release* (January 10, 1992).

27. *Baptists Today* (April 23, 1992), 1.

28. "Sherman Accepts Invitation to Be Fellowship Coordinator," in *Baptist Standard* (February 5, 1992), 3.

29. *Southern Baptist Convention Annuals, 1979, 1991*, 83, 67, 120, 299.

30. Roy A. Jones, II, *Abilene Reporter News* (April 23, 1992).

31. Editorial cartoon in *News and Observer* (Raleigh, N.C.: April 23, 1992).

32. "Church Refuses Seminary President for Membership," *Ft. Worth Star Telegram* (February 3, 1993).

33. *Indiana Baptist* (February 25, 1992), 20.

34. Greg Warner, "Sherman Denounces Homosexuality to Preempt Criticism of Fellowship," in *Baptist Press* (April 1, 1993), 4.

35. Ammerman, Nancy T., "Share My Dreams For Cooperative Fellowship," in *Baptists Today* (April 23, 1992), 2.

36. Editorial, *Baptists Today* (April 23, 1992), 6.

37. Warner, *Baptist Press* (May 14, 1992).

38. Debbie Moore, "Nelson Price Asks Open Convention," in *Baptist Standard* (April 29, 1992), 5.

39. *Alabama Baptist* (May 7, 1992), 10.

40. Roy A. Jones, III, "Fired Baptist Editor Finds Job with SBC," *Abilene Reporter News* (June 21, 1992), 2.

41. Ibid.

42. "Parks Asks Convention to End Controversy," *Convention Press Release* (June 10, 1992).

43. *The Baptist Program* (Sept. 1992), 9.

44. James Davison Hunter, "Culture Wars: The Struggle to Define America," cited by Terry Mattingly of Scripps Howard News Service in the *Knoxville New Sentinel* (June 14, 1992).

45. Ken Camp, "Evangelical Organization Backs Bush/Quayle," in *Baptist Standard* (September 2, 1992), 5.

46. Louis A. Moore, "Light," published by the Christian Life Commission of the Southern Baptist Convention, Nashville, Tenn. (September-October, 1992).

47. Charles Lavine, "Letters to Editor," *Baptist Standard* (August 5, 1992), 2.

48. *Baptists Today* (November 26, 1992), 1.

49. Richard Land, *The Christian Life Commission,* (November 12, 1992), 1.

50. "SBC leaders to pray, work with Clinton," based on *Baptist Press* release, in *Baptists Today* (November 26, 1992), 3.

51. David Smith, "Indiana Baptist, Little Rock's Immanuel Baptist to Be Home Church of a President," in *Baptist Press* (February 2, 1993), 8.

52. Art Toalston, "Agencies ask 8 million more SBC Cooperative Program," in *Baptist Courier* (October 1, 1992), 8.

53. Chip Alford, "SSB Head Fields Editor's Questions," in *The Baptist Messenger* (October 8, 1992), 4.

54. "Young Appoints 19 for In-depth Studies," in *The Baptist Messenger* (October 1, 1992), 3.

55. Ibid.

56. Russell Dilday, *Southwestern News* (September-October, 1992), 3.

57. *Baptists Today* (December 15, 1992), 3.

58. Walker L. Knight, "Year of Crucial Meetings," in *Baptists Today* (February 4, 1993), .7

59. *The Christian Century* (September 9-16, 1992), 796.

60. Ferrell Foster, "Criswell Discusses SBC Strife, Future of First Baptist, Dallas," in *Baptist Press* (February 4, 1993), 2.

61. Ferrell Foster, "Gregory Says He's at Peace Over Resigning Dallas Pulpit," in *Baptist Press* (March 15, 1993), 3.

62. Ibid.

63. Ibid.

64. R. Keith Parks, "Letter to Missionary Colleagues," in *Baptist Press* release (October 23, 1992), 1.

65. *Baptist Standard* (November 4, 1992), 3.

66. Erich Bridges, *Baptist Press* (November 3, 1992).

67. Cecil Sherman, "The Emerging CBF," in *Baptists Today* (February 4, 1993), 19.

68. Art Toalston, "Baptist Press," reported in the *Baptist Standard* (November 25, 1992), 3.

69. *The Commission* (October-November 1992), 34.

70. Leland Webb, "The Parks Era in Missions: Shifting to a Global Strategy," in *The Commission* (October-November 1992), 30.

71. Ibid.

72. Ibid.

73. Ibid.

74. *News Release* on Executive Committee survey.

75. Ibid.

76. Ibid.

77. Foreign Mission Board Minutes, (October 14, 1992), 1.

78. Warner, *Baptists Today* (December 15, 1992), 3.

79. Toalson, *Baptist Press*, in the *Baptist Standard* (November 25, 1992), 3.

80. *Baptist Press, ABP and WMU* press releases (January 10, 1993).

81. Greg Warner, in *Baptists Today* (January 21, 1993), 8.

82. Greg Warner, "FMB Chairman Compares WMU Move to Committing Adultery," in *Baptist Standard* (February 3, 1993), 5.

83. "News in Brief" in *Baptist Standard* (February 3, 1993), 4.

84. George Gaston, "Letters to the Editor," in *Baptist Standard* (February 3, 1993), 2.

85. "WMU executive offers reasons for board actions," in *Biblical Recorder* (January 20, 1993), 10.

86. Susan Doyle, "WMU Sends Video Message Reassuring Missionaries," *Baptist Press* (March 5, 1993), 2.

87. "HMB Asks WMU to Limit Work to Only SBC Agencies," *Baptist Standard* (March 24, 1993), 5.

88. Gary Ledbetter, "WMU's New Friend," *Indiana Baptist* (March 2, 1993), 2.

89. David E. Anderson, "Southern Baptist Woman's Auxiliary Told to Submit to Conservatism," in *Dallas Morning News* (March 6, 1993), 45a.

90. Herb Hollinger, "Adrian Rogers Is Critical of Persons Speaking for Him," *Baptist Press* (March 11, 1993), 6.

91. Charles Willis, "Draper Cites Concerns, Actions in State of the Board Address," in *Baptist Press* (Feb. 9, 1993), 1.

92. Ibid.

93. Paul Simmons, "A Personal Reflection on Theological Education and the Politically Correct," in *Baptists Today* (March 18, 1993), 9.

94. Art Toalston, "To Maintain Pro-Life Convictions, Theology Revival Needed, Professor Says," in *Baptist Press* (March 4, 1993).

95. Art Toalston, "Survey Shows Top Priority Is Evangelism," in *Baptist Press* (March 10, 1993), 18.

96. Michael J. Clingenpeel, "Southern Seminary in Chaos," in *The Religious Herald*, (April 29, 1993), 4.

97. Jon Walker, "Unsettled Convicitions Can Yield to Apostasy, Mohler Tells Grads," in *Baptist Press* (May 19, 1993), 3.

98. Mark McCormick, "Southern's Mohler Challenges 'Fundamentalism of the Left,'" in *Baptist Press* (May 17, 1993), 3.

99. Amy Greene, "Alliance Meets in Daytona Beach, Simplifies Vision, Clarifies Goals," in *Baptist Today* (March 18, 1993), 1.

100. Stan Hastey, "Thoughts On Our Present Untidy State," in *Baptists Today* (May 13, 1993), 15.

101. Ibid.

102. Mark Wingfield, "Women Gain Ground in USA Ministry Roles," in *Baptist Today* (March 18, 1993), 16.

103. Ibid.

104. "Trustee resigns," in *Baptist Standard* (March 24, 1993), 10.

105. Toby Druin, "Baylor to Open Truett Seminary in Fall, '94," in *Baptist Standard*(May 26, 1993), 4.

106. Herb Hollinger, "CBF OK's Budget, 'Blesses' 22 Missionaries," in *Baptist Standard* (May 26, 1993), 3 and 5.

107. Tami Ledbetter, "Parks Video Ignores FMB Inroads To World A," in *Indiana Baptist* (May 25, 1993) and 10.

108. Hardy Clemons, "Letter from a Birmingham Sheraton," in *Baptists Today* (May 27, 1993), 4.

109. Robert O'Brien, "Jerry Rankin Nominated as Next Foreign Mission Board President," *Foreign Mission Board Release* (May 25, 1993).

110. Greg Warner, "'Dark Horse' Jerry Rankin Chosen as FMB Nominee," in *Associated Baptist Press Release* (May 25, 1993), 1.

111. Ed Briggs, "Mission Panel Taps Singapore Veteran," in *Richmond Times-Dispatch* (May 26, 1993).

112. Thomas E. Miller, Jr., "Annuity Board Trustees Mark 75th Year, Get Kmart Update," in *Baptist Press* (March 5, 1993), 10.

113. "Baptist Briefs," in *Baptist Standard* (February 24, 1993), 4.

114. Lloyd Elder, "Calling the Family Back Together" (Nashville: Lloyd Elder & Associates, May 8, 1993).

115. Art Toalston, "Chapman says Elder plans for SBC 'unwise and unneeded,'" in *The Baptist Standard* (June 9, 1993), 5.

116. Greg Warner, "Movement may jeopardize Rankin election," in *The Baptist Standard* (June 9, 1993), 5.

117. Tammi Ledbetter and Scott Collins, "Rankin outlines vision for FMB 'to focus on what God is doing,'" 1993 Southern Baptist Convention News Release (June 14, 1993).

118. Steve Brunsman, "Clinton's hometown minister denounces SBC 'witch hunt,'" in *Houston Post* (June 15, 1993), 1.

119. Timothy George and Roy L. Honeycutt, "Report of the Theological Study Committee," in *Southern Baptist Watchman* (1993 Convention Issue), 1–4.

120. "No CBF Supporters Nominated," in *Baptist Standard* (May 12, 1993), 4.

Chapter 10

1. Art Toalston, in *The Baptist Standard* (November 25, 1992), 3.
2. George, *Beyond Impasse*, 198.
3. Randall Lolley, "Church and Change Is the Baptist Challenge," in *Baptists Today* (February 4, 1993), 15.
4. Criswell, Foster article, 1.
5. Lolley, "Church and Change," 15.
6. Russell Dilday, "Future Offers New Day, New Days for the SBC," in *Southwestern News* (January–February, 1993), 3.
7. George, *Beyond Impasse*, 198.
8. McBeth, *Heritage*, 66.
9. William L. Lumpkin, "The Nature and Authority of Baptist Confessions of Faith," in *Review and Expositor* 76 (Winter 1979), 24.
10. Baker, *Source Book*, 120.
11. George, *Beyond Impasse*, 198.
12. Ibid., quoting from Boyce Inaugural, 204.
13. Slayden Yarbrough, "Is Creedalism a Threat to Southern Baptists?" in *Baptist History and Heritage* (April, 1993), 31.
14. Taylor, *Broadus*, 119–21.
15. *Baptists Today* (December 15, 1992), 17.
16. Warner, "Parks indicates," in *The Baptist Standard* (December 2, 1992), 3.
17. W. W. Barnes, *The Southern Baptist Convention: A Study in the Developement of Ecclesiology* (Ft.. Worth, Tex.: W. W. Barnes, 1934), 75–76.
18. Patterson, "Vision," 46.
19. Nancy Ammerman, "After the Battles: Emerging Organizational Forms," in *Southern Baptists Observed*, 306.
20. Ibid.
21. Claude Howe, Jr., "Factors Affecting Cooperation Since 1945," in *Baptist History and Heritage* (January 1989), 30.
22. David Dockery, "Recent Theological Developements," audio–tape from previously cited Louisville Institute conference.
23. Ibid.
24. Newman, vol. 2, 328.
25. Greg Warner, "Hobbs urges SBC leaders to share power," in *The Baptist Standard* (February 24, 1993), 3.
26. Wayne Keely, "Claremore Pastor Responds to Critical Letters," in *Oklahoma Baptist Messenger* (February 11, 1993).
27. See chapter 4 on SWBTS founding.
28. James Davidson Hunter, *Culture Wars: The Struggle to Define America* (New York: Basic Books, 1991), 42–43.
29. Donald G. Bloesch, "A Theology for Confronting the Cultural Captivity of Evangelicalism," in *Academic Alert* (Winter 1993), IVP's Book Bulletin for Professors, 3.
30. Ibid.
31. *Southern Baptist Convention Annual, 1988,* 68–69.

32. "1992 Profile of the Typical Southern Baptist Church," in *Research Review,* Home Mission Board (Summer 1993), 2.

33. R. Scott Walker, *The Freedom Factor* (San Francisco: Harper and Row, Publishers, 1989), xiii.

34. Walter B. Shurden, *The Baptist Identity: Four Fragile Freedoms* (Macon: Smyth & Helwys, 1993). See also James M. Dunn, "Shurden volume describes essence of 'Baptistness,'" in *Baptists Today* (August 26, 1993), 18.

35. Mathew Brady, "Garrett: "Baptist Distinctives are in Danger" in *The Baptist Standard* (Sept. 11, 1991), 4.

36. Elliot, *Genesis Controversy,* 177.

37. James M. Wall, "Images of Southern Baptists in Contemporary America," in *Baptist History and Heritage* (July 1980), 2.

Bibliography

A history of Southern Baptists depends upon many sources. These include those who have attempted such before and the sources available to them and new materials that have either subsequently come to light or have been generated around events that have taken place since their publication. As the acknowledgments indicate, this author is grateful for those who have done this task before either in overview or in particular.

A Southern Baptist history originally planned for the centennial, though not completed until 1954, *The Southern Baptist Convention,* by W. W. Barnes; and the 1972 work, *The Southern Baptist Convention and Its People,* by Robert A. Baker, not only laid groundwork but delineated key sources. Larger histories of Baptists, including David Benedict's, A. H. Newman's, Robert Torbet's, and most recently, Leon McBeth's contributed to Baptist backgrounds and the larger Baptist environment. Uniquely valuable to such an effort is the four volume *Encyclopedia of Southern Baptists.* Its myriad of contributors, however uneven their work, are due real gratitude.

Particularly helpful because of convenience are the "Source Books" that have been gathered by such Southern Baptist historians as William Lumpkin, Robert A. Baker, and Leon McBeth.

Of course, any work such as this must begin with an analysis of the minutes and reports of Southern Baptist work found in its *Annuals.* If there is a primary source, this is it. But background to this material is crucial to its understanding and is found in Baptist state paper articles, journals, and periodicals, as well as collections of letters and papers of the principal players found in libraries and other repositories.

Agency histories, though generally congratulatory, help; and Baptist state convention histories which have been produced for most cooperating states and biographies, both critical and hagiographic, lend color and point to often overlooked sources for the larger picture.

Plowing by furrow rather than by field, Southern Baptist scholars have contributed a wealth of material germane to this study for publication in such periodicals as Southern's *Review and Expositor,* Southwestern's *Journal of Theology,* New Orleans's *Theological Educator,* and the Southern Baptist Historical Commission's *Baptist History and Heritage.* Still others are mentioned in connection with particular articles cited.

An on-going movie of Southern Baptist life has been and continues to be produced by state Baptist papers which, though often beholden to their state constituencies, have been surprisingly objective about Southern Baptists. Any mention of these publications risks oversight, but special note is due the older publications and some of the more aggressive newer journals. Citations are specific as to quotes, but not complete as to helpfulness.

Key repositories include the Historical Commission's Southern Baptist Historical Library and Archives, the Sunday School Board's Dargan Research Center, Southern Baptist Theological Seminary's Boyce library, and Southwestern Baptist Theological Seminary's Roberts library. The directors, librarians, and archivists in these repositories are living sources in their awareness of relevant materials that rivals their increasingly sophisticated computer services.

A host of recent works analyzing Southern Baptist life in its immediate past contribute significantly, including Nancy Ammerman's sociological study, *Baptist Battles,* and her more recent collection of essays by a panel of scholars entitled *Southern Baptists Observed: Multiple Perspectives on a Changing Denomination,* and Bill Leonard's *God's Last & Only Hope.* Chronicles focusing on the conservative point of view by James Hefley including the five volume *Truth in Crisis* series and a wrap-up volume have offered data not found elsewhere. His point of view is balanced by a work edited by Rob James and a more recent book, *What Happened to the Southern Baptist Convention?* by Grady Cothen. An openness to offering contrasting views by Broadman Press exemplified by the collection edited by James and Dockery, *Beyond the Impasse,* offers new insights into Baptist dynamics. And, of course, a plethora of articles and publications from outside Southern Baptist life, while seldom sympathetic and occasionally guilty of caricature, offer objective and scholarly perspective.

Surprisingly helpful to this effort has been the unpublished dissertations emerging from graduate studies in seminaries and universities both in and outside Southern Baptist life. These studies not only yielded important perspective but also pointed to key sources.

The author's commitment to cite only from published works or catalogued unpublished works and collections available to the public represents a personal bias. Interviews as source have been studiously avoided even when accessioned in established libraries as oral history because of the lack of opportunity for challenge, balance, or verification. The author is indebted, however, for the help of a number of individuals who have pointed to relevant publications or collections.

Papers on subjects related to this history and on file at Hardin-Simmons University were helpful, as was the dialogue with their writers who were students of the authors in a Southern Baptist history class in the fall of 1992. Special thanks are due Monica Austin, Tony Celleli, Chris Dikes, Randy Evans, Donnie Harbors, Paul Irby, Chris May, Jonathon Owen, Sean Parmer, Randy Perkins, Shawn Powers, Tony Roberts, and Jerry Shields.

Books

Abington, E. Butler. *Perpetuity of Baptist Churches.* Eureka Springs, Ark.: Times-Echo Press, 1962.

Allen, Catherine B. *A Century to Celebrate.* Birmingham, Ala: Woman's Missionary Union, 1987.

———. *Laborers Together with God.* Birmingham, Ala.: Woman's Missionary Union, 1987.

———. *The New Lottie Moon Story.* Nashville: Broadman Press, 1980.

Alley, Ruben Edward. *A History of Baptists in Virginia.* Richmond: Virginia Baptist General Board, 1974.

Ammerman, Nancy T. *Baptist Battles: Social Change and Religious Conflict in the Southern Baptist Convention.* New Bruinswick: Rutgers University Press, 1990.

———. *Southern Baptists Observed: Multiple Perspectives on a Changing Denomination.* Knoxville: University of Tennessee Press, 1993.

Armitage, Thomas. *A History of the Baptists.* New York: Bryan, Taylor, & Company, 1887.

Backus, Isaac. *A History of New England with Particular Reference to the Denomination of Christians Called Baptists.* Newton: Backus Historical Society, 1871.

Bailey, Thomas A. and David M. Kennedy. *The American Pageant.* Lexington: D.C. Heath and Company, 1983.

Baker, James T. *Brook Hays.* Macon: Mercer University Press, 1989.

Baker, Robert A. *A Baptist Source Book.* Nashville: Broadman Press, 1966.

———. and Paul J. Craven, Jr. *Adventure in Faith: The First 300 Years of First Baptist Church, Charleston, South Carolina.* Nashville: Broadman Press, 1982.

———. *The Blossoming Desert.* Waco: Word Publisher, 1970.

———. *Tell the Generations Following.* Nashville: Broadman Press, 1983.

———. *Relations Between Northern and Southern Baptists.* Ft. Worth: Marvin D. Evans Printing Company, 1954.

———. *The Southern Baptist Convention and Its People 1607–1972.* Nashville: Broadman Press, 1974.

Barnes, W.W. *The Southern Baptist Convention 1845–1953.* Nashville: Broadman Press, 1954.

———. *The Southern Baptist Convention: A Study in the Development of Ecclesiology.* Ft. Worth: Southwestern Seminary Press, 1934.

Beales, David O. *SBC: House of Sand?* Greenville, S.C.: Unusual Publications, 1985.

Beck, Rosalie. *The Whitsitt Controversy: A Denomination in Crisis.* Ann Arbor: University Microfilms International, 1985.

Belew, M. Wendell. *A Missions People: The Southern Baptist Pilgrimage.* Nashville: Broadman Press, 1989.

Benedict, David A. *A General History of the Baptist Denomination in America and in Other Parts of the World.* Vol. 1. Boston: Lincoln & Edwards, 1813.

Brackney, William Henry. *Baptist Life and Thought: 1600–1980, A Source Book.* Valley Forge: Judson Press, 1983.

———. *The Baptists.* New York: Greenwood Press, 1988.

Bradford, William. *Of Plymouth Plantation, 1620–1647.* New York: Alfred A. Knopf, 1959.

Broadus, John A. *Memoir of James Petigru Boyce.* Nashville: Sunday School Board of the Southern Baptist Convention, 1927.

Buck, Paul H. *The Road to Reunion.* New York: Vintage Books, 1937.

Burgess, Walter H. *John Smith the Se-Baptist, Thomas Helwys and the First Baptist Church in England.* London: James Clarke & Company, 1911.

Burton, Joe W. *Epochs of Home Missions.* Atlanta: Home Mission Board, 1945.

———. *Road to Augusta.* Nashville: Broadman Press, 1976.

Carey, John J. *Carlyle Marney: A Pilgrim's Progress*. Macon, Ga.: Mercer University Press, 1980.

Cauthen, Baker James. *Advance: A History of Southern Baptist Foreign Missions*. Nashville: Broadman Press, 1970.

———. and Frank K. Means. *Advance to Bold Mission Thrust—1845–1980*. Nashville: Foreign Mission Board of the Southern Baptist Convention, 1981.

Coggins, James Robert. *John Smyth's Congregation*. Waterloo, Ontario: Herald Press, 1991.

Combs, James O., ed. *Roots and Origins of Baptist Fundamentalism*. Springfield, Mo.: John the Baptist Press, 1984.

Cothen, Grady. *What Happened to the Southern Baptist Convention?* Macon, Ga.: Smyth & Helwys, 1993.

Cox, Norman Wade. *Encyclopedia of Southern Baptists, Vol. I & II*. Nashville: Broadman Press, 1958.

Dana, H.E. *Lee Rutland Scarborough: A Life of Service*. Nashville: Broadman Press, 1942.

Dexter, Henry M. *The True Story of John Smyth*. Boston: Lee and Shepherd, 1818.

Dilday, Russell H., Jr. *The Doctrine of Biblical Authority*. Nashville: Convention Press, 1982.

Dobbins, Gaines S. *Great Teachers Make a Difference*. Nashville: Broadman Press, 1965.

Draper, James T., Jr. *Authority: The Critical Issue for Southern Baptists*. Old Tappan, N.J.: Fleming H. Revell, 1984.

Eighmy, John Lee. *Churches in Cultural Captivity*. Knoxville: University of Tennessee Press, 1972.

Eitel, Keith E. and James Madison Pendleton. *Baptist Theologians*. Edited by Timothy George and David S. Dockery. Nashville: Broadman Press, 1990.

Elliot, Ralph H. *The Genesis Controversy and Continuity in Southern Baptist Chaos—A Eulogy for a Great Tradition*. Macon, Ga.: Mercer University Press, 1992.

Estep, William R. *The Anabaptist Story*. Nashville: Broadman Press, 1963.

Fletcher, Jesse C. *Baker James Cauthen—A Man for All Nations*. Nashville: Broadman Press, 1977.

———. *Bill Wallace of China*. Nashville: Broadman Press, 1963.

———. *Living Sacrifices: A Missionary Odyssey*. Nashville: Broadman Press, 1974.

Foster, L.S. *Fifty Years in China*. Nashville: Bayless-Pullen Company, 1909.

Fuller, Richard and Francis Wayland. *Domestic Slavery Considered as a Scriptural Institution*. New York: Lewis Colby, 1845.

Garraty, John A. and Peter Gay, ed. *The Columbia History of the World*. New York: Harper and Row, 1972.

George, Timothy. *Faithful Witness: The Life and Mission of William Carey*. Birmingham, Ala.: New Hope, 1991.

———. and David S. Dockery, eds. *Baptist Theologians*. Nashville: Broadman Press, 1990.

Graves, J.R. *Old Landmarkism: What Is It?* Texarkana: Baptist Sunday School Committee, 1880.

Hefley, James. *The Conservative Resurgence in the Southern Baptist Convention*. Hannibal, Mo.: Hannibal Books, 1991.

———. *Truth In Crisis*. Vols. 1–5. Hannibal, Mo.: Hannibal Books, 1986–1989.

Hinson, Glenn E. *A History of Baptists in Arkansas 1818–1978*. Little Rock: Arkansas Baptist State Convention, 1979.

Hunt, Alma. *History of Woman's Missionary Union*. Nashville: Convention Press, 1964.

Hunter, James Davidson. *Cultural Wars: The Struggle to Define America*. New York: Basic Books, 1991.

Hyatt, Irwin T. *Our Ordered Lives Confess*. Cambridge: Harvard University Press, 1976.

James, Powhatan W. *George W. Truett: A Biography*. New York: Macmillan Company, 1939.

James, Robinson B. and David S. Dockery. *Beyond the Impasse.* Nashville: Broadman Press, 1992.

James, Rob. *The Takeover in the Southern Baptist Convention.* Decatur, Ga.: SBC Today, 1989.

Jeter, Jeremiah Bell. *The Recollections of a Long Life.* New York: Arno Press, 1880.

Keith, Billy Phegan, *W. A. Criswell: The Authorized Biography.* Old Tappan, N.J.: Fleming Revell, 1973.

King, Joe M. *A History of South Carolina Baptists.* Columbia: The General Board of the South Carolina Convention, 1964.

Knowles, James D. *Memoir of Mrs. Ann H. Judson.* Boston: Lincoln and Edmands, 1829.

Lackey, Margaret. *Decade of W.M.U. Service, 1913–1923.* Nashville: Sunday School Board, 1924.

Land, Richard. *The Christian Life Commission.* November 12, 1992.

Lindsell, Harold. *The Battle for the Bible.* Grand Rapids: Zondervan Publishing, 1976.

Lumpkin, William L. *Baptist Confessions of Faith.* Philadelphia: Judson Press, 1959.

———. *Baptist Foundations in the South.* Nashville: Broadman Press, 1961.

May, Lynn Edward, Jr., ed. *Encyclopedia of Southern Baptists* vol. 4., Nashville: Broadman Press, 1982.

———. *The First Baptist Church of Nashville, Tennessee 1820–1970.* Nashville: First Baptist Church, 1970.

McBeth, H. Leon. *The First Baptist Church of Dallas.* Grand Rapids: Zondervan Publishing, 1968.

———. *The Baptist Heritage: Four Centuries of Baptist Witness.* Nashville: Broadman Press, 1987.

———. *Sourcebook for Baptist Heritage.* Nashville: Broadman Press.

———. *Women in Baptist Life.* Nashville: Broadman Press, 1979.

McClellan, Albert. *The Executive Committee of the Southern Baptist Convention—1917–1984.* Nashville: Broadman Press, 1985.

Masters, Victor I. *A Historical Sketch.* Atlanta: Home Mission Board, 1912.

Mueller, William A. *A History of Southern Baptist Theological Seminary.* Nashville: Broadman Press, 1959.

Mullins, E.Y. *Freedom and Authority in Religion.* Philadelphia: Griffeth and Rowland, 1913.

Neil, Anne Thomas and Virginia Garrrett Neely. *The New Has Come.* Washington, D.C.: Southern Baptist Alliance, 1989.

Newman, Albert Henry. *A History of the Baptist Churches in the United States.* Philadelphia: American Baptist Publication, 1915.

———. *A Manual of Church History.* vol. 1 and 2. Philadelphia: The American Baptist Publication Society, 1902.

Nowlin, William D. *Kentucky Baptist History 1770–1922.* n.p.: Baptist Book Concern, 1922.

Orchard, G.H. *A Concise History of Foreign Baptists.* Nashville: Graves and Marks & Co., 1838.

Pair, C.L. *A History of the Arizona Baptist Convention 1928–1984.* Arizona Baptist Convention, 1989.

Patterson, Morgan W. *Baptist Successionism.* Valley Forge: Judson Press, 1969.

Patterson, Roberta Turner. *Candle by Night.* Dallas, Tex.: Woman's Missionary Union of Texas, 1955.

Penrose, St. Amant. *A Short History of Lousiana Baptists.* Nashville: Broadman Press, 1948.

Reid, A.H. *Baptists in Alabama.* Montgomery: Alabama State Convention, 1967.

Reimers, David M. *White Protestantism and the Negro.* New York: Oxford University Press, 1965.

Robertson, Archibald T. *Life and Letters of John Albert Broadus.* Philadelphia: American Baptist Publication.

Rogers, James A. *Richard Furman: Life and Legacy.* Macon, Ga.: Mercer University Press, 1985.

Rosenberg, Ellen M. *The Southern Baptists: A Subculture in Transition.* Knoxville: University Press, 1989.

Rutledge, Author B. *Mission to America: A Century and a Quarter of Southern Baptist Home Missions.* Nashville: Broadman Press, 1969.

Sanford, Don A. *A Choosing People: The History of Seventh Day Baptists.* Nashville: Broadman Press, 1992.

Shurden, Walter B. *Associationalism Among Baptists in America: 1707–1814.* New York: Arno Press, 1980.

———. *Not A Silent People,* Nashville: Broadman Press, 1972.

———. ed. *The Struggle for the Soul of the SBC.* Macon, Ga.: Mercer University Press, 1993.

———. *The Baptist Identity: Four Fragile Freedoms.* Macon: Smyth & Helwys, 1993.

Stackhouse, Yvonne. *Hardin-Simmons University—A Centennial History.* Abilene: Hardin-Simmons University, 1991.

Sullivan, James L. *Baptist Polity As I See It.* Nashville: Broadman Press, 1983.

Taylor, George B. *Life and Times of James B. Taylor.* Philadelphia: The Bible and Publication Society, 1872.

Torbet, Robert G. *A History of the Baptists.* Philadelphia: Judson Press, 1950.

Townsend, Leah. *South Carolina Baptists 1670–1805.* Baltimore: Geneological Publishing Company, 1978.

Toy, C.H. *The Claims of Biblical Interpretation on Baptists.* New York: Lange & Hillman, 1869.

Tull, James E. *A Study of Southern Baptist Landmarkism in the Light of Historical Baptist Ecclesiology.* New York: Arno Press, 1980.

Underwood, A.C. *A History of English Baptists.* London: The Carey Kingsgate Press, 1956.

Walker, R. Scott. *The Freedom Factor.* San Francisco: Harper and Row, 1989.

Weatherspoon, J. M. *M. Theron Rankin: Apostle of Advance.* Nashville: Broadman Press, 1958.

Whaley, Lois. *Edwin Dozier of Japan: Man of the Way.* Birmingham: Woman's Missionary Union, 1983.

Whitely, W.T. *A History of British Baptists.* London: Charles Griffin & Company, 1923.

Winslow, Ola Elizabeth. *Master Roger Williams.* New York: The Macmillan Company, 1957.

Woodson, Hortense. *Giant in the Land.* Nashville: Broadman Press, 1950.

Woolley, Davis Collier, ed. *Encyclopedia of Southern Baptists. Vol. III.* Nashville: Broadman Press, 1971.

———. *Baptist Advance.* Nashville: Broadman Press, 1964.

Articles

Allison, B. Gray. "Notable Achievements in Missions and Evangelism Since 1845." *Baptist History and Heritage.* (July 1989).

Ammerman, Nancy. "The SBC: Retrospect and Prospect."*Review and Expositor* (1991).

———. "Share My Dreams for Cooperative Fellowship." *Baptists Today* (April 23, 1992).

Anderson, David E. "Southern Baptist Woman's Auxiliary Told to Submit to Conservatism." *Dallas Morning News* (March 6, 1993).

Baker, Robert A. "Factors Encouraging the Rise of Landmarkism." *Baptist History and Heritage* (January 1975).

———. "The Magnificent Years—1917–1931." *Baptist History and Heritage* (July 1973).

Bird, Craig. "Baylor President Denounces SBC 'College of Cardinals.'" *Baptist Standard* (October 17, 1984).

Bloesch, Donald G. "A Theology for Confronting the Cultural Captivity of Evangelicalism." *Academic Alert* (Winter 1993). IVP's Book Bulletin for Professors.

Briggs, Ed. "Mission Panel Taps Singapore Veteran." *Richmond Times Dispatch* (May 26, 1993).

Brunsman, Steve. "Clinton's hometown minister denounces SBC 'witch hunt.'" *Houston Post* (June 15, 1993).

Camp, Ken. "Evangelical Organization Backs Bush/Quayle." *The Baptist Standard* (September 2, 1992).

Carter, James E. "A Review of Confessions of Faith Adopted by Major Baptist bodies in the United States." *Baptist History and Heritage* (April 1977).

———. "The Fraternal Address of Southern Baptists." *Baptist History and Heritage* (October, 1977).

Carver, W. O. "William Whitsitt: The Seminary Martyr." *Review and Expositor* (October 1954).

Cattau, Daniel. "Carter declares support for Southern Baptist moderate group." *The Dallas Morning News* (May 22, 1993).

Clemons, Hardy. "Letter from a Birmingham Sheraton." *Baptists Today* (May 27, 1993).

Clingenpeel, Michael J. "Southern Seminary in Chaos." *The Religious Herald* (April 29, 1993).

Compton, Bob. "J. M. Pendleton: A Nineteenth-Century Statesman." *Baptist History and Heritage* (January 1975).

Cranfill, J.B. "The Greatest Convention of All." *Baptist Standard* (November 1901).

Davis, C. Anne. "Women in Southern Baptist History." *Baptist History and Heritage* (July 1987).

Deweese, Charles W. "Southern Baptists and Church Covenants." *Baptist History and Heritage* (January 1977).

———. "Deaconesses in Baptist History: A Preliminary Study." *Baptist History and Heritage* (January 1977).

Dilday, Russell. "Future Offers New Day, New Days for the SBC." *Southwestern News* (January–February 1993).

Doyle, Susan. "WMU Sends Video Message Reassuring Missionaries." *Baptist Press* (March 5, 1993).

Druin, Toby. "Graham Wanted No Word on Stanley Support." *Baptist Standard* (June 26, 1985).

———. "SBC: A Fundamental-Conservative Sweep." *Baptist Standard* (June 18, 1986).

———. "Motion to Fire Elder Discussed, Withdrawn." *Baptist Standard* (August 16, 1989).

———. "Baylor Changes Charter: 'Regents' will Govern." *Baptist Standard* (September 26, 1990).

———. "Cooperative Baptist Fellowship Organized." *Baptist Standard* (May 15, 1991).

———. "Parks: Decision Positive, But He Had Reasons." *Baptist Standard* (April 1, 1992).

———. "Baylor to Open Truett Seminary in Fall, '94." *Baptist Standard* (May 26, 1993).

Dye, Harold E. "Matchless California." *The Quarterly Review* (April–June, 1961).

Elder, Lloyd. "Calling the Family Back Together." *Lloyd Elder and Associates* (May 8, 1993).

Estep, William R. "Anabaptists and the Rise of English Baptists." *The Quarterly Review* (October-December 1968 and January-March, 1969).

———. "Southern Baptists in Search of an Identity." *The Lord's Free People in a Free Land*. Ft. Worth: Evans Press, 1976.

———. "Biblical Authority in Baptist Confessions of Faith." *Baptists History and Heritage* (October 1987).

Falwell, Jerry. "The SBC: Revived and Rebuilding." *Fundamentalist Journal* (July-August 1989).

Fletcher, Jesse C. "The Development of Foreign Mission Board Strategy, 1845–1974." *Baptist History and Heritage* (October 1974).

———. "Letters From Burma: The Personal Side." *The Quarterly Review* (April, May, June, 1964).

Foster, Ferrell. "Criswell Discusses SBC Strife, Future of First Baptist, Dallas." *Baptist Press* (February 4, 1993).

————. "Gregory Says He's at Peace Over Resigning Dallas Pulpit." *Baptist Press* (March 15, 1993).

Gambrell, J.B. "A Long Look for Baptists." *Baptist Standard* (May 8, 1919).

Garrett, James Leo. "Restitution and Dissent Among Early English Baptists." *Baptist History and Heritage* (April, 1978).

————. "Baptist Distinctives Threatened." *The Baptist Standard* (1991).

Gaston, George. "Letter to the Editor." *Baptist Standard* (February 3, 1993).

George, Timothy. "Conflict and Identity in the SBC: The Quest for a New Consensus." *Beyond Impasse,* edited by James and Dockery. Nashville: Broadman Press, 1992.

————. and Roy L. Honeycutt, "Report of the Theological Study Committee." *Southern Baptist Watchman* (1993 Convention Issue).

Greene, Amy. "Alliance Meets in Daytona Beach, Simplifies Vision, Clarifies Goals." *Baptists Today* (March 18, 1993).

Hastey, Stan. "Peace Committee Emerges From Scarred SBC." *Baptist Standard* (June 19, 1985).

————. "Thoughts on our Present Untidy State." *Baptists Today* (May 13, 1993).

Hinson, Glen E. "Between Two Worlds." *Baptist History and Heritage* (April, 1985).

Hobbs, Herschel H. "The Baptist Faith and Message—Anchored but Free." *Baptist History and Heritage* (July 1978).

————. "Southern Baptists and Confessionalism: A Comparison of the Origin and Contents of the 1925 and 1963 Confessions." *Review and Expositor* (Winter 1979).

Hollinger, Herb. "Adrian Rogers Is Critical of Persons Speaking for Him." *Baptist Press* (March 11, 1993).

————. "CBF OK's Budget, 'Blesses' 22 Missionaries." *Baptist Standard* (May 26, 1993).

Howe, Claude. Jr. "Factors Affecting Cooperation Since 1945." *Baptist History and Heritage* (January 1989).

Hunt, Angela Elwell. "SBC Looks to the Past for Future Success." *Fundamentalist Journal* (July-August 1989).

Jetter, J.B. "Southern Baptist Convention." *Religious Herald* (May 20, 1869).

Jones, Jim. "Baptists' fight over Masons has steep cost." *Fort Worth Star Telegram* (May 30, 1993).

Jones, Roy A. III. "Fired Baptist Editor Finds Job with SBC." *Abilene Reporter News,* Abilene, Texas (June 21, 1992).

Kammerdiener, Don. "Mission and the Church." *The Commission* (September 1991).

Kelly, Wayne. "Claremore Pastor Responds to Critical Letters." *Oklahoma Baptist Messenger* (February 11, 1993).

Kliever, Lonnie D. "General Baptist Origins: The Question of Anabaptist Influence." *Mennonite Quarterly Review* (1962).

Knight, Walker L. "Moderate Organizations." *Baptists Today* (December 15, 1992).

————. "Moderate Organizations Fill Vacuums in SBC." *Baptists Today* (December 15, 1992).

————. "Year of Crucial Meetings." *Baptists Today* (February 4, 1993).

Knox, Marv. "New Seminary Approved at Alliance Annual Meeting." *Biblical Recorder* (March 18, 1989).

————. "Trustees Cancel Book on Sunday School Board." *Baptist Standard* (August 22, 1990).

Lavine, Charles. "Letters to the Editor." *Baptist Standard* (August 5, 1992).

Ledbetter, Gary. "WMU's New Friend." *Indiana Baptist* (March 2, 1993).

Ledbetter, Tami. "Shackleford, Martin Fired by Executive Committee." *Indiana Baptist* (July 31, 1991).

————. "Parks Video Ignores FMB Inroads to World A." *Indiana Baptist* (May 25, 1993).

———— and Scott Collins. "Rankin outlines vision for FMB 'to focus in what God is doing.'" *1993 Southern Baptist Convention News Release* (June 14, 1993).

Lindsey, Jonathon A. "Basil Manly: Protean Man." *Baptist History and Heritage* (July 1973).

Lolley, Randall. "Church and Change is the Baptist Challenge." *Baptists Today* (Feb. 4, 1993).

Lumpkin, William L. "The Nature and Authority of Baptist Confessions of Faith." *Review and Expositor* (Winter 1979).

McClellan, Albert H. "The Leadership Heritage of Southern Baptists." *Baptist History and Heritage* (January 1985).

————. "The Southern Baptist Convention, 1965–1985." *Baptist History and Heritage* (October 1985).

McCormick, Mark. "Southern's Mohler Challenges 'Fundamentalism Of the Left.'" *Baptist Press* (May 17, 1993).

McSwain, Larry L. "Anatomy of the SBC Institutional Crisis." *Review and Expositor* (Winter 1991).

Manley, Kenneth Ross. "Origin of the Baptists: The Case for the Development from Puritan-Separatism." *Baptist History and Heritage* (October 1987).

Marsden, George. "The New Paganism." *Reformed Journal* (January 1988).

Martin, Dan. "Bisagno to Nominate Chapman New Orleans." *Baptist Standard* (February 14, 1990).

————. "Elder, Sunday School Board Trustees Agree to 'Retirement.'" *Associated Baptist Press Release* (January 17, 1993).

Miller, Thomas E., Jr. "Annuity Board Trustees Mark 75th Year, Get Kmart Update." *Baptist Press* (March 5, 1993).

Moore, Debbie. "Nelson Price Asks Open Convention." *Baptist Standard* (April 29, 1992).

Morgan, David T. "Upheaval the Southern Baptist Convention." *Perspectives Religious Studies, Journal of NABPR.*

Newton, Jim and William Fletcher Allen. "Moderate fellowship moves to alternate funding." *Baptist and Reflector* (August 29, 1990), 1.

Noricks, Ronald H. "Misguided Missionaries: New Englanders View Frontier Baptists, 1804–1831." *Baptist History and Heritage* (January 1993).

Norris, J. Frank. "Fort Worth Gives $200,000 for Seminary." *Baptist Standard* (November 11, 1909).

O'Brien, Robert. "FMB Leaders of Europe will Retire Early." *Baptist Standard* (January 15, 1992).

————. "Parks shares his heart with FMB staff," *Florida Baptist Witness* (April 2, 1992).

————. "Jerry Rankin Nominated as Next Foreign Mission Board President." *Foreign Mission Board Release* (May 25, 1993).

Parks, R. Keith. "Letter to Missionary Colleagues." *Baptist Press Release* (October 23, 1992).

Patterson, Paige. "My Vision of the Twenty-First Century SBC." *Review and Expositor* (Winter 1991).

Pentecost, Julian. "A Century to Celebrate, A Future to Fulfill." *The Religious Herald* (May 19, 1988).

Pollard, E. B. "Life and Work of Whitsitt." *Review and Expositor* (April 1912).

Romo, Oscar I. "Ethnic Southern Baptists: Contexts, Trends, Contributions." *Baptist History and Heritage* (July 1983).

Sehested, Ken. "The Birmingham Confession." *Baptist Peacemaker* (Summer 1993).

Sherman, Cecil. "The Emerging CBF." *Baptists Today* (February 4, 1993).

Shurden, Walter B. "The Southern Baptist Synthesis: Is It Cracking?" *Baptist History and Heritage* (April 1981).

Simmons, Paul. "A Personal Reflection on Theological Education and the Politically Correct." *Baptist Today* (March 18, 1993).

Smith, David. "Little Rock's Immanuel Baptist to be Home Church of a President." *Indiana Baptist* (Feb. 2, 1993).

Smith, Harold S. "The Life and Work of J. R. Graves." *Baptist History and Heritage* (January 1975).

Sorrill, Bobbie. "Southern Baptist Laywomen in Missions." *Baptist History and Heritage* (July 1987).

Stinson, Roddy. "And there was unity at the Alamo after the battle, too." *San Antonio Express-News* (June 18, 1993).

Sumners, Bill. "Southern Baptists and the Liquor Question 1910–20." *Baptist History and Heritage* (April, 1983).

Terry, Bobby S. "Southern Baptist News Media 1945: Purpose, History and Influence." *Baptist History and Heritage* (July 1993).

Toalston, Art and Eric Miller. "Ordained Couple Turned Down by FMB Trustees." *Baptist and Reflector* (July 5, 1989).

———. "To Maintain Pro-life Convictions, Theology Revival Needed, Professor Says." *Baptist Press* (March 4, 1993).

———. "Survey Shows Top Priority is Evangelism." *Baptist Press* (March 10, 1993).

———. "Jesse Helms Defends Freemasonry Against Texas Baptist's Claims." *Baptist Press Release* (May 20, 1993).

———. "Chapman says Elder plans for SBC 'Unwise and unneeded.'" *The Baptist Standard* (June 9, 1993).

Torbet, Robert G. "Historical Background of the Southern Baptist Invasion." *Foundations* (October 1959).

Tull, James E. "The Landmark Movement: An Historical and Theological Appraisal." *Baptist History and Heritage* (January 1975).

Vestal, Dan. "Quest for Renewal." *Review and Expositor* (Winter 1991).

Vickers, Gregory. "Models of Womanhood and the Early Woman's Missionary Union." *Baptist History and Heritage* (January 1989).

Walker, Jon. "Unsettled Convictions Can Yield to Apostasy, Mohler Tells Graduates." *Baptist Press Release* (May 19, 1993).

Wall, James M. "Images of Southern Baptists in Contemporary America." *Baptist History and Heritage* (July 1980).

Wamble, G. Hugh. "History of Messengers to Baptist Denominational Bodies." *Baptist History and Heritage* (April 1987).

———. "The Leadership of Southern Baptist Presidents." *Baptist History and Heritage* (January 1985).

Warner, Greg. "3000 in Atlanta Approve Alternate Funding Plan." *Baptist Standard* (August 29, 1990).

———. "Parks Indicates..." *Baptist Standard* (December 2, 1992).

———. "FMB Chairman Compares WMU Move to Committing Adultery." *Baptist Standard.* (February 3, 1993).

———. "Hobbs Urges SBC Leaders to Share Power." *Baptist Standard* (February 24, 1993).

———. "Sherman Denounces Homosexuality to Preempt Criticism of Fellowship." *Baptist Press* (April 1, 1993).

———. "'Dark Horse' Jerry Rankin Chosen As FMB Nominee." *Associated Baptist Press Release* (May 25, 1993).

———. "Movement may jeopardize Rankin election." *The Baptist Standard* (June 9, 1993).

Webb, Leland. "The Parks Era: Shifting to Global Strategy." *The Commission* (October-November 1992).

White, K. Owen. "Death in the Pot." *Baptist Standard* (January 10, 1962).

Whittington, Tony B. "Christ's Wider Kingdom." *The Adventure* (November-December 1992).

Willis, Charles. "Draper Cites Concerns, Actions in State of the Board Address." *Baptist Press* (February 9, 1993).

Wingfield, Mark. "Criswell Comments on Divorce, America, SBC." *Baptist Standard* (March 25, 1992).

———. "Women Gain Ground in USA Ministry Roles." *Baptists Today* (March 18, 1993).

Womack, Paula, "Baptist group confesses racisim to historic church group." *Baptists Today* (August 26, 1993).

Yarbrough, Slayden A. "The Origins of Baptist Associations Among the English Particular Baptists." *Baptist History and Heritage* (April 1988).

———. "Is Creedalism a Threat to Southern Baptist?" *Baptist History and Heritage* (April 1993).

Unpublished Material

Beck, Rosalie. "The Whitsitt Controversy." Ph.D. diss., Baylor University, 1989.

Bugg, Charles B. "The Whitsitt Controversy: A Study in Denominational Conflict." Th.D. diss., Southern Baptist Theological Seminary, 1972.

Carter, James C. "The Southern Baptist Convention and Confessions of Faith," 1845–1945. Ph.D. diss., Southwestern Baptist Theological Seminary, 1964.

Carson, Glenn Thomas. "Lee Rutland Scarborough." Ph.D. diss., Southwestern Baptist Theological Seminary, 1992.

Cobbs, Louis R. "The Student Worker as 21st Century Missionary." Lectures to Korean Baptist Student Workers, 1992. Papers contained in Southern Baptist History Collection, Hardin-Simmons University.

Cox, J.P. "A Study of the Life and Work of Basil Manly, Jr." Doctoral diss., Southern Baptist Theological Seminary, 1954.

Hernandez, Jose A. "Training Hispanic Leaders in the United States," Ph. D. diss., Southwestern Baptist Theological Seminary, 1985.

Hunt, Billy Grey. "Crawford Howell Toy: Interpreter of the Old Testament." Th.D. diss., Southern Baptist Theological Seminary, 1965.

Lefever, Alan J. "The Life and Work of Benajah Harvey Carroll." Ph.D. diss., Southwestern Baptist Theological Seminary, 1992.

Loftis, John Franklin. "Factors in Southern Baptist Identity As Reflected by Ministerial Role Models, 1750–1925." Ph.D. diss., Southern Baptist Theological Seminary.

McBeth, H. Leon. "Celebrating History and Hope." Unpublished manuscript in the Hardin-Simmons University File of Southern Baptist History, 1990.

Neely, H.K. "The Territorial Expansion of the Southern Baptist Convention—1894–1959." Th. D. diss., Southwestern Baptist Theological Seminary, 1963.

O'Brien, William R. "Southern Baptists' Changing Age," Paper delivered to the Baptist Public Relations Society, San Francisco, April 23, 1991.

———. "Serampore's Shadows: Means or Models?" Response paper delivered to the American Society of Missiology's annual meeting, June 11–14, 1992.

Ray, Cecil and Susan. "Roots and Change in Southern Baptist Life." Unpublished manuscript, 1989.

Weatherford, Kenneth Vaughn. "The Graves-Howell Controversy." Ph.D. diss., Baylor University, 1991.

Index

M

Y

Z